SOCIAL THOUGHT IN AMERICA AND EUROPE

Readings in Comparative Intellectual History

SOCIAL THOUGHT IN AMERICA AND EUROPE

Readings in Comparative Intellectual History

edited by

DAVID M. KENNEDY, *Stanford University*

and

PAUL A. ROBINSON, *Stanford University*

LITTLE, BROWN AND COMPANY

BOSTON

LIBRARY OF CONGRESS CATALOG CARD NUMBER: 72-112756

FIRST PRINTING

Published simultaneously in Canada
by Little, Brown & Company (Canada) Limited

PRINTED IN THE UNITED STATES OF AMERICA

for
H. Stuart Hughes
and
Norman Holmes Pearson

ACKNOWLEDGMENTS

This anthology grew from a graduate seminar the authors taught together on comparative European and American intellectual history. Accordingly, much of our thinking was first tested on the students in that seminar: Lenox Anderson, Charles Bergquist, Robert Eager, Jacques Depelchin, Dolores Donovan, Jack Hickling, Roy Hoyer, John Noller, Timothy Patterson, and Rosalind Rosenberg. We should like here to express our appreciation for their conscientious participation in the seminar, and our thanks for their valuable comments on many of the topics that this book considers.

CONTENTS

INTRODUCTION

This anthology compares ideas and intellectual systems of the highest, most explicit sort. Accordingly, we have included writings from professional intellectuals, rather than documents that represent popular attitudes. This variety of intellectual history deals with what John Higham has called the "internal" rather than the "external" history of ideas: the "relationship between what some men write or say and what other men write or say," rather than "the connections between thought and deed." [1] We are concerned, that is, with ideas themselves rather than with their consequences.

We have chosen to focus on one kind of thinking: general social thought. Under this rubric fall ideas about psychology, society, and history. Thus, we have for the most part passed over readings from technical philosophers, theologians, natural scientists, and literary figures, though we recognize that such documents furnish important information for the student of intellectual history. For the sake of cohesion and focus, however, it seemed sensible to emphasize social thought, broadly conceived.[2]

The intellectual historian does not merely recount and interpret past ideas. He also attempts to locate those ideas historically, to relate them to other ideas in both a logical and a chronological fashion. His essential task is to determine how discrete intellectual enterprises are to be understood as parts of larger movements of thought, exhibiting common assumptions and located in specific historical periods. Thus, for example, intellectual historians have agreed, after years of debate, that

[1] John Higham, "Intellectual History and its Neighbors," *Journal of the History of Ideas,* XV, 3 (June, 1954), 341.

[2] In taking general social thought as the essential subject matter of intellectual history we are following the example of several prominent contemporary practitioners of the art, among them H. Stuart Hughes, *Consciousness and Society: The Reorientation of European Social Thought, 1890–1930* (New York: Alfred A. Knopf, 1958), and Morton White, *Social Thought in America: The Revolt Against Formalism* (New York: Viking Press, 1949). See in particular, Hughes, *Consciousness and Society,* p. 13.

from the fourteenth to the sixteenth centuries in Europe there developed a body of ideas sharing certain preconceptions and concerns, to which we can assign the label "the Renaissance." The definition of such epochs in the history of thought, and the demonstration of connections between various intellectual activities within each period, comprise the principal job of the intellectual historian. In effect he attempts to determine the climate of opinion, the intellectual style, the unspoken assumptions behind articulate expression, of successive epochs—to trace changes in what might be called "the spirit of the times." [3]

European historians have reached a viable, though by no means definitive, consensus about the major stages in the development of modern European thought, a consensus that has determined the organization of this anthology. By the order of the readings we hope to suggest—and this is perhaps the central argument of the anthology—that during the past two centuries American thought has followed a course of development that closely parallels European thought. As the predilections and concerns of European thinkers have changed, so have those of Americans. The dates that mark off distinctive periods in European intellectual history delineate similar phases in the history of ideas in America. Both substantively and chronologically, Europe and America have experienced a striking intellectual congruence. Comparative examination, by revealing this common experience, illuminates in a new fashion the contours of American intellectual history.

In suggesting that American and European intellectual developments parallel one another, we are not arguing that American thought followed the course it did because of the direct influence of European ideas. Obviously European intellectuals influenced Americans (and vice versa), but influence does not adequately explain their affinity. Indeed, we have focussed especially on the period from the late eighteenth century to the First World War—roughly the first century and a half of American nationhood—because during that period the factor of influence appears to have been at a minimum. By way of contrast, before 1790 and again after 1930 the impact of European ideas on American thought was of paramount importance. The American Puritans, and to a lesser extent the American *philosophes*, still thought of themselves as English subjects, the bearers of European culture in the New World, and they re-

[3] John C. Greene has succinctly formulated this particular objective of intellectual history: "The primary function of the intellectual historian is to delineate the presuppositions of thought in given historical epochs and to explain the changes which those presuppositions undergo from epoch to epoch." "Objectives and Methods in Intellectual History," *The Mississippi Valley Historical Review*, XLIV (June, 1957), 59. John Higham has reached a similar conclusion: "The largest distinctive aim of the intellectual historian . . . is to describe and explain the spirit of an age." "American Intellectual History: A Critical Appraisal," *American Quarterly*, XIII (Summer, 1961), 221.

mained in close intellectual contact with their counterparts across the Atlantic. After 1930 the massive emigration of central European intellectuals to the United States, initiated by the Nazi rise to power in Germany, effected a virtual transplant of many European ideas to America.

In the nineteenth century, however, particularly in its early years, American intellectuals deliberately repudiated European influence. They self-consciously determined to fashion a uniquely American polity and culture. Many American intellectual historians, working without benefit of the comparative perspective, have too readily assumed the success of that endeavor. But while American thinkers may have avoided explicit capture by imported European ideas, we believe that their success in establishing a distinctively American intellectual tradition was highly qualified. The history of ideas in America shows the same general pattern as the history of ideas in Europe.

The selections in the first portion of the anthology suggest that the history of both European and American social thought from the mid-eighteenth century to the First World War falls into five main periods. The eighteenth century itself was dominated, in both Europe and America, by a set of attitudes that historians group under the rubric "Enlightenment": the ideal of a rational organization of social and political life, a belief in civil liberties, and a commitment to a secular, scientific world view. The last years of the eighteenth century and the early decades of the nineteenth were characterized, on both sides of the Atlantic, by a reaction against the Enlightenment inheritance. In those years the belief in reason and science typical of the Enlightenment gave way to a characteristically Romantic concern for emotion, tradition, and religion, and political conservatism emerged as an explicit ideological posture.

During the middle years of the nineteenth century, the values of the Enlightenment experienced something of a revival, focussed now on an economic analysis of the emerging industrial civilization. European and American intellectuals sought to explain how the eighteenth-century ideal of a humane, pacified existence might be reconciled with the harsh realities of the Industrial Revolution. The closing decades of the nineteenth century found both European and American thinkers preoccupied with the achievements and aspirations of science, as epitomized in the application of principles derived from Darwinian biology to the analysis of social phenomena. That era was followed in turn by an early twentieth-century reaction against the complacent scientism of the late nineteenth century, a reaction that has been described as a "revolt against positivism" in Europe by H. Stuart Hughes and as a "revolt against formalism" in America by Morton White. Both European and American thinkers fought against deterministic, mechanistic modes of thought and turned their attention to the psychological, often unconscious, aspects of human behavior. As at the beginning of the nineteenth century, the rationalist heritage of the Enlightenment was again called into question.

We are still too close to most twentieth-century developments to have formed a satisfactory notion of their exact shape or significance. However, certain characteristic preoccupations can be identified, and we have included the last four sections of readings to illustrate recent European and American critiques of the collective, industrial nation-state.

A satisfactory explanation for the parallel development of European and American thought would require a much more extensive argument than can be presented in a short introductory essay of this sort. We might, however, indicate two possible lines of approach to the problem. These could be called the idealist and the materialist interpretations, or, alternatively, the Hegelian and the Marxian interpretations. The idealist interpretation would contend that the European and American intellectual traditions are in fact two variants of a larger, unitary experience, the Western intellectual tradition, which traces its origins back to the fusion of Greek and Judeo-Christian thought during the later centuries of the Roman Empire. The idealist would further argue that this tradition possesses an inherent historical logic or dialectic. Occidental culture thus follows an inevitable course of development in which the intellectual constructs typical of one period give rise to those of the next—perhaps by a mechanism of action and reaction (thesis and antithesis), as can be seen in the relation of the Romantic movement of the nineteenth century to the Enlightenment of the eighteenth. Moreover, since this evolutionary dialectic is built into the Western intellectual tradition, it works itself out wherever that tradition implants itself, regardless of the presence or absence of direct contact between the different branches of the tradition. Thus the parallel development of European and American ideas follows, according to the idealist explanation, from the logic implicit in their common intellectual inheritance.

The materialist, or Marxian, explanation, on the other hand, would direct attention to the common social, political, and particularly economic experience of Europeans and Americans during the last two hundred years. The specific features of this experience that might be singled out for emphasis would vary from historian to historian, but certainly one could point to the evolution in both Europe and America of a democratic political order, an industrialized capitalist economy, a mechanized technology, and a society in which status has come to be measured in terms of occupation and wealth, rather than in terms of inherited position. The materialist historian would then argue that certain ideological constructs reflect different stages in the evolution of such a civilization, and that the common course of European and American intellectual history follows from this shared practical experience.

We offer these (admittedly overly schematic) scenarios for their suggestive value only. The selections that follow do not pretend to substantiate either the idealist or the materialist interpretation. We are satisfied if, through the comparative method, they succeed in establishing the fact of Europe's and America's common intellectual experience, whatever its causes.

It is not our sole intention, however, to emphasize the essential congruence of the histories of European and American ideas. Intellectual history attempts to discern the elements that unify the thought of a given epoch, but it has another objective as well: the identification of those perennial preoccupations, assumptions, and ideas that, over time, unify the thought of a given place. The intellectual historian is concerned, that is, with the nature and development of intellectual traditions. It is in detecting and characterizing such traditions that comparison finds its most valuable application. While it discloses the general and discourages the parochial, it also illuminates the truly unique. This anthology, accordingly, hopes to encourage comparative examination of those factors that have been judged by many to define a distinctly American intellectual tradition.

Several historians have suggested ways in which American social thought is unique. Although not all of them have been expressly concerned with intellectual history, they have identified circumstances peculiar to the American experience and have argued or implied that the ideas issuing from those circumstances constituted important elements in a characteristically American intellectual style. Few of these historians have been systematically comparative in their method. The selections that follow, therefore, afford the reader an opportunity to test in a comparative context some of the major hypotheses about American uniqueness.

One circumstance that has differentiated the American experience from the European is reflected in the historical name for the Western hemisphere: the New World. America was not simply geographically separate from Europe; its civilization was also new in time, free from the weight of Old World history. R. W. B. Lewis has provided the best description of the intellectual consequences of that fact in *The American Adam*. Lewis argues that in the crucial period of the early nineteenth century, in the infancy of the nation, American intellectuals contrived an image of "the authentic American as a figure of heroic innocence and vast potentialities, poised at the start of a new history." [4] That image,

[4] R. W. B. Lewis, *The American Adam: Innocence, Tragedy, and Tradition in the Nineteenth Century* (Chicago: University of Chicago Press, 1955), 1.

says Lewis, dominated and unified American thought and gave it its unique character: American thinkers rejected Calvinistic notions of human sinfulness, questioned the basis of institutions and traditional ways of doing things, and fashioned their social thought largely without reference to the history of Europe and against the backdrop of a virgin continent to the west.

The attitude that encompassed those themes certainly informed the deliberately anti-Old World thinking of Thomas Jefferson and Ralph Waldo Emerson; but did it significantly differentiate Jefferson from the European *philosophes* or Emerson from the European Romantics? Can a sense of history similar to the one Lewis describes be seen in the political writings of John Adams, and does it meaningfully distinguish him from his great English counterpart, Edmund Burke? In general terms, do the notions of newness, innocence, potentiality, and freedom from history mark a substantially distinct American intellectual style in the nineteenth century, or do they simply define ephemeral variations on a succession of commonly European and American themes? A similar question might well be addressed to all theories of a uniquely American tradition of social thought.

David M. Potter, in *People of Plenty* (Chicago: University of Chicago Press, 1954), has identified another factor that has shaped the distinctive character of American history: economic abundance. In many ways, says Potter, abundance has made possible a "new history" for Americans, one freed from the conditions of scarcity that characterized all past societies. Though he does not deal primarily with intellectual history, Potter nevertheless suggests ways in which the existence of a prosperous economy has shaped American social thought.

Specifically, Potter notes that abundance has spared American society serious class conflict. The absence of social antagonism, he suggests, has denied American thinkers the necessity and hence the aptitude to think systematically in terms of conflict or antithesis. European thought, especially radical thought, says Potter, reflects the tensions of European society. It therefore tends toward complex, tension-ridden, dialectical constructions, as in the works of Hegel, Marx, Freud, or Sartre. American thought, in contrast, lacks such a dialectical dimension. It characteristically emphasizes unity and harmony. Karl Marx touched the same theme in 1852 when he complained that a leading American economist, Henry C. Carey (see Section V), was teaching that industrialism promoted harmony between social classes. Carey's views could not be raised to a general principle, Marx said, because they derived from observation of the peculiarly prosperous conditions in America. Conversely, it has become commonplace to attribute the indifference to Marxian ideas in America at least in part to economic prosperity.

Potter's argument gives support to the interpretation of American political thought advanced by Daniel Boorstin in *The Genius of American Politics*. "The peculiar strengths of American life," Boorstin says, "have saved us from the European preoccupation with political dogmas and left us inept and uninterested in political theory." [5] For Boorstin, that felicitous ineptitude derives principally from the erroneous but tenacious conviction that the Founding Fathers bequeathed to later generations a fully articulated political theory. Ever since the formation of the Republic, the deep belief in the continuity of our history from a fixed starting point, as well as our general prosperity, has discouraged the kind of ideological system-building that in Europe has produced Nazism, Fascism, and Communism. Americans were profoundly pragmatic, Boorstin suggests, well before William James elaborated the notion; from the beginning they eschewed dogma and fitted theory to fact. Thus Boorstin, like Potter, finds the characteristic trait of American social thought to be a sort of intellectual anemia, a salutary aversion to highly refined, monolithic theories of society or politics.

In *The Liberal Tradition in America*, the most explicitly comparative analysis of American and European social thought, Louis Hartz discusses a similar anemia. Essentially, Hartz elaborates Alexis de Tocqueville's insight in the 1830's that Americans were "reaping the fruits of the democratic revolution which we [Europeans] are undergoing, without having had the revolution itself." [6] Americans, says Hartz, echoing Tocqueville, were "born equal." They came to nationhood free from the heritage of a feudal past. Lacking an aristocratic right, America never developed a socialist left. She harbored only Lockian liberals, successful sons of the Enlightenment whose very success spelled their intellectual truncation: without meaningful opposition, they had no need to develop a rich intellectual dialogue as Europeans had done.

Thus, since the eighteenth century, Hartz maintains, America has enjoyed but one intellectual tradition: the liberal tradition. In politics that tradition comprised a belief in the rule of law, in civil liberties, and in a democratic form of government. It also entailed a distinct antipathy to power and the associated belief that society was best served if power was widely and evenly distributed. In economic and social terms the liberal tradition included a commitment to the institution of private property, to the ideal of a self-regulating capitalism, and to the definition of status by achievement rather than by birth. Intellectually the liberal tradition implied a dogmatic empiricism and corresponding hostility to

[5] Daniel Boorstin, *The Genius of American Politics* (Chicago: University of Chicago Press, 1953), 4.

[6] Alexis de Tocqueville, *Democracy in America*, ed. Richard D. Heffner (New York: New American Library, 1956), 36.

abstract conceptual systems. That latent anti-intellectualism, inherent in the European liberal tradition, was accentuated in America by the peculiar exclusiveness of American liberalism.

All supposedly antagonistic schools of thought in America, Hartz argues, have represented only minor variations on a single theme, at least when compared with the genuine diversity of the European intellectual tradition. Where Europe can boast of authentic revolutionaries and equally authentic reactionaries, America has produced only liberals. The fact that some of our intellectuals are called conservatives and others radicals Hartz attributes either to myopia or to simple convenience. Similarly, Hartz suggests that the periodization of American intellectual history into epochs dominated by progressive or regressive intellectual styles represents a spurious effort to lend contour and drama to an essentially one-dimensional and prosaic tale. All of our important intellectuals, from Thomas Jefferson to John C. Calhoun to William Graham Sumner to John Dewey, have remained liberals.[7]

All these studies have produced provocative hypotheses about the distinctive elements of the American experience: the newness of the North American continent; the constant reality of economic abundance; a fixed beginning in time, which fostered the faith that our ideological origins were so articulate as to require no further elaboration; the absence of a feudal period in our development. They have correspondingly suggested unique characteristics of the American mind: a sense of innocence and freedom from history; an incapacity to think dialectically; a pragmatic disregard for ideology; a one-dimensional liberalism; a general flatness and attenuation in our social thought. These themes will recur throughout the readings from American intellectuals that follow. With them, perhaps, should be mentioned two older customary schemes for explaining the American intellectual tradition: as a succession of escapes from a rigid, moralistic Puritanism, and as a progressively richer articulation of the democratic ethos.

Except Louis Hartz, none of the historians who have put forward these hypotheses has derived this theory from rigorously comparative

[7] Hartz is concerned in his book almost exclusively with political intellectuals. He does not argue that all aspects of American cultural history have been as monolithic as the history of American political theory. And yet Hartz's thesis of one-dimensionality reflects a characteristic European attitude toward American culture in its larger contours: the conviction that by European standards our intellectual history has been a distinctly narrow, even impoverished, affair. Strictly speaking, of course, comparative judgments about American culture ought to be made against the example of a single European nation—say, France—rather than against European culture as a whole. Such a national comparison might prove illuminating, but we have preferred to follow Hartz in treating Europe itself as the unit of comparison.

analysis. One can never be certain, therefore, that the themes they describe as characteristically American warrant the use of the adjective "American" more than they warrant the use of such other qualifiers as "Western" or "Anglo-Saxon" or simply "modern." To that liability the present anthology should serve as a corrective. But whether American thought is best understood as a mere variation of European thought, or whether it possesses enough genuine distinctiveness to justify discussion of a separate American intellectual tradition are questions this book can only raise. The reader must supply the answers.

SOCIAL THOUGHT
IN AMERICA AND EUROPE

Readings in Comparative Intellectual History

I

THE ENLIGHTENMENT

The Enlightenment is the name given by historians to the great intellectual movement of the eighteenth century in which European and American thinkers severed the ties binding them to the Christian past and articulated the basic precepts of a modern secular world view. The leading figures of the movement styled themselves philosophes *(French for "philosophers"), announcing thereby that they chose reason and experience as the best guides to correct belief and conduct. In other words, nothing was to be accepted uncritically on the basis of authority, tradition, or revelation.*

In the realm of religion and morals, the typical philosophe *was a deist, as is evidenced by the selections here from François Marie Arouet de Voltaire (1694–1778), Benjamin Franklin (1706–1790), and Thomas Jefferson (1743–1826). For the elaborate doctrines and rituals of orthodox Christianity, the deist substituted a simple belief in a benevolent Creator, who demanded of men nothing more than that they lead virtuous lives. Some of the European* philosophes *— David Hume, Denis Diderot, Baron Holbach — passed beyond deism to full-fledged atheism or agnosticism. However, for the majority of Enlightenment thinkers, deism — which was, in reality, a halfway house between traditional faith and modern scepticism — remained the most comfortable religious stance.*

It is difficult to define a characteristic Enlightenment position in politics and social theory. Voltaire's essay on "Democracy," from the Philosophical Dictionary, *indicates that European intellectuals often felt more equivocal about popular government than did their American confreres. Indeed although Voltaire moved closer to democracy as he grew older, he remained throughout his career an advocate of enlightened despotism; he believed that the best political system was a monarchy ruled by a philosopher-king. Jefferson's* Notes on the State of Virginia *make clear how repugnant such a notion was to the mind of the American Enlightenment.*

Even though European and American philosophes *might have disagreed about the most desirable form of government, there nevertheless existed among them a broad consensus in social and political attitudes. There was, for example, the conviction that the state had no business in certain areas of individual life, that it should not constrain religious belief or inhibit the free expression and dissemination of ideas. There was also a marked hostility to legally sanctioned inequalities, a strong antipathy, that is, toward aristocratic or hierarchical social arrangements, an attitude represented here especially clearly in the selection from Jean-Jacques Rousseau (1712–1778). In general, the Americans were more thoroughgoing in their egalitarianism than the Europeans, although, as Jefferson's* Notes *reveal, their commitment to social equality was profoundly compromised by the institution of Negro slavery.*

The social theorists of the late eighteenth and early nineteenth centuries — the men whose writings will concern us in Section II of this anthology — came to regard the philosophes' *ideas as dangerously subversive. In fact, they concluded that those ideas were the primary moving force behind the catastrophe of the French Revolution. Whether or not they were correct in this judgment, it is undoubtedly the case that the ideas of the Enlightenment, in both Europe and America, were essentially critical and, therefore, at least potentially revolutionary. However, in America the bearers of enlightened attitudes were, for the most part, members of the country's establishment — leading statesmen, educators, journalists, even generals — whereas in Europe the* philosophes *were almost always outsiders, sometimes even to the point, as with Voltaire, of spending a good portion of their lives in exile. It is this contrast that Louis Hartz has in mind when he claims that in America conservatism and liberalism converge. In a word, our* philosophes *are also our Founding Fathers.*

Philosophical Dictionary

(1750)

FRANÇOIS MARIE AROUET DE VOLTAIRE

Democracy

Le pire des états, c'est l'état populaire.
That sway is worst, in which the people rule.

Such is the opinion which Cinna gave Augustus. But on the other hand, Maximus maintains, that

Le pire des états, c'est l'état monarchique.
That sway is worst, in which a monarch rules.

Bayle,[1] in his "Philosophical Dictionary," after having repeatedly advocated both sides of the question, gives, under the article on "Pericles," a most disgusting picture of democracy, and more particularly that of Athens.

A republican, who is a stanch partisan of democracy, and one of our "proposers of questions," sends us his refutation of Bayle and his apology for Athens. We will adduce his reasons. It is the privilege of every writer to judge the living and the dead; he who thus sits in judgment will be himself judged by others, who, in their turn, will be judged also; and thus, from age to age, all sentences are, according to circumstances, reversed or reformed.

Bayle, then, after some common-place observations, uses these words: "A man would look in vain into the history of Macedon for as much tyranny as he finds in the history of Athens." . . .

It is difficult to weigh, in an exquisitely nice balance, the iniquities of the republic of Athens and of the court of Macedon. We still upbraid the Athenians with the banishment of Cimon, Aristides, Themistocles, and Alcibiades, and the sentences of death upon Phocion and Socrates; sentences similar in absurdity and cruelty to those of some of our own tribunals.

In short, what we can never pardon in the Athenians is the execution of their six victorious generals, condemned because they had not time to

From William Fleming, tr., *The Works of Voltaire* (New York: The St. Hubert Guild, 1901), vol. IV, 75–79; vol. VI, 131–134; vol. VII, 181–185.

[1] [Pierre Bayle (1647–1706), acerbic critic of Christianity who lived in exile in Holland, was recognized by the eighteenth-century *philosophes* as one of their great forbears. His *Philosophical Dictionary* served as a model for Voltaire. — Eds.]

bury their dead after the victory, and because they were prevented from doing so by a tempest. The sentence is at once so ridiculous and barbarous, it bears such a stamp of superstition and ingratitude, that those of the Inquisition, those delivered against Urbain Grandier, against the wife of Marshal d'Ancre, against Montrin, and against innumerable sorcerers and witches, etc., are not, in fact, fooleries more atrocious.

It is in vain to say, in excuse of the Athenians, that they believed, like Homer before them, that the souls of the dead were always wandering, unless they had received the honors of sepulture or burning. A folly is no excuse for a barbarity.

A dreadful evil, indeed, for the souls of a few Greeks to ramble for a week or two on the shores of the ocean! The evil is, in consigning living men to the executioner; living men who have won a battle for you; living men, to whom you ought to be devoutly grateful.

Thus, then, are the Athenians convicted of having been at once the most silly and the most barbarous judges in the world. But we must now place in the balance the crimes of the court of Macedon; we shall see that that court far exceeds Athens in point of tyranny and atrocity.

There is ordinarily no comparison to be made between the crimes of the great, who are always ambitious, and those of the people, who never desire, and who never can desire, anything but liberty and equality. These two sentiments, "liberty and equality," do not *necessarily* lead to calumny, rapine, assassination, poisoning, and devastation of the lands of neighbors; but, the towering ambition and thirst for power of the great precipitate them headlong into every species of crime in all periods and all places.

In this same Macedon, the virtue of which Bayle opposes to that of Athens, we see nothing but a tissue of tremendous crimes for a series of two hundred years.

It is Ptolemy, the uncle of Alexander the Great, who assassinates his brother Alexander to usurp the kingdom. It is Philip, his brother, who spends his life in guilt and perjury, and ends it by a stab from Pausanias.

Olympias orders Queen Cleopatra and her son to be thrown into a furnace of molten brass. She assassinates Aridæus. Antigonus assassinates Eumenes. Antigonus Gonatas, his son, poisons the governor of the citadel of Corinth, marries his widow, expels her, and takes possession of the citadel. Philip, his grandson, poisons Demetrius, and defiles the whole of Macedon with murders. Perseus kills his wife with his own hand, and poisons his brother. These perfidies and cruelties are authenticated in history.

Thus, then, for two centuries, the madness of despotism converts Macedon into a theatre for every crime; and in the same space of time you see the popular government of Athens stained only by five or six acts of judicial iniquity, five or six certainly atrocious judgments, of which the people in every instance repented, and for which they made, as far as they could, honorable expiation (*amende honorable*). They asked pardon of Socrates after his death, and erected to his memory the small temple called *Socrateion*. They asked pardon of Phocion, and raised a statue to his honor. They asked pardon of the six generals, so ridiculously condemned and so basely executed. They confined in chains the principal accuser, who, with difficulty, escaped from public vengeance. The Athenian people, therefore, appear to have had good natural dispositions, connected, as they were, with great versatility and frivolity. In what despotic state has the injustice of precipitate decrees ever been thus ingenuously acknowledged and deplored?

Bayle, then, is for this once in the wrong. My republican has reason on his side. Popular government, therefore, is in itself iniquitous, and less abominable than monarchical despotism. . . .

Liberty of the Press

. . . In general, we have as natural a right to make use of our pens as our language, at our peril, risk, and fortune. I know many books which fatigue, but I know of none which have done real evil. Theologians, or pretended politicians, cry: "Religion is destroyed, the government is lost, if you print certain truths or certain paradoxes. Never attempt to think, till you have demanded permission from a monk or an officer. It is against good order for a man to think for himself. Homer, Plato, Cicero, Virgil, Pliny, Horace, never published anything but with the approbation of the doctors of the Sorbonne and of the holy Inquisition."

"See into what horrible decay the liberty of the press brought England and Holland. It is true that they possess the commerce of the whole world, and that England is victorious on sea and land; but it is merely a false greatness, a false opulence: they hasten with long strides to their ruin. An enlightened people cannot exist."

None can reason more justly, my friends; but let us see, if you please, what state has been lost by a book. The most dangerous, the most pernicious of all, is that of Spinoza. Not only in the character of a Jew he attacks the New Testament, but in the character of a scholar he ruins the Old; his system of atheism is a thousand times better composed and reasoned than those of Straton and of Epicurus. We have need of the most profound sagacity to answer to the arguments by which he endeavors to prove that one substance cannot form another.

Like yourself, I detest this book, which I perhaps understand better than you, and to which you have very badly replied; but have you discovered that this book has changed the face of the world? Has any preacher lost a florin of his income by the publication of the works of Spinoza? Is there a bishop whose rents have diminished? On the contrary, their revenues have doubled since his time: all the ill is reduced to a small number of peaceable readers, who have examined the arguments of Spinoza in their closets, and have written for or against them works but little known.

For yourselves, it is of little consequence to have caused to be printed "*ad usum Delphini*," the atheism of Lucretius — as you have already been reproached with doing — no trouble, no scandal, has ensued from it: so leave Spinoza to live in peace in Holland. Lucretius was left in repose at Rome.

But if there appears among you any new book, the ideas of which shock your own — supposing you have any — or of which the author may be of a party contrary to yours — or what is worse, of which the author may not be of any party at all — then you cry out "Fire!" and let all be noise, scandal, and uproar in your small corner of the earth. There is an abominable man who has printed that if we had no hands we could not make shoes nor stockings. Devotees cry out, furred doctors assemble, alarms multiply from college to college, from house to house, and why? For five or six pages, about which there no longer will be a question at the end of three months. Does a book displease you? refute it. Does it tire you? read it not.

Oh! say you to me, the books of Luther and Calvin have destroyed the Roman Catholic religion in one-half of Europe? Why say not also, that the books of the patriarch Photius have destroyed this Roman religion in Asia, Africa, Greece, and Russia?

You deceive yourself very grossly, when you think that you have been ruined by books. The empire of Russia is two thousand leagues in extent, and there are not six men who are aware of the points disputed by the Greek and Latin Church. If the monk Luther, John Calvin, and the vicar Zuinglius had been content with writing, Rome would yet subjugate all the states that it has lost; but these people and their adherents ran from town to town, from house to house, exciting the women, and were maintained by princes. Fury, which tormented Amata, and which, according to Virgil, whipped her like a top, was not more turbulent. Know, that one enthusiastic, factious, ignorant, supple, vehement Capuchin, the emissary of some ambitious monks, preaching, confessing, communicating, and caballing, will much sooner overthrow a province than a hundred authors can enlighten it. It was not the Koran which caused Mahomet to succeed: it was Mahomet who caused the success of the Koran.

No! Rome has not been vanquished by books; it has been so by having caused Europe to revolt at its rapacity; by the public sale of indulgences; for having insulted men, and wishing to govern them like domestic animals; for having abused its power to such an extent that it is astonishing a single village remains to it. Henry VIII., Elizabeth, the duke of Saxe, the landgrave of Hesse, the princes of Orange, the Condés and Colignys, have done all, and books nothing. Trumpets have never gained battles, nor caused any walls to fall except those of Jericho.

You fear books, as certain small cantons fear violins. Let us read, and let us dance — these two amusements will never do any harm to the world. . . .

Sect

Every sect, of whatever opinion it may be, is a rallying point for doubt and error. Scotists, Thomists, Realists, Nominalists, Papists, Calvinists, Molinists, and Jansenists, are only warlike appellations.

There is no sect in geometry; we never say: A Euclidian, an Archimedian. When truth is evident, it is impossible to divide people into parties and factions. Nobody disputes that it is broad day at noon.

That part of astronomy which determines the course of the stars, and the return of eclipses, being now known, there is no longer any dispute among astronomers.

It is similar with a small number of truths, which are similarly established; but if you are a Mahometan, as there are many men who are not Mahometans, you may possibly be in error.

What would be the true religion, if Christianity did not exist? That in which there would be no sects; that in which all minds necessarily agreed.

Now, in what doctrine are all minds agreed? In the adoration of one God, and in probity. All the philosophers who have professed a religion have said at all times: "There is a God, and He must be just." Behold then the universal religion, established throughout all time and among all men! The point then in which all agree is true; the systems in regard to which all differ are false. . . .

When Zoroaster, Hermes, Orpheus, Minos, and all the great men say: Let us worship God, and be just, no one laughs; but all the world sneers at him who pretends, that to please God it is proper to die holding a cow by the tail; at him who cuts off a particle of foreskin for the same purpose; at him who consecrates crocodiles and onions; at him who attaches eternal salvation to the bones of dead men carried underneath the shirt, or to a plenary indulgence purchased at Rome for two sous and a half.

Whence this universal assemblage of laughing and hissing from one end of the universe to the other? It must be that the things which all the world derides are not evident truths. What shall we say to a secretary of Sejanus, who dedicates to Petronius a book, in a confused and involved style, entitled "The Truth of the Sibylline Oracles, Proved from Facts."

This secretary at first proves to you, that God sent upon earth many Sibyls, one after the other, having no other means of instructing men. It is demonstrated, that God communicated with these Sibyls, because the word "sibyl" signifies "Council of God." They ought to live a long time, for this privilege at least belongs to persons with whom God communicates. They amounted to twelve, because this number is sacred. They certainly predicted all the events in the world, because Tarquin the Proud bought their book from an old woman for a hundred crowns. What unbeliever, exclaims the secretary, can deny all these evident facts, which took place in one corner of the earth, in the face of all the world? Who can deny the accomplishment of their prophecies? Has not Virgil himself cited the predictions of the Sibyls? If we have not the first copies of the Sibylline books, written at a time when no one could read and write, we have authentic copies. Impiety must be silent before such proofs. . . .

Sect and error are synonymous terms. Thou art a peripatetic and I a Platonist; we are therefore both in the wrong; for thou opposest Plato, because his chimeras repel thee; and I fly from Aristotle, because it appears to me that he knew not what he said. If the one or the other had demonstrated the truth, there would have been an end of sect. To declare for the opinion of one in opposition to that of another, is to take part in a civil war. There is no sect in mathematics or experimental philosophy: a man who examines the relation between a cone and a sphere is not of the sect of Archimedes; and he who perceived that the square of the hypotenuse of a right-angled triangle is equal to the sum of the squares of the other two sides, is not in consequence a Pythagorean.

When we say that the blood circulates, that the air is weighty, that the rays of the sun are a bundle of seven refrangible rays, it follows not that we are of the sect of Harvey, of Torricelli, or of Newton; we simply acquiesce in the truths which they demonstrate, and the whole universe will be of the same opinion.

Such is the character of truth, which belongs to all time and to all men. It is only to be produced to be acknowledged, and admits of no opposition. A long dispute signifies that both parties are in error.

A *Discourse upon the Origin and the Foundation of the Inequality Among Mankind* (1755)

JEAN-JACQUES ROUSSEAU

. . . I conceive two species of inequality among men; one which I call natural, or physical inequality, because it is established by nature, and consists in the difference of age, health, bodily strength, and the qualities of

From *The Harvard Classics* (New York: P. F. Collier and Son, 1910), vol. XXXIV, 165, 194, 220–228.

the mind, or of the soul; the other which may be termed moral, or political inequality, because it depends on a kind of convention, and is established, or at least authorized, by the common consent of mankind. This species of inequality consists in the different privileges which some men enjoy, to the prejudice of others, such as that of being richer, more honoured, more powerful, and even that of exacting obedience from them. . . .

. . . We may easily perceive that among the differences which distinguish men, several pass for natural, which are merely the work of habit and the different kinds of life adopted by men living in a social way. Thus a robust or delicate constitution, and the strength and weakness which depend on it, are oftener produced by the hardy or effeminate manner in which a man has been brought up, than by the primitive constitution of his body. It is the same thus in regard to the forces of the mind; and education not only produces a difference between those minds which are cultivated and those which are not, but even increases that which is found among the first in proportion to their culture; for let a giant and a dwarf set out in the same path, the giant at every step will acquire a new advantage over the dwarf. Now, if we compare the prodigious variety in the education and manner of living of the different orders of men in a civil state, with the simplicity and uniformity that prevails in the animal and savage life, where all the individuals make use of the same aliments, live in the same manner, and do exactly the same things, we shall easily conceive how much the difference between man and man in the state of nature must be less than in the state of society, and how much every inequality of institution must increase the natural inequalities of the human species. . . .

The various forms of government owe their origin to the various degrees of inequality between the members at the time they first coalesced into a political body. Where a man happened to be eminent for power, for virtue, for riches, or for credit, he became sole magistrate, and the state assumed a monarchical form; if many of pretty equal eminence outtopped all the rest, they were jointly elected, and this election produced an aristocracy; those, between whose fortune or talents there happened to be no such disproportion, and who had deviated less from the state of nature, retained in common the supreme administration, and formed a democracy. Time demonstrated which of these forms suited mankind best. Some remained altogether subject to the laws; others soon bowed their necks to masters. The former laboured to preserve their liberty; the latter thought of nothing but invading that of their neighbours, jealous at seeing others enjoy a blessing which themselves had lost. In a word, riches and conquest fell to the share of the one, and virtue and happiness to that of the other.

In these various modes of government the offices at first were all elective; and when riches did not preponderate, the preference was given to merit, which gives a natural ascendant, and to age, which is the parent of deliberateness in council, and experience in execution. The ancients among the Hebrews, the Geronts of Sparta, the Senate of Rome, nay, the very etymology of our word seigneur, show how much gray hairs were formerly respected. The oftener the choice fell upon old men, the oftener it became necessary to repeat it, and the more the trouble of such repetitions became sensible; electioneering took place; factions arose; the parties contracted ill-blood; civil wars blazed forth; the lives of the citizens were sacrificed to the pretended happiness of the state; and things at last came to such a pass, as to be ready to relapse into their primitive confusion. The ambition of the principal men induced them to take advantage of these circumstances to perpetuate the hitherto temporary charges in their families; the people already inured to dependence, accustomed to ease and the conveniences of life, and too much enervated to break their fetters, consented to the increase of their slavery for the sake of securing their tranquillity; and it is thus that chiefs, become hereditary, contracted the habit of considering magistracies as a family estate, and themselves as proprietors of those communities, of which at first they were but mere officers; to call their fellow-citizens their slaves; to look upon them, like so many cows or sheep, as a part of their substance; and to style themselves the peers of Gods, and Kings of Kings.

By pursuing the progress of inequality in these different revolutions, we shall discover that the establishment of laws and of the right of property was the first stage; the institution of magistrates the second; and the third and last the changing of legal into arbitrary power; so that the different states of rich and poor were authorized by the first epoch; those of powerful and weak by the second; and by the third those of master and slave, which formed the last degree of inequality, and the term in which all the rest at last end, till new revolutions entirely dissolve the government, or bring it back nearer to its legal constitution. . . .

Were this a proper place to enter into details, I could easily explain in what manner inequalities in point of credit and authority become unavoidable among private persons the moment that, united into one body, they are obliged to compare themselves one with another, and to note the differences which they find in the continual use every man must make of his neighbour. These differences are of several kinds; but riches, nobility or rank, power and personal merit, being in general the principal distinctions by which men in society measure each other, I could prove that the harmony or conflict between these different forces is the surest indication of the good or bad original constitution of any state: I could make it appear that, as among these four kinds of inequality, personal qualities are the source of all the rest, riches is that in which they ultimately terminate, because, being the most immediately useful to the prosperity of individuals, and the most easy to communicate, they are made use of to purchase every other distinction. By this observation we are enabled to judge with tolerable exactness how much any people has deviated from its primitive institution, and what steps it has still to make to the extreme term of corruption. I could show how much this universal desire of reputation, of honours, of preference, with which we are all devoured, exercises and compares our talents and our forces: how much it excites and multiplies our passions; and, by creating a universal competition, rivalship, or rather enmity among men, how many disappointments, successes, and catastrophes of every kind it daily causes among the innumerable pretenders whom it engages in the same career. I could show that it is to this itch of being spoken of, to this fury of distinguishing ourselves which seldom or never gives us a moment's respite, that we owe both the best and the worst things among us, our virtues and our vices, our sciences and our errors, our conquerors and our philosophers; that is to say, a great many bad things to a very few good ones. I could prove, in short, that if we behold a handful of rich and powerful men seated on the pinnacle of fortune and greatness, while the crowd grovel in obscurity and want, it is merely because the first prize what they enjoy, but in the same degree that others want it, and that, without changing their condition, they would cease to be happy the minute the people ceased to be miserable.

But these details would alone furnish sufficient matter for a more considerable work, in which might be weighed the advantages and disadvantages of every species of government relatively to the rights of man in a state of nature, and might likewise be unveiled all the different faces under which inequality has appeared to this day, and may hereafter appear to the end of time, according to the nature of these several governments, and the revolutions time must unavoidably occasion in them. We should then see the multitude oppressed by domestic tyrants in consequence of those very precautions taken by them to guard against foreign masters. We should see oppression increase continually without its being ever possible for the oppressed to know where it would stop, nor what lawful means they had left to check its progress. We should see the rights of citizens and the liberties of nations extinguished by slow degrees, and the groans and protestations and appeals of the weak treated as seditious murmurings. We should see policy confine to a mercenary portion of the people the honour of defending the common cause.[1] We should see imposts made necessary by such measures, the disheartened husbandman desert his field even in time of peace, and quit the plough to take up the sword. We should see fatal and whimsical rules laid down concerning the point of honour. We should see the champions of their country sooner or later

[1] [Rousseau refers to the practice, common in the eighteenth century, of hiring private armies to fight national wars. — Eds.]

become her enemies, and perpetually holding their poniards to the breasts of their fellow citizens. . . .

'Tis from the bosom of this disorder and these revolutions, that despotism gradually rearing up her hideous crest, and devouring in every part of the state all that still remained sound and untainted, would at last issue to trample upon the laws and the people, and establish herself upon the ruins of the republic. The times immediately preceding this last alteration would be times of calamity and trouble: but at last everything would be swallowed up by the monster; and the people would no longer have chiefs or laws, but only tyrants. At this fatal period all regard to virtue and manners would likewise disappear; for despotism . . . tolerates no other master, whenever it reigns; the moment it speaks, probity and duty lose all their influence, and the blindest obedience is the only virtue the miserable slaves have left them to practice.

This is the last term of inequality, the extreme point which closes the circle and meets that from which we set out. 'Tis here that all private men return to their primitive equality, because they are no longer of any account; and that, the subjects having no longer any law but that of their master, nor the master any other law but his passions, all notions of good and principles of justice again disappear. 'Tis here that everything returns to the sole law of the strongest, and of course to a new state of nature different from that with which we began, in as much as the first was the state of nature in its purity, and the last the consequence of excessive corruption. There is, in other respects, so little difference between these two states, and the contract of government is so much dissolved by despotism, that the despot is no longer master than he continues the strongest, and that, as soon as his slaves can expel him, they may do it without his having the least right to complain of their using him ill. The insurrection, which ends in the death or dethroning of a sultan, is as juridical an act as any by which the day before he disposed of the lives and fortunes of his subjects. Force alone upheld him, force alone overturns him. Thus all things take place and succeed in their natural order; and whatever may be the upshot of these hasty and frequent revolutions, no one man has reason to complain of another's injustice but only of his own indiscretion or bad fortune. . . .

. . . Savage man and civilised man differ so much at bottom in point of inclinations and passions, that what constitutes the supreme happiness of the one would reduce the other to despair. The first sighs for nothing but repose and liberty; he desires only to live, and to be exempt from labour; nay, the quietude of the most confirmed Stoic falls short of his consummate indifference for every other object. On the contrary, the citizen, always in motion, is perpetually sweating and toiling, and racking his brains to find out occupations still more laborious: He continues a drudge to his last minute; nay, he courts death to be able to live, or renounces life to acquire immortality. He cringes to men in power whom he hates, and to rich men whom he despises; he sticks at nothing to have the honour of serving them; he is not ashamed to value himself on his own weakness and the protection they afford him; and proud of his chains, he speaks with disdain of those who have not the honour of being the partner of his bondage. What a spectacle must the painful and envied labours of a European minister of state form in the eyes of a Caribbean! How many cruel deaths would not this indolent savage prefer to such a horrid life, which very often is not even sweetened by the pleasure of doing good? But to see the drift of so many cares, his mind should first have affixed some meaning to these words power and reputation; he should be apprised that there are men who consider as something the looks of the rest of mankind, who know how to be happy and satisfied with themselves on the testimony of others sooner than upon their own. In fact, the real source of all those differences is that the savage lives within himself, whereas the citizen, constantly beside himself, knows only how to live in the opinion of others; insomuch that it is, if I may say so, merely from their judgment that he derives the consciousness of his own existence. It is foreign to my subject to show how this disposition engenders so much indifference for good and evil, notwithstanding so many and such fine discourses of morality; how everything, being reduced to appearances, becomes mere art and mummery: honour, friendship, virtue, and often vice itself, which we at last learn the secret to boast of; how, in short, ever inquiring of others what we are, and never daring to question ourselves on so delicate a point, in the midst of so much philosophy, humanity, and politeness, and so many sublime maxims, we have nothing to show for ourselves but a deceitful and frivolous exterior, honour without virtue, reason without wisdom, and pleasure without happiness. It is sufficient that I have proved that this is not the original condition of man, and that it is merely the spirit of society, and the inequality which society engenders, that thus change and transform all our natural inclinations.

I have endeavoured to exhibit the origin and progress of inequality, the institution and abuse of political societies, as far as these things are capable of being deduced from the nature of man by the mere light of reason, and independently of those sacred maxims which give to the sovereign authority the sanction of divine right. It follows from this picture, that as there is scarce any inequality among men in a state of nature, all that which we now behold owes its force and its growth to the development of our faculties and the improvement of our understanding, and at last becomes permanent and lawful by the establishment of property and of laws. It likewise follows that moral inequality, authorised by any right that is merely positive, clashes with natural right, as often as it does not combine in the same proportion with physical inequality: a distinction which sufficiently determines what we ought to think in that respect of the kind of inequality which obtains in all civilised nations, since it is evidently against the law of nature that infancy should command old age, folly conduct wisdom, and a handful of men should be ready to choke with superfluities, while the famished multitude want the commonest necessaries of life.

The Autobiography
(1771)

BENJAMIN FRANKLIN

Before I enter upon my public appearance in business, it may be well to let you know the then state of my mind with regard to my principles and morals, that you may see how far those influenc'd the future events of my life. My parents had early given me religious impressions, and brought me through my childhood piously in the Dissenting way. But I was scarce fifteen, when, after doubting by turns of several points, as I found them disputed in the different books I read, I began to doubt of Revelation itself. Some books against Deism fell into my hands; they were said to be the substance of sermons preached at Boyle's Lectures. It happened that they wrought an effect on me quite contrary to what was intended by them; for the arguments of the Deists, which were quoted to be refuted, appeared to me much stronger than the refutations; in short, I soon became a thorough Deist. . . .

I grew convinc'd that *truth, sincerity* and *integrity* in dealings between man and man were of the utmost importance to the felicity of life; and I form'd written resolutions, which still remain in my journal book, to practice them ever while I lived. Revelation had indeed no weight with me, as such; but I entertain'd an opinion that, though certain actions might not be bad *because* they were forbidden by it, or good *because* it commanded them, yet probably these actions might be forbidden *because* they were bad for us, or commanded *because* they were beneficial to us, in their own natures, all the circumstances of things considered. And this persuasion, with the kind hand of Providence, or some guardian angel, or accidental favourable circumstances and situations, or all together, preserved me, thro' this dangerous time of youth, and the hazardous situations I was sometimes in among strangers, remote from the eye and

From Albert Henry Smyth, ed., *The Writings of Benjamin Franklin* (New York: Macmillan, 1905), vol. I, 295–297, 324–331.

advice of my father, without any willful gross immorality or injustice, that might have been expected from my want of religion. I say willful, because the instances I have mentioned had something of *necessity* in them, from my youth, inexperience, and the knavery of others. I had therefore a tolerable character to begin the world with; I valued it properly, and determin'd to preserve it. . . .

I had been religiously educated as a Presbyterian; and tho' some of the dogmas of that persuasion, such as *the eternal decrees of God, election, reprobation*, etc., appeared to me unintelligible, others doubtful, and I early absented myself from the public assemblies of the sect, Sunday being my studying day, I never was without some religious principles. I never doubted, for instance, the existence of the Deity; that he made the world, and govern'd it by his Providence; that the most acceptable service of God was the doing good to man; that our souls are immortal; and that all crime will be punished, and virtue rewarded, either here or hereafter. These I esteem'd the essentials of every religion; and, being to be found in all the religions we had in our country, I respected them all, tho' with different degrees of respect, as I found them more or less mix'd with other articles, which, without any tendency to inspire, promote, or confirm morality, serv'd principally to divide us, and make us unfriendly to one another. This respect to all, with an opinion that the worst had some good effects, induc'd me to avoid all discourse that might tend to lessen the good opinion another might have of his own religion; and as our province increas'd in people, and new places of worship were continually wanted, and generally erected by voluntary contribution, my mite for such purpose, whatever might be the sect, was never refused.

Tho' I seldom attended any public worship, I had still an opinion of its propriety, and of its utility when rightly conducted, and I regularly paid my annual subscription for the support of the only Presbyterian minister or meeting we had in Philadelphia. He us'd to visit me sometimes as a friend, and admonish me to attend his administrations, and I was now and then prevail'd on to do so, once for five Sundays successively. Had he been in my opinion a good preacher, perhaps I might have continued, notwithstanding the occasion I had for the Sunday's leisure in my course of study; but his discourses were chiefly either polemic arguments, or explications of the peculiar doctrines of our sect, and were all to me very dry, uninteresting, and unedifying, since not a single moral principle was inculcated or enforc'd, their aim seeming to be rather to make us Presbyterians than good citizens.

At length he took for his text that verse of the fourth chapter of Philippians, "*Finally, brethren, whatsoever things are true, honest, just, pure, lovely, or of good report, if there be any virtue, or any praise, think on these things.*" And I imagin'd, in a sermon on such a text, we could not miss of having some morality. But he confin'd himself to five points only, as meant by the apostle, viz.: 1. Keeping holy the Sabbath day.

2. Being diligent in reading the holy Scriptures. 3. Attending duly the publick worship. 4. Partaking of the Sacrament. 5. Paying a due respect to God's ministers. These might be all good things; but, as they were not the kind of good things that I expected from that text, I despaired of ever meeting with them from any other, was disgusted, and attended his preaching no more. I had some years before compos'd a little Liturgy, or form of prayer, for my own private use (viz., in 1728), entitled, *Articles of Belief and Acts of Religion.* I return'd to the use of this, and went no more to the public assemblies. My conduct might be blameable, but I leave it, without attempting further to excuse it; my present purpose being to relate facts, and not to make apologies for them.

It was about this time I conceiv'd the bold and arduous project of arriving at moral perfection. I wish'd to live without committing any fault at any time; I would conquer all that either natural inclination, custom, or company might lead me into. As I knew, or thought I knew, what was right and wrong, I did not see why I might not always do the one and avoid the other. But I soon found I had undertaken a task of more difficulty than I had imagined. While my care was employ'd in guarding against one fault, I was often surprised by another; habit took the advantage of inattention; inclination was sometimes too strong for reason. I concluded, at length, that the mere speculative conviction that it was our interest to be completely virtuous, was not sufficient to prevent our slipping; and that the contrary habits must be broken, and good ones acquired and established, before we can have any dependence on a steady, uniform rectitude of conduct. For this purpose I therefore contrived the following method.

In the various enumerations of the moral virtues I had met with in my reading, I found the catalogue more or less numerous, as different writers included more or fewer ideas under the same name. Temperance, for example, was by some confined to eating and drinking, while by others it was extended to mean the moderating every other pleasure, appetite, inclination, or passion, bodily or mental, even to our avarice and ambition. I propos'd to myself, for the sake of clearness, to use rather more names, with fewer ideas annex'd to each, than a few names with more ideas; and I included under thirteen names of virtues all that at that time occurr'd to me as necessary or desirable, and annexed to each a short precept, which fully express'd the extent I gave to its meaning.

These names of virtues, with their precepts, were:

1. TEMPERANCE. Eat not to dullness; drink not to elevation.
2. SILENCE. Speak not but what may benefit others or yourself; avoid trifling conversation.
3. ORDER. Let all your things have their places; let each part of your business have its time.

4. RESOLUTION. Resolve to perform what you ought; perform without fail what you resolve.
5. FRUGALITY. Make no expense but to do good to others or yourself; *i.e.*, waste nothing.
6. INDUSTRY. Lose no time; be always employ'd in something useful; cut off all unnecessary actions.
7. SINCERITY. Use no hurtful deceit; think innocently and justly, and, if you speak, speak accordingly.
8. JUSTICE. Wrong none by doing injuries, or omitting the benefits that are your duty.
9. MODERATION. Avoid extreams; forbear resenting injuries so much as you think they deserve.
10. CLEANLINESS. Tolerate no uncleanliness in body, cloaths, or habitation.
11. TRANQUILLITY. Be not disturbed at trifles, or at accidents common or unavoidable.
12. CHASTITY. Rarely use venery but for health or offspring, never to dulness, weakness, or the injury of your own or another's peace or reputation.
13. HUMILITY. Imitate Jesus and Socrates.

My intention being to acquire the *habitude* of all these virtues, I judg'd it would be well not to distract my attention by attempting the whole at once, but to fix it on one of them at a time; and, when I should be master of that, then to proceed to another, and so on, till I should have gone thro' the thirteen; and, as the previous acquisition of some might facilitate the acquisition of certain others, I arrang'd them with that view, as they stand above. Temperance first, as it tends to procure that coolness and clearness of head, which is so necessary where constant vigilance was to be kept up, and guard maintained against the unremitting attraction of ancient habits, and the force of perpetual temptations. This being acquir'd and establish'd, Silence would be more easy; and my desire being to gain knowledge at the same time that I improv'd in virtue, and considering that in conversation it was obtain'd rather by the use of the ears than of the tongue, and therefore wishing to break a habit I was getting into of prattling, punning, and joking, which only made me acceptable to trifling company, I gave *Silence* the second place. This and the next, *Order*, I expected would allow me more time for attending to my project and my studies. *Resolution*, once become habitual, would keep me firm in my endeavours to obtain all the subsequent virtues; *Frugality* and Industry freeing me from my remaining debt, and producing affluence and independence, would make more easy the practice of Sincerity and Justice, etc., etc. Conceiving then, that, agreeably to the advice of Pythagoras in his Golden Verses, daily examination would be necessary, I contrived the following method for conducting that examination.

I made a little book, in which I allotted a page for each of the virtues. I rul'd each page with red ink, so as to have seven columns, one for each day of the week, marking each column with a letter for the day. I cross'd these columns with thirteen red lines, marking the beginning of each line with the first letter of one of the virtues, on which line, and in its proper column, I might mark, by a little black spot, every fault I found upon examination to have been committed respecting that virtue upon that day.

I determined to give a week's strict attention to each of the virtues successively. Thus, in the first week, my great guard was to avoid every the least offence against *Temperance*, leaving the other virtues to their ordinary chance, only marking every evening the faults of the day. Thus, if in the first week I could keep my first line, marked T, clear of spots, I suppos'd the habit of that virtue so much strengthen'd, and its opposite weaken'd, that I might venture extending my attention to include the next, and for the following week keep both lines clear of spots. Proceeding thus to the last, I could go thro' a course compleat in thirteen weeks, and four courses in a year. And like him who, having a garden to weed, does not attempt to eradicate all the bad herbs at once, which would exceed his reach and his strength, but works on one of the beds at a time, and, having accomplish'd the first, proceeds to a second, so I should have, I hoped, the encouraging pleasure of seeing on my pages the progress I made in virtue, by clearing successively my lines of their spots, till in the end, by a number of courses, I should be happy in viewing a clean book, after a thirteen weeks' daily examination.

Notes on the State of Virginia

(1782)

THOMAS JEFFERSON

The following notes were written in Virginia in the year 1781, and somewhat corrected and enlarged in the winter of 1782, in answer to queries proposed to the Author, by a Foreigner of Distinction, then re-

From Andrew A. Lipscomb, ed., *The Writings of Thomas Jefferson* (Washington, D.C.: The Thomas Jefferson Memorial Association, 1904), vol. II, 50, 160–163, 173–176, 190–201, 203–208, 220–225.

siding among us. The subjects are all treated imperfectly; some scarcely touched on. To apologize for this by developing the circumstances of the time and place of their composition, would be to open wounds which have already bled enough. To these circumstances some of their imperfections may with truth be ascribed; the great mass to the want of information and want of talents in the writer. He had a few copies printed, which he gave among his friends; and a translation of them has been lately published in France, but with such alterations as the laws of the press in that country rendered necessary. They are now offered to the public in their original form and language. . . .

Query XIII. The Constitution of the State and Its Several Charters?

This constitution was formed when we were new and unexperienced in the science of government. It was the first, too, which was formed in the whole United States. No wonder then that time and trial have discovered very capital defects in it.

1. The majority of the men in the State, who pay and fight for its support, are unrepresented in the legislature, the roll of freeholders entitled to vote not including generally the half of those on the roll of the militia, or of the tax-gatherers.

2. Among those who share the representation, the shares are very unequal. Thus the county of Warwick, with only one hundred fighting men, has an equal representation with the county of Loudon, which has one thousand seven hundred and forty-six. So that every man in Warwick has as much influence in the government as seventeen men in Loudon. . . .

3. The senate is, by its constitution, too homogeneous with the house of delegates. Being chosen by the same electors, at the same time, and out of the same subjects, the choice falls of course on men of the same description. The purpose of establishing different houses of legislation is to introduce the influence of different interests or different principles. Thus in Great Britain it is said their constitution relies on the house of commons for honesty, and the lords for wisdom; which would be a rational reliance, if honesty were to be bought with money, and if wisdom were hereditary. In some of the American States, the delegates and senators are so chosen, as that the first represent the persons, and the second the property of the State. But with us, wealth and wisdom have equal chance for admission into both houses. We do not, therefore, derive from the separation of our legislature into two houses, those benefits which a proper complication of principles are capable of producing, and those which alone can compensate the evils which may be produced by their dissensions.

4. All the powers of government, legislative, executive, and judiciary, result to the legislative body. The concentrating these in the same hands

is precisely the definition of despotic government. It will be no alleviation that these powers will be exercised by a plurality of hands, and not by a single one. One hundred and seventy-three despots would surely be as oppressive as one. Let those who doubt it turn their eyes on the republic of Venice. As little will it avail us that they are chosen by ourselves. An *elective despotism* was not the government we fought for, but one which should not only be founded on free principles, but in which the powers of government should be so divided and balanced among several bodies of magistracy, as that no one could transcend their legal limits, without being effectually checked and restrained by the others. For this reason that convention which passed the ordinance of government, laid its foundation on this basis, that the legislative, executive, and judiciary departments should be separate and distinct, so that no person should exercise the powers of more than one of them at the same time. But no barrier was provided between these several powers. The judiciary and executive members were left dependent on the legislative, for their subsistence in office, and some of them for their continuance in it. . . .

In enumerating the defects of the Constitution, it would be wrong to count among them what is only the error of particular persons. In December 1776, our circumstances being much distressed, it was proposed in the house of delegates to create a *dictator*, invested with every power legislative, executive, and judiciary, civil and military, of life and of death, over our persons and over our properties; and in June 1781, again under calamity, the same proposition was repeated, and wanted a few votes only of being passed. One who entered into this contest [1] from a pure love of liberty, and a sense of injured rights, who determined to make every sacrifice, and to meet every danger, for the re-establishment of those rights on a firm basis, who did not mean to expend his blood and substance for the wretched purpose of changing this matter for that, but to place the powers of governing him in a plurality of hands of his own choice, so that the corrupt will of no one man might in future oppress him, must stand confounded and dismayed when he is told, that a considerable portion of that plurality had mediated the surrender of them into a single hand, and, in lieu of a limited monarchy, to deliver him over to a despotic one! How must we find his efforts and sacrifices abused and baffled, if he may still, by a single vote, be laid prostrate at the feet of one man! In God's name, from whence have they derived this power? Is it from our ancient laws? None such can be produced. Is it from any principle in our new Constitution expressed or implied? Every lineament expressed or implied, is in full opposition to it. Its fundamental principle is, that the State shall be governed as a commonwealth. It provides a republican organization, proscribes under the name of *prerogative*

[1] [The war against Great Britain. — Eds.]

the exercise of all powers undefined by the laws; places on this basis the whole system of our laws; and by consolidating them together, chooses that they should be left to stand or fall together, never providing for any circumstances, nor admitting that such could arise, wherein either should be suspended; no, not for a moment. Our ancient laws expressly declare, that those who are but delegates themselves shall not delegate to others powers which require judgment and integrity in their exercise. Or was this proposition moved on a supposed right in the movers, of abandoning their posts in a moment of distress? The same laws forbid the abandonment of that post, even on ordinary occasions; and much more a transfer of their powers into other hands and other forms, without consulting the people. They never admit the idea that these, like sheep or cattle, may be given from hand to hand without an appeal to their own will. Was it from the necessity of the case? Necessities which dissolve a government, do not convey its authority to an oligarchy or a monarchy. They throw back, into the hands of the people, the powers they had delegated, and leave them as individuals to shift for themselves. A leader may offer, but not impose himself, nor be imposed on them. Much less can their necks be submitted to his sword, their breath to be held at his will or caprice. The necessity which should operate these tremendous effects should at least be palpable and irresistible. Yet in both instances, where it was feared, or pretended with us, it was belied by the event. It was belied, too, by the preceding experience of our sister States, several of whom had grappled through greater difficulties without abandoning their forms of government. When the proposition was first made, Massachusetts had found even the government of committees sufficient to carry them through an invasion. But we at the time of that proposition, were under no invasion. When the second was made, there had been added to this example those of Rhode Island, New York, New Jersey, and Pennsylvania, in all of which the republican form had been found equal to the task of carrying them through the severest trials. In this State alone did there exist so little virtue, that fear was to be fixed in the hearts of the people, and to become the motive of their exertions, and principle of their government? The very thought alone was treason against the people; was treason against mankind in general; as riveting forever the chains which bow down their necks, by giving to their oppressors a proof, which they would have trumpeted through the universe, of the imbecility of republican government, in times of pressing danger, to shield them from harm. . . .

Query XIV. The Administration of Justice and the Description of the Laws?

. . . Many of the laws which were in force during the monarchy being relative merely to that form of government, or inculcating principles inconsistent with republicanism, the first assembly which met after the establishment of the commonwealth appointed a committee to revise the whole code, to reduce it into proper form and volume, and report it to the assembly. . . .

The plan of the revisal was this. The common law of England, by which is meant, that part of the English law which was anterior to the date of the oldest statutes extant, is made the basis of the work. It was thought dangerous to attempt to reduce it to a text; it was therefore left to be collected from the usual monuments of it. Necessary alterations in that, and so much of the whole body of the British statutes, and of acts of assembly, as were thought proper to be retained, were digested into one hundred and twenty-six new acts, in which simplicity of style was aimed at, as far as was safe. The following are the most remarkable alterations proposed:

To change the rules of descent, so as that the lands of any person dying intestate shall be divisible equally among all his children, or other representatives, in equal degree.

To make slaves distributable among the next of kin, as other movables.

To have all public expenses, whether of the general treasury, or of a parish or county, (as for the maintenance of the poor, building bridges, court-houses, etc.,) supplied by assessment on the citizens, in proportion to their property.

To hire undertakers for keeping the public roads in repair, and indemnify individuals through whose lands new roads shall be opened.

To define with precision the rules whereby aliens should become citizens, and citizens make themselves aliens.

To establish religious freedom on the broadest bottom.

To emancipate all slaves born after the passing [of] the act. The bill reported by the revisers does not itself contain this proposition; but an amendment containing it was prepared, to be offered to the legislature whenever the bill should be taken up, and farther directing, that they should continue with their parents to a certain age, then to be brought up, at the public expense, to tillage, arts, or sciences, according to their geniuses, till the females should be eighteen, and the males twenty-one years of age, when they should be colonized to such place as the circumstances of the time should render most proper, sending them out with arms, implements of household and of the handicraft arts, seeds, pairs of the useful domestic animals, etc., to declare them a free and independent people, and extend to them our alliance and protection, till they have acquired strength; and to send vessels at the same time to other parts of the world for an equal number of white inhabitants; to induce them to migrate hither proper encouragements were to be proposed. It will probably be asked, Why not retain and incorporate the blacks into the

State, and thus save the expense of supplying by importation of white settlers, the vacancies they will leave? Deep-rooted prejudices entertained by the whites; ten thousand recollections, by the blacks, of the injuries they have sustained; new provocations; the real distinctions which nature has made; and many other circumstances, will divide us into parties, and produce convulsions, which will probably never end but in the extermination of the one or the other race. To these objections, which are political, may be added others, which are physical and moral. The first difference which strikes us is that of color. Whether the black of the negro resides in the reticular membrane between the skin and scarf-skin, or in the scarf-skin itself; whether it proceeds from the color of the blood, the color of the bile, or from that of some other secretion, the difference is fixed in nature, and is as real as if its seat and cause were better known to us. And is this difference of no importance? Is it not the foundation of a greater or less sharc of beauty in the two races? Are not the fine mixtures of red and white, the expressions of every passion by greater or less suffusions of color in the one, preferable to that external monotony, which reigns in the countenances, that immovable veil of black which covers the emotions of the other race? Add to these, flowing hair, a more elegant symmetry of form, their own judgment in favor of the whites, declared by their preference of them, as uniformly as is the preference of the Oran-ûtan for the black woman over those of his own species. The circumstance of superior beauty, is thought worthy attention in the propagation of our horses, dogs, and other domestic animals; why not in that of man? Besides those of color, figure, and hair, there are other physical distinctions proving a difference of race. They have less hair on the face and body. They secrete less by the kidneys, and more by the glands of the skin, which gives them a very strong and disagreeable odor. This greater degree of transpiration, renders them more tolerant of heat, and less so of cold than the whites. Perhaps, too, a difference of structure in the pulmonary apparatus, which a late ingenious experimentalist has discovered to be the principal regulator of animal heat, may have disabled them from extricating, in the act of inspiration, so much of that fluid from the outer air, or obliged them in expiration, to part with more of it. They seem to require less sleep. A black after hard labor through the day, will be induced by the slightest amusements to sit up till midnight, or later, though knowing he must be out with the first dawn of the morning. They are at least as brave, and more adventuresome. But this may perhaps proceed from a want of fore-thought, which prevents their seeing a danger till it be present. When present, they do not go through it with more coolness or steadiness than the whites. They are more ardent after their female; but love seems with them to be more an eager desire, than a tender delicate mixture of sentiment and sensation. Their griefs are transient. Those numberless afflictions, which render it doubtful whether heaven has given life to us in mercy or wrath, are less felt, and sooner forgotten with them. In general, their existence appears to participate more of sensation than reflection. To this must be ascribed their disposition to sleep when abstracted from their diversions, and unemployed in labor. An animal whose body is at rest, and who does not reflect must be disposed to sleep of course. Comparing them by their faculties of memory, reason, and imagination, it appears to me that in memory they are equal to the whites; in reason much inferior, as I think one could scarcely be found capable of tracing and comprehending the investigations of Euclid; and that in imagination they are dull, tasteless, and anomalous. It would be unfair to follow them to Africa for this investigation. We will consider them here, on the same stage with the whites, and where the facts are not apocryphal on which a judgment is to be formed. It will be right to make great allowances for the difference of condition, of education, of conversation, of the sphere in which they move. Many millions of them have been brought to, and born in America. Most of them, indeed, have been confined to tillage, to their own homes, and their own society; yet many have been so situated, that they might have availed themselves of the conversation of their masters; many have been brought up to the handicraft arts, and from that circumstance have always been associated with the whites. Some have been liberally educated, and all have lived in countries where the arts and sciences are cultivated to a considerable degree, and all have had before their eyes samples of the best works from abroad. The Indians, with no advantages of this kind, will often carve figures on their pipes not destitute of design and merit. They will crayon out an animal, a plant, or a country, so as to prove the existence of a germ in their minds which only wants cultivation. They astonish you with strokes of the most sublime oratory; such as prove their reason and sentiment strong, their imagination glowing and elevated. But never yet could I find that a black had uttered a thought above the level of plain narration; never saw even an elementary trait of painting or sculpture. In music they are more generally gifted than the whites with accurate ears for tune and time, and they have been found capable of imagining a small catch. Whether they will be equal to the composition of a more extensive run of melody, or of complicated harmony, is yet to be proved. Misery is often the parent of the most affecting touches in poetry. Among the blacks is misery enough, God knows, but no poetry. Love is the peculiar œstrum of the poet. Their love is ardent, but it kindles the senses only, not the imagination. . . . The improvement of the blacks in body and mind, in the first instance of their mixture with the whites, has been observed by every one, and proves that their inferiority is not the effect merely of their condition of life. We know that among the Romans, about the Augustan age especially, the condition of their slaves was much more deplorable than that of the blacks on the continent of America. . . . Yet notwithstanding these . . . discouraging circumstances among the Romans, their slaves were often their rarest artists. They excelled too in science, insomuch as to be usually employed as tutors to their master's children. Epictetus, Terence, and Phædrus, were slaves. But they were of the race of whites. It is not their condition then, but nature, which has produced the distinction. Whether further observation will or will not verify the conjecture, that nature has been less bountiful to them in the endowments of the head, I believe that in those of the heart she will be found to have done them justice. That disposition to theft with which they have been branded, must be ascribed to their situation, and not to any depravity of the moral sense. The man in whose favor no laws of property exist, probably feels himself less bound to respect those made in favor of others. When arguing for ourselves, we lay it down as a fundamental, that laws, to be just, must give a reciprocation of right; that, without this, they are mere arbitrary rules of conduct, founded in force, and not in conscience; and it is a problem which I give to the master to solve, whether the religious precepts against the violation of property were not framed for him as well as his slave? And whether the slave may not as justifiably take a little from one who has taken all from him, as he may slay one who would slay him? . . .

. . . Notwithstanding these considerations which must weaken their respect for the laws of property, we find among them numerous instances of the most rigid integrity, and as many as among their better instructed masters, of benevolence, gratitude, and unshaken fidelity. The opinion that they are inferior in the faculties of reason and imagination, must be hazarded with great diffidence. To justify a general conclusion, requires many observations, even where the subject may be submitted to the anatomical knife, to optical glasses, to analysis by fire or by solvents. How much more then where it is a faculty, not a substance, we are examining; where it eludes the research of all the senses; where the conditions of its existence are various and variously combined; where the effects of those which are present or absent bid defiance to calculation; let me add too, as a circumstance of great tenderness, where our conclusion would degrade a whole race of men from the rank in the scale of beings which their Creator may perhaps have given them. To our reproach it must be said, that though for a century and a half we have had under our eyes the races of black and of red men, they have never yet been viewed by us as subjects of natural history. I advance it, therefore, as a suspicion only, that the blacks, whether originally a distinct race, or made distinct by time and circumstances, are inferior to the whites in the endowments both of body and mind. It is not against experience to suppose that different species of the same genus, or varieties of the same species, may possess different qualifications. Will not a lover of natural history then, one who views the gradations in all the races of animals with the eye of philosophy, excuse an effort to keep those in the department of man as distinct as nature has formed them? This unfortunate difference of color, and perhaps of faculty, is a powerful obstacle to the emancipation of these people. Many of their advocates, while they wish to vindicate the liberty of human nature, are anxious also to preserve its dignity and beauty. Some of these, embarrassed by the question, "What further is to be done with them?" join themselves in opposition with those who are actuated by sordid avarice only. Among the Romans emancipation required but one effort. The slave, when made free, might mix with, without staining the blood of his master. But with us a second is necessary, unknown to history. When freed, he is to be removed beyond the reach of mixture. . . .

Another object of the revisal is to diffuse knowledge more generally through the mass of the people. This bill proposes to lay off every country into small districts of five or six miles square, called hundreds, and in each of them to establish a school for teaching, reading, writing, and arithmetic. The tutor to be supported by the hundred, and every person in it entitled to end their children three years gratis, and as much longer as they please, paying for it. These schools to be under a visitor who is annually to choose the boy of best genius in the school, of those whose parents are too poor to give them further education, and to send him forward to one of the grammar schools, of which twenty are proposed to be erected in different parts of the country, for teaching Greek, Latin, Geography, and the higher branches of numerical arithmetic. Of the boys thus sent in one year, trial is to be made at the grammar schools one or two years, and the best genius of the whole selected, and continued six years, and the residue dismissed. By this means twenty of the best geniuses will be raked from the rubbish annually, and be instructed, at the public expense, so far as the grammar schools go. At the end of six years' instruction, one half are to be discontinued (from among whom the grammar schools will probably be supplied with future masters); and the other half, who are to be chosen for the superiority of their parts and disposition, are to be sent and continued three years in the study of such sciences as they shall choose, at William and Mary college, the plan of which is proposed to be enlarged, as will be hereafter explained, and extended to all the useful sciences. The ultimate result of the whole scheme of education would be the teaching all the children of the State reading, writing, and common arithmetic; turning out ten annually, of superior genius, well taught in Greek, Latin, Geography, and the higher branches of arithmetic; turning out ten others annually, of still superior parts, who, to those branches of learning, shall have added such of the sciences as their genius shall have led them to; the furnishing to the wealthier part of the people convenient schools at which their children may be educated at their own expense. The general objects of this law are to provide an education adapted to the years, to the capacity, and the condition of every one, and directed to their freedom and happiness. Specific details were not proper for the law. These must be the business of the visitors entrusted with its execution. The first stage of this education being the schools of the hundreds, wherein the great mass of the people will receive their instruction, the principal foundations of future order will be laid here. Instead, therefore, of putting the Bible and Testament into the hands of the children at an age when their judgments are not sufficiently matured for religious inquiries, their memories may here be stored with the most useful facts from Grecian, Roman, European and American history. The first elements of morality too may be instilled into their minds; such as, when further developed as their judgments advance in strength, may teach them how to work out their own greatest happiness, by showing them that it does not depend on the condition of life in which chance has placed them, but is always the result of a good conscience, good health, occupation, and freedom in all just pursuits. Those whom either the wealth of their parents or the adoption of the State shall destine to higher degrees of learning, will go on to the grammar schools, which constitute the next stage, there to be instructed in the languages. . . . As soon as they are of sufficient age, it is supposed they will be sent on from the grammar schools to the university, which constitutes our third and last stage, there to study those sciences which may be adapted to their views. By that part of our plan which prescribes the selection of the youths of genius from among the classes of the poor, we hope to avail the State of those talents which nature has sown as liberally among the poor as the rich, but which perish without use, if not sought for and cultivated. But of the views of this law none is more important, none more legitimate, than that of rendering the people the safe, as they are the ultimate, guardians of their own liberty. For this purpose the reading in the first stage, where *they* will receive their whole education, is proposed, as has been said, to be chiefly historical. History, by apprizing them of the past, will enable them to judge of the future; it will avail them of the experience of other times and other nations; it will qualify them as judges of the actions and designs of men; it will enable them to know ambition under every disguise it may assume; and knowing it, to defeat its views. In every government on earth is some trace of human weakness, some germ of corruption and degeneracy, which cunning will discover, and wickedness insensibly open, cultivate and improve. Every government degenerates when trusted to the rulers of the people alone. The people themselves therefore are its only safe depositories. And to render even them safe, their minds must be improved to a certain degree. This indeed is not all that is necessary, though it be essentially necessary. An amendment of our constitution must here come in aid of the public education. The influence over government must be shared among all the people. If every individual which composes their mass participates of the ultimate authority, the government will be safe; because the corrupting the whole mass will exceed any private resources of wealth; and public ones cannot be provided but by levies on the people. In this case every man would have to pay his own price. The government of Great Britain has been corrupted, because but one man in ten has a right to vote for members of parliament. The sellers of the government, therefore, get nine-tenths of their price clear. It has been thought that corruption is restrained by confining the right of suffrage to a few of the wealthier of the people; but it would be more effectually restrained by an extension of that right to such members as would bid defiance to the means of corruption.

Lastly, it is proposed, by a bill in this revisal, to begin a public library and gallery, by laying out a certain sum annually in books, paintings, and statues. . . .

Query XVII. The Different Religions Received into That State?

. . . By our own act of assembly of 1705, c. 30, if a person brought up in the Christian religion denies the being of a God, or the Trinity, or asserts there are more gods than one, or denies the Christian religion to be true, or the scriptures to be of divine authority, he is punishable on the first offence by incapacity to hold any office or employment ecclesiastical, civil, or military; on the second by disability to sue, to take any gift or legacy, to be guardian, executor, or administrator, and by three years' imprisonment without bail. A father's right to the custody of his own children being founded in law on his right of guardianship, this being taken away, they may of course be severed from him, and put by the authority of a court into more orthodox hands. This is a summary view of that religious slavery under which a people have been willing to remain, who have lavished their lives and fortunes for the establishment of their civil freedom. The error seems not sufficiently eradicated, that the operations of the mind, as well as the acts of the body, are subject to the coercion of the laws. But our rulers can have no authority over such natural rights, only as we have submitted to them. The rights of conscience we never submitted, we could not submit. We are answerable for them to our God. The legitimate powers of government extend to such acts only as are injurious to others. But it does me no injury for my neighbor to say there are twenty gods, or no God. It neither picks my pocket nor breaks my leg. If it be said, his testimony in a court of justice cannot be relied on, reject it then, and be the stigma on him. Constraint may make him worse by making him a hypocrite, but it will never make him a truer man. It may fix him obstinately in his errors, but will not cure them. Reason and free inquiry are the only effectual agents against error. Give a loose to them, they will support the true religion by bringing every false one to their tribunal, to the test of their investigation. They are the natural enemies of error, and of error only. Had not the Roman government permitted free inquiry, Christianity could never have been introduced. Had not free inquiry been indulged at the era of the Reformation, the corruptions of Christianity could not have been purged away. If it be restrained now, the present corruptions will be protected, and new ones encouraged. Was the government to prescribe to us our medicine and diet, our bodies would be in such keeping as our souls are now. Thus in France the emetic was once forbidden as a medicine, and the potato as an article of food. Government is just as infallible, too, when it fixes systems in physics. Galileo was sent to the Inquisition for affirming that the earth was a sphere; the government had declared it to be as flat as a trencher, and Galileo was obliged to abjure his error. This error, however, at length prevailed, the earth became a globe, and Descartes declared it was whirled around its axis by a vortex. The government in which he lived was wise enough to see that this was no question of civil jurisdiction, or we should all have been involved by authority in vortices. In fact, the vortices have been exploded, and the Newtonian principle of gravitation is now more firmly established, on the basis of reason, than it would be were the government to step in, and to make it an article of necessary faith. Reason and experiment have been indulged, and error has fled before them. It is error alone which needs the support of government. Truth can stand by itself. Subject opinion to coercion: whom will you make your inquisitors? Fallible men; men governed by bad passions, by private as well as public reasons. And why subject it to coercion? To produce uniformity. But is uniformity of opinion desirable? No more than of face and stature. Introduce the bed of Procrustes then, and as there is danger that the large men may beat the small, make us all of a size, by lopping the former and stretching the latter. Difference of opinion is advantageous in religion. The several sects perform the office of a *censor morum* over such other. Is uniformity attainable? Millions of innocent men, women, and children, since the introduction of Christianity, have been burnt, tortured, fined, imprisoned; yet we have not advanced one inch towards uniformity. What has been the effect of coercion? To make one half the world fools, and the other half hypocrites. To support roguery and error all over the earth. Let us reflect that it is inhabited by a thousand millions of people. That these profess probably a thousand different systems of religion. That ours is but one of that thousand. That if there be but one right, and ours that one, we should wish to see the nine hundred and ninety-nine wandering sects gathered into the fold of truth. But against such a majority we cannot effect this by force. Reason and persuasion are the only practicable instruments. To make way for these, free inquiry must be indulged; and how can we wish others to indulge it while we refuse it ourselves. But every State, says an inquisitor, has established some religion. No two, say I, have established the same. Is this a proof of the infallibility of establishments? Our sister States of Pennsylvania and New York, however, have long subsisted without any establishment at all. The experiment was new and doubtful when they made it. It has answered beyond conception. They flourish infinitely. Religion is well supported; of various kinds, indeed, but all good enough; all sufficient to preserve peace and order; or if a sect arises, whose tenets would subvert morals, good sense has fair play, and reasons and laughs it out of doors, without suffering the State to be troubled with it. They do not hang more malefactors than we do. They are not more disturbed with religious dissensions. On the contrary, their harmony is unparalleled, and can be ascribed to nothing but their unbounded tolerance, because there is no other circumstance in which they differ from every nation on earth. They have made the happy discovery, that the way to silence religious disputes, is to take no notice of them. Let us too give this experiment fair play, and get rid, while we may, of those tyrannical laws. It is true, we are as yet secured against them by the spirit of the times. I doubt whether the people of this country would suffer an execution for heresy, or a three years' imprisonment for not comprehending the mysteries of the Trinity. But is the spirit of the people an infallible, a permanent reliance? Is it government? Is this the kind of protection we receive in return for the rights we give up? Besides, the spirit of the times may alter, will alter. Our rulers will become corrupt, our people careless. A single zealot may commence persecutor, and better men be his victims. It can never be too often repeated, that the time for fixing every essential right on a legal basis is while our rulers are honest, and ourselves united. From the conclusion of this war we shall be going down hill. It will not then be necessary to resort every moment to the people for support. They will be forgotten, therefore, and their rights disregarded. They will forget themselves, but in the sole faculty of making money, and will never think of uniting to effect a due respect for their rights. The shackles, therefore, which shall not be knocked off at the conclusion of this war, will remain on us long, will be made heavier and heavier, till our rights shall revive or expire in a convulsion.

II

THE REVOLT AGAINST THE ENLIGHTENMENT: CONSERVATISM

John Adams (1735–1826) and Edmund Burke (1729–1797) became, in their mature years, leading representatives of the conservative revolt against the Enlightenment, a reaction that dominated the intellectual life of Europe and America during the late eighteenth and early nineteenth centuries. The principal themes of this revolt were a new emphasis on history and tradition as the standards of political judgment, and a corresponding hostility to abstract, rationalistic political theorizing; an insistence on the organic and hierarchical character of society; a revitalized Christianity; and a pessimistic assessment of human nature. Burke and Adams both exhibit these attitudes, although to different degrees and in different ways.

Burke's Reflections, *as their full title indicates, were written in response to the French Revolution of 1789. They placed the blame for that upheaval on the "political metaphysicians" of the Enlightenment. Similarly, Adams's* Defense *was directed against what he held to be the dangerously abstract egalitarian doctrines of Anne Robert Jacques Turgot (1727–1781), one of the most prominent and theoretical of the French* philosophes, *whose anti-aristocratic ideas Adams feared might inspire democratic insurrections like Shays's Rebellion in western Massachusetts.*

If it seems strange that John Adams, a leading participant in the American Revolution, should be labeled a conservative, the reader ought to bear in mind that Edmund Burke also was a staunch supporter of the American colonies in their struggle against Britain. The selection from Friedrich von Gentz (1764–1832), a close adviser of Prince Metternich and secretary to the Congress of Vienna, indicates how European and American conservatives attempted to distinguish the American Revolution from the French. Gentz's essay made a strong impression on John Adams's son, John Quincy Adams, who translated it into English and secured its publication in 1800, the same year Gentz wrote it.

Finally, Alexander Hamilton's second contribution to the Federalist Papers *illustrates the important role conservative attitudes played in the debate over the Constitution. Hamilton apparently shared Burke's and Adams's rather dismal estimation of human nature and their distrust of political visionaries.*

Reflections on the Revolution in France (1790)

EDMUND BURKE

It may not be unnecessary to inform the reader that the following Reflections had their origin in a correspondence between the author and a very young gentleman at Paris, who did him the honor of desiring his opinion upon the important transactions which then, and ever since have, so much occupied the attention of all men. . . .

On the forenoon of the fourth of November last, Doctor Richard Price, a Non-Conforming minister of eminence, preached at the Dissenting meeting-house of the Old Jewry, to his club or society, a very extraordinary miscellaneous sermon, in which there are some good moral and religious sentiments, and not ill expressed, mixed up with a sort of porridge of various political opinions and reflections: but the Revolution in France is the grand ingredient in the caldron. I consider the address transmitted by the Revolution Society to the National Assembly, through Earl Stanhope, as originating in the principles of the sermon, and as a corollary from them. It was moved by the preacher of that discourse. It was passed by those who came reeking from the effect of the sermon, without any censure or qualification, expressed or implied. If, however, any of the gentlemen concerned shall wish to separate the sermon from

From *The Writings and Speeches of Edmund Burke* (Boston: Little, Brown, 1901), vol. III, 233, 244–245, 248–249, 251–252, 271–272, 274–276, 295–299, 308–313, 316, 346–348, 350–352.

the resolution, they know how to acknowledge the one and to disavow the other. They may do it: I cannot.

For my part, I looked on the sermon as the public declaration of a man much connected with literary caballers and intriguing philosophers, with political theologians and theological politicians, both at home and abroad. I know they set him up as a sort of oracle; because, with the best intentions in the world, he naturally *philippizes,* and chants his prophetic song in exact unison with their designs. . . .

. . . He tells the Revolution Society, in this political sermon, that his Majesty "is almost the *only* lawful king in the world, because the *only* one who owes his crown to *the choice of his people*." As to the kings of *the world,* all of whom (except one) this arch-pontiff of the *rights of men,* with all the plenitude and with more than the boldness of the Papal deposing power in its meridian fervor of the twelfth century, puts into one sweeping clause of ban and anathema, and proclaims usurpers by circles of longitude and latitude over the whole globe, it behooves them to consider how they admit into their territories these apostolic missionaries, who are to tell their subjects they are not lawful kings. That is their concern. It is ours, as a domestic interest of some moment, seriously to consider the solidity of the *only* principle upon which these gentlemen acknowledge a king of Great Britain to be entitled to their allegiance.

This doctrine, as applied to the prince now on the British throne, either is nonsense, and therefore neither true nor false, or it affirms a most unfounded, dangerous, illegal, and unconstitutional position. According to this spiritual doctor of politics, if his Majesty does not owe his crown to the choice of his people, he is no *lawful* king. Now nothing can be more untrue than that the crown of this kingdom is so held by his Majesty. Therefore, if you follow their rule, the king of Great Britain, who most certainly does not owe his high office to any form of popular election, is in no respect better than the rest of the gang of usurpers, who reign, or rather rob, all over the face of this our miserable world, without any sort of right or title to the allegiance of their people. The policy of this general doctrine, so qualified, is evident enough. The propagators of this political gospel are in hopes their abstract principle (their principle that a popular choice is necessary to the legal existence of the sovereign magistracy) would be overlooked, whilst the king of Great Britain was not affected by it. In the mean time the ears of their congregations would be gradually habituated to it, as if it were a first principle admitted without dispute. For the present it would only operate as a theory, pickled in the preserving juices of pulpit eloquence, and laid by for future use. . . .

Whatever may be the success of evasion in explaining away the gross error of *fact,* which supposes that his Majesty (though he holds it in concurrence with the wishes) owes his crown to the choice of his people, yet nothing can evade their full, explicit declaration concerning the principle of a right in the people to choose, — which right is directly maintained, and tenaciously adhered to. All the oblique insinuations concerning election bottom in this proposition, and are referable to it. Lest the foundation of the king's exclusive legal title should pass for a mere rant of adulatory freedom, the political divine proceeds dogmatically to assert, that, by the principles of the Revolution, the people of England have acquired three fundamental rights, all of which, with him, compose one system, and lie together in one short sentence: namely, that we have acquired a right

1. "To choose our own governors."
2. "To cashier them for misconduct."
3. "To frame a government for ourselves."

This new, and hitherto unheard-of bill of rights, though made in the name of the whole people, belongs to those gentlemen and their faction only. The body of the people of England have no share in it. They utterly disclaim it. They will resist the practical assertion of it with their lives and fortunes. They are bound to do so by the laws of their country, made at the time of that very Revolution which is appealed to in favor of the fictitious rights claimed by the society which abuses its name.[1] . . .

The third head of right asserted by the pulpit of the Old Jewry, namely, the "right to form a government for ourselves," has, at least, as little countenance from anything done at the Revolution, either in precedent or principle, as the two first of their claims. The Revolution was made to preserve our *ancient* indisputable laws and liberties, and that *ancient* constitution of government which is our only security for law and liberty. If you are desirous of knowing the spirit of our Constitution, and the policy which predominated in that great period which has secured it to this hour, pray look for both in our histories, in our records, in our acts of Parliament and journals of Parliament, and not in the sermons of the Old Jewry, and the after-dinner toasts of the Revolution Society. In the former you will find other ideas and another language. Such a claim is as ill-suited to our temper and wishes as it is unsupported by any appearance of authority. The very idea of the fabrication of a new government is enough to fill us with disgust and horror. We wished at the period of the Revolution, and do now wish, to derive all we possess as *an inheritance from our forefathers*. Upon that body and stock of inheritance we have taken care

[1] [The Revolution of 1688, in which the last of the Stuarts, James II, was deposed in favor of the Protestant William of Orange. Burke, as a member of the Whig party — the party most closely associated with the Revolution of 1688 — was anxious to distinguish that "glorious" event from the French Revolution of 1789 — and from the ideas of Dr. Price's sermons. — Eds.]

not to inoculate any scion alien to the nature of the original plant. All the reformations we have hitherto made have proceeded upon the principle of reference to antiquity; and I hope, nay, I am persuaded, that all those which possibly may be made hereafter will be carefully formed upon analogical precedent, authority, and example. . . .

You will observe, that, from Magna Charta to the Declaration of Right, it has been the uniform policy of our Constitution to claim and assert our liberties as an *entailed inheritance* derived to us from our forefathers, and to be transmitted to our posterity, — as an estate specially belonging to the people of this kingdom, without any reference whatever to any other more general or prior right. By this means our Constitution preserves an unity in so great a diversity of its parts. We have an inheritable crown, an inheritable peerage, and a House of Commons and a people inheriting privileges, franchises, and liberties from a long line of ancestors.

This policy appears to me to be the result of profound reflection, — or rather the happy effect of following Nature, which is wisdom without reflection, and above it. A spirit of innovation is generally the result of a selfish temper and confined views. People will not look forward to posterity, who never look backward to their ancestors. Besides, the people of England well know that the idea of inheritance furnishes a sure principle of conservation, and a sure principle of transmission, without at all excluding a principle of improvement. It leaves acquisition free; but it secures what it acquires. Whatever advantages are obtained by a state proceeding on these maxims are locked fast as in a sort of family settlement, grasped as in a kind of mortmain forever. By a constitutional policy working after the pattern of Nature, we receive, we hold, we transmit our government and our privileges, in the same manner in which we enjoy and transmit our property and our lives. The institutions of policy, the goods of fortune, the gifts of Providence, are handed down to us, and from us, in the same course and order. Our political system is placed in a just correspondence and symmetry with the order of the world, and with the mode of existence decreed to a permanent body composed of transitory parts, — wherein, by the disposition of a stupendous wisdom, moulding together the great mysterious incorporation of the human race, the whole, at one time, is never old or middle-aged or young, but, in a condition of unchangeable constancy, moves on through the varied tenor of perpetual decay, fall, renovation, and progression. Thus, by preserving the method of Nature in the conduct of the state, in what we improve we are never wholly new, in what we retain we are never wholly obsolete. By adhering in this manner and on those principles to our forefathers, we are guided, not by the superstition of antiquarians, but by the spirit of philosophic analogy. In this choice of inheritance we have given to our frame of polity the image of a relation in blood: binding up the Constitution of our country with our dearest domestic ties; adopting our fundamental laws into the bosom of our family affections; keeping inseparable, and cherishing with the warmth of all their combined and mutually reflected charities, our state, our hearths, our sepulchres, and our altars. . . .

Through the same plan of a conformity to Nature in our artificial institutions, and by calling in the aid of her unerring and powerful instincts to fortify the fallible and feeble contrivances of our reason, we have derived several other, and those no small benefits, from considering our liberties in the light of an inheritance. Always acting as if in the presence of canonized forefathers, the spirit of freedom, leading in itself to misrule and excess, is tempered with an awful gravity. This idea of a liberal descent inspires us with a sense of habitual native dignity, which prevents that upstart insolence almost inevitably adhering to and disgracing those who are the first acquirers of any distinction. By this means our liberty becomes a noble freedom. It carries an imposing and majestic aspect. It has a pedigree and illustrating ancestors. It has its bearings and its ensigns armorial. It has its gallery of portraits, its monumental inscriptions, its records, evidences, and titles. We procure reverence to our civil institutions on the principle upon which Nature teaches us to revere individual men: on account of their age, and on account of those from whom they are descended. All your sophisters cannot produce anything better adapted to preserve a rational and manly freedom than the course that we have pursued, who have chosen our nature rather than our speculations, our breasts rather than our inventions, for the great conservatories and magazines of our rights and privileges. . . .

. . . Believe me, Sir, those who attempt to level never equalize. In all societies consisting of various descriptions of citizens, some description must be uppermost. The levellers, therefore, only change and pervert the natural order of things: they load the edifice of society by setting up in the air what the solidity of the structure requires to be on the ground. The associations of tailors and carpenters, of which the republic (of Paris, for instance) is composed, cannot be equal to the situation into which, by the worst of usurpations, an usurpation on the prerogatives of Nature, you attempt to force them.

The Chancellor of France, at the opening of the States, said, in a tone of oratorial flourish, that all occupations were honorable. If he meant only that no honest employment was disgraceful, he would not have gone beyond the truth. But in asserting that anything is honorable, we imply some distinction in its favor. The occupation of a hair-dresser, or of a working tallow-chandler, cannot be a matter of honor to any person, — to say nothing of a number of other more servile employments. Such descriptions of men ought not to suffer oppression from the state; but the state suffers oppression, if such as they, either individually or collectively, are permitted to rule. In this you think you are combating prejudice, but you are at war with Nature. . . .

Nothing is a due and adequate representation of a state, that does not represent its ability, as well as its property. But as ability is a vigorous and active principle, and as property is sluggish, inert, and timid, it never can be safe from the invasions of ability, unless it be, out of all proportion, predominant in the representation. It must be represented, too, in great masses of accumulation, or it is not rightly protected. The characteristic essence of property, formed out of the combined principles of its acquisition and conservation, is to be *unequal*. The great masses, therefore, which excite envy, and tempt rapacity, must be put out of the possibility of danger. Then they form a natural rampart about the lesser properties in all their gradations. The same quantity of property which is by the natural course of things divided among many has not the same operation. Its defensive power is weakened as it is diffused. In this diffusion each man's portion is less than what, in the eagerness of his desires, he may flatter himself to obtain by dissipating the accumulations of others. The plunder of the few would, indeed, give but a share inconceivably small in the distribution to the many. But the many are not capable of making this calculation; and those who lead them to rapine never intend this distribution.

The power of perpetuating our property in our families is one of the most valuable and interesting circumstances belonging to it, and that which tends the most to the perpetuation of society itself. It makes our weakness subservient to our virtue; it grafts benevolence even upon avarice. The possessors of family wealth, and of the distinction which attends hereditary possession, (as most concerned in it,) are the natural securities for this transmission. With us the House of Peers is formed upon this principle. It is wholly composed of hereditary property and hereditary distinction, and made, therefore, the third of the legislature, and, in the last event, the sole judge of all property in all its subdivisions. The House of Commons, too, though not necessarily, yet in fact, is always so composed, in the far greater part. Let those large proprietors be what they will, (and they have their chance of being amongst the best,) they are, at the very worst, the ballast in the vessel of the commonwealth. For though hereditary wealth, and the rank which goes with it, are too much idolized by creeping sycophants, and the blind, abject admirers of power, they are too rashly slighted in shallow speculations of the petulant, assuming, short sighted coxcombs of philosophy. Some decent, regulated preëminence, some preference (not exclusive appropriation) given to birth, is neither unnatural, nor unjust, nor impolitic. . . .

Far am I from denying in theory, full as far is my heart from withholding in practice, (if I were of power to give or to withhold,) the *real* rights of men. In denying their false claims of right, I do not mean to injure those which are real, and are such as their pretended rights would totally destroy. If civil society be made for the advantage of man, all the advantages for which it is made become his right. It is an institution of beneficence; and law itself is only beneficence acting by a rule. Men have a right to live by that rule; they have a right to justice, as between their fellows, whether their fellows are in politic function or in ordinary occupation. They have a right to the fruits of their industry, and to the means of making their industry fruitful. They have a right to the acquisitions of their parents, to the nourishment and improvement of their offspring, to instruction in life and to consolation in death. Whatever each man can separately do, without trespassing upon others, he has a right to do for himself; and he has a right to a fair portion of all which society, with all its combinations of skill and force, can do in his favor. In this partnership all men have equal rights; but not to equal things. He that has but five shillings in the partnership has as good a right to it as he that has five hundred pounds has to his larger proportion; but he has not a right to an equal dividend in the product of the joint stock. And as to the share of power, authority, and direction which each individual ought to have in the management of the state, that I must deny to be amongst the direct original rights of man in civil society; for I have in my contemplation the civil social man, and no other. It is a thing to be settled by convention.

If civil society be the offspring of convention, that convention must be its law. That convention must limit and modify all the descriptions of constitution which are formed under it. Every sort of legislative, judicial, or executory power are its creatures. They can have no being in any other state of things; and how can any man claim, under the conventions of civil society, rights which do not so much as suppose its existence, — rights which are absolutely repugnant to it? One of the first motives to civil society, and which becomes one of its fundamental rules, is, *that no man should be judge in his own cause*. By this each person has at once divested himself of the first fundamental right of uncovenanted man that is, to judge for himself, and to assert his own cause. He abdicates all right to be his own governor. He inclusively, in a great measure, abandons the right of self-defence, the first law of Nature. Men cannot enjoy the rights of an uncivil and of a civil state together. That he may obtain justice, he gives up his right of determining what it is in points the most essential to him. That he may secure some liberty, he makes a surrender in trust of the whole of it.

Government is not made in virtue of natural rights, which may and do exist in total independence of it, — and exist in much greater clearness, and in a much greater degree of abstract perfection: but their abstract perfection is their practical defect. By having a right to everything they want everything. Government is a contrivance of human wisdom to provide for human *wants*. Men have a right that these wants should be provided for by this wisdom. Among these wants is to be reckoned the want, out of civil society, of a sufficient restraint upon their passions. Society requires not only that the passions of individuals should be subjected, but that even in the mass and body, as well as in the individuals, the inclinations of men should frequently be thwarted, their will controlled, and their passions brought into subjection. This can only be done *by a power out of themselves*, and not, in the exercise of its function, subject to that will and to those passions which it is its office to bridle and subdue. In this sense the restraints on men, as well as their liberties, are to be reckoned among their rights. But as the liberties and the restrictions vary with times and circumstances, and admit of infinite modifications, they cannot be settled upon any abstract rule; and nothing is so foolish as to discuss them upon that principle.

The moment you abate anything from the full rights of men each to govern himself, and suffer any artificial, positive limitation upon those rights, from that moment the whole organization of government becomes a consideration of convenience. This it is which makes the constitution of a state, and the due distribution of its powers, a matter of the most delicate and complicated skill. It requires a deep knowledge of human nature and human necessities, and of the things which facilitate or obstruct the various ends which are to be pursued by the mechanism of civil institutions. The state is to have recruits to its strength and remedies to its distempers. What is the use of discussing a man's abstract right to food or medicine? The question is upon the method of procuring and administering them. In that deliberation I shall always advise to call in the aid of the farmer and the physician, rather than the professor of metaphysics.

The science of constructing a commonwealth, or renovating it, or reforming it, is, like every other experimental science, not to be taught *a priori*. Nor is it a short experience that can instruct us in that practical science; because the real effects of moral causes are not always immediate, but that which in the first instance is prejudicial may be excellent in its remoter operation, and its excellence may arise even from the ill effects it produces in the beginning. The reverse also happens; and very plausible schemes, with very pleasing commencements, have often shameful and lamentable conclusions. In states there are often some obscure and almost latent causes, things which appear at first view of little moment, on which a very great part of its prosperity or adversity may most essentially depend. The science of government being, therefore, so practical in itself, and intended for such practical purposes, a matter which requires experience, and even more experience than any person can gain in his whole life, however sagacious and observing he may be, it is with infinite caution that any man ought to venture upon pulling down an edifice which has answered in any tolerable degree for ages the common purposes of society, or on building it up again without having models and patterns of approved utility before his eyes.

These metaphysic rights entering into common life, like rays of light which pierce into a dense medium, are, by the laws of Nature, refracted from their straight line. Indeed, in the gross and complicated mass of human passions and concerns, the primitive rights of men undergo such a variety of refractions and reflections that it becomes absurd to talk of them as if they continued in the simplicity of their original direction. The nature of man is intricate; the objects of society are of the greatest possible complexity: and therefore no simple disposition or direction of power can be suitable either to man's nature or to the quality of his affairs. When I hear the simplicity of contrivance aimed at and boasted of in any new political constitutions, I am at no loss to decide that the artificers are grossly ignorant of their trade or totally negligent of their duty. The simple governments are fundamentally defective, to say no worse of them. If you were to contemplate society in but one point of view, all these simple modes of polity are infinitely captivating. In effect each would answer its single end much more perfectly than the more complex is able to attain all its complex purposes. But it is better that the whole should be imperfectly and anomalously answered than that while some parts are provided for with great exactness, others might be totally neglected, or perhaps materially injured, by the over-care of a favorite member.

The pretended rights of these theorists are all extremes; and in proportion as they are metaphysically true, they are morally and politically false. The rights of men are in a sort of *middle*, incapable of definition, but not impossible to be discerned. The rights of men in governments are their advantages; and these are often in balances between differences of good, — in compromises sometimes between good and evil, and sometimes between evil and evil. Political reason is a computing principle: adding, subtracting, multiplying, and dividing, morally, and not metaphysically or mathematically, true moral denominations. . . .

In France you are now in the crisis of a revolution, and in the transit from one form of government to another: you cannot see that character of men exactly in the same situation in which we see it in this country. With us it is militant, with you it is triumphant; and you know how it can act, when its power is commensurate to its will. I would not be supposed to confine those observations to any description of men, or to comprehend all men of any description within them, — no, far from it! I am as incapable of that injustice as I am of keeping terms with those who profess principles of extremes, and who, under the name of religion, teach little else than wild and dangerous politics. The worst of these politics of revolution is this: they temper and harden the breast, in order to prepare it for the desperate strokes which are sometimes used in extreme occasions. But as these occasions may never arrive, the mind receives a gratuitous taint; and the moral sentiments suffer not a little, when no political purpose is served by the depravation. This sort of people are so taken up with their theories about the rights of man, that they have totally forgot his nature. Without opening one new avenue to the understanding, they have succeeded in stopping up those that lead to the heart. They have perverted in themselves, and in those that attend to them, all the well-placed sympathies of the human breast. . . .

You see, Sir, that in this enlightened age I am bold enough to confess that we are generally men of untaught feelings: that, instead of casting away all our old prejudices, we cherish them to a very considerable degree; and, to take more shame to ourselves, we cherish them because they are prejudices; and the longer they have lasted, and the more generally they have prevailed, the more we cherish them. We are afraid to put men to live and trade each on his own private stock of reason; because we suspect that the stock in each man is small, and that the individuals would do better to avail themselves of the general bank and capital of nations and of ages. Many of our men of speculation, instead of exploding general prejudices, employ their sagacity to discover the latent wisdom which prevails in them. If they find what they seek, (and they seldom fail,) they think it more wise to continue the prejudice, with the reason involved, than to cast away the coat of prejudice, and to leave nothing but the naked reason; because prejudice, with its reason, has a motive to give action to that reason, and an affection which will give it permanence. Prejudice is of ready application in the emergency; it previously engages the mind in a steady course of wisdom and virtue, and does not leave the man hesitating in the moment of decision, skeptical, puzzled, and unresolved. Prejudice renders a man's virtue his habit, and not a series of unconnected acts. Through just prejudice, his duty becomes a part of his nature.

Your literary men, and your politicians, and so do the whole clan of the enlightened among us, essentially differ in these points. They have no respect for the wisdom of others; but they pay it off by a very full measure of confidence in their own. With them it is a sufficient motive to destroy an old scheme of things, because it is an old one. As to the new, they are in no sort of fear with regard to the duration of a building run up in haste; because duration is no object to those who think little or nothing has been done before their time, and who place all their hopes in discovery. They conceive, very systematically, that all things which give perpetuity are mischievous, and therefore they are at inexpiable war with all establishments. They think that government may vary like modes of dress, and with as little ill effect; that there needs no principle of attachment, except a sense of present conveniency, to any constitution of the state. They always speak as if they were of opinion that there is a singular species of compact between them and their magistrates, which binds the magistrate, but which has nothing reciprocal in it, but that the majesty of the people has a right to dissolve it without any reason but its will. Their attachment to their country itself is only so far as it agrees with some of their fleeting projects: it begins and ends with that scheme of polity which falls in with their momentary opinion.

These doctrines, or rather sentiments, seem prevalent with your new statesmen. But they are wholly different from those on which we have always acted in this country. . . .

We know, and, what is better, we feel inwardly, that religion is the basis of civil society, and the source of all good, and of all comfort. In England we are so convinced of this, that there is no rust of superstition, with which the accumulated absurdity of the human mind might have crusted it over in the course of ages, that ninety-nine in a hundred of the people of England would not prefer to impiety. We shall never be such fools as to call in an enemy to the substance of any system to remove its corruptions, to supply its defects, or to perfect its construction. If our religious tenets should ever want a further elucidation, we shall not call on Atheism to explain them. We shall not light up our temple from that unhallowed fire. It will be illuminated with other lights. It will be perfumed with other incense than the infectious stuff which is imported by the smugglers of adulterated metaphysics. If our ecclesiastical establishment should want a revision, it is not avarice or rapacity, public or private, that we shall employ for the audit or receipt or application of its consecrated revenue. Violently condemning neither the Greek nor the Armenian, nor, since heats are subsided, the Roman system of religion, we prefer the Protestant: not because we think it has less of the Christian religion in it, but because, in our judgment, it has more. We are Protestants, not from indifference, but from zeal.

We know, and it is our pride to know, that man is by his constitution a religious animal; that atheism is against, not only our reason, but our instincts; and that it cannot prevail long. But if, in the moment of riot, and in a drunken delirium from the hot spirit drawn out of the alembic of hell, which in France is now so furiously boiling, we should uncover our nakedness, by throwing off that Christian religion which has hitherto been our boast and comfort, and one great source of civilization amongst us, and among many other nations, we are apprehensive (being well aware that the mind will not endure a void) that some uncouth, pernicious, and degrading superstition might take place of it.

For that reason, before we take from our establishment the natural, human means of estimation, and give it up to contempt, as you have done, and in doing it have incurred the penalties you well deserve to suffer, we desire that some other may be presented to us in the place of it. We shall then form our judgment.

On these ideas, instead of quarrelling with establishments, as some do, who have made a philosophy and a religion of their hostility to such institutions, we cleave closely to them. We are resolved to keep an established church, an established monarchy, an established aristocracy, and an established democracy, each in the degree it exists, and in no greater. . . .

Origin and Principles of the American Revolution, Compared with the French Revolution

(1800)

FRIEDRICH VON GENTZ

The Revolution of North America, had, in the course of events, been the nearest neighbour to that of France. A very considerable part of those, who were contemporaries and witnesses of the latter had likewise survived the former. Some of the most important personages, who made a figure in the French revolution, scarce ten years before, had been active on the theatre of that in America. The example of this undertaking, crowned with the most complete success, must have had a more immediate and powerful influence upon those, who destroyed the old government of France, than the example of any earlier European revolution: the circumstances, in which France was, at the breaking out of her revolution, had been, if not wholly, yet for the greatest part brought on by the part she had taken in that of America. In the conduct and language of most of the founders of the French revolution, it was impossible not to perceive an endeavour to imitate the course, the plans, the measures, the forms, and, in part, the language of those, who had conducted that of America; and to consider this, upon all occasions, as at once the model, and the justification of their own.

From all these causes, but especially because the recollection of the American revolution was yet fresh in every mind; because the principles to which it had given currency still sounded in every ear; because the preparatory temper of mind, which it had every where in Europe excited and left behind, favoured every similar, or only seemingly similar under-

From Stefan T. Possony, ed., *Three Revolutions* (Chicago: Henry Regnery Co., 1959), 5–6, 52–57, 60, 62–63, 65–72.

taking, it became so easy for those, who felt an evident interest in seeing the French revolution superficially compared, and thereby placed on the same ground, and confounded with that of America, to draw the great majority of the public into this fundamentally false point of view. . . .

The American revolution was from beginning to end, on the part of the Americans, merely a *defensive revolution;* the French was from beginning to end, in the highest sense of the word, *an offensive revolution.*

This difference of itself is essential and decisive; upon it rests, perhaps more than upon any other, the peculiar character, which has distinguished these two revolutions.

The British government began the revolution in America by resolves, for which they could shew no right; the colonies endeavoured by all means in their power to repel them. The colonies wished to maintain their old constitution; the government destroyed it. The resistance, which the colonies opposed against the mother country, was, in every period of this unhappy contest, exactly commensurate with the attack; the total separation was not resolved, until the utter impossibility of preserving the ancient condition was proved.

The stamp-act threw America into the most violent commotion; tumultuous scenes, though attended with no acts of bloody violence, broke out in all the provinces. But they were no where formally sanctioned by the approbation of the legislative authorities. The little congress of 28 deputies of several colonies, who in the year 1765 assembled at New-York, and served as the model for the subsequent larger assembly, passed no other resolution than that "the colonies could only be taxed by their representatives," and expressed this perfectly lawful resolve, in *petitions* to the king. The single general measure, which was then offered, the non-importation agreement, was a voluntary engagement, sanctioned by no public authority. . . .

The resistance against the impost taxes of 1767, was of the same nature, as that which the stamp-tax had experienced. This new grievance of the colonies, was accompanied with circumstances of the most odious kind: the augmentation of the troops, the conduct of a part of them, the harshness of some governors, the frequent adjournments and violent dissolution of the provincial assemblies, all was calculated to put the patience of the Americans to dangerous proof. And yet they never overstepped the boundaries, which the constitution and the laws prescribed to them; and in their numerous addresses and protestations, adhered rigorously to what was allowed by law. When in the year 1770, a violent quarrel arose between some of the royal soldiers, and certain citizens of Boston, which ended in the first bloody scene the colonies had in their contest with England yet witnessed, the courts of law, with a glorious impartiality, acquitted the greatest part of the accused and indicted soldiers.

The continuation of the tax upon tea in the year 1770, had no other consequence than to strengthen the voluntary agreement against the importation of English tea; the resolve in the year 1773; which authorised the East-India company to the exportation of their stores of tea, free from duty, and the actual execution of this resolve, could not, indeed but produce a still more unfavourable operation. This measure was altogether calculated to provoke the colonies to a general insurrection. Yet did they keep themselves rigorously within the limits of a necessary defence. The destruction of the tea at Boston was, in fact, no other than a defensive operation. The sale of this tea, or only a part of it, would have involved the compulsive levy of a tax, by the payment of which the constitution of the colonies and all their rights would have been lost. Yet, even then, they proceeded not beyond what was unavoidable, and measured the resistance as exactly as possible by the attack. The tea was thrown into the sea, and not a single hostile step followed upon this undertaking. Nay, although the public authorities of Boston, and of the whole province, held it for necessary, as much as every single citizen, yet they always undeniably discovered themselves ready to grant the fullest indemnity to the East-India company. . . .

The appearance of the act, which closed the port of Boston, of that which, immediately after, took away the Massachusetts charter, the account of all what had passed in parliament upon that occasion, the visible impossibility of eradicating peaceably such deep rooted bitterness — all these circumstances concurred to render a sudden explosion probable; many of the resolves of parliament were indisputably of a nature to furnish sufficient motive for such an explosion. But the provincial assemblies contented themselves with sending deputies to a general congress. Not one over hasty step disturbed the pacific and lawful character of their conduct in this hard and trying period. . . .

When, finally, the congress resolved upon the general arming of the country, *defence* was still their single, and exclusive object. The constitution had been long since, without their fault, torn to pieces; they might have proclaimed immediately a new one upon its ruins; but they appealed to arms, to maintain the same constitution, of which the colonies had been, with so much violence, deprived. . . .

The revolution of America was, therefore, in every sense of the word, a revolution of necessity: England, alone, had by violence effected it: America had contended ten years long, not against England, but against the revolution: America sought not a revolution; she yielded to it, compelled by necessity, not because she wished to extort a better condition than she had before enjoyed, but because she wished to avert a worse one, prepared for her.

Exactly contrary of all this, was the case in France. The French revolution was *offensive* in its origin, offensive in its progress, offensive in its whole compass, and in every single characteristic moment of its existence. As the American revolution had exhibited a model of moderation in defence, so the French one displayed an unparalleled example of violence and inexorable fury in attack. As the former had always kept the vigour of its defensive measures in rigorous proportion to the exigency, so the latter, from the weakness of the resistance made against it, became more and more violent and terrible, the more cause it had to grow milder. . . .

If we follow this revolution through all its periods, we shall find that the strongest motive for effecting any greater usurpation, for maintaining any greater injustice, for committing any greater crime, constantly was, that a smaller one had immediately before succeeded. The single motive for using persecutions, was, that the victims had already suffered others. This was the character of the French revolution, in wholesale and in retail. The sufferers were punishable, merely because they had suffered; in this bitterest of all offensive wars, they seemed so cautiously to shun every thing that made a shew of resistance, that they sooner forgave a struggling, than a defenceless, enemy.

The relics of the old constitution were not so much boundaries to the omnipotent desolating power of the revolution, as land-marks, designating its victorious progress. The constitution, of 1791, was only a short and voluntary pause; a sort of resting point, at which nobody meant long to wait. The second national assembly did not make a pass, no, not one, which was not an attack upon some ruin or other of the monarchy. The establishment of the republic did not satisfy its authors. The execution of the king scarcely appeased the ravenousness of his butchers, for a single instant. In the year 1793 the thirst for destruction had gone so far, that it was at a loss for an object. The well known saying, that Robespierre meant to reduce the population of France by one half, had its foundation in the lively sense of the impossibility of satisfying the hitherto insatiate revolution, with any thing less, than such a hecatomb.

When there was nothing more left in the country to attack, the offensive frenzy turned itself against the neighbouring states, and finally declared war in solemn decrees against all civil society. It was certainly not the want of will in those, who then conducted this war, if Europe preserved any thing, besides "bread and iron." Fortunately, no strength was great enough long to support such a will. The unavoidable exhaustion of the assailants, and not the power or the merit of the resistance made, saved society; and, finally, brought the work shops themselves, where the weapons for its destruction were forged, within its beneficent bonds again.

As the American revolution was a defensive revolution, it was of course finished, at the moment, when it had overcome the attack, by which it had been occasioned. The French revolution, true to the character of a most violent offensive revolution, could not but proceed so long as there remained objects for it to attack, and it retained strength for the assault.

The American revolution, at every stage of its duration, had a fixed and definite object, and moved within definite limits, and by a definite direction towards this object. The French revolution never had a definite object; and in a thousand various directions, continually crossing each other, ran through the unbounded space of a fantastic arbitrary will, and of a bottomless anarchy.

It lay in the very nature of a defensive revolution, like that of America, to proceed from definite objects, and to pursue definite ends. The peculiar situation, and the peculiar character of the North-Americans confirmed and secured this moderate and beneficent quality to the progress of their revolution.

In the course of it, two principal periods may be observed; *that,* from the first breaking out of the contests in 1765, until the declaration of independence in 1776, and *that,* from this declaration, until the peace with England.

In the first period, the single towns and provinces, and afterwards the members of the general congress, had for their declared and sole object the salvation of their constitution, and of their rights and liberties, as they then stood, from the oppressive usurpations of the British parliament. . . . every step they took, during that critical period was calculated for preservation, not for conquest, for resistance against innovations, not for ardour after them; for defence, not for attack.

In the second period, indeed, a new object came in the place of that, which they had until then pursued: the British parliament had compelled the congress to proclaim the independence of the colonies; but, even this decisive measure by no means threw America into the precipice of lawlessness, into the horrible gulph of an unmeasurable interregnum, or into the slippery career of wild and chimerical theories — The machine of government was, and remained, completely organized: the revolution had taken from the king his negative upon legislative acts, almost the only essential prerogative, which as sovereign of the colonies he immediately exercised: but every province took care that this important function should be performed by another authority, distinct from the legislature, and Georgia and Pennsylvania, were the only ones, which entrusted the legislative powers to an undivided senate. The royal governors, who till then had stood at the head of the executive power, were replaced by others, chosen by the provinces themselves; and as the former governors, owing to their great distance from the mother country, had always held powers in the highest degree discretionary and independent, this alteration could not be much felt — The great and immediate exigencies of social life, the local administration, the police, and course of judicial proceeding were continued as before. Nothing but the loose tie, which had connected America with England, was broken; none of the internal relations were discomposed; all the laws remained in force; the condition of persons and of property suffered no other revolution, than that which was necessarily brought with it! "The people," says that very well informed American historian Dr. Ramsay "scarcely perceived that an alteration in their political constitution had taken place."

As the founders and conductors of the American revolution, from the beginning, knew exactly how far they were to go, and where they must stop; as the new existence of their country, the constitutions of the several provinces, and even the organization of the federal government, at least in its principles was definitely prescribed to them; as their purpose was in no sort to create, but only to preserve, not to erect a new building, but to free the old one from an external, burdensome, straitening scaffolding, and as it never occurred to them, in the rigorous sense of the word, to *reform,* even their own country, much less the whole world, they escaped the most dangerous of all the rocks, which in our times threaten the founders of any great revolution, the deadly passion for making political experiments with abstract theories, and untried systems. It is of the utmost importance, in judging the American revolution, never to lose sight of this point, and by so much the more important, as certain expressions in the early resolves of congress, the maxims of single writers, but especially the frequent appeals of the first leaders of the French revolution to the example of their predecessors in America, have encouraged, and spread abroad the opinion that these, in truth, opened the wide field of revolutionary speculations, and of systematic anarchy — True it is, that the declaration of independence published by the congress, in the name of the colonies, is proceeded by an introduction, in which the *natural* and *unalienable* rights of mankind are considered as the foundation of all government; that after this assertion, so indefinite, and so exposed to the greatest misconstructions, follow certain principles, no less indefinite, no less liable to be abused, from which an inference might be drawn of the unlimited right of the people to change their form of government, and what in the new revolutionary language, is called their *sovereignty.* It is likewise true, that most of the constitutions of the United States, are preceded by those idle *declarations of rights,* so dangerous in their application, from which so much misery has at a later period been derived upon France, and the whole civilized world. Much, however, as it were to be wished, that the legislators of America had disdained this empty pomp of words, that they had exclusively confined themselves within the clear and lawful motives of their resistance; a resistance at first constitutional, and afterwards necessary, and within the limits of their uncontrovertible rights, yet it cannot escape the observation of those, who attentively study the history of their revolution, that they allowed to these speculative ideas, no visible influence upon their practical measures and resolves — They erroneously believed them necessary to justify their first steps; but here the dominion of empty speculation, was forever abandoned — Never, in the whole course of the American revolution, were the *rights of man*, appealed to, for the destruction of the *rights of a citizen;* never was the sovereignty of the people used as a pretext to undermine the respect, due to the laws, or the foundations of social security; no example was ever seen of an individual, or a whole class of individuals, or even the representatives of this, or that single state, who recurred to the declaration of rights, to escape from positive obligation, or to renounce obedience to the common sovereign; finally, never did it enter the head of any legislator, or statesman in America, to combat the lawfulness of foreign constitutions, and to set up the American revolution, as a new epocha in the general relations of civil society.

A Defense of the Constitutions of Government of the United States of America (1787)

JOHN ADAMS

Three writers in Europe of great abilities, reputation, and learning, M. Turgot, the Abbé de Mably, and Dr. Price, have turned their attention to the constitutions of government in the United States of America, and have written and published their criticisms and advice. They all had the most amiable characters, and unquestionably the purest intentions. They all had experience in public affairs, and ample information respecting the nature of man, the necessities of society, and the science of government.

There are in the productions of all of them, among many excellent things, some sentiments, however, that it will be difficult to reconcile to reason, experience, the constitution of human nature, or to the uniform testimony of the greatest statesmen, legislators, and philosophers of all enlightened nations, ancient and modern.

M. Turgot, in his letter to Dr. Price, confesses, "that he is not satisfied with the constitutions which have hitherto been formed for the

From Charles Francis Adams, ed., *The Works of John Adams* (Boston: Little, Brown, 1851), vol. IV, 299–302, 379–380, 391–398; vol. VI, 6, 64–66, 68–69, 114–115.

different states of America." He observes, "that by most of them the customs of England are imitated, without any particular motive. Instead of collecting all authority into one centre, that of the nation, they have established different bodies, a body of representatives, a council, and a governor, because there is in England a house of commons, a house of lords, and a king. They endeavor to balance these different powers, as if this equilibrium, which in England may be a necessary check to the enormous influence of royalty, could be of any use in republics founded upon the equality of all the citizens, and as if establishing different orders of men was not a source of divisions and disputes."

There has been, from the beginning of the revolution in America, a party in every state, who have entertained sentiments similar to these of M. Turgot. Two or three of them have established governments upon his principle; and, by advices from Boston, certain committees of counties have been held, and other conventions proposed in the Massachusetts, with the express purpose of deposing the governor and senate as useless and expensive branches of the constitution; and as it is probable that the publication of M. Turgot's opinion has contributed to excite such discontents among the people, it becomes necessary to examine it, and, if it can be shown to be an error, whatever veneration the Americans very justly entertain for his memory, it is to be hoped they will not be misled by his authority.

M. Turgot is offended because the customs of England are imitated in most of the new constitutions in America, without any particular motives. But, if we suppose English customs to be neither good nor evil in themselves, and merely indifferent; and the people, by their birth, education, and habits, were familiarly attached to them; would not this be a motive particular enough for their preservation, rather than to endanger the public tranquillity, or unanimity, by renouncing them? If those customs were wise, just, and good, and calculated to secure the liberty, property, and safety of the people, as well, or better, than any other institutions, ancient or modern, would M. Turgot have advised the nation to reject them, merely because it was at that time justly incensed against the English government? What English customs has it retained which may with any propriety be called evil? M. Turgot has instanced only one, namely, — "that a body of representatives, a council, and a governor, have been established, because there is in England a house of commons, a house of lords, and a king." It was not so much because the legislature in England consisted of three branches, that such a division of power was adopted by the states, as because their own assemblies had ever been so constituted. It was not so much from attachment by habit to such a plan of power that it was continued, as from conviction that it was founded in nature and reason.

M. Turgot seems to be of a different opinion, and is for "collecting all authority into one centre, the nation." It is easily understood how all authority may be collected into "one centre" in a despot or monarch; but how it can be done when the centre is to be the nation, is more difficult to comprehend. Before we attempt to discuss the notions of an author, we should be careful to ascertain his meaning. It will not be easy, after the most anxious research, to discover the true sense of this extraordinary passage. If, after the pains of "collecting all authority into one centre," that centre is to be the nation, we shall remain exactly where we began, and no collection of authority at all will be made. The nation will be the authority, and the authority the nation. The centre will be the circle, and the circle the centre. When a number of men, women, and children, are simply congregated together, there is no political authority among them; nor any natural authority, but that of parents over their children. To leave the women and children out of the question for the present, the men will all be equal, free, and independent of each other. Not one will have any authority over any other. The first "collection" of authority must be an unanimous agreement to form themselves into a *nation, people, community*, or *body politic*, and to be governed by the majority of suffrages or voices. But even in this case, although the authority is collected into one centre, that centre is no longer the nation, but the majority of the nation. Did M. Turgot mean that the people of Virginia, for example, half a million of souls scattered over a territory of two hundred leagues square, should stop here, and have no other authority by which to make or execute a law, or judge a cause, but by a vote of the whole people, and the decision of a majority! Where is the plain large enough to hold them; and what are the means, and how long would be the time, necessary to assemble them together?

A simple and perfect democracy never yet existed among men. If a village of half a mile square, and one hundred families, is capable of exercising all the legislative, executive, and judicial powers, in public assemblies of the whole, by unanimous votes, or by majorities, it is more than has ever yet been proved in theory or experience. In such a democracy, for the most part, the moderator would be king, the town-clerk legislator and judge, and the constable sheriff; and, upon more important occasions, committees would be only the counsellors of both the former, and commanders of the latter.

Shall we suppose, then, that M. Turgot intended that an assembly of representatives should be chosen by the nation, and vested with all the powers of government; and that this assembly should be the centre in which all the authority was to be collected, and should be virtually deemed the nation? After long reflection, I have not been able to discover any other sense in his words, and this was probably his real meaning. To examine this system in detail may be thought as trifling an occupation as the labored reasonings of Sidney and Locke, to show the absurdity of

Filmer's superstitious notions, appeared to Mr. Hume to be in his enlightened day. Yet the mistakes of great men, and even the absurdities of fools, when they countenance the prejudices of numbers of people, especially in a young country and under new governments, cannot be too fully confuted. I shall not then esteem my time misspent, in placing this idea of M. Turgot in all his lights; in considering the consequences of it; and in collecting a variety of authorities against it. . . .

As we have taken a cursory view of those countries in Europe where the government may be called, in any reasonable construction of the word, republican, let us now pause a few moments, and reflect upon what we have seen.

Among every people, and in every species of republics, we have constantly found *a first magistrate, a head, a chief*, under various dominations, indeed, and with different degrees of authority, with the title of stadtholder, burgomaster, avoyer, doge, gonfaloniero, president, syndic, mayor, alcalde, capitaneo, governor, or king; in every nation we have met with a distinguished officer. If there is no example, then, in any free government, any more than in those which are not free, of a society without a principal personage, we may fairly conclude that the body politic cannot subsist, any more than the animal body, without a head. If M. Turgot had made any discovery which had escaped the penetration of all the legislators and philosophers who have lived before him, he ought at least to have communicated it to the world for their improvement; but as he has never hinted at any such invention, we may safely conclude that he had none; and, therefore, that the Americans are not justly liable to censure for instituting *governors*.

In every form of government we have seen a *senate*, or *little council*, a composition, generally, of those officers of state who have the most experience and power, and of a few other members selected from the highest ranks and most illustrious reputations. On these lesser councils, with the first magistrate at their head, generally rests the principal burden of administration, a share in the legislative, as well as executive and judicial authority of government. The admission of such senates to a participation of these three kinds of power, has been generally observed to produce in the minds of their members an ardent aristocratical ambition, grasping equally at the prerogatives of the first magistrate, and the privileges of the people, and ending in the nobility of a few families, and a tyrannical oligarchy. But in those states, where the senates have been debarred from all executive power, and confined to the legislative, they have been observed to be firm barriers against the encroachments of the crown, and often great supporters of the liberties of the people. The Americans, then, who have carefully confined their senates to the legislative power, have done wisely in adopting them.

We have seen, in every instance, another and a larger assembly, composed of the body of the people, in some little states; of representatives chosen by the people, in others; of members appointed by the senate, and supposed to represent the people, in a third sort; and of persons appointed by themselves or the senate, in certain aristocracies; to prevent them from becoming oligarchies. The Americans, then, whose assemblies are the most adequate, proportional, and equitable representations of the people, that are known in the world, will not be thought mistaken in appointing houses of representatives.

In every republic, — in the smallest and most popular, in the larger and more aristocratical, as well as in the largest and most monarchical, — we have observed a multitude of curious and ingenious inventions to balance, in their turn, all those powers, to check the passions peculiar to them, and to control them from rushing into those exorbitancies to which they are most addicted. The Americans will then be no longer censured for endeavoring to introduce an equilibrium, which is much more profoundly meditated, and much more effectual for the protection of the laws, than any we have seen, except in England. We may even question whether that is an exception. . . .

Let us now return to M. Turgot's idea of a government consisting in a single assembly. He tells us our republics are "founded on the equality of all the citizens, and, therefore, 'orders' and 'equilibriums' are unnecessary, and occasion disputes." But what are we to understand here by equality? Are the citizens to be all of the same age, sex, size, strength, stature, activity, courage, hardiness, industry, patience, ingenuity, wealth, knowledge, fame, wit, temperance, constancy, and wisdom? Was there, or will there ever be, a nation, whose individuals were all equal, in natural and acquired qualities, in virtues, talents, and riches? The answer of all mankind must be in the negative. It must then be acknowledged, that in every state, in the Massachusetts, for example, there are inequalities which God and nature have planted there, and which no human legislator ever can eradicate. I should have chosen to have mentioned Virginia, as the most ancient state, or indeed any other in the union, rather than the one that gave me birth, if I were not afraid of putting suppositions which may give offence, a liberty which my neighbors will pardon. Yet I shall say nothing that is not applicable to all the other twelve.

In this society of Massachusettensians then, there is, it is true, a moral and political equality of rights and duties among all the individuals, and as yet no appearance of artificial inequalities of condition, such as hereditary dignities, titles, magistracies, or legal distinctions; and no established marks, as stars, garters, crosses, or ribbons; there are, nevertheless, inequalities of great moment in the consideration of a legislator, because they have a natural and inevitable influence in society. Let us enumerate some of them: — 1. There is an inequality of wealth; some individuals, whether by descent from their ancestors, or from greater skill, industry, and success in business, have estates both in lands and goods of great value; others have no property at all; and of all the rest of society, much the greater number are possessed of wealth, in all the variety of degrees between these extremes; it will easily be conceived that all the rich men will have many of the poor, in the various trades, manufactures, and other occupations in life, dependent upon them for their daily bread; many of smaller fortunes will be in their debt, and in many ways under obligations to them; others, in better circumstances, neither dependent nor in debt, men of letters, men of the learned professions, and others, from acquaintance, conversation, and civilities, will be connected with them and attached to them. Nay, farther, it will not be denied, that among the wisest people that live, there is a degree of admiration, abstracted from all dependence, obligation, expectation, or even acquaintance, which accompanies splendid wealth, insures some respect, and bestows some influence. 2. Birth. Let no man be surprised that this species of inequality is introduced here. Let the page in history be quoted, where any nation, ancient or modern, civilized or savage, is mentioned, among whom no difference was made between the citizens, on account of their extraction. The truth is, that more influence is allowed to this advantage in free republics than in despotic governments, or than would be allowed to it in simple monarchies, if severe laws had not been made from age to age to secure it. The children of illustrious families have generally greater advantages of education, and earlier opportunities to be acquainted with public characters, and informed of public affairs, than those of meaner ones, or even than those in middle life; and what is more than all, an habitual national veneration for their names, and the characters of their ancestors described in history, or coming down by tradition, removes them farther from vulgar jealousy and popular envy, and secures them in some degree the favor, the affection, and respect of the public. Will any man pretend that the name of Andros, and that of Winthrop, are heard with the same sensations in any village of New England? Is not gratitude the sentiment that attends the latter, and disgust the feeling excited by the former? In the Massachusetts, then, there are persons descended from some of their ancient governors, counsellors, judges, whose fathers, grandfathers, and great-grandfathers, are remembered with esteem by many living, and who are mentioned in history with applause, as benefactors to the country, while there are others who have no such advantage. May we go a step farther, — Know thyself, is as useful a precept to nations as to men. Go into every village in New England, and you will find that the office of justice of the peace, and even the place of representative, which has ever depended only on the freest election of the people, have generally descended from generation to generation, in three or four families at most. The present subject is one of those which all men respect, and all men deride. It may be said of this part of our nature, as Pope said of the whole: —

> "Of human nature, wit her worst may write,
> We all revere it in our own despite."

If, as Harrington says, the ten commandments were voted by the people of Israel, and have been enacted as laws by all other nations; and if we should presume to say, that nations had a civil right to repeal them, no nation would think proper to repeal the fifth, which enjoins honor to parents. If there is a difference between right and wrong; if any thing can be sacred; if there is one idea of moral obligation; the decree of nature must force upon every thinking being and upon every feeling heart the conviction that honor, affection, and gratitude are due from children to those who gave them birth, nurture, and education. The sentiments and affections which naturally arise from reflecting on the love, the cares, and the blessings of parents, abstracted from the consideration of duty, are some of the most forcible and most universal. When religion, law, morals, affection, and even fashion, thus conspire to fill every mind with attachment to parents, and to stamp deep upon the heart their impressions, is it to be expected that men should reverence their parents while they live, and begin to despise or neglect their memories as soon as they are dead? This is in nature impossible. On the contrary, every little unkindness and severity is forgotten, and nothing but endearments remembered with pleasure.

The son of a wise and virtuous father finds the world about him sometimes as much disposed as he himself is, to honor the memory of his father; to congratulate him as the successor to his estate; and frequently to compliment him with elections to the offices he held. A sense of duty, his passions and his interest, thus conspiring to prevail upon him to avail himself of this advantage, he finds a few others in similar circumstances with himself; they naturally associate together, and aid each other. This is a faint sketch of the source and rise of the family spirit; very often the disposition to favor the family is as strong in the town, country, province, or kingdom, as it is in the house itself. The enthusiasm is indeed sometimes wilder, and carries away, like a torrent, all before it.

These observations are not peculiar to any age; we have seen the effects of them in San Marino, Biscay, and the Grisons, as well as in Poland and all other countries. Not to mention any notable examples which have lately happened near us, it is not many months since I was witness to a conversation between some citizens of Massachusetts. One was haranguing on the jealousy which a free people ought to entertain of their liberties, and was heard by all the company with pleasure. In less than ten minutes, the conversation turned upon their governor; and the jealous republican was very angry at the opposition to him. "The present governor," says he, "has done us such services, that he ought to rule us, he and his posterity after him, for ever and ever." "Where is your jealousy of liberty?" demanded the other. "Upon my honor," replies the orator, "I had forgot that; you have caught me in an inconsistency; for I cannot know whether a child of five years old will be a son of liberty or a tyrant." His jealousy was the dictate of his understanding. His confidence and enthusiasm the impulse of his heart.

The pompous trumpery of ensigns, armorials, and escutcheons are not, indeed, far advanced in America. Yet there is a more general anxiety to know their originals, in proportion to their numbers, than in any nation of Europe; arising from the easier circumstances and higher spirit of the common people. And there are certain families in every state equally attentive to all the proud frivolities of heraldry. That kind of pride, which looks down on commerce and manufacturers as degrading, may, indeed, in many countries of Europe, be a useful and necessary quality in the nobility. It may prevent, in some degree, the whole nation from being entirely delivered up to the spirit of avarice. It may be the cause why honor is preferred by some to money. It may prevent the nobility from becoming too rich, and acquiring too large a proportion of the landed property. In America, it would not only be mischievous, but would expose the highest pretensions of the kind to universal ridicule and contempt. Those other hauteurs, of keeping the commons at a distance, and disdaining to converse with any but a few of a certain race, may in Europe be a favor to the people, by relieving them from a multitude of assiduous attentions and humiliating compliances, which would be troublesome. It may prevent the nobles from caballing with the people, and gaining too much influence with them in elections and otherwise. In America, it would justly excite universal indignation; the vainest of all must be of the people, or be nothing. While every office is equally open to every competitor, and the people must decide upon every pretension to a place in the legislature, that of governor and senator, as well as representative, no such airs will ever be endured. At the same time, it must be acknowledged, that some men must take more pains to deserve and acquire an office than others, and must behave better in it, or they will not hold it.

We cannot presume that a man is good or bad, merely because his father was one or the other; and we should always inform ourselves first, whether the virtues and talents are inherited, before we yield our confidence. Wise men beget fools, and honest men knaves; but these instances, although they may be frequent, are not general. If there is often a likeness in feature and figure, there is generally more in mind and heart, because education contributes to the formation of these as well as nature. The influence of example is very great, and almost universal, especially that of parents over their children. In all countries it has been observed, that vices, as well as virtues, very often run down in families from age to age. Any man may go over in his thoughts the circle of his acquaintance, and he will probably recollect instances of a disposition to mischief, malice, and revenge, descending in certain breeds from grandfather to father and son. A young woman was lately convicted at Paris of a trifling theft, barely within the law which decreed a capital punishment. There were circumstances, too, which greatly alleviated her fault; some things in her behavior that seemed innocent and modest; every spectator, as well as the judges, was affected at the scene, and she was advised to petition for a pardon, as there was no doubt it would be granted. "No," says she; "my grandfather, father, and brother were all hanged for stealing; it runs in the blood of our family to steal, and be hanged. If I am pardoned now, I shall steal again in a few months more inexcusably; and, therefore, I will be hanged now." An hereditary passion for the halter is a strong instance, to be sure, and cannot be very common; but something like it too often descends, in certain breeds, from generation to generation.

If vice and infamy are thus rendered less odious, by being familiar in a family, by the example of parents and by education, it would be as unhappy as unaccountable, if virtue and honor were not recommended and rendered more amiable to children by the same means.

There are, and always have been, in every state, numbers possessed of some degree of family pride, who have been invariably encouraged, if not flattered in it, by the people. These have most acquaintance, esteem, and friendship with each other, and mutually aid each other's schemes of interest, convenience, and ambition. Fortune, it is true, has more influence than birth. A rich man, of an ordinary family and common decorum of conduct, may have greater weight than any family merit commonly confers without it.

It will be readily admitted, there are great inequalities of merit, or talents, virtues, services, and what is of more moment, very often of reputation. Some, in a long course of service in an army, have devoted their time, health, and fortunes, signalized their courage and address, exposed themselves to hardships and dangers, lost their limbs, and shed their blood, for the people. Others have displayed their wisdom, learning, and eloquence in council, and in various other ways acquired the confidence and affection of their fellow-citizens to such a degree, that the public have settled into a kind of habit of following their example and taking their advice.

There are a few, in whom all these advantages of birth, fortune, and fame are united.

These sources of inequality, which are common to every people, and can never be altered by any, because they are founded in the constitution of nature; this natural aristocracy among mankind, has been dilated on, because it is a fact essential to be considered in the institution of a government. It forms a body of men which contains the greatest collection of virtues and abilities in a free government, is the brightest ornament and glory of the nation, and may always be made the greatest blessing of society, if it be judiciously managed in the constitution. But if this be not done, it is always the most dangerous; nay, it may be added, it never fails to be the destruction of the commonwealth. . . .

There is but one expedient yet discovered, to avail the society of all the benefits from this body of men, which they are capable of affording, and at the same time, to prevent them from undermining or invading the public liberty; and that is, to throw them all, or at least the most remarkable of them, into one assembly together, in the legislature; to keep all the executive power entirely out of their hands as a body; to erect a first magistrate over them, invested with the whole executive authority; to make them dependent on that executive magistrate for all public executive employments; to give that first magistrate a negative on the legislature, by which he may defend both himself and the people from all their enterprises in the legislature; and to erect on the other side an impregnable barrier against them, in a house of commons, fairly, fully, and adequately representing the people, who shall have the power both of negativing all their attempts at encroachment in the legislature, and of withholding from them and from the crown all supplies, by which they may be paid for their services in executive offices, or even the public service may be carried on to the detriment of the nation.

We have seen, both by reasoning and in experience, what kind of equality is to be found or expected in the simplest people in the world. There is not a city nor a village, any more than a kingdom or a commonwealth, in Europe or America; not a horde, clan, or tribe, among the negroes of Africa, or the savages of North or South America; nor a private club in the world, in which inequalities are not more or less visible. There is, then, a certain degree of weight, which property, family, and merit, will have in the public opinion and deliberations. If M. Turgot had discovered a mode of ascertaining the quantity which they ought to have, and had revealed it to mankind, so that it might be known to every citizen, he would have deserved more of gratitude than is due to all the inventions of philosophers. But, as long as human nature shall have passions and imagination, there is too much reason to fear that these advantages, in many instances, will have more influence than reason and equity can justify. . . .

Marchamont Nedham [1] lays it down as a fundamental principle and an undeniable rule, "that the people, (that is, such as shall be successively

[1] [The author of *The Excellency of a Free State* (1656), which, like Turgot's letter to Dr. Price, defended the idea of pure democracy. — Eds.]

chosen to represent the people,) are the best keepers of their own liberties, and that for many reasons. First, because they never think of usurping over other men's rights, but mind which way to preserve their own." . . .

It is agreed that the people are the best keepers of their own liberties, and the only keepers who can be always trusted; and, therefore, the people's fair, full, and honest consent, to every law, by their representatives, must be made an essential part of the constitution; but it is denied that they are the best keepers, or any keepers at all, of their own liberties, when they hold collectively, or by representation, the executive and judicial power, or the whole and uncontrolled legislative; on the contrary, the experience of all ages has proved, that they instantly give away their liberties into the hand of grandees, or kings, idols of their own creation. The management of the executive and judicial powers together always corrupts them; and throws the whole power into the hands of the most profligate and abandoned among themselves. The honest men are generally nearly equally divided in sentiment, and, therefore, the vicious and unprincipled, by joining one party, carry the majority; and the vicious and unprincipled always follow the most profligate leader, him who bribes the highest, and sets all decency and shame at defiance. It becomes more profitable, and reputable too, except with a very few, to be a party man than a public-spirited one.

It is agreed that "the end of all government is the good and ease of the people, in a secure enjoyment of their rights, without oppression;" but it must be remembered, that the rich are *people* as well as the poor; that they have rights as well as others; that they have as clear and as *sacred* a right to their large property as others have to theirs which is smaller; that oppression to them is as possible and as wicked as to others; that stealing, robbing, cheating, are the same crimes and sins, whether committed against them or others. The rich, therefore, ought to have an effectual barrier in the constitution against being robbed, plundered, and murdered, as well as the poor; and this can never be without an independent senate. The poor should have a bulwark against the same dangers and oppressions; and this can never be without a house of representatives of the people. But neither the rich nor the poor can be defended by their respective guardians in the constitution, without an executive power, vested with a negative, equal to either, to hold the balance even between them, and decide when they cannot agree. If it is asked, When will this negative be used? it may be answered, Perhaps never. The known existence of it will prevent all occasion to exercise it; but if it has not a being, the want of it will be felt every day. If it has not been used in England for a long time past, it by no means follows that there have not been occasions when it might have been employed with propriety. But one thing is very certain, that there have been many occasions since the Revolution, when the constitution would have been overturned if the negative had not been an indubitable prerogative of the crown.

It is agreed that the people are "most sensible of their own burdens; and being once put into a capacity and freedom of acting, are the most likely to provide remedies for their own relief." For this reason they are an essential branch of the legislature, and have a negative on all laws, an absolute control over every grant of money, and an unlimited right to accuse their enemies before an impartial tribunal. Thus far they are most sensible of their burdens, and are most likely to provide remedies. But it is affirmed that they are not only incapable of managing the executive power, but would be instantly corrupted by it in such numbers, as would destroy the integrity of all elections. It is denied that the legislative power can be wholly intrusted in their hands with a moment's safety. The poor and the vicious would instantly rob the rich and virtuous, spend their plunder in debauchery, or confer it upon some idol, who would become the despot; or, to speak more intelligibly, if not more accurately, some of the rich, by debauching the vicious to their corrupt interest, would plunder the virtuous, and become more rich, until they acquired all the property, or a balance of property and of power, in their own hands, and domineered as despots in an oligarchy.

It is agreed that the "people know where the shoe wrings, what grievances are most heavy," and, therefore, they should always hold an independent and essential part in the legislature, and be always able to prevent the shoe from wringing more, and the grievances from being made more heavy; they should have a full hearing of all their arguments, and a full share of all consultations, for easing the foot where it is in pain, and for lessening the weight of grievances or annihilating them. But it is denied that they have right, or that they should have power to take from one man his property to make another easy, and that they *only* know "what fences they stand in need of to shelter them from the injurious assaults of those powers that are above them"; meaning, by the powers above them, senators and magistrates, though, properly speaking, there are no powers above them but the law, which is above all men, governors and senators, kings, and nobles, as well as commons. . . .

Our author is not explicit. If he meant that a fundamental law should be made, that no man should be chosen more than one year, he has nowhere said so. He knew the nation would not have borne it. Cromwell and his creatures would all have detested it; nor would the members of the Long Parliament, or their constituents, have approved it. The idea would have been universally unpopular. No people in the world will bear to be deprived, at the end of one year, of the service of their best men, and be obliged to confer their suffrages, from year to year, on the next best, until the rotation brings them to the worst. The men of greatest interest and influence, moreover, will govern; and if they cannot be chosen themselves, they will generally influence the choice of others so decidedly, that they may be said to have the appointment. If it is true that "the strongest obligation that can be laid upon a man in public matters, is to see that he engage in nothing but what must either offensively or beneficially reflect upon himself," it is equally true at least in a mixed government as in a simple democracy. It is, indeed, more clearly and universally true, because in the first the representatives of the people being the special guardians of equality, equity, and liberty, for the people, will not consent to unequal laws; but in the second, where the great and rich will have the greatest influence in the public councils, they will continually make unequal laws in their own favor, unless the poorer majority unite, which they rarely do, set up an opposition to them, and run them down by making unequal laws against them. In every society where property exists, there will ever be a struggle between rich and poor. Mixed in one assembly, equal laws can never be expected. They will either be made by numbers, to plunder the few who are rich, or by influence, to fleece the many who are poor. Both rich and poor, then, must be made independent, that equal justice may be done, and equal liberty enjoyed by all. To expect that in a single sovereign assembly no load shall be laid upon any but what is common to all, nor to gratify the passions of any, but only to supply the necessities of their country, is altogether chimerical. Such an assembly, under an awkward, unwieldy form, becomes at once a simple monarchy in effect. Some one overgrown genius, fortune, or reputation, becomes a despot, who rules the state at his pleasure, while the deluded nation, or rather a deluded majority, thinks itself free; and in every resolve, law, and act of government, you see the interest, fame, and power of that single individual attended to more than the general good. . . .

If Socrates and Plato, Cicero and Seneca, Hutcheson and Butler are to be credited, reason is rightfully supreme in man, and, therefore, it would be most suitable to the reason of mankind to have no civil or political government at all. The moral government of God, and his vicegerent, Conscience, ought to be sufficient to restrain men to obedience, to justice, and benevolence, at all times and in all places; we must therefore descend from the dignity of our nature, when we think of civil government at all. But the nature of mankind is one thing, and the reason of mankind another; and the first has the same relation to the last as the whole to a part. The passions and appetites are parts of human nature, as well as reason and the moral sense. In the institution of government, it must be remembered that, although reason ought always to govern individuals, it certainly never did since the Fall, and never will, till the Millennium; and human nature must be taken as it is, as it has been, and will be. If, as Cicero says, "man is a noble creature, born with affections to rule rather than obey, there being in every man a natural desire of principality," it is yet certain that every man ought to obey as well as to rule, . . . and that every man cannot rule alone. Each man must be content with his share of empire; and if the nature and reason of mankind, the nobleness of his qualities and affections, and his natural desires, prove his right to a share in the government, they cannot surely prove more than the constitutions of the United States have allowed, — an annual election of the whole legislative and executive, the governor, senate, and house. If we admit them to prove more, they would prove that every man has every year a right to be governor, senator, and representative; which, being impossible, is absurd.

The Federalist. No. VI.

(1787)

ALEXANDER HAMILTON

To the People of the State of New York:

The three last numbers of this paper have been dedicated to an enumeration of the dangers to which we should be exposed, in a state of disunion, from the arms and arts of foreign nations. I shall now proceed to delineate dangers of a different and, perhaps, still more alarming kind — those which will in all probability flow from dissensions between the States themselves, and from domestic factions and convulsions. These have been already in some instances slightly anticipated; but they deserve a more particular and more full investigation.

A man must be far gone in Utopian speculations who can seriously doubt that, if these States should either be wholly disunited, or only united in partial confederacies, the subdivisions into which they might be thrown would have frequent and violent contests with each other. To presume a want of motives for such contests as an argument against their existence, would be to forget that men are ambitious, vindictive, and rapacious. To look for a continuation of harmony between a number of independent, unconnected sovereignties in the same neighborhood, would be to disregard the uniform course of human events, and to set at defiance the accumulated experience of ages.

From Henry Cabot Lodge, ed., *The Federalist* (New York: G. P. Putnam's Sons, 1911), 26–32.

The causes of hostility among nations are innumerable. There are some which have a general and almost constant operation upon the collective bodies of society. Of this description are the love of power or the desire of pre-eminence and dominion — the jealousy of power, or the desire of equality and safety. There are others which have a more circumscribed though an equally operative influence within their spheres. Such are the rivalships and competitions of commerce between commercial nations. And there are others, not less numerous than either of the former, which take their origin entirely in private passions; in the attachments, enmities, interests, hopes, and fears of leading individuals in the communities of which they are members. Men of this class, whether the favorites of a king or of a people, have in too many instances abused the confidence they possessed; and assuming the pretext of some public motive, have not scrupled to sacrifice the national tranquillity to personal advantage or personal gratification.

The celebrated Pericles, in compliance with the resentment of a prostitute, at the expense of much of the blood and treasure of his countrymen, attacked, vanquished, and destroyed the city of the *Samnians*. The same man, stimulated by private pique against the *Megarensians*, another nation of Greece, or to avoid a prosecution with which he was threatened as an accomplice in a supposed theft of the statuary Phidias, or to get rid of the accusations prepared to be brought against him for dissipating the funds of the state in the purchase of popularity, or from a combination of all these causes, was the primitive author of that famous and fatal war, distinguished in the Grecian annals by the name of the *Peloponnesian* war; which, after various vicissitudes, intermissions, and renewals, terminated in the ruin of the Athenian commonwealth.

The ambitious cardinal, who was prime minister to Henry VIII., permitting his vanity to aspire to the triple crown,[1] entertained hopes of succeeding in the acquisition of that splendid prize by the influence of the Emperor Charles V. To secure the favor and interest of this enterprising and powerful monarch, he precipitated England into a war with France, contrary to the plainest dictates of policy, and at the hazard of the safety and independence, as well of the kingdom over which he presided by his counsels, as of Europe in general. For if there ever was a sovereign who bid fair to realize the project of universal monarchy, it was the Emperor Charles V., of whose intrigues Wolsey was at once the instrument and the dupe. . . .

To multiply examples of the agency of personal considerations in the production of great national events, either foreign or domestic, according to their direction, would be an unnecessary waste of time. Those who have but a superficial acquaintance with the sources from which they

[1] Worn by the popes. — PUBLIUS.

are to be drawn, will themselves recollect a variety of instances; and those who have a tolerable knowledge of human nature will not stand in need of such lights, to form their opinion either of the reality or extent of that agency. Perhaps, however, a reference, tending to illustrate the general principle, may with propriety be made to a case which has lately happened among ourselves. If Shays had not been a *desperate debtor*, it is much to be doubted whether Massachusetts would have been plunged into a civil war.

But notwithstanding the concurring testimony of experience, in this particular, there are still to be found visionary or designing men, who stand ready to advocate the paradox of perpetual peace between the States, though dismembered and alienated from each other. The genius of republics (say they) is pacific; the spirit of commerce has a tendency to soften the manners of men, and to extinguish those inflammable humors which have so often kindled into wars. Commercial republics, like ours, will never be disposed to waste themselves in ruinous contentions with each other. They will be governed by mutual interest, and will cultivate a spirit of mutual amity and concord.

Is it not (we may ask these projectors in politics) the true interest of all nations to cultivate the same benevolent and philosophic spirit? If this be their true interest, have they in fact pursued it? Has it not, on the contrary, invariably been found that momentary passions, and immediate interests, have a more active and imperious control over human conduct than general or remote considerations of policy, utility, or justice? Have republics in practice been less addicted to war than monarchies? Are not the former administered by *men* as well as the latter? Are there not aversions, predilections, rivalships, and desires of unjust acquisitions, that affect nations as well as kings? Are not popular assemblies frequently subject to the impulses of rage, resentment, jealousy, avarice, and of other irregular and violent propensities? It is not well known that their determinations are often governed by a few individuals in whom they place confidence, and are, of course, liable to be tinctured by the passions and views of those individuals? Has commerce hitherto done any thing more than change the objects of war? Is not the love of wealth as domineering and enterprising a passion as that of power or glory? Have there not been as many wars founded upon commercial motives since that has become the prevailing system of nations, as were before occasioned by the cupidity of territory or dominion? Has not the spirit of commerce, in many instances, administered new incentives to the appetite, both for the one and for the other? Let experience, the least fallible guide of human opinions, be appealed to for an answer to these inquiries.

Sparta, Athens, Rome, and Carthage were all republics; two of them, Athens and Carthage, of the commercial kind. Yet were they as often engaged in wars, offensive and defensive, as the neighboring monarchies of the same times. Sparta was little better than a well-regulated camp; and Rome was never sated on carnage and conquest.

Carthage, though a commercial republic, was the aggressor in the very war that ended in her destruction. Hannibal had carried her arms into the heart of Italy and to the gates of Rome, before Scipio, in turn, gave him an overthrow in the territories of Carthage, and made a conquest of the commonwealth. . . .

The provinces of Holland, till they were overwhelmed in debts and taxes, took a leading and conspicuous part in the wars of Europe. They had furious contests with England for the dominion of the sea, and were among the most persevering and most implacable of the opponents of Louis XIV.

In the government of Britain the representatives of the people compose one branch of the national legislature. Commerce has been for ages the predominant pursuit of that country. Few nations, nevertheless, have been more frequently engaged in war; and the wars in which that kingdom has been engaged have, in numerous instances, proceeded from the people.

There have been, if I may so express it, almost as many popular as royal wars. The cries of the nation and the importunities of their representatives have, upon various occasions, dragged their monarchs into war, or continued them in it, contrary to their inclinations, and sometimes contrary to the real interests of the state. In that memorable struggle for superiority between the rival houses of *Austria* and *Bourbon*, which so long kept Europe in a flame, it is well known that the antipathies of the English against the French, seconding the ambition, or rather the avarice, of a favorite leader,[2] protracted the war beyond the limits marked out by sound policy, and for a considerable time in opposition to the views of the court.

The wars of these two last-mentioned nations have in a great measure grown out of commercial considerations, — the desire of supplanting and the fear of being supplanted, either in particular branches of traffic or in the general advantages of trade and navigation.

From this summary of what has taken place in the other countries, whose situations have borne the nearest resemblance to our own, what reason can we have to confide in those reveries which would seduce us into an expectation of peace and cordiality between the members of the present confederacy, in a state of separation? Have we not already seen enough of the fallacy and extravagance of those idle theories which have amused us with promises of an exemption from the imperfections, weaknesses, and evils incident to society in every shape? Is it not time to awake from the deceitful dream of a golden age, and to adopt as a

[2] The Duke of Marlborough. — PUBLIUS.

practical maxim for the direction of our political conduct that we, as well as the other inhabitants of the globe, are yet remote from the happy empire of perfect wisdom and perfect virtue?

Let the point of extreme depression to which our national dignity and credit have sunk, let the inconveniences felt everywhere from a lax and ill administration of government, let the revolt of a part of the State of North Carolina, the late menacing disturbances in Pennsylvania, and the actual insurrections and rebellions in Massachusetts, declare —— !

So far is the general sense of mankind from corresponding with the tenents of those who endeavor to lull asleep our apprehensions of discord and hostility between the States, in the event of disunion, that it has from long observation of the progress of society become a sort of axiom in politics, that vicinity, or nearness of situation, constitutes nations natural enemies. An intelligent writer expresses himself on this subject to this effect: "NEIGHBORING NATIONS [says he] are naturally enemies of each other, unless their common weakness forces them to league in a CONFEDERATIVE REPUBLIC, and their constitution prevents the differences that neighborhood occasions, extinguishing that secret jealousy which disposes all states to aggrandize themselves at the expense of their neighbors." This passage, at the same time, points out the EVIL and suggests the REMEDY.

PUBLIUS.

III

THE REVOLT AGAINST THE ENLIGHTENMENT: ROMANTICISM

Romanticism denotes one of those great tendencies in intellectual history that, because of their inclusiveness, are extremely difficult to define. Most interpreters agree that Romanticism emerged in the first half of the nineteenth century as part of the reaction against the Enlightenment. Most also agree that Romanticism was essentially an aesthetic movement; its great monuments were, to name only a few obvious examples, the poetry of Wordsworth, the novels of Cooper, the paintings of Delacroix, and the symphonies of Beethoven. As an aesthetic movement Romanticism entailed a preference for content over form, for the exotic and disorderly over the familiar and regular, for extravagance over moderation, for nature over culture, and for the pleasures of sensuality and emotion over those of reason. However, one can also speak of a characteristically Romantic theory of human nature and society, and the following readings are intended to illustrate this dimension of Romanticism.

Alexis de Tocqueville (1805–1859) has long been acknowledged the most incisive foreign interpreter of American society. In recent years he has also achieved growing recognition as one of the great innovative minds in the history of European social theory. However, he is not very often considered a Romantic. Neither is Ralph Waldo Emerson (1803–1882), the dean of American transcendentalists, very often taken seriously as a social theorist. Yet the selections from Tocqueville and Emerson illustrate what can legitimately be called a Romantic response to the democratic social and political doctrines of the American and French Revolutions. Both intellectuals exhibit a typically Romantic concern for the fate of individual creativity and excellence in democratic times (times that both men seem to associate with materialism and crass commercial-

ism), and both regret the lost heroic virtues of an aristocratic order. However, the reader will have to ask himself to what extent Tocqueville and Emerson mean the same thing when they speak of aristocracy. Is Emerson's aristocracy the privileged social order of pre-revolutionary Europe that Tocqueville, for all his hard-headed realism about the inevitability of democracy, continues to regard as the best bulwark against political tyranny and cultural philistinism? Or is Emerson speaking of an aristocracy of the spirit, an aristocracy of isolated individuals?

Democracy in America

(1835, 1840)

ALEXIS DE TOCQUEVILLE

Amongst the novel objects that attracted my attention during my stay in the United States, nothing struck me more forcibly than the general equality of condition among the people. I readily discovered the prodigious influence which this primary fact exercises on the whole course of society; it gives a peculiar direction to public opinion, and a peculiar tenor to the laws; it imparts new maxims to the governing authorities, and peculiar habits to the governed.

I soon perceived that the influence of this fact extends far beyond the political character and the laws of the country, and that it has no less empire over civil society than over the government; it creates opinions, gives birth to new sentiments, founds novel customs, and modifies whatever it does not produce. The more I advanced in the study of American society, the more I perceived that this equality of condition is the fundamental fact from which all others seem to be derived, and the central point at which all my observations constantly terminated.

I then turned my thoughts to our own hemisphere, and thought that I discerned there something analogous to the spectacle which the New World presented to me. I observed that equality of condition, though it has not there reached the extreme limit which it seems to have attained in the United States, is constantly approaching it; and that the democracy which governs the American communities appears to be rapidly rising into power in Europe. . . .

From Francis Bowen, ed., Henry Reeve, tr., *Democracy in America* (Boston: John Allyn, 1876), vol. I, 1–2, 7–13, 16, 302–307, 318–323; vol. II, 40–46.

It is evident to all alike that a great democratic revolution is going on amongst us; but all do not look at it in the same light. To some it appears to be novel but accidental, and, as such, they hope it may still be checked; to others it seems irresistible, because it is the most uniform, the most ancient, and the most permanent tendency which is to be found in history. . . .

In no country in Europe has the great social revolution which I have just described made such rapid progress as in France; but it has always advanced without guidance. The heads of the state have made no preparation for it, and it has advanced without their consent or without their knowledge. The most powerful, the most intelligent, and the most moral classes of the nation have never attempted to take hold of it in order to guide it. The democracy has consequently been abandoned to its wild instincts, and it has grown up like those children who have no parental guidance, who receive their education in the public streets, and who are acquainted only with the vices and wretchedness of society. Its existence was seemingly unknown, when suddenly it acquired supreme power. Every one then submitted to its caprices; it was worshipped as the idol of strength; and when afterwards it was enfeebled by its own excesses, the legislator conceived the rash project of destroying it, instead of instructing it and correcting its vices. No attempt was made to fit it to govern, but all were bent on excluding it from the government.

The consequence has been, that the democratic revolution has taken place in the body of society, without that concomitant change in the laws, ideas, customs, and manners, which was necessary to render such a revolution beneficial. Thus we have a democracy, without anything to lessen its vices and bring out its natural advantages; and although we already perceive the evils it brings, we are ignorant of the benefits it may confer.

While the power of the crown, supported by the aristocracy, peaceably governed the nations of Europe, society, in the midst of its wretchedness, had several sources of happiness which can now scarcely be conceived or appreciated. The power of a part of his subjects was an insurmountable barrier to the tyranny of the prince; and the monarch, who felt the almost divine character which he enjoyed in the eyes of the multitude, derived a motive for the just use of his power from the respect which he inspired. The nobles, high as they were placed above the people, could not but take that calm and benevolent interest in their fate which the shepherd feels towards his flock; and without acknowledging the poor as their equals, they watched over the destiny of those whose welfare Providence had intrusted to their care. The people, never having conceived the idea of a social condition different from their own, and never expecting to become equal to their leaders, received benefits from them without discussing their rights. They became attached to them when they were clement and just, and submitted to their exactions without resistance or servility, as to the inevitable visitations of the Deity. Custom and the manners of the time, moreover, had established certain limits to oppression, and put a sort of legal restraint upon violence.

As the noble never suspected that any one would attempt to deprive him of the privileges which he believed to be legitimate, and as the serf looked upon his own inferiority as a consequence of the immutable order of nature, it is easy to imagine that some mutual exchange of good-will took place between two classes so differently gifted by fate. Inequality and wretchedness were then to be found in society; but the souls of neither rank of men were degraded. . . .

On the one side were wealth, strength, and leisure, accompanied by the refinements of luxury, the elegance of taste, the pleasures of wit, and the cultivation of the arts; on the other, were labor, clownishness, and ignorance. But in the midst of this coarse and ignorant multitude it was not uncommon to meet with energetic passions, generous sentiments, profound religious convictions, and wild virtues.

The social state thus organized might boast of its stability, its power, and, above all, its glory.

But the scene is now changed. Gradually the distinctions of rank are done away; the barriers which once severed mankind are falling down; property is divided, power is shared by many, the light of intelligence spreads, and the capacities of all classes are equally cultivated. The State becomes democratic, and the empire of democracy is slowly and peaceably introduced into the institutions and the manners of the nation.

I can conceive of a society in which all men would feel an equal love and respect for the laws of which they consider themselves as the authors; in which the authority of the government would be respected as necessary, though not as divine; and in which the loyalty of the subject to the chief magistrate would not be a passion, but a quiet and rational persuasion. Every individual being in the possession of rights which he is sure to retain, a kind of manly confidence and reciprocal courtesy would arise between all classes, alike removed from pride and servility. The people, well acquainted with their own true interests, would understand that, in order to profit by the advantages of society, it is necessary to satisfy its requisitions. The voluntary association of the citizens might then take the place of the individual exertions of the nobles, and the community would be alike protected from anarchy and from oppression.

I admit that, in a democratic state thus constituted, society would not be stationary. But the impulses of the social body might there be regulated and made progressive. If there were less splendor than in the midst of an aristocracy, the contrast of misery would also be less frequent; the pleasures of enjoyment might be less excessive, but those of comfort would be more general; the sciences might be less perfectly cultivated, but ignorance would be less common; the impetuosity of the feelings would be repressed, and the habits of the nation softened; there would be more vices and fewer great crimes.

In the absence of enthusiasm and an ardent faith, great sacrifices may be obtained from the members of a commonwealth by an appeal to their understandings and their experience; each individual will feel the same necessity of union with his fellows to protect his own weakness; and as he knows that he can obtain their help only on condition of helping them, he will readily perceive that his personal interest is identified with the interests of the whole community. The nation, taken as a whole, will be less brilliant, less glorious, and perhaps less strong; but the majority of the citizens will enjoy a greater degree of prosperity, and the people will remain quiet, not because they despair of a change for the better, but because they are conscious that they are well off already.

If all the consequences of this state of things were not good or useful, society would at least have appropriated all such as were useful and good; and having once and for ever renounced the social advantages of aristocracy, mankind would enter into possession of all the benefits which democracy can afford.

But here it may be asked what we have adopted in the place of those institutions, those ideas, and those customs of our forefathers which we have abandoned.

The spell of royalty is broken, but it has not been succeeded by the majesty of the laws. The people have learned to despise all authority, but they still fear it; and fear now extorts more than was formerly paid from reverence and love.

I perceive that we have destroyed those individual powers which were able, single-handed, to cope with tyranny; but it is the government that has inherited the privileges of which families, corporations, and individuals have been deprived; to the power of a small number of persons — which, if it was sometimes oppressive, was often conservative — has succeeded the weakness of the whole community. . . .

We have, then, abandoned whatever advantages the old state of things afforded, without receiving any compensation from our present condition; we have destroyed an aristocracy, and we seem inclined to survey its ruins with complacency, and to fix our abode in the midst of them. . . .

There is a country in the world where the great social revolution which I am speaking of seems to have nearly reached its natural limits. It has been affected with ease and quietness; say rather that this country is reaping the fruits of the democratic revolution which we are undergoing, without having the revolution itself.

The emigrants who colonized the shores of America in the beginning of the seventeenth century somehow separated the democratic principle from all the principles which it had to contend with in the old communities of Europe, and transplanted it alone to the New World. It has there been able to spread in perfect freedom, and peaceably to determine the character of the laws by influencing the manners of the country.

It appears to me beyond a doubt that, sooner or later, we shall arrive, like the Americans, at an almost complete equality of condition. But I do not conclude from this, that we shall ever be necessarily led to draw the same political consequences which the Americans have derived from a similar social organization. I am far from supposing that they have chosen the only form of government which a democracy may adopt; but as the generative cause of laws and manners in the two countries is the same, it is of immense interest for us to know what it has produced in each of them.

It is not, then, merely to satisfy a legitimate curiosity that I have examined America; my wish has been to find there instruction by which we may ourselves profit. Whoever should imagine that I have intended to write a panegyric would be strangely mistaken, and on reading this book, he will perceive that such was not my design: nor has it been my object to advocate any form of government in particular, for I am of opinion that absolute excellence is rarely to be found in any system of laws. I have not even pretended to judge whether the social revolution, which I believe to be irresistible, is advantageous or prejudicial to mankind. I have acknowledged this revolution as a fact already accomplished, or on the eve of its accomplishment; and I have selected the nation, from amongst those which have undergone it, in which its development has been the most peaceful and the most complete, in order to discern its natural consequences, and to find out, if possible, the means of rendering it profitable to mankind. I confess that, in America, I saw more than America; I sought there the image of democracy itself, with its inclinations, its character, its prejudices, and its passions, in order to learn what we have to fear or to hope from its progress. . . .

What Are the Real Advantages Which American Society Derives from a Democratic Government

. . . The defects and weaknesses of a democratic government may readily be discovered; they are demonstrated by flagrant instances, whilst its salutary influence is insensible, and, so to speak, occult. A glance suffices to detect its faults, but its good qualities can be discerned only by long observation. The laws of the American democracy are frequently defective or incomplete; they sometimes attack vested rights, or sanction others which are dangerous to the community; and even if they were good, their frequency would still be a great evil. How comes it, then, that the American republics prosper and continue? . . .

Democratic laws generally tend to promote the welfare of the greatest possible number; for they emanate from the majority of the citizens, who are subject to error, but who cannot have an interest opposed to their own advantage. The laws of an aristocracy tend, on the contrary, to concentrate wealth and power in the hands of the minority; because an aristocracy, by its very nature, constitutes a minority. It may therefore be asserted, as a general proposition, that the purpose of a democracy in its legislation is more useful to humanity than that of an aristocracy. This is, however, the sum total of its advantages.

Aristocracies are infinitely more expert in the science of legislation than democracies ever can be. They are possessed of a self-control which protects them from the errors of temporary excitement; and they form far-reaching designs, which they know how to mature till a favorable opportunity arrives. Aristocracy government proceeds with the dexterity of art; it understands how to make the collective force of all its laws converge at the same time to a given point. Such is not the case with democracies, whose laws are almost always ineffective or inopportune. The means of democracy are therefore more imperfect than those of aristocracy, and the measures which it unwittingly adopts are frequently opposed to its own cause; but the object it has in view is more useful. . . .

The men who are intrusted with the direction of public affairs in the United States are frequently inferior, both in capacity and morality, to those whom an aristocracy would raise to power. But their interest is identified and confounded with that of the majority of their fellow-citizens. They may frequently be faithless, and frequently mistaken; but they will never systematically adopt a line of conduct hostile to the majority; and they cannot give a dangerous or exclusive tendency to the government.

The maladministration of a democratic magistrate, moreover, is an isolated fact, which has influence only during the short period for which he is elected. Corruption and incapacity do not act as common interests, which may connect men permanently with one another. A corrupt or incapable magistrate will not concert his measures with another magistrate, simply because the latter is as corrupt and incapable as himself; and these two men will never unite their endeavors to promote the corruption and inaptitude of their remote posterity. The ambition and the manœuvres of the one will serve, on the contrary, to unmask the other. The vices of a magistrate, in democratic states, are usually wholly personal.

But under aristocratic governments, public men are swayed by the interest of their order, which, if it is sometimes confounded with the interests of the majority, is very frequently distinct from them. This interest is the common and lasting bond which unites them together; it induces them to coalesce and combine their efforts to attain an end which is not always the happiness of the greatest number: and it serves not only to connect the persons in authority with each other, but to unite them with a considerable portion of the community, since a numerous body of citizens belong to the aristocracy, without being invested with official functions. The aristocratic magistrate is therefore constantly supported by a portion of the community, as well as by the government of which he is a member. . . .

The English aristocracy is perhaps the most liberal which has ever existed, and no body of men has ever, uninterruptedly, furnished so many honorable and enlightened individuals to the government of a country. It cannot, however, escape observation, that, in the legislation of England, the interests of the poor have been often sacrificed to the advantage of the rich, and the rights of the majority to the privileges of a few. The consequence is, that England, at the present day, combines the extremes of good and evil fortune in the bosom of her society; and the miseries and privations of her poor almost equal her power and renown.

In the United States, where the public officers have no class-interests to promote, the general and constant influence of the government is beneficial, although the individuals who conduct it are frequently unskilful, and sometimes contemptible. There is, indeed, a secret tendency in democratic institutions, which makes the exertions of the citizens subservient to the prosperity of the community, in spite of their vices and mistakes; whilst in aristocratic institutions, there is a secret bias, which, notwithstanding the talents and virtues of those who conduct the government, leads them to contribute to the evils which oppress their fellow-creatures. In aristocratic governments, public men may frequently do harm without intending it; and in democratic states, they bring about good results which they never thought of. . . .

It is not impossible to conceive the surprising liberty which the Americans enjoy; some idea may likewise be formed of their extreme equality; but the political activity which pervades the United States must be seen in order to be understood. No sooner do you set foot upon American ground, than you are stunned by a kind of tumult; a confused clamor is heard on every side; and a thousand simultaneous voices demand the satisfaction of their social wants. Everything is in motion around you; here, the people of one quarter of a town are met to decide upon the building of a church; there, the election of a representative is going on; a little further, the delegates of a district are posting to the town in order to consult upon some local improvements; in another place, the laborers of a village quit their ploughs to deliberate upon the project of a road or a public school. Meetings are called for the sole purpose of declaring their disapprobation of the conduct of the government; whilst in other assemblies, citizens salute the authorities of the day as the fathers of their country. Societies are formed which regard drunkenness as the principal cause of the evils of the state, and solemnly bind themselves to give an example of temperance. . . .

This ceaseless agitation which democratic government has introduced into the political world, influences all social intercourse. I am not sure that, upon the whole, this is not the greatest advantage of democracy; and I am less inclined to applaud it for what it does, than for what it causes to be done.

It is incontestable that the people frequently conduct public business very ill; but it is impossible that the lower orders should take a part in public business without extending the circle of their ideas, and quitting the ordinary routine of their thoughts. The humblest individual who cooperates in the government of society acquires a certain degree of self-respect; and as he possesses authority, he can command the services of minds more enlightened than his own. He is canvassed by a multitude of applicants, and, in seeking to deceive him in a thousand ways, they really enlighten him. He takes a part in political undertakings which he did not originate, but which give him a taste for undertakings of the kind. New improvements are daily pointed out to him in the common property, and this gives him the desire of improving that property which is his own. He is perhaps neither happier nor better than those who came before him, but he is better informed and more active. I have no doubt that the democratic institutions of the United States, joined to the physical constitution of the country, are the cause (not the direct, as is so often asserted, but the indirect cause) of the prodigious commercial activity of the inhabitants. It is not created by the laws, but the people learn how to promote it by the experience derived from legislation.

When the opponents of democracy assert that a single man performs what he undertakes better than the government of all, it appears to me that they are right. The government of an individual, supposing an equality of knowledge on either side, is more consistent, more persevering, and more accurate in details, than that of a multitude, and selects with more discrimination the men whom it employs. If any deny this, they have never seen a democratic government, or have judged upon partial evidence. It is true that, even when local circumstances and the dispositions of the people allow democratic institutions to exist, they do not display a regular and methodical system of government. Democratic liberty is far from accomplishing all its projects with the skill of an adroit despotism. It frequently abandons them before they have borne their fruits, or risks them when the consequences may be dangerous; but in the end, it produces more than any absolute government; if it does fewer things well, it does a greater number of things. Under its sway, the grandeur is not in what the public administration does, but in what is done without it or outside of it. Democracy does not give the people the most skilful government, but it produces what the ablest governments are frequently unable to create; namely, an all-pervading and restless activity, a superabundant force, and an energy which is inseparable from it, and which may, however unfavorable circumstances may be, produce wonders. These are the true advantages of democracy.

In the present age, when the destinies of Christendom seem to be in suspense, some hasten to assail democracy as a hostile power, whilst it is yet growing; and others already adore this new deity which is springing forth from chaos. But both parties are imperfectly acquainted with the object of their hatred or their worship; they strike in the dark, and distribute their blows at random.

We must first understand what is wanted of society and its government. Do you wish to give a certain elevation to the human mind, and teach it to regard the things of this world with generous feelings, to inspire men with a scorn of mere temporal advantages, to form and nourish strong convictions, and keep alive the spirit of honorable devotedness? Is it your object to refine the habits, embellish the manners, and cultivate the arts, to promote the love of poetry, beauty, and glory? Would you constitute a people fitted to act powerfully upon all other nations, and prepared for those high enterprises which, whatever be their results, will leave a name forever famous in history? If you believe such to be the principal object of society, avoid the government of the democracy, for it would not lead you with certainty to the goal.

But if you hold it expedient to divert the moral and intellectual activity of man to the production of comfort, and the promotion of general well-being; if a clear understanding be more profitable to man than genius; if your object be not to stimulate the virtues of heroism, but the habits of peace; if you had rather witness vices than crimes, and are content to meet with fewer noble deeds, provided offences be diminished in the same proportion; if, instead of living in the midst of a brilliant society, you are contented to have prosperity around you; if, in short, you are of opinion that the principal object of a government is not to confer the greatest possible power and glory upon the body of the nation, but to insure the greatest enjoyment, and to avoid the most misery, to each of the individuals who compose it, — if such be your desire, then equalize the conditions of men, and establish democratic institutions.

But if the time be past at which such a choice was possible, and if some power superior to that of man already hurries us, without consulting our wishes, towards one or the other of these two governments, let us endeavor to make the best of that which is allotted to us, and, by finding out both its good and its evil tendencies, be able to foster the former and repress the latter to the utmost.

The Example of the Americans Does Not Prove That a Democratic People Can Have No Aptitude and No Taste for Science, Literature, or Art

It must be acknowledged that in few of the civilized nations of our time have the higher sciences made less progress than in the United

States; and in few have great artists, distinguished poets, or celebrated writers, been more rare. Many Europeans, struck by this fact, have looked upon it as a natural and inevitable result of equality; and they have thought that, if a democratic state of society and democratic institutions were ever to prevail over the whole earth, the human mind would gradually find its beacon-lights grow dim, and men would relapse into a period of darkness.

To reason thus is, I think, to confound several ideas which it is important to divide and examine separately: it is to mingle, unintentionally, what is democratic with what is only American.

The religion professed by the first emigrants, and bequeathed by them to their descendants, — simple in its forms, austere and almost harsh in its principles, and hostile to external symbols and to ceremonial pomp, — is naturally unfavorable to the fine arts, and only yields reluctantly to the pleasures of literature. The Americans are a very old and a very enlightened people, who have fallen upon a new and unbounded country, where they may extend themselves at pleasure, and which they may fertilize without difficulty. This state of things is without a parallel in the history of the world. In America, every one finds facilities unknown elsewhere for making or increasing his fortune. The spirit of gain is always on the stretch, and the human mind, constantly diverted from the pleasures of imagination and the labors of the intellect, is there swayed by no impulse but the pursuit of wealth. Not only are manufacturing and commercial classes to be found in the United States, as they are in all other countries; but, what never occurred elsewhere, the whole community are simultaneously engaged in productive industry and commerce.

But I am convinced that, if the Americans had been alone in the world, with the freedom and the knowledge acquired by their forefathers, and the passions which are their own, they would not have been slow to discover that progress cannot long be made in the application of the sciences without cultivating the theory of them; that all the arts are perfected by one another: and, however absorbed they might have been by the pursuit of the principal object of their desires, they would speedily have admitted that it is necessary to turn aside from it occasionally, in order the better to attain it in the end.

The taste for the pleasures of mind is moreover so natural to the heart of civilized man, that amongst the polite nations, which are least disposed to give themselves up to these pursuits, a certain number of persons are always to be found who take part in them. This intellectual craving, once felt, would very soon have been satisfied.

But at the very time when the Americans were naturally inclined to require nothing of science but its special applications to the useful arts and the means of rendering life comfortable, learned and literary Europe was engaged in exploring the common sources of truth, and in improving at the same time all that can minister to the pleasures or satisfy the wants of man.

At the head of the enlightened nations of the Old World the inhabitants of the United States more particularly distinguished one, to which they were closely united by a common origin and by kindred habits. Amongst this people they found distinguished men of science, able artists, writers of eminence, and they were enabled to enjoy the treasures of the intellect without laboring to amass them. In spite of the ocean which intervenes, I cannot consent to separate America from Europe. I consider the people of the United States as that portion of the English people who are commissioned to explore the forests of the New World; whilst the rest of the nation, enjoying more leisure and less harassed by the drudgery of life, may devote their energies to thought, and enlarge in all directions the empire of mind.

The position of the Americans is therefore quite exceptional, and it may be believed that no democratic people will ever be placed in a similar one. Their strictly Puritanical origin, — their exclusively commercial habits, — even the country they inhabit, which seems to divert their minds from the pursuit of science, literature, and the arts, — the proximity of Europe, which allows them to neglect these pursuits without relapsing into barbarism, — a thousand special causes, of which I have only been able to point out the most important, — have singularly concurred to fix the mind of the American upon purely practical objects. His passions, his wants, his education, and everything about him, seem to unite in drawing the native of the United States earthward: his religion alone bids him turn, from time to time, a transient and distracted glance to heaven. Let us cease, then, to view all democratic nations under the example of the American people, and attempt to survey them at length with their own features.

It is possible to conceive a people not subdivided into any castes or scale of ranks; among whom the law, recognizing no privileges, should divide inherited property into equal shares; but which, at the same time, should be without knowledge and without freedom. Nor is this an empty hypothesis: a despot may find that it is his interest to render his subjects equal and to leave them ignorant, in order more easily to keep them slaves. Not only would a democratic people of this kind show neither aptitude nor taste for science, literature, or art, but it would probably never arrive at the possession of them. The law of descent would of itself provide for the destruction of large fortunes at each succeeding generation; and no new fortunes would be acquired. The poor man, without either knowledge of freedom, would not so much as conceive the idea of raising himself to wealth; and the rich man would allow himself to be degraded to poverty, without a notion of self-defence. Between these two members of the community complete and invincible equality would soon be established. No one would then have time or taste to devote himself to the pursuits of pleasures of the intellect; but all men would remain paralyzed in a state of common ignorance and equal servitude.

When I conceive a democratic society of this kind, I fancy myself in one of those low, close, and gloomy abodes, where the light which breaks in from without soon faints and fades away. A sudden heaviness overpowers me, and I grope through the surrounding darkness, to find an opening which will restore me to the air and the light of day. But all this is not applicable to men already enlightened who retain their freedom, after having abolished those peculiar and hereditary rights which perpetuated the tenure of property in the hands of certain individuals or certain classes.

When men living in a democratic state of society are enlightened, they readily discover that they are not confined and fixed by any limits which constrain them to take up with their present fortune. They all, therefore, conceive the idea of increasing it, — if they are free, they all attempt it; but all do not succeed in the same manner. The legislature, it is true, no longer grants privileges, but nature grants them. As natural inequality is very great, fortunes become unequal as soon as every man exerts all his faculties to get rich.

The law of descent prevents the establishment of wealthy families,[1] but it does not prevent the existence of wealthy individuals. It constantly brings back the members of the community to a common level, from which they as constantly escape; and the inequality of fortunes augments in proportion as their knowledge is diffused and their liberty increased. . . .

Free and democratic communities, then, will always contain a multitude of people enjoying opulence or a competency. The wealthy will not be so closely linked to each other as the members of the former aristocratic class of society; their inclinations will be different, and they will scarcely ever enjoy leisure as secure or complete; but they will be far more numerous than those who belonged to that class of society could ever be. These persons will not be strictly confined to the cares of practical life; and they will still be able, though in different degrees, to indulge in the pursuits and pleasure of the intellect. In those pleasures they will indulge; for, if it be true that the human mind leans on one side to the limited, the material, and the useful, it naturally rises on the other to the infinite, the spiritual, and the beautiful. Physical wants confine it to the earth; but, as soon as the tie is loosened, it will rise of itself.

Not only will the number of those who can take an interest in the productions of mind be greater, but the taste for intellectual enjoyment will

[1] [Tocqueville believed, mistakenly, that in America a man's estate was by law divided equally among his heirs, thus preventing the accumulation of large family fortunes. — Eds.]

descend, step by step, even to those who, in aristocratic societies, seem to have neither time nor ability to indulge in them. When hereditary wealth, the privileges of rank, and the prerogatives of birth have ceased to be, and when every man derives his strength from himself alone, it becomes evident that the chief cause of disparity between the fortunes of men is the mind. Whatever tends to invigorate, to extend, or to adorn the mind, instantly rises to a high value. The utility of knowledge becomes singularly conspicuous even to the eyes of the multitude: those who have no taste for its charms set store upon its results, and make some efforts to acquire it.

In free and enlightened democratic times there is nothing to separate men from each other, or to retain them in their place: they rise or sink with extreme rapidity. All classes live in continual intercourse, from their great proximity to each other. They communicate and intermingle every day; they imitate and emulate one another: this suggests to the people many ideas, notions, and desires which they would never have entertained if the distinctions of rank had been fixed, and society at rest. In such nations, the servant never considers himself as an entire stranger to the pleasures and toils of his master, nor the poor man to those of the rich; the rural population assimilates itself to that of the towns, and the provinces to the capital. No one easily allows himself to be reduced to the mere material cares of life; and the humblest artisan casts at times an eager and a furtive glance into the higher regions of the intellect. People do not read with the same notions or in the same manner as they do in aristocratic communities; but the circle of readers is unceasingly expanded, till it includes all the people.

As soon as the multitude begin to take an interest in the labors of the mind, it finds out that to excel in some of them is a powerful means of acquiring fame, power, or wealth. The restless ambition which equality begets instantly takes this direction, as it does all others. The number of those who cultivate science, letters, and the arts, becomes immense. The intellectual world starts into prodigious activity: every one endeavors to open for himself a path there, and to draw the eyes of the public after him. Something analogous occurs to what happens in society in the United States politically considered. What is done is often imperfect, but the attempts are innumerable; and, although the results of individual effort are commonly very small, the total amount is always very large.

It is therefore not true to assert, that men living in democratic times are naturally indifferent to science, literature, and the arts: only it must be acknowledged that they cultivate them after their own fashion, and bring to the task their own peculiar qualifications and deficiencies.

Aristocracy
(1848)

RALPH WALDO EMERSON

There is an attractive topic, which never goes out of vogue and is impertinent in no community, — the permanent traits of the Aristocracy. It is an interest of the human race, and, as I look at it, inevitable, sacred and to be found in every country and in every company of men. My concern with it is that concern which all well-disposed persons will feel, that there should be model men, — true instead of spurious pictures of excellence, and, if possible, living standards. . . .

If one thinks of the interest which all men have in beauty of character and manners; that it is of the last importance to the imagination and affection, inspiring as it does that loyalty and worship so essential to the finish of character, — certainly, if culture, if laws, if primogeniture, if heraldry, if money could secure such a result as superior and finished men, it would be the interest of all mankind to see that the steps were taken, the pains incurred. No taxation, no concession, no conferring of privileges never so exalted would be a price too large.

The old French Revolution attracted to its first movement all the liberality, virtue, hope and poetry in Europe. By the abolition of kingship and aristocracy, tyranny, inequality and poverty would end. Alas! no; tyranny, inequality, poverty, stood as fast and fierce as ever. We likewise put faith in Democracy; in the Republican principle carried out to the extremes of practice in universal suffrage, in the will of majorities. The young adventurer finds that the relations of society, the position of classes, irk and sting him, and he lends himself to each malignant party that assails what is eminent. He will one day know that this is not removable, but a distinction in the nature of things; that neither the caucus, nor the newspaper, nor the Congress, nor the mob, nor the guillotine, nor fire, nor all together, can avail to outlaw, cut out, burn, or destroy the offense of superiority in persons. The manners, the pretension, which annoy me so much, are not superficial, but built on a real distinction in the nature of my companion. The superiority in him is inferiority in me, and if this particular companion were wiped by a sponge out of nature, my inferiority would still be made evident to me by other persons everywhere and every day. . . .

The existence of an upper class is not injurious, as long as it is dependent on merit. For so long it is provocation to the bold and generous.

From *Emerson's Complete Works* (Boston: Houghton Mifflin, 1883), 35, 38–39, 42–67.

These distinctions exist, and they are deep, not to be talked or voted away. If the differences are organic, so are the merits, that is to say the power and excellence we describe are real. Aristocracy is the class eminent by personal qualities, and to them belongs without assertion a proper influence. Men of aim must lead the aimless; men of invention the uninventive. I wish catholic men, who by their science and skill are at home in every latitude and longitude, who carry the world in their thoughts; men of universal politics, who are interested in things in proportion to their truth and magnitude; who know the beauty of animals and the laws of their nature, whom the mystery of botany allures, and the mineral laws; who see general effects and are not too learned to love the Imagination, the power and the spirits of Solitude; — men who see the dance in men's lives as well as in a ball-room, and can feel and convey the sense which is only collectively or totally expressed by a population; men who are charmed by the beautiful Nemesis as well as by the dire Nemesis, and dare trust their inspiration for their welcome; who would find their fellows in persons of real elevation of whatever kind of speculative or practical ability. We are fallen on times so acquiescent and traditionary that we are in danger of forgetting so simple a fact that the basis of all aristocracy must be truth, — the doing what elsewhere is pretended to be done. One would gladly see all our institutions rightly aristocratic in this wise.

I enumerate the claims by which men enter the superior class.

1. A commanding talent. In every company one finds the best man; and if there be any question, it is decided the instant they enter into any practical enterprise. If the finders of glass, gunpowder, printing, electricity, — if the healer of small-pox, the contriver of the safety lamp, of the aqueduct, of the bridge, of the tunnel; if the finders of parallax, of new planets, of steam power for boat and carriage, the finder of sulphuric ether and the electric telegraph, — if these men should keep their secrets, or only communicate them to each other, must not the whole race of mankind serve them as gods? It only needs to look at the social aspect of England and America and France, to see the rank which original practical talent commands.

Every survey of the dignified classes, in ancient or modern history, imprints universal lessons, and establishes a nobility of a prouder creation. And the conclusion which Roman Senators, Indian Brahmins, Persian Magians, European Nobles and great Americans inculcate, — that which they preach out of their material wealth and glitter, out of their old war and modern land-owning, even out of sensuality and sneers, is, that the radical and essential distinctions of every aristocracy are moral. Do not hearken to the men, but to the Destiny in the institutions. An aristocracy is composed of simple and sincere men for whom nature and ethics are strong enough, who say what they mean and go straight to their objects. It is essentially real.

The multiplication of monarchs known by telegraph and daily news from all countries to the daily papers, and the effect of freer institutions in England and America, has robbed the title of king of all its romance, as that of our commercial consuls as compared with the ancient Roman. We shall come to add "Kings" in the "Contents" of the Directory, as we do "Physicians," "Brokers," etc. In simple communities, in the heroic ages, a man was chosen for his knack; got his name, rank and living for that; and the best of the best was the aristocrat or king. In the Norse Edda it appears as the curious but excellent policy of contending tribes, when tired of war, to exchange hostages, and in reality each to adopt from the other a first-rate man, who thus acquired a new country; was at once made a chief. And no wrong was so keenly resented as any fraud in this transaction. In the heroic ages, as we call them, the hero uniformly has some real talent. Ulysses in Homer is represented as a very skilful carpenter. He builds the boat with which he leaves Calypso's isle, and in his own palace carves a bedstead out of the trunk of a tree and inlays it with gold and ivory. Epeus builds the wooden horse. The English nation down to a late age inherited the reality of the Northern stock. In 1373, in writs of summons of members of Parliament, the sheriff of every county is to cause "two dubbed knights, or the most worthy esquires, the most expert in feats of arms, and no others; and of every city, two citizens, and of every borough, two burgesses, such as have greatest skill in shipping and merchandising, to be returned."

The ancients were fond of ascribing to their nobles gigantic proportions and strength. The hero must have the force of ten men. The chief is taller by a head than any of his tribe. Douglas can throw the bar a greater cast. Richard can sever the iron bolt with his sword. The horn of Roland, in the romance, is heard sixty miles. The Cid has a prevailing health that will let him nurse the leper, and share his bed without harm. And since the body is the pipe through which we tap all the succors and virtues of the material world, it is certain that a sound body must be at the root of any excellence in manners and actions; a strong and supple frame which yields a stock of strength and spirits for all the needs of the day, and generates the habit of relying on a supply of power for all extraordinary exertions. When Nature goes to create a national man, she puts a symmetry between the physical and intellectual powers. She moulds a large brain, and joins to it a great trunk to supply it; as if a fine alembic were fed with liquor for its distillations from broad full vats in the vaults of the laboratory.

Certainly, the origin of most of the perversities and absurdities that disgust us is, primarily, the want of health. Genius is health and Beauty is health and Virtue is health. The petty arts which we blame in the half-great seem as odious to them also; — the resources of weakness and despair. And the manners betray the like puny constitution. Temperament is fortune, and we must say it so often. In a thousand cups of life, only one is the right mixture, — a fine adjustment to the existing elements. When that befalls, when the well-mixed man is born, with eyes not too dull nor too good, with fire enough and earth enough, capable of impressions from all things, and not too susceptible, — then no gift need be bestowed on him, he brings with him fortune, followers, love, power. . . .

An aristocracy could not exist unless it were organic. Men are born to command, and — it is even so — "come into the world booted and spurred to ride." The blood royal never pays, we say. It obtains service, gifts, supplies, furtherance of all kinds from the love and joy of those who feel themselves honored by the service they render.

Dull people think it Fortune that makes one rich and another poor. Is it? Yes, but the fortune was earlier than they think, namely, in the balance or adjustment between devotion to what is agreeable to-day and the forecast of what will be valuable to-morrow.

Certainly I am not going to argue the merits of gradation in the universe; the existing order of more or less. Neither do I wish to go into a vindication of the justice that disposes the variety of lot. I know how steep the contrast of condition looks; such excess here and such destitution there; like entire chance, like the freaks of the wind, heaping the snow-drift in gorges, stripping the plain; such despotism of wealth and comfort in banquet-halls, whilst death is in the pots of the wretched, — that it behooves a good man to walk with tenderness and heed amidst so much suffering. I only point in passing to the order of the universe, which makes a rotation, — not like the coarse policy of the Greeks, ten generals, each commanding one day and then giving place to the next, or like our democratic politics, my turn now, your turn next, — but the constitution of things has distributed a new quality or talent to each mind, and the revolution of things is always bringing the need, now of this, now of that, and is sure to bring home the opportunity to every one.

The only relief that I know against the invidiousness of superior position is, that you exert your faculty; for whilst each does that, he excludes hard thoughts from the spectator. All right activity is amiable. I never feel that any man occupies my place, but that the reason why I do not have what I wish, is, that I want the faculty which entitles. All spiritual or real power makes its own place.

We pass for what we are, and we prosper or fail by what we are. There are men who may dare much and will be justified in their daring. But it is because they know they are in their place. As long as I am in my place, I am safe. "The best lightning-rod for your protection is your own spine." Let a man's social aims be proportioned to his means and power. I do not pity the misery of a man underplaced: that will right itself presently: but I pity the man overplaced. A certain quantity of power belongs to a certain quantity of faculty. Whoever wants more power than is the legitimate attraction of his faculty, is a politician, and must pay for that excess; must truckle for it. This is the whole game of society and the politics of the world. . . .

It will be agreed everywhere that society must have the benefit of the best leaders. How to obtain them? Birth has been tried and failed. Caste in India has no good result. Ennobling of one family is good for one generation; not sure beyond. Slavery had mischief enough to answer for, but it had this good in it, — the pricing of men. In the South a slave was bluntly but accurately valued at five hundred to a thousand dollars, if a good field-hand; if a mechanic, as carpenter or smith, twelve hundred or two thousand. In Rome or Greece what sums would not be paid for a superior slave, a confidential secretary and manager, an educated slave; a man of genius, a Moses educated in Egypt? I don't know how much Epictetus was sold for, or Æsop, or Toussaint l'Ouverture, and perhaps it was not a good market-day. Time was, in England, when the state stipulated beforehand what price should be paid for each citizen's life, if he was killed. Now, if it were possible, I should like to see that appraisal applied to every man, and every man made acquainted with the true number and weight of every adult citizen, and that he be placed where he belongs, with so much power confided to him as he could carry and use.

In the absence of such anthropometer I have a perfect confidence in the natural laws. I think that the community, — every community, if obstructing laws and usages are removed, — will be the best measure and the justest judge of the citizen, or will in the long run give the fairest verdict and reward; better than any royal patronage; better than any premium on race; better than any statute elevating families to hereditary distinction, or any class to sacerdotal education and power. The verdict of battles will best prove the general; the town-meeting, the Congress, will not fail to find out legislative talent. The prerogatives of a right physician are determined, not by his diplomas, but by the health he restores to body and mind; the powers of a geometer by solving his problem; of a priest by the act of inspiring us with a sentiment which disperses the grief from which we suffered. When the lawyer tries his case in court he himself is also on trial and his own merits appear as well as his client's. When old writers are consulted by young writers who have written their first book, they say, Publish it by all means; so only can you certainly know its quality.

But we venture to put any man in any place. It is curious how negligent the public is of the essential qualifications of its representatives. They ask if a man is a republican, a democrat? Yes. Is he a man of talent? Yes. Is he honest and not looking for an office or any manner of bribe? He is honest. Well then choose him by acclamation. And they go home and tell their wives with great satisfaction what a good thing they have done. But they forgot to ask the fourth question, not less important than either of the others, and without which the others do not avail. Has he a will? Can he carry his points against opposition? Probably not. It is not sufficient that your work follows your genius, or is organic, to give you the magnetic power over men. More than taste and talent must go to the Will. That must also be a gift of nature. It is in some; it is not in others. But I should say, if it is not in you, you had better not put yourself in places where not to have it is to be a public enemy.

The expectation and claims of mankind indicate the duties of this class. Some service they must pay. We do not expect them to be saints, and it is very pleasing to see the instinct of mankind on this matter, — how much they will forgive to such as pay substantial service and work energetically after their kind; but they do not extend the same indulgence to those who claim and enjoy the same prerogative but render no returns. The day is darkened when the golden river runs down into mud; when genius grows idle and wanton and reckless of its fine duties of being Saint, Prophet, Inspirer to its humble fellows, baulks their respect and confounds their understanding by silly extravagances. To a right aristocracy, to Hercules, to Theseus, Odin, the Cid, Napoleon; to Sir Robert Walpole, to Fox, Chatham, Mirabeau, Jefferson, O'Connell; — to the men, that is, who are incomparably superior to the populace in ways agreeable to the populace, showing them the way they should go, doing for them what they wish done and cannot do; — of course everything will be permitted and pardoned, — gaming, drinking, fighting, luxury. These are the heads of party, who can do no wrong, — everything short of infamous crime will pass. But if those who merely sit in their places and are not, like them, able; if the dressed and perfumed gentleman, who serves the people in no wise and adorns them not, is not even *not afraid of them,* if such an one go about to set ill examples and corrupt them, who shall blame them if they burn his barns, insult his children, assault his person, and express their unequivocal indignation and contempt? He eats their bread, he does not scorn to live by their labor, and after breakfast he cannot remember that there are human beings. To live without duties is obscene.

2. Genius, what is so called in strictness, — the power to affect the Imagination, as possessed by the orator, the poet, the novelist, or the artist, — has a royal right in all possessions and privileges being itself representative and accepted by all men as their delegate. It has indeed the best right, because it raises men above themselves, intoxicates them with beauty. They are honored by rendering it honor, and the reason of this allowance is that Genius unlocks for all men the chains of use, temperament and drudgery, and gives them a sense of delicious liberty and power.

The first example that occurs is an extraordinary gift of eloquence. A man who has that possession of his means and that magnetism that he can at all times carry the convictions of a public assembly, we must respect, and he is thereby ennobled. He has the freedom of the city. He is entitled to neglect trifles. Like a great general, or a great poet, or a millionaire, he may wear his coat out at elbows, and his hat on his feet, if he will. He has established relation, representativeness. The best feat of genius is to bring all the varieties of talent and culture into its audience; the mediocre and the dull are reached as well as the intelligent. I have seen it conspicuously shown in a village. Here are classes which day by day have no intercourse, nothing beyond perhaps a surly nod in passing. But I have seen a man of teeming brain come among these men, so full of his facts, so unable to suppress them, that he has poured out a river of knowledge to all comers, and drawing all these men round him, all sorts of men, interested the whole village, good and bad, bright and stupid, in his facts; the iron boundary lines had all faded away; the stupid had discovered that they were not stupid; the coldest had found themselves drawn to their neighbors by interest in the same things. This was a naturalist.

The more familiar examples of this power certainly are those who establish a wider dominion over men's minds than any speech can; who think, and paint, and laugh, and weep, in their eloquent closets, and then convert the world into a huge whispering gallery, to report the tale to all men, and win smiles and tears from many generations. The eminent examples are Shakspeare, Cervantes, Bunyan, Burns, Scott, and now we must add Dickens. In the fine arts, I find none in the present age who have any popular power, who have achieved any nobility by ennobling the people.

3. Elevation of sentiment, refining and inspiring the manners, must really take the place of every distinction whether of material power or of intellectual gifts. The manners of course must have that depth and firmness of tone to attest their centrality in the nature of the man. I mean the things themselves shall be judges, and determine. In the presence of this nobility even genius must stand aside. For the two poles of nature are Beauty and Meanness, and noble sentiment is the highest form of Beauty. He is beautiful in face, in port, in manners, who is absorbed in objects which he truly believes to be superior to himself. Is there any parchment or any cosmetic or any blood that can obtain homage like that security of air presupposing so undoubtingly the sympathy of men in his designs? What is it that makes the true knight? Loyalty to his thought. That makes the beautiful scorn, the elegant simplicity, the directness, the commanding port which all men admire and which men not noble affect. For the thought has no debts, no hunger, no lusts, no low obligations or relations, no intrigue or business, no murder, no envy, no crime, but large leisures and an inviting future.

The service we receive from the great is a mutual deference. If you deal with the vulgar, life is reduced to beggary indeed. The astronomers are very eager to know whether the moon has an atmosphere; I am only concerned that every man have one. I observe however that it takes two to make an atmosphere. I am acquainted with persons who go attended with this ambient cloud. It is sufficient that they come. It is not important what they say. The sun and the evening sky are not calmer. They seem to have arrived at the fact, to have got rid of the show, and to be serene. Their manners and behavior in the house and in the field are those of men at rest: what have they to conceal? what have they to exhibit? Others I meet, who have no deference, and who denude and strip one of all attributes but material values. As much health and muscle as you have, as much land, as much house-room and dinner, avails. Of course a man is a poor bag of bones. There is no gracious interval, not an inch allowed. Bone rubs against bone. Life is thus a Beggar's Bush. I know nothing which induces so base and forlorn a feeling as when we are treated for our utilities, as economists do, starving the imagination and the sentiment. In this impoverishing animation, I seem to meet a Hunger, a wolf. Rather let us be alone whilst we live, than encounter these lean kine. Man should emancipate man. He does so, not by jamming him, but by distancing him. The nearer my friend, the more spacious is our realm, the more diameter our spheres have. It is a measure of culture, the number of things taken for granted. When a man begins to speak, the churl will take him up by disputing his first words, so he cannot come at his scope. The wise man takes all for granted until he sees the parallelism of that which puzzled him with his own view.

I will not protract this discourse by describing the duties of the brave and generous. And yet I will venture to name one, and the same is almost the sole condition on which knighthood is to be won; this, namely, loyalty to your own order. The true aristocrat is he who is at the head of his own order, and disloyalty is to mistake other chivalries for his own. Let him not divide his homage, but stand for that which he was born and set to maintain. It was objected to Gustavus that he did not better distinguish between the duties of a carabine and a general, but exposed himself to all dangers and was too prodigal of a blood so precious. For a soul on which elevated duties are laid will so realize its special and lofty duties as not to be in danger of assuming through a low generosity those which do not belong to it.

There are all degrees of nobility, but amid the levity and giddiness of people one looks round, as for a tower of strength, on some self-dependent mind, who does not go abroad for an estimate, and has long ago made up its conclusion that it is impossible to fail. The great Indian sages had a lesson for the Brahmin, which every day returns to mind, "All that depends on another gives pain; all that depends on himself gives pleasure; in these few words is the definition of pleasure and pain." The noble mind is here to teach us that failure is a part of success. Prosperity and poundcake are for very young gentlemen, whom such things content; but a hero's, a man's success is made up of failures, because he experiments and ventures every day, and "the more falls he gets, moves faster on;" defeated all the time and yet to victory born. I have heard that in horsemanship he is not the good rider who never was thrown, but rather that a man never will be a good rider until he is thrown; then he will not be haunted any longer by the terror that he shall tumble, and will ride; — that is his business, — to *ride*, whether with falls or whether with none, to ride unto the place whither he is bound. And I know no such unquestionable badge and ensign of a sovereign mind, as that tenacity of purpose which, through all change of companions, of parties, of fortunes, — changes never, bates no jot of heart or hope, but wearies out opposition, and arrives at its port. In his consciousness of deserving success, the caliph Ali constantly neglected the ordinary means of attaining it; and to the grand interests, a superficial success is of no account. It prospers as well in mistake as in luck, in obstruction and nonsense, as well as among the angels; it reckons fortunes mere paint; difficulty is its delight: perplexity is its noonday: minds that make their way without winds and against tides. But these are rare and difficult examples, we can only indicate them to show how high is the range of the realm of Honor.

I know the feeling of the most ingenious and excellent youth in America; I hear the complaint of the aspirant that we have no prizes offered to the ambition of virtuous young men; that there is no Theban Band; no stern exclusive Legion of Honor, to be entered only by long and real service and patient climbing up all the steps. We have a rich men's aristocracy, plenty of bribes for those who like them; but a grand style of culture, which, without injury, an ardent youth can propose to himself as a Pharos through long dark years, does not exist, and there is no substitute. The youth, having got through the first thickets that oppose his entrance into life, having got into decent society, is left to himself, and falls abroad with too much freedom. But in the hours of insight we rally against this skepticism. We then see that if the ignorant are around us, the great are much more near; that there is an order of men, never quite absent, who enroll no names in their archives but of such as are capable of truth. They are gathered in no one chamber; no chamber would hold them; but, out of the vast duration of man's race, they tower like mountains, and are present to every mind in proportion to its likeness to theirs. The solitariest man who shares their spirit walks environed by them; they talk to him, they comfort him, and happy is he who prefers these associates to profane companions. They also take shape in men, in women. There is no heroic trait, no sentiment or thought that will not sometime embody itself in the form of a friend. That highest good of rational existence is always coming to such as reject mean alliances.

One trait more we must celebrate, the self-reliance which is the patent of royal natures. It is so prized a jewel that it is sure to be tested. The rules and discipline are ordered for that. The Golden Table never lacks members; all its seats are kept full; but with this strange provision, that the members are carefully withdrawn into deep niches, so that no one of them can see any other of them, and each believes himself alone. In the presence of the Chapter it is easy for each member to carry himself royally and well; but in the absence of his colleagues and in the presence of mean people he is tempted to accept the low customs of towns. The honor of a member consists in an indifferency to the persons and practices about him, and in the pursuing undisturbed the career of a Brother, as if always in their presence, and as if no other existed. Give up, once for all, the hope of approbation from the people in the street, if you are pursuing great ends. How can they guess your designs?

All reference to models, all comparison with neighboring abilities and reputations, is the road to mediocrity. The generous soul, on arriving in a new port, makes instant preparation for a new voyage. By experiment, by original studies, by secret obedience he has made a place for himself in the world; stands there a real, substantial, unprecedented person, and when the great come by, as always there are angels walking in the earth, they know him at sight. Effectual service in his own legitimate fashion distinguishes the true man. For he is to know that the distinction of a royal nature is a great heart; that not Louis Quatorze, not Chesterfield, nor Byron, nor Bonaparte is the model of the Century, but, wherever found, the old renown attaches to the virtues of simple faith and staunch endurance and clear perception and plain speech, and that there is a master grace and dignity communicated by exalted sentiments to a human form, to which utility and even genius must do homage. And it is the sign and badge of this nobility, the drawing his counsel from his own breast. For to every gentleman, grave and dangerous duties are proposed. Justice always wants champions. The world waits for him as its defender, for he will find in the well-dressed crowd, yet, in the civility of whole nations, vulgarity of sentiment. In the best parlors of modern society he will find the laughing devil, the civil sneer; in English palaces the London twist, derision, coldness, contempt of the masses, contempt of Ireland, dislike of the Chartist.[1] The English House of Commons is the proudest assembly of gentlemen in the world, yet the genius of the House of Commons, its legitimate expression, is a sneer. In America he shall find depreciation of purism on all questions touching the morals of trade and of social customs, and the narrowest contraction of ethics to the one duty of paying money. Pay that, and you may play the tyrant at discretion and

[1] [The Chartist movement of the 1830's and 1840's represented the interests of the English lower middle classes and workingmen; it sought universal (male) suffrage through public petitions and mass meetings. — Eds.]

never look back to the fatal question, — where had you the money that you paid?

I know the difficulties in the way of the man of honor. The man of honor is a man of taste and humanity. By tendency, like all magnanimous men, he is a democrat. But the revolution comes, and does he join the standard of Chartist and outlaw? No, for these have been dragged in their ignorance by furious chiefs to the Red Revolution; they are full of murder, and the student recoils, — and joins the rich. If he cannot vote with the poor, he should stay by himself. Let him accept the position of armed neutrality, abhorring the crimes of the Chartist, abhorring the selfishness of the rich, and say, "The time will come when these poor *enfans perdus* of revolution will have instructed their party, if only by their fate, and wiser counsels will prevail; the music and the dance of liberty will come up to bright and holy ground and will take me in also. Then I shall not have forfeited my right to speak and act for mankind." Meantime shame to the fop of learning and philosophy who suffers a vulgarity of speech and habit to blind him to the grosser vulgarity of pitiless selfishness, and to hide from him the current of Tendency; who abandons his right position of being priest and poet of these impious and unpoetic doers of God's work. You must, for wisdom, for sanity, have some access to the mind and heart of the common humanity. The exclusive excludes himself. No great man has existed who did not rely on the sense and heart of mankind as represented by the good sense of the people, as correcting the modes and over-refinements and class-prejudices of the lettered men of the world.

There are certain conditions in the highest degree favorable to the tranquillity of spirit and to that magnanimity we so prize. And mainly the habit of considering large interests, and things in masses, and not too much in detail. The habit of directing large affairs generates a nobility of thought in every mind of average ability. For affairs themselves show the way in which they should be handled; and a good head soon grows wise, and does not govern too much.

Now I believe in the closest affinity between moral and material power. Virtue and genius are always on the direct way to the control of the society in which they are found. It is the interest of society that good men should govern, and there is always a tendency so to place them. But, for the day that now is, a man of generous spirit will not need to administer public offices or to direct large interests of trade, or war, or politics, or manufacture, but he will use a high prudence in the conduct of life to guard himself from being dissipated on many things. There is no need that he should count the pounds of property or the numbers of agents whom his influence touches; it suffices that his aims are high, that the interest of intellectual and moral beings is paramount with him, that he comes into what is called fine society from higher ground, and he has an elevation of habit which ministers of empires will be forced to see and to remember.

I do not know whether that word Gentleman, although it signifies a leading idea in recent civilization, is a sufficiently broad generalization to convey the deep and grave fact of self-reliance. To many the word expresses only the outsides of cultivated men, — only graceful manners, and independence in trifles; but the fountains of that thought are in the deeps of man, a beauty which reaches through and through, from the manners to the soul; an honor which is only a name for sanctity, a self-trust which is a trust in God himself. Call it man of honor, or call it Man, the American who would serve his country must learn the beauty and honor of perseverance, he must reinforce himself by the power of character, and revisit the margin of that well from which his fathers drew waters of life and enthusiasm, the fountain I mean of the moral sentiments, the parent fountain from which this goodly Universe flows as a wave.

IV

THE INDIVIDUAL IN INDUSTRIAL SOCIETY

The Industrial Revolution, which got under way in England in the late eighteenth century and reached continental Europe and the United States in the middle years of the nineteenth century, effected the most thoroughgoing transformation in the life style of Western man since the development of agriculture. It was inevitable therefore that European and American intellectuals would, in the course of the nineteenth century, devote increasing attention to the character and implications of this great event. The readings here reproduced from John Ruskin and Henry David Thoreau present one variety of intellectual response to industrialization: a critique of its impact on the quality of individual life. It is a response almost identical to that articulated by the young Karl Marx in his Economic and Philosophical Manuscripts *of 1844. In particular, both Ruskin and Thoreau stress the manner in which people are transformed into things, a process that Marx termed "reification" (from the Latin noun "res," meaning "thing").*

John Ruskin (1819–1900) was essentially an aesthetician, not a social critic. However, in "The Nature of Gothic" (a chapter from his most famous work, The Stones of Venice*) he uses his analysis of medieval architecture as the occasion for some incisive observations about the psychological and social implications of modern industrial production. Ruskin, like Thoreau, was a Romantic. He exemplified the Romantics' preoccupation with the world of beautiful objects, as well as their enthusiasm for the hierarchical society and Gothic art of the Middle Ages. (It would be interesting in this respect to compare Ruskin's essay with Henry Adams's great book on medieval architecture and society,* Mont-Saint-Michel and Chartres.*) Ruskin's critique of industrial society thus differed significantly from that of Marx and his followers in so far as the latter accepted the industrial mode of production and demanded only a rearrangement of property relations.*

Ruskin's American contemporary Henry David Thoreau (1817–1862) was a critic not so much of industrial civilization as of the economic ethic — Max Weber would later call it the Protestant ethic — that found its ultimate expression in industrialism. Some passages of Walden *seem to suggest that the individual is responsible for his own reification. But, elsewhere, particularly in the magnificent description of the railroad and its impact on man and nature, Thoreau comes closer to Ruskin's and Marx's sense of the larger historical factors shaping modern existence. If we recall R. W. B. Lewis's thesis about the distinguishing features of the American mind, we will perhaps find it significant that Thoreau's critique of modern civilization takes the form of a retreat into the wilderness, while Ruskin's that of a retreat into the past.*

The Nature of Gothic
(1853)

JOHN RUSKIN

If the reader will look . . . to the division of our subject which was made in the first chapter of the first volume [of *The Stones of Venice*], he will find that we are now about to enter upon the examination of that school of Venetian architecture which forms an intermediate step between the Byzantine and Gothic forms; but which I find may be conveniently considered in its connexion with the latter style. In order that we may discern the tendency of each step of this change, it will be wise in the outset to endeavor to form some general idea of its final result. We know already what the Byzantine architecture is from which the transition was made, but we ought to know something of the Gothic architecture into which it led. I shall endeavor therefore to give the reader in this chapter an idea, at once broad and definite, of the true nature of *Gothic* architecture, properly so called; not of that of Venice only, but of universal Gothic: for it will be one of the most interesting parts of our subsequent inquiry, to find out how far Venetian architecture reached the universal or perfect type of Gothic, and how far it either fell short of it, or assumed foreign and independent forms.

From John Ruskin, *The Stones of Venice* (Philadelphia: Reuwee, Wattley and Walsh, n.d.), vol. II, 152–170.

The principal difficulty in doing this arises from the fact that every building of the Gothic period differs in some important respect from every other; and many include features which, if they occurred in other buildings, would not be considered Gothic at all; so that all we have to reason upon is merely, if I may be allowed so to express it, a greater or less degree of *Gothicness* in each building we examine. And it is this Gothicness, — the character which, according as it is found more or less in a building, makes it more or less Gothic, — of which I want to define the nature; and I feel the same kind of difficulty in doing so which would be encountered by any one who undertook to explain, for instance, the nature of Redness, without any actual red thing to point to, but only orange and purple things. Suppose he had only a piece of heather and a dead oak-leaf to do it with. He might say, the color which is mixed with the yellow in this oak-leaf, and with the blue in this heather, would be red, if you had it separate; but it would be difficult, nevertheless, to make the abstraction perfectly intelligible: and it is so in a far greater degree to make the abstraction of the Gothic character intelligible, because that character itself is made up of many mingled ideas, and can consist only in their union. That is to say, pointed arches do not constitute Gothic, nor vaulted roofs, nor flying buttresses, nor grotesque sculptures; but all or some of these things, and many other things with them, when they come together so as to have life.

Observe also, that, in the definition proposed, I shall only endeavor to analyze the idea which I suppose already to exist in the reader's mind. We all have some notion, most of us a very determined one, of the meaning of the term Gothic; but I know that many persons have this idea in their minds without being able to define it: that is to say, understanding generally that Westminster Abbey is Gothic, and St. Paul's is not, that Strasburg Cathedral is Gothic, and St. Peter's is not, they have, nevertheless, no clear notion of what it is that they recognize in the one or miss in the other, such as would enable them to say how far the work at Westminster or Strasburg is good and pure of its kind: still less to say of any nondescript building, like St. James's Palace or Windsor Castle, how much right Gothic element there is in it, and how much wanting. And I believe this inquiry to be a pleasant and profitable one; and that there will be found something more than usually interesting in tracing out this grey, shadowy, many-pinnacled image of the Gothic spirit within us; and discerning what fellowship there is between it and our Northern hearts. And if, at any point of the inquiry, I should interfere with any of the reader's previously formed conceptions, and use the term Gothic in any sense which he would not willingly attach to it, I do not ask him to accept, but only to examine and understand, my interpretation, as necessary to the intelligibility of what follows in the rest of the work.

We have, then, the Gothic character submitted to our analysis, just as the rough mineral is submitted to that of the chemist, entangled with many other foreign substances, itself perhaps in no place pure, or ever to be obtained or seen in purity for more than an instant; but nevertheless a thing of definite and separate nature, however inextricable or confused in appearance. Now observe: the chemist defines his mineral by two separate kinds of character; one external, its crystalline form, hardness, lustre, etc.; the other internal, the proportions and nature of its constituent atoms. Exactly in the same manner, we shall find that Gothic architecture has external forms, and internal elements. Its elements are certain mental tendencies of the builders, legibly expressed in it; as fancifulness, love of variety, love of richness, and such others. Its external forms are pointed arches, vaulted roofs, etc. And unless both the elements and the forms are there, we have no right to call the style Gothic. It is not enough that it has the Form, if it have not also the power and life. It is not enough that it has the Power, if it have not the form. We must therefore inquire into each of these characters successively; and determine first, what is the Mental Expression, and secondly, what the Material Form, of Gothic architecture, properly so called. . . .

I believe, then, that the characteristic or moral elements of Gothic are the following, placed in the order of their importance:

1. Savageness.
2. Changefulness.
3. Naturalism.
4. Grotesqueness.
5. Rigidity.
6. Redundance.

These characters are here expressed as belonging to the building; as belonging to the builder, they would be expressed thus: 1. Savageness, or Rudeness. 2. Love of Change. 3. Love of Nature. 4. Disturbed Imagination. 5. Obstinacy. 6. Generosity. And I repeat, that the withdrawal of any one, or any two, will not at once destroy the Gothic character of a building, but the removal of a majority of them will. I shall proceed to examine them in their order.

1. Savageness. I am not sure when the word "Gothic" was first generically applied to the architecture of the North; but I presume that, whatever the date of its original usage, it was intended to imply reproach, and express the barbaric character of the nations among whom that architecture arose. It never implied that they were literally of Gothic lineage, far less that their architecture had been originally invented by the Goths themselves; but it did imply that they and their buildings together exhibited a degree of sternness and rudeness, which, in contradistinction to the character of Southern and Eastern nations, appeared like a perpetual reflection of the contrast between the Goth and the Roman in their first encounter. And when that fallen Roman, in the utmost importance of his luxury, and insolence of his guilt, became the model for the imitation of civilized Europe, at the close of the so-called Dark

ages, the word Gothic became a term of unmitigated contempt, not unmixed with aversion. From that contempt, by the exertion of the antiquaries and architects of this century, Gothic architecture has been sufficiently vindicated; and perhaps some among us, in our admiration of the magnificent science of its structure, and sacredness of its expression, might desire that the term of ancient reproach should be withdrawn, and some other, of more apparent honorableness, adopted in its place. There is no chance, as there is no need, of such a substitution. As far as the epithet was used scornfully, it was used falsely; but there is no reproach in the word, rightly understood; on the contrary, there is a profound truth, which the instinct of mankind almost unconsciously recognizes. It is true, greatly and deeply true, that the architecture of the North is rude and wild; but it is not true, that, for this reason, we are to condemn it, or despise. Far otherwise: I believe it is in this very character that it deserves our profoundest reverence.

The charts of the world which have been drawn up by modern science have thrown into a narrow space the expression of a vast amount of knowledge, but I have never yet seen any one pictorial enough to enable the spectator to imagine the kind of contrast in physical character which exists between Northern and Southern countries. We know the differences in detail, but we have not that broad glance and grasp which would enable us to feel them in their fulness. We know that gentians grow on the Alps, and olives on the Apennines; but we do not enough conceive for ourselves that variegated mosaic of the world's surface which a bird sees in its migration, that difference between the district of the gentian and of the olive which the stork and the swallow see far off, as they lean upon the sirocco wind. Let us, for a moment, try to raise ourselves even above the level of their flight, and imagine the Mediterranean lying beneath us like an irregular lake, and all its ancient promontories sleeping in the sun: here and there an angry spot of thunder, a grey stain of storm, moving upon the burning field; and here and there a fixed wreath of white volcano smoke, surrounded by its circle of ashes; but for the most part a great peacefulness of light, Syria and Greece, Italy and Spain, laid like pieces of a golden pavement into the sea-blue, chased, as we stoop nearer to them, with bossy beaten work of mountain chains, and glowing softly with terraced gardens, and flowers heavy with frankincense, mixed among masses of laurel, and orange and plumy palm, that abate with their grey-green shadows the burning of the marble rocks, and of the ledges of porphyry sloping under lucent sand. Then let us pass farther towards the north, until we see the orient colors change gradually into a vast belt of rainy green, where the pastures of Switzerland, and poplar valleys of France, and dark forests of the Danube and Carpathians stretch from the mouths of the Loire to those of the Volga, seen through clefts in grey swirls of rain-cloud and flaky veils of the mist of the brooks, spreading low along the pasture lands: and then, farther north still, to see the earth heave into mighty masses of leaden rock and heathy moor, bordering with a broad waste of gloomy purple that belt of field and wood, and splintering into irregular and grisly islands amidst the northern seas, beaten by storm and chilled by ice-drift, and tormented by furious pulses of contending tide, until the roots of the last forests fail from among the hill ravines, and the hunger of the north wind bites their peaks into barrenness; and, at last, the wall of ice, durable like iron, sets, deathlike, its white teeth against us out of the polar twilight. And, having once traversed in thought its gradation of the zoned iris of the earth in all its material vastness, let us go down nearer to it, and watch the parallel change in the belt of animal life: the multitudes of swift and brilliant creatures that glance in the air and sea, or tread the sands of the southern zone; striped zebras and spotted leopards, glistening serpents, and birds arrayed in purple and scarlet. Let us contrast their delicacy and brilliancy of color, and swiftness of motion, with the frost-cramped strength, and shaggy covering, and dusky plumage of the northern tribes; contrast the Arabian horse with the Shetland, the tiger and leopard with the wolf and bear, the antelope with the elk, the bird of paradise with the osprey: and then, submissively acknowledging the great laws by which the earth and all that it bears are ruled throughout their being, let us not condemn, but rejoice at the expression by man of his own rest in the statutes of the lands that gave him birth. Let us watch him with reverence as he sets side by side the burning gems, and smoothes with soft sculpture the jasper pillars, that are to reflect a ceaseless sunshine, and rise into a cloudless sky: but not with less reverence let us stand by him, when, with rough strength and hurried stroke, he smites an uncouth animation out of the rocks which he has torn from among the moss of the moor-land, and heaves into the darkened air the pile of iron buttress and rugged wall, instinct with work of an imagination as wild and wayward as the northern sea; creations of ungainly shape and rigid limb, but full of wolfish life; fierce as the winds that beat, and changeful as the clouds that shade them.

There is, I repeat, no degradation, no reproach in this, but all dignity and honorableness; and we should err grievously in refusing either to recognise as an essential character of the existing architecture of the North, or to admit as a desirable character in that which it yet may be, this wildness of thought, and roughness of work; this look of mountain brotherhood between the cathedral and the Alp; this magnificence of sturdy power, put forth only the more energetically because the fine finger-touch was chilled away by the frosty wind, and the eye dimmed by the moor-mist, or blinded by the hail; this out-speaking of the strong spirit of men who may not gather redundant fruitage from the earth, nor bask in dreamy benignity of sunshine, but must break the rock for bread, and cleave the forest for fire, and show, even in what they did for their delight, some of the hard habits of the arm and heart that grew on them as they swung the axe or pressed the plough.

If, however, the savagesness of Gothic architecture, merely as an expression of its origin among Northern nations, may be considered, in some sort, a noble character, it possesses a higher nobility still, when considered as an index, not of climate, but of religious principle.

In the 13th and 14th paragraphs of Chapter XXI. of the first volume of [*The Stones of Venice*], it was noticed that the systems of architectural ornament, properly so called, might be divided into three: — 1. Servile ornament, in which the execution or power of the inferior workman is entirely subjected to the intellect of the higher: — 2. Constitutional ornament, in which the executive inferior power is, to a certain point, emancipated and independent, having a will of its own, yet confessing its inferiority and rendering obedience to higher powers; — and 3. Revolutionary ornament, in which no executive inferiority is admitted at all. I must here explain the nature of these divisions at somewhat greater length.

Of Servile ornament, the principal schools are the Greek, Ninevite, and Egyptian; but their servility is of different kinds. The Greek master-workman was far advanced in knowledge and power above the Assyrian or Egyptian. Neither he nor those for whom he worked could endure the appearance of imperfection in anything; and, therefore, what ornament he appointed to be done by those beneath him was composed of mere geometrical forms, — balls, ridges, and perfectly symmetrical foliage, — which could be executed with absolute precision by line and rule, and were as perfect in their way when completed, as his own figure sculpture. The Assyrian and Egyptian, on the contrary, less cognizant of accurate form in anything, were content to allow their figure sculpture to be executed by inferior workmen, but lowered the method of its treatment to a standard which every workman could reach, and then trained him by discipline so rigid, that there was no chance of his falling beneath the standard appointed. The Greek gave to the lower workman no subject which he could not perfectly execute. The Assyrian gave him subjects which he could only execute imperfectly, but fixed a legal standard for his imperfection. The workman was, in both systems, a slave.[1]

But in the mediæval, or especially Christian, system of ornament, this

[1] The third kind of ornament, the Renaissance, is that in which the inferior detail becomes principal, the executor of every minor portion being required to exhibit skill and possess knowledge as great as that which is possessed by the master of the design; and in the endeavor to endow him with this skill and knowledge, his own original power is overwhelmed, and the whole building becomes a wearisome exhibition of well-educated imbecility. We must fully inquire into the nature of this form of error, when we arrive at the examination of the Renaissance schools.

slavery is done away with altogether; Christianity having recognized, in small things as well as great, the individual value of every soul. But it not only recognizes its value; it confesses its imperfection, in only bestowing dignity upon the acknowledgment of unworthiness. That admission of lost power and fallen nature, which the Greek or Ninevite felt to be intensely painful, and, as far as might be, altogether refused, the Christian makes daily and hourly, contemplating the fact of it without fear, as tending, in the end, to God's greater glory. Therefore, to every spirit which Christianity summons to her service, her exhortation is: Do what you can, and confess frankly what you are unable to do; neither let your effort be shortened for fear of failure, nor your confession silenced for fear of shame. And it is, perhaps, the principal admirableness of the Gothic schools of architecture, that they thus receive the results of the labor of inferior minds; and out of fragments full of imperfection, and betraying that imperfection in every touch, indulgently raise up a stately and unaccusable whole.

But the modern English mind has this much in common with that of the Greek, that it intensely desires, in all things, the utmost completion or perfection compatible with their nature. This is a noble character in the abstract, but becomes ignoble when it causes us to forget the relative dignities of the nature itself, and to prefer the perfectness of the lower nature to the imperfection of the higher; not considering that as, judged by such a rule, all the brute animals would be preferable to man, because more perfect in their functions and kind, and yet are always held inferior to him, so also in the works of man, those which are more perfect in their kind are always inferior to those which are, in their nature, liable to more faults and shortcomings. For the finer the nature, the more flaws it will show through the clearness of it; and it is a law of this universe, that the best things shall be seldomest seen in their best form. The wild grass grows well and strongly, one year with another; but the wheat is, according to the greater nobleness of its nature, liable to the bitterer blight. And therefore, while in all things that we see, or do, we are to desire perfection, and strive for it, we are nevertheless not to set the meaner thing, in its narrow accomplishment, above the nobler thing, in its mighty progress; not to esteem smooth minuteness above shattered majesty; not to prefer mean victory to honorable defeat; not to lower the level of our aim, that we may the more surely enjoy the complacency of success. But, above all, in our dealings with the souls of other men, we are to take care how we check, by severe requirement or narrow caution, efforts which might otherwise lead to a noble issue; and, still more, how we withhold our admiration from great excellences, because they are mingled with rough faults. Now, in the make and nature of every man, however rude or simple, whom we employ in manual labor, there are some powers for better things: some tardy imagination, torpid capacity of emotion, tottering steps of thought, there are, even at the worst; and in most cases it is all our own fault that they *are* tardy or torpid. But they cannot be strengthened, unless we are content to take them in their feebleness, and unless we prize and honor them in their imperfection above the best and most perfect manual skill. And this is what we have to do with all our laborers; to look for the *thoughtful* part of them, and get that out of them, whatever we lose for it, whatever faults and errors we are obliged to take with it. For the best that is in them cannot manifest itself, but in company with much error. Understand this clearly: You can teach a man to draw a straight line, and to cut one; to strike a curved line, and to carve it; and to copy and carve any number of given lines or forms, with admirable speed and perfect precision; and you find his work perfect of its kind: but if you ask him to think about any of those forms, to consider if he cannot find any better in his own head, he stops; his execution becomes hesitating; he thinks, and ten to one he thinks wrong; ten to one he makes a mistake in the first touch he gives to his work as a thinking being. But you have made a man of him for all that. He was only a machine before, an animated tool.

And observe, you are put to stern choice in this matter. You must either make a tool of the creature, or a man of him. You cannot make both. Men were not intended to work with the accuracy of tools, to be precise and perfect in all their actions. If you will have that precision out of them, and make their fingers measure degrees like cog-wheels, and their arms strike curves like compasses, you must unhumanize them. All the energy of their spirits must be given to make cogs and compasses of themselves. All their attention and strength must go to the accomplishment of the mean act. The eye of the soul must be bent upon the finger-point, and the soul's force must fill all the invisible nerves that guide it, ten hours a day, that it may not err from its steely precision, and so soul and sight may be worn away, and the whole human being be lost at last — a heap of sawdust, so far as its intellectual work in this world is concerned; saved only by its Heart, which cannot go into the form of cogs and compasses, but expands, after the ten hours are over, into fireside humanity. On the other hand, if you will make a man of the working creature, you cannot make a tool. Let him but begin to imagine, to think, to try to do anything worth doing; and the engine-turned precision is lost at once. Out come all his roughness, all his dulness, all his incapability; shame upon shame, failure upon failure, pause after pause: but out comes the whole majesty of him also; and we know the height of it only, when we see the clouds settling upon him. And, whether the clouds be bright or dark, there will be transfiguration behind and within them.

And now, reader, look round this English room of yours, about which you have been proud so often, because the work of it was so good and strong, and the ornaments of it so finished. Examine again all those accurate mouldings, and perfect polishings, and unerring adjustments of the seasoned wood and tempered steel. Many a time you have exulted over them, and thought how great England was, because her slightest work was done so thoroughly. Alas! if read rightly, these perfectnesses are signs of slavery in our England a thousand times more bitter and more degrading than that of the scourged African, or helot Greek. Men may be beaten, chained, tormented, yoked like cattle, slaughtered like summer flies, and yet remain in one sense, and the best sense, free. But to smother their souls within them, to blight and hew into rotting pollards the suckling branches of their human intelligence, to make the flesh and skin which, after the worm's work on it, is to see God, into leathern thongs to yoke machinery with, — this it is to be slave-masters indeed; and there might be more freedom in England, though her feudal lords' lightest words were worth men's lives, and though the blood of the vexed husbandman dropped in the furrows of her fields, than there is while the animation of her multitudes is sent like fuel to feed the factory smoke, and the strength of them is given daily to be wasted into the fineness of a web, or racked into the exactness of a line.

And, on the other hand, go forth again to gaze upon the old cathedral front, where you have smiled so often at the fantastic ignorance of the old sculptors: examine once more those ugly goblins, and formless monsters, and stern statues, anatomiless and rigid; but do not mock at them, for they are signs of the life and liberty of every workman who struck the stone; a freedom of thought, and rank in scale of being, such as no laws, no charters, no charities can secure; but which it must be the first aim of all Europe at this day to regain for her children.

Let me not be thought to speak wildly or extravagantly. It is verily this degradation of the operative into a machine, which, more than any other evil of the times, is leading the mass of the nations everywhere into vain, incoherent, destructive struggling for a freedom of which they cannot explain the nature to themselves. Their universal outcry against wealth, and against nobility, is not forced from them either by the pressure of famine, or the sting of mortified pride. These do much, and have done much in all ages; but the foundations of society were never yet shaken as they are at this day. It is not that men are ill fed, but that they have no pleasure in the work by which they make their bread and therefore look to wealth as the only means of pleasure. It is not that men are pained by the scorn of the upper classes, but they cannot endure their own; for they feel that the kind of labor to which they are condemned is verily a degrading one, and makes them less than men. Never had the upper classes so much sympathy with the lower, or charity for them, as they have at this day, and yet never were they so much hated by them; for, of old, the separation between the noble and the poor was merely a wall built by law; now it is a veritable difference in level of standing, a precipice between upper and lower grounds in the field of humanity, and there is pestilential air at the bottom of it. I know not if a day is ever to come when the nature of right freedom will be understood, and when men will see that to obey another man, to labor for him, yield reverence to him or to his place, is not slavery. It is often the best kind of liberty, — liberty from care. The man who says to one, Go, and he goeth, and to another, Come, and he cometh, has, in most cases, more sense of restraint and difficulty than the man who obeys him. The movements of the one are hindered by the burden on his shoulder; of the other, by the bridle on his lips: there is no way by which the burden may be lightened; but we need not suffer from the bridle if we do not champ at it. To yield reverence to another, to hold ourselves and our lives at his disposal, is not slavery; often, it is the noblest state in which a man can live in this world. There is, indeed, a reverence which is servile, that is to say, irrational or selfish: but there is also noble reverence, that is to say, reasonable and loving; and a man is never so noble as when he is reverent in this kind; nay, even if the feeling pass the bounds of mere reason, so that it be loving, a man is raised by it. . . . And therefore, in all ages and all countries, reverence has been paid and sacrifice made by men to each other, not only without complaint, but rejoicingly; and famine, and peril, and sword, and all evil, and all shame, have been borne willingly in the causes of masters and kings; for all these gifts of the heart ennobled the men who gave, not less than the men who received them, and nature prompted, and God rewarded the sacrifice. But to feel their souls withering within them, unthanked, to find their whole being sunk into an unrecognized abyss, to be counted off into a heap of mechanism, numbered with its wheels, and weighed with its hammer strokes; — this nature bade not, — this God blesses not, — this humanity for no long time is able to endure.

We have much studied and much perfected, of late, the great civilized invention of the division of labor; only we give it a false name. It is not, truly speaking, the labor that is divided; but the men: — Divided into mere segments of men — broken into small fragments and crumbs of life; so that all the little piece of intelligence that is left in a man is not enough to make a pin, or a nail, but exhausts itself in making the point of a pin, or the head of a nail. Now it is a good and desirable thing, truly, to make many pins in a day; but if we could only see with what crystal sand their points were polished, — sand of human soul, much to be magnified before it can be discerned for what it is, — we should think there might be some loss in it also. And the great cry that rises from all our manufacturing cities, louder than their furnace blast, is all in very deed for this, — that we manufacture everything there except men; we blanch cotton, and strengthen steel, and refine sugar, and shape pottery; but to brighten, to strengthen, to refine, or to form a single living spirit, never enters into our estimate of advantages. And all the evil to which that cry is urging our myriads can be met only in one way: not by teaching nor preaching, for to teach them is but to show them their misery, and to preach to them, if we do nothing more than preach, is to mock at it. It can be met only by a right understanding, on the part of all classes, of what kinds of labor are good for men, raising them, and making them happy; by a determined sacrifice of such convenience, or beauty, or cheapness as is to be got only by the degradation of the workman; and by equally determined demand for the products and results of healthy and ennobling labor.

And how, it will be asked, are these products to be recognized, and this demand to be regulated? Easily: by the observance of three broad and simple rules:

1. Never encourage the manufacture of any article not absolutely necessary, in the production of which *Invention* has no share.
2. Never demand an exact finish for its own sake, but only for some practical or noble end.
3. Never encourage imitation or copying of any kind, except for the sake of preserving record of great works.

The second of these principles is the only one which directly rises out of the consideration of our immediate subject; but I shall briefly explain the meaning and extent of the first also, reserving the enforcement of the third for another place.

1. Never encourage the manufacture of anything not necessary, in the production of which invention has no share.

For instance. Glass beads are utterly unnecessary, and there is no design or thought employed in their manufacture. They are formed by first drawing out the glass into rods; these rods are chopped up into fragments of the size of beads by the human hand, and the fragments are then rounded in the furnace. The men who chop up the rods sit at their work all day, their hands vibrating with a perpetual and exquisitely timed palsy, and the beads dropping beneath their vibration like hail. Neither they, nor the men who draw out the rods, or fuse the fragments, have the smallest occasion for the use of any single human faculty; and every young lady, therefore, who buys glass beads is engaged in the slave-trade, and in a much more cruel one than that which we have so long been endeavoring to put down.

But glass cups and vessels may become the subjects of exquisite invention; and if in buying these we pay for the invention, that is to say for the beautiful form, or color, or engraving, and not for mere finish of execution, we are doing good to humanity. . . .

I shall perhaps press this law farther elsewhere, but our immediate concern is chiefly with the second, namely, never to demand an exact finish, when it does not lead to a noble end. For observe, I have only dwelt upon the rudeness of Gothic, or any other kind of imperfectness, as admirable, where it was impossible to get design or thought without it. If you are to have the thought of a rough and untaught man, you must have it in a rough and untaught way; but from an educated man, who can without effort express his thoughts in an educated way, take the graceful expression, and be thankful. Only *get* the thought, and do not silence the peasant because he cannot speak good grammar, or until you have taught him his grammar. Grammar and refinement are good things, both, only to be sure of the better thing first. And thus in art, delicate finish is desirable from the greatest masters, and is always given by them. In some places Michael Angelo, Leonardo, Phidias, Perugino, Turner, all finished with the most exquisite care; and the finish they give always leads to the fuller accomplishment of their noble purposes. But lower men than these cannot finish, for it requires consummate knowledge to finish consummately, and then we must take their thoughts as they are able to give them. So the rule is simple: Always look for invention first, and after that, for such execution as will help the invention, and as the inventor is capable of without painful effort, and *no more*. Above all, demand no refinement of execution where there is no thought, for that is slaves' work, unredeemed. Rather choose rough work than smooth work, so only that the practical purpose be answered, and never imagine there is reason to be proud of anything that may be accomplished by patience and sandpaper.

I shall only give one example, which however will show the reader what I mean, from the manufacture already alluded to, that of glass. Our modern glass is exquisitely clear in its substance, true in its form, accurate in its cutting. We are proud of this. We ought to be ashamed of it. The old Venice glass was muddy, inaccurate in all its forms, and clumsily cut, if at all. And the old Venetian was justly proud of it. For there is this difference between the English and Venetian workman, that the former thinks only of accurately matching his patterns, and getting his curves perfectly true and his edges perfectly sharp, and becomes a mere machine for rounding curves and sharpening edges, while the old Venetian cared not a whit whether his edges were sharp or not, but he invented a new design for every glass that he made, and never moulded a handle or a lip without a new fancy in it. And therefore, though some Venetian glass is ugly and clumsy enough, when made by clumsy and uninventive workmen, other Venetian glass is so lovely in its forms that no price is too great for it; and we never see the same form in it twice. Now you cannot have the finish and the varied form too. If the workman is thinking about his edges, he cannot be thinking of his design; if of his design, he cannot think of his edges. Choose whether you will pay for the lovely form or the perfect finish, and choose at the same moment whether you will make the worker a man or a grindstone.

Nay, but the reader interrupts me, — "If the workman can design beautifully, I would not have him kept at the furnace. Let him be taken away and made a gentleman, and have a studio, and design his glass there, and I will have it blown and cut for him by common workmen, and so I will have my design and my finish too."

All ideas of this kind are founded upon two mistaken suppositions: the first, that one man's thoughts can be, or ought to be, executed by another man's hands; the second, that manual labor is a degradation, when it is governed by intellect.

On a large scale, and in work determinable by line and rule, it is indeed both possible and necessary that the thoughts of one man should be carried out by the labor of others; in this sense I have already defined the best architecture to be the expression of the mind of manhood by the hands of childhood. But on a smaller scale, and in a design which cannot be mathematically defined, one man's thoughts can never be expressed by another: and the difference between the spirit of touch of the man who is inventing, and of the man who is obeying directions, is often all the difference between a great and a common work of art. How wide the separation is between original and second-hand execution, I shall endeavor to show elsewhere; it is not so much to our purpose here as to mark the other and more fatal error of despising manual labor when governed by intellect; for it is no less fatal an error to despise it when thus regulated by intellect, than to value it for its own sake. We are always in these days endeavoring to separate the two; we want one man to be always thinking, and another to be always working, and we call one a gentleman, and the other an operative; whereas the workman ought often to be thinking, and the thinker often to be working, and both should be gentlemen, in the best sense. As it is, we make both ungentle, the one envying, the other despising, his brother; and the mass of society is made up of morbid thinkers, and miserable workers. Now it is only by labor that thought can be made healthy, and only by thought that labor can be made happy, and the two cannot be separated with impunity. It would be well if all of us were good handicraftsmen in some kind, and the dishonor of manual labor done away with altogether; so that though there should still be a trenchant distinction of race between nobles and commoners, there should not, among the latter, be a trenchant distinction of employment, as between idle and working men, or between men of liberal and illiberal professions. All professions should be liberal, and there should be less pride felt in peculiarity of employment, and more in excellence of achievement. And yet more, in each several profession, no master should be too proud to do its hardest work. The painter should grind his own colors; the architect work in the mason's yard with his men; the master-manufacturer be himself a more skilful operative than any man in his mills; and the distinction between one man and another be only in experience and skill, and the authority and wealth which these must naturally and justly obtain.

Walden
(1854)

HENRY DAVID THOREAU

ECONOMY

When I wrote the following pages, or rather the bulk of them, I lived alone, in the woods, a mile from any neighbor, in a house which I had built myself, on the shore of Walden Pond, in Concord, Massachusetts, and earned my living by the labor of my hands only. I lived there two years and two months. At present I am a sojourner in civilized life again.

I should not obtrude my affairs so much on the notice of my readers if very particular inquiries had not been made by my townsmen concerning my mode of life, which some would call impertinent, though they do not appear to me at all impertinent, but, considering the circumstances, very natural and pertinent. Some have asked what I got to eat; if I did not feel lonesome; if I was not afraid; and the like. Others have been curious to learn what portion of my income I devoted to charitable purposes; and some, who have large families, how many poor children I maintained. I will therefore ask those of my readers who feel no particular interest in me to pardon me if I undertake to answer some of these questions. . . .

I would fain say something, not so much concerning the Chinese and Sandwich Islanders as you who read these pages, who are said to live in New England; something about your condition, especially your outward condition or circumstances in this world, in this town, what it is, whether it is necessary that it be as bad as it is, whether it cannot be improved as well as not. I have travelled a good deal in Concord; and everywhere, in shops, and offices, and fields, the inhabitants have appeared to me to be doing penance in a thousand remarkable ways. What I have heard of Bramins sitting exposed to four fires and looking in the face of the sun; or hanging suspended, with their heads downward, over flames; or looking at

From *The Writings of Henry David Thoreau* (Boston: Houghton Mifflin, 1893), vol. II, 7–15, 53–62, 65–66, 74–78, 143–150, 153–155, 179–186.

the heavens over their shoulders "until it becomes impossible for them to resume their natural position, while from the twist of the neck nothing but liquids can pass into the stomach"; or dwelling, chained for life, at the foot of a tree; or measuring with their bodies, like caterpillars, the breadth of vast empires; or standing on one leg on the tops of pillars, — even these forms of conscious penance are hardly more incredible and astonishing than the scenes which I daily witness. The twelve labors of Hercules were trifling in comparison with those which my neighbors have undertaken; for they were only twelve, and had an end; but I could never see that these men slew or captured any monster or finished any labor. They have no friend Iolas to burn with a hot iron the root of the hydra's head, but as soon as one head is crushed, two spring up.

I see young men, my townsmen, whose misfortune it is to have inherited farms, houses, barns, cattle, and farming tools; for these are more easily acquired than got rid of. Better if they had been born in the open pasture and suckled by a wolf, that they might have seen with clearer eyes what field they were called to labor in. Who made them serfs of the soil? Why should they eat their sixty acres, when man is condemned to eat only his peck of dirt? Why should they begin digging their graves as soon as they are born? They have got to live a man's life, pushing all these things before them, and get on as well as they can. How many a poor immortal soul have I met well nigh crushed and smothered under its load, creeping down the road of life, pushing before it a barn seventy-five feet by forty, its Augean stables never cleansed, and one hundred acres of land, tillage, mowing, pasture, and wood-lot! The portionless, who struggle with no such unnecessary inherited encumbrances, find it labor enough to subdue and cultivate a few cubic feet of flesh.

But men labor under a mistake. The better part of the man is soon ploughed into the soil for compost. By a seeming fate, commonly called necessity, they are employed, as it says in an old book, laying up treasures which moth and rust will corrupt and thieves break through and steal. It is a fool's life, as they will find when they get to the end of it, if not before. . . .

Most men, even in this comparatively free country, through mere ignorance and mistake, are so occupied with the factitious cares and superfluously coarse labors of life that its finer fruits cannot be plucked by them. Their fingers, from excessive toil, are too clumsy and tremble too much for that. Actually, the laboring man has not leisure for a true integrity day by day; he cannot afford to sustain the manliest relations to men; his labor would be depreciated in the market. He has no time to be anything but a machine. How can he remember well his ignorance — which his growth requires — who has so often to use his knowledge? We should feed and clothe him gratuitously sometimes, and recruit him with our cordials, before we judge of him. The finest qualities of our nature, like the bloom on fruits, can be preserved only by the most delicate handling. Yet we do not treat ourselves nor one another thus tenderly.

Some of you, we all know, are poor, find it hard to live, are sometimes, as it were, gasping for breath. I have no doubt that some of you who read this book are unable to pay for all the dinners which you have actually eaten, or for the coats and shoes which are fast wearing or are already worn out, and have come to this page to spend borrowed or stolen time, robbing your creditors of an hour. It is very evident what mean and sneaking lives many of you live, for my sight has been whetted by experience; always on the limits, trying to get into business and trying to get out of debt, a very ancient slough, called by the Latins *œs alienum*, another's brass, for some of their coins were made of brass; still living, and dying, and buried by this other's brass; always promising to pay, promising to pay, to-morrow, and dying to-day, insolvent; seeking to curry favor, to get custom, by how many modes, only not state-prison offences; lying, flattering, voting, contracting yourselves into a nutshell of civility, or dilating into an atmosphere of thin and vaporous generosity, that you may persuade your neighbor to let you make his shoes, or his hat, or his coat, or his carriage, or import his groceries for him; making yourselves sick, that you may lay up something against a sick day, something to be tucked away in an old chest, or in a stocking behind the plastering, or, more safely, in the brick bank; no matter where, no matter how much or how little.

I sometimes wonder that we can be so frivolous, I may almost say, as to attend to the gross but somewhat foreign form of servitude called Negro Slavery, there are so many keen and subtle masters that enslave both North and South. It is hard to have a Southern overseer; it is worse to have a Northern one; but worst of all when you are the slave-driver of yourself. Talk of a divinity in man! Look at the teamster on the highway, wending to market by day or night; does any divinity stir within him? His highest duty to fodder and water his horses! What is his destiny to him compared with the shipping interests? Does not he drive for Squire Make-a-stir? How godlike, how immortal, is he? See how he cowers and sneaks, how vaguely all the day he fears, not being immortal nor divine, but the slave and prisoner of his own opinion of himself, a fame won by his own deeds. Public opinion is a weak tyrant compared with our own private opinion. What a man thinks of himself, that it is which determines, or rather indicates, his fate. . . .

The mass of men lead lives of quiet desperation. What is called resignation is confirmed desperation. From the desperate city you go into the desperate country, and have to console yourself with the bravery of minks and muskrats. A stereotyped but unconscious despair is concealed even under what are called the games and amusements of mankind. There is no play in them, for this comes after work. But it is a characteristic of wisdom not to do desperate things. . . .

When I consider my neighbors, the farmers of Concord, who are at least as well off as the other classes, I find that for the most part they have been toiling twenty, thirty, or forty years, that they may become the real owners of their farms, which commonly they have inherited with encumbrances, or else bought with hired money, — and we may regard one third of that toil as the cost of their houses, — but commonly they have not paid for them yet. It is true, the encumbrances sometimes outweigh the value of the farm, so that the farm itself becomes one great encumbrance, and still a man is found to inherit it, being well acquainted with it, as he says. On applying to the assessors, I am surprised to learn that they cannot at once name a dozen in the town who own their farms free and clear. If you would know the history of these homesteads, inquire at the bank where they are mortgaged. The man who has actually paid for his farm with labor on it is so rare that every neighbor can point to him. . . .

And when the farmer has got his house, he may not be the richer but the poorer for it, and it be the house that has got him. As I understand it, that was a valid objection urged by Momus against the house which Minerva made, that she "had not made it movable, by which means a bad neighborhood might be avoided"; and it may still be urged, for our houses are such unwieldy property that we are often imprisoned rather than housed in them; and the bad neighborhood to be avoided is our own scurvy selves. I know one or two families, at least, in this town, who, for nearly a generation, have been wishing to sell their houses in the outskirts and move into the village, but have not been able to accomplish it, and only death will set them free.

Granted that the *majority* are able at last either to own or hire the modern house with all its improvements. While civilization has been improving our houses, it has not equally improved the men who are to inhabit them. It has created palaces, but it was not so easy to create noblemen and kings. And *if the civilized man's pursuits are no worthier than the savage's, if he is employed the greater part of his life in obtaining gross necessaries and comforts merely, why should he have a better dwelling than the former?*

But how do the poor *minority* fare? Perhaps it will be found that just in proportion as some have been placed in outward circumstances above the savage, others have been degraded below him. The luxury of one class is counterbalanced by the indigence of another. On the one side is the palace, on the other are the almshouse and "silent poor." The myriads who built the pyramids to be the tombs of the Pharaohs were fed on garlic, and it may be were not decently buried themselves. The mason who finishes the cornice of the palace returns at night perchance to a hut not so good as a wigwam. It is a mistake to suppose that, in a country where the usual evidences of civilization exist, the condition of a very large body of the inhabitants may not be as degraded as that of savages. I refer to the degraded poor, not now to the degraded rich. To know this I should not need to look farther than to the shanties which everywhere border our railroads, that last improvement in civilization; where I see in my daily walks human beings living in sties, and all winter with an open door, for the sake of light, without any visible, often imaginable, wood pile, and the forms of both old and young are permanently contracted by the long habit of shrinking from cold and misery, and the development of all their limbs and faculties is checked. It certainly is fair to look at that class by whose labor the works which distinguish this generation are accomplished. Such too, to a greater or less extent, is the condition of the operatives of every denomination in England, which is the great workhouse of the world. Or I could refer you to Ireland, which is marked as one of the white or enlightened spots on the map. Contrast the physical condition of the Irish with that of the North American Indian, or the South Sea Islander, or any other savage race before it was degraded by contact with the civilized man. Yet I have no doubt that that people's rulers are as wise as the average of civilized rulers. Their condition only proves what squalidness may consist with civilization. I hardly need refer now to the laborers in our Southern States who produce the staple exports of this country, and are themselves a staple production of the South. But to confine myself to those who are said to be in *moderate* circumstances.

Most men appear never to have considered what a house is, and are actually though needlessly poor all their lives because they think that they must have such a one as their neighbors have. As if one were to wear any sort of coat which the tailor might cut out for him, or, gradually leaving off palmleaf hat or cap of woodchuck skin, complain of hard times because he could not afford to buy him a crown! It is possible to invent a house still more convenient and luxurious than we have, which yet all would admit that man could not afford to pay for. Shall we always study to obtain more of these things, and not sometimes to be content with less? Shall the respectable citizen thus gravely teach, by precept and example, the necessity of the young man's providing a certain number of superfluous glow-shoes, and umbrellas, and empty guest chambers for empty guests, before he dies? Why should not our furniture be as simple as the Arab's or the Indian's? When I think of the benefactors of the race, whom we have apotheosized as messengers from heaven, bearers of divine gifts to man, I do not see in my mind any retinue at their heels, any car-load of fashionable furniture. Or what if I were to allow — would it not be a singular allowance? — that our furniture should be more complex than the Arab's, in proportion as we are morally and intellectually his superiors! At present our houses are cluttered and defiled with it, and a good housewife would sweep out the greater part into the dust hole, and not leave her morning's work undone. Morning work! By the blushes of Aurora and the music of Memnon, what should be man's *morning work* in this world? I had three pieces of limestone on my desk, but I was terrified to find that they required to be dusted daily, when the furniture of my mind was all undusted still, and I threw them out the window in disgust. How, then, could I have a furnished house? I would rather sit in the open air, for no dust gathers on the grass, unless where man has broken ground.

It is the luxurious and dissipated who set the fashions which the herd so diligently follow. The traveller who stops at the best houses, so called, soon discovers this, for the publicans presume him to be a Sardanapalus, and if he resigned himself to their tender mercies he would soon be completely emasculated. I think that in the railroad car we are inclined to spend more on luxury than on safety and convenience, and it threatens without attaining these to become no better than a modern drawing room, with its divans, and ottomans, and sunshades, and a hundred other oriental things, which we are taking west with us, invented for the ladies of the harem and the effeminate natives of the Celestical Empire, which Jonathan should be ashamed to know the names of. I would rather sit on a pumpkin and have it all to myself than be crowded on a velvet cushion. I would rather ride on earth in an ox cart, with a free circulation, than go to heaven in the fancy car of an excursion train and breathe a *malaria* all the way.

The very simplicity and nakedness of man's life in the primitive ages imply this advantage, at least, that they left him still but a sojourner in nature. When he was refreshed with food and sleep he contemplated his journey again. He dwelt, as it were, in a tent in this world, and was either threading the valleys, or crossing the plains, or climbing the mountain tops. But lo! men have become the tools of their tools. The man who independently plucked the fruits when he was hungry is become a farmer; and he who stood under a tree for shelter, a housekeeper. We now no longer camp as for a night, but have settled down on earth and forgotten heaven. We have adopted Christianity merely as an improved method of *agri*-culture. We have built for this world a family mansion, and for the next a family tomb. The best works of art are the expression of man's struggle to free himself from this condition, but the effect of our art is merely to make this low state comfortable and that higher state to be forgotten. There is actually no place in this village for a work of *fine* art, if any had come down to us, to stand, for our lives, our houses and streets, furnish no proper pedestal for it. There is not a nail to hang a picture on, nor a shelf to receive the bust of a hero or a saint. When I consider how our houses are built and paid for, or not paid for, and their internal economy managed and sustained, I wonder that the floor does not give way under the visitor while he is admiring the gewgaws upon the mantelpiece, and let him through into the cellar, to some solid and honest though earthy foundation. . . .

. . . When I think of acquiring for myself one of our luxurious dwellings, I am deterred, for, so to speak, the country is not yet adapted to *human* culture, and we are still forced to cut our *spiritual* bread far thinner than our forefathers did their wheaten. Not that all architectural ornament is to be neglected even in the rudest periods; but let our houses first be lined with beauty, where they come in contact with our lives, like the tenement of the shell-fish, and not overlaid with it. But, alas! I have been inside one or two of them, and know what they are lined with.

Though we are not so degenerate but that we might possibly live in a cave or a wigwam or wear skins to-day, it certainly is better to accept the advantages, though so dearly bought, which the invention and industry of mankind offer. In such a neighborhood as this, boards and shingles, lime and bricks, are cheaper and more easily obtained than suitable caves, or whole logs, or bark in sufficient quantities, or even well-tempered clay or flat stones. I speak understandingly on this subject, for I have made myself acquainted with it both theoretically and practically. With a little more wit we might use these materials so as to become richer than the richest now are, and make our civilization a blessing. The civilized man is a more experienced and wiser savage. . . .

It would be worth the while to build still more deliberately than I did, considering, for instance, what foundation a door, a window, a cellar, a garret, have in the nature of man, and perchance never raising any superstructure until we found a better reason for it than our temporal necessities even. There is some of the same fitness in a man's building his own house that there is in a bird's building its own nest. Who knows but if men constructed their dwellings with their own hands, and provided food for themselves and families simply and honestly enough, the poetic faculty would be universally developed, as birds universally sing when they are so engaged? But alas! we do like cowbirds and cuckoos, which lay their eggs in nests which other birds have built, and cheer no traveller with their chattering and unmusical notes. Shall we forever resign the pleasure of construction to the carpenter? What does architecture amount to in the experience of the mass of men? I never in all my walks came across a man engaged in so simple and natural an occupation as building his house. We belong to the community. It is not the tailor alone who is the ninth part of a man; it is as much the preacher, and the merchant, and the farmer. Where is this division of labor to end? and what object does it finally serve? No doubt another *may* also think for me; but it is not therefore desirable that he should do so to the exclusion of my thinking for myself.

True, there are architects so called in this country, and I have heard of one at least possessed with the idea of making architectural ornaments have a core of truth, a necessity, and hence a beauty, as if it were a revelation to him. All very well perhaps from his point of view, but only a little better than the common dilettantism. A sentimental reformer in architecture, he began at the cornice, not at the foundation. It was only now to put a core of truth within the ornaments, that every sugar plum in fact might have an almond or caraway seed in it, — though I hold that almonds are most wholesome without the sugar, — and not how the inhabitant, the indweller, might build truly within and without, and let the ornaments take care of themselves. What reasonable man ever supposed that ornaments were something outward and in the skin merely, — that the tortoise got his spotted shell, or the shellfish its mother-o'-pearl tints, by such a contract as the inhabitants of Broadway their Trinity Church? But a man has no more to do with the style of architecture of his house than a tortoise with that of its shell: nor need the soldier be so idle as to try to paint the precise *color* of his virtue on his standard. The enemy will find it out. He may turn pale when the trial comes. This man seemed to me to lean over the cornice, and timidly whisper his half truth to the rude occupants who really knew it better than he. What of architectural beauty I now see, I know has gradually grown from within outward, out of the necessities and character of the indweller, who is the only builder, — out of some unconscious truthfulness, and nobleness, without ever a thought for the appearance; and whatever additional beauty of this kind is destined to be produced will be preceded by a like unconscious beauty of life. The most interesting dwellings in this country, as the painter knows, are the most unpretending, humble log huts and cottages of the poor commonly; it is the life of the inhabitants whose shells they are, and not any peculiarity in their surfaces merely, which makes them *picturesque;* and equally interesting will be the citizen's suburban box, when his life shall be as simple and as agreeable to the imagination, and there is as little straining after effect in the style of his dwelling. A great proportion of architectural ornaments are literally hollow, and a September gale would strip them off, like borrowed plumes, without injury to the substantials. They can do without *architecture* who have no olives nor wines in the cellar. What if an equal ado were made about the ornaments of style in literature, and the architects of our bibles spent as much time about their cornices as the architects of our churches do? So are made the *belles-lettres* and the *beaux-arts* and their professors. Much it concerns a man, forsooth, how a few sticks are slanted over him or under him, and what colors are daubed upon his box. It would signify somewhat, if, in any earnest sense, *he* slanted them and daubed it; but the spirit having departed out of the tenant, it is of a piece with constructing his own coffin, — the architecture of the grave, and "carpenter," is but another name for "coffin-maker." One man says, in his despair or indifference to life, take up a handful of the earth at your feet, and paint your house that color. Is he thinking of his last and narrowhouse? Toss up a copper for it as well. What an abundance of leisure he must have! Why do you take up a handful of dirt? Better paint your house your own complexion; let it turn pale or blush for you. An enterprise to improve the style of cottage architecture! When you have got my ornaments ready I will wear them. . . .

What I Lived For

I went to the woods because I wished to live deliberately, to front only the essential facts of life, and see if I could not learn what it had to teach, and not, when I came to die, discover that I had not lived. I did not wish to live what was not life, living is so dear; nor did I wish to practise resignation, unless it was quite necessary. I wanted to live deep and suck out all the marrow of life, to live so sturdily and Spartan-like as to put to rout all that was not life, to cut a broad swath and shave close, to drive life into a corner, and reduce it to its lowest terms, and, if it proved to be mean, why then to get the whole and genuine meanness of it, and publish its meanness to the world; or if it were sublime, to know it by experience, and be able to give a true account of it in my next excursion. For most men, it appears to me, are in a strange uncertainty about it, whether it is of the devil or of God, and have *somewhat hastily* concluded that it is the chief end of man here to "glorify God and enjoy him forever."

Still we live meanly, like ants; though the fable tells us that we were long ago changed into men; like pygmies we fight with cranes; it is error upon error, and clout upon clout, and our best virtue has for its occasion a superfluous and evitable wretchedness. Our life is frittered away by detail. An honest man has hardly need to count more than his ten fingers, or in extreme cases he may add his ten toes, and lump the rest. Simplicity, simplicity, simplicity! I say, let your affairs be as two or three, and not a hundred or a thousand; instead of a million count half a dozen, and keep your accounts on your thumb nail. In the midst of this chopping sea of civilized life, such are the clouds and storms and quicksands and thousand-and-one items to be allowed for, that a man has to live, if he would not founder and go to the bottom and not make his port at all, by dead reckoning, and he must be a great calculator indeed who succeeds. Simplify, simplify. Instead of three meals a day, if it be necessary eat but one; instead of a hundred dishes, five; and reduce other things in proportion. Our life is like a German Confederacy, made up of petty states, with its boundary forever fluctuating, so that even a German cannot tell you how it is bounded at any moment. The nation itself, with all its so-called internal improvements, which, by the way are all external and superficial, is just such an unwieldy and overgrown establishment, cluttered with furniture and tripped up by its own traps, ruined by luxury and heedless expense, by want of calculation and a worthy aim, as the million households in the land; and the only cure for it as for them is in a rigid economy, a stern and more than Spartan simplicity of life and elevation of purpose. It lives too fast. Men think that it is essential that the *Nation* have commerce, and export ice, and talk through a telegraph, and ride thirty miles an hour, without a doubt, whether *they* do or not; but whether we should live like baboons or like men, is a little uncertain. If we do not get out sleepers, and forge rails, and devote days and nights to the work, but go to tinkering upon our *lives* to improve *them*, who will build railroads? And if railroads are not built, how shall we get to heaven in season? But if we stay at home and mind our business, who will want railroads? We do not ride on the railroad; it rides upon us. Did you ever think what those sleepers are that underlie the railroad? Each one is a man, an Irishman, or a Yankee man. The rails are laid on them, and they are covered with sand, and the cars run smoothly over them. They are sound sleepers, I assure you. And every few years a new lot is laid down and run over; so that, if some have the pleasure of riding on a rail, others have the misfortune to be ridden upon. And when they run over a man that is walking in his sleep, a supernumerary sleeper in the wrong position, and wake him up, they suddenly stop the cars, and make a hue and cry about it, as if this were an exception. I am glad to know that it takes a gang of men for every five miles to keep the sleepers down and level in their beds as it is, for this is a sign that they may sometime get up again.

Why should we live with such hurry and waste of life? We are determined to be starved before we are hungry. Men say that a stitch in time saves nine, and so they take a thousand stitches to-day to save nine to-morrow. As for *work*, we have n't any of any consequence. We have the Saint Vitus' dance, and cannot possibly keep our heads still. If I should only give a few pulls at the parish bell-rope, as for a fire, that is, without setting the bell, there is hardly a man on his farm in the outskirts of Concord, notwithstanding that press of engagements which was his excuse so many times this morning, nor a boy, nor a woman, I might almost say, but would forsake all the follow that sound, not mainly to save property from the flames, but, if we will confess the truth, much more to see it burn, since burn it must, and we, be it known, did not set it on fire, — or to see it put out, and have a hand in it, if that is done as handsomely; yes, even if it were the parish church itself. Hardly a man takes a half hour's nap after dinner, but when he wakes he holds up his head and asks, "What's the news?" as if the rest of mankind had stood his sentinels. Some give directions to be waked every half hour, doubtless for no other purpose; and then, to pay for it, they tell what they have dreamed. After a night's sleep the news is as indispensable as the breakfast. "Pray tell me anything new that has happened to a man anywhere on this globe," — and he reads it over his coffee and rolls, that a man has had his eyes gouged out this morning on the Wachito River; never dreaming the while that he lives in the dark unfathomed mammoth cave of this world, and has but the rudiment of an eye himself.

For my part, I could easily do without the post-office. I think that there are very few important communications made through it. To speak critically, I never received more than one or two letters in my life — I wrote this some years ago — that were worth the postage. The penny-post is, commonly, an institution through which you seriously offer a man that penny for his thoughts which is so often safely offered in jest. And I am sure that I never read any memorable news in a newspaper. If we read of one man robbed, or murdered, or killed by accident, or one house burned, or one vessel wrecked, or one steamboat blown up, or one cow run over on the Western Railroad, or one mad dog killed, or one lot of grasshoppers in the winter, — we never need read of another. One is enough. If you are acquainted with the principle, what do you care for a myriad instances and applications? To a philosopher all *news*, as it is called, is gossip, and they who edit and read it are old women over their tea. Yet not a few are greedy after this gossip. There was such a rush, as I hear, the other day at one of the offices to learn the foreign news by the last arrival, that several large squares of plate glass belonging to the establishment were broken by the pressure, — news which I seriously think a ready wit might write a twelvemonth or twelve years beforehand with sufficient accuracy. As for Spain, for instance, if you know how to throw in Don Carlos and the Infanta, and Don Pedro and Seville and Granada, from time to time in the right proportions, — they may have changed the names a little since I saw the papers, — and serve up a bull-fight when other entertainments fail, it will be true to the letter, and give us as good an idea of the exact state or ruin of things in Spain as the most succinct and lucid reports under this head in the newspapers: and as for England, almost the last significant scrap of news from that quarter was the revolution of 1649; and if you have learned the history of her crops for an average year, you never need attend to that thing again, unless your speculations are of a merely pecuniary character. If one may judge who rarely looks into the newspapers, nothing new does ever happen in foreign parts, a French revolution not excepted. . . .

Let us spend one day as deliberately as Nature, and not be thrown off the track by every nutshell and mosquito's wing that falls on the rails. Let us rise early and fast, or break fast, gently and without perturbation;

let company come and let company go, let the bells ring and the children cry, — determined to make a day of it. Why should we knock under and go with the stream? Let us not be upset and overwhelmed in that terrible rapid and whirlpool called a dinner, situated in the meridian shallows. Weather this danger and you are safe, for the rest of the way is down hill. With unrelaxed nerves, — with morning vigor, sail by it, looking another way, tied to the mast like Ulysses. If the engine whistles, let it whistle till it is hoarse and its pains. If the bell rings, why should we run? We will consider what kind of music they are like. Let us settle ourselves, and work and wedge our feet downward through the mud and slush of opinion, and prejudice, and tradition, and delusion, and appearance, that allusion which covers the globe, through Paris and London, through New York and Boston and Concord, through church and state, through poetry and philosophy and religion, till we come to a hard bottom and rocks in place, which we can call *reality*, and say, This is, and no mistake; and then begin, having a *point d'appui*, below freshet and frost and fire, a place where you might found a wall or a state, or set a lamp-post safely, or perhaps a gauge, not a Nilometer, but a Realometer, that future ages might know how deep a freshet of shams and appearances had gathered from time to time. If you stand right fronting and face to face to a fact, you will see the sun glimmer on both its surfaces, as if it were a cimeter, and feel its sweet edge dividing you through the heart and marrow, and so you will happily conclude your mortal career. Be it life or death, we crave only reality. If we are really dying, let us hear the rattle in our throats and feel cold in the extremities; if we are alive, let us go about our business.

Time is but the stream I go a-fishing in. I drink at it; but while I drink I see the sandy bottom and detect how shallow it is. Its thin current slides away, but eternity remains. I would drink deeper; fish in the sky, whose bottom is pebbly with stars. I cannot count one. I know not the first letter of the alphabet. I have always been regretting that I was not as wise as the day I was born. The intellect is a cleaver; it discerns and rifts its way into the secret of things. I do not wish to be any more busy with my hands than is necessary. My head is hands and feet. I feel all my best faculties concentrated in it. My instinct tells me that my head is an organ for burrowing, as some creatures use their snout and fore-paws, and with it I would mine and burrow my way through these hills. I think that the richest vein is somewhere hereabouts; so by the divining rod and thin rising vapors I judge; and here I will begin to mine. . . .

Sounds

As I sit at my window this summer afternoon, hawks are circling about my clearing; the tantivy of wild pigeons, flying by twos and threes athwart my view, or perching restless on the white-pine boughs behind my house, gives a voice to the air; a fishhawk dimples the glassy surface of the pond and brings up a fish; a mink steals out of the marsh before my door and seizes a frog by the shore; the sedge is bending under the weight of the reed-birds flitting hither and thither; and for the last half hour I have heard the rattle of railroad cars, now dying away and then reviving like the beat of a partridge, conveying travellers from Boston to the country. For I did not live so out of the world as that boy, as I hear, was put out to a farmer in the east part of the town, but ere long ran away and came home again, quite down at the heel and homesick. He had never seen such a dull and out-of-the way place; the folks were all gone off; why, you could n't even hear the whistle! I doubt if there is such a place in Massachusetts now: —

> "In truth, our village has become a butt
> For one of those fleet railroad shafts, and o'er
> Our peaceful plain its soothing sound is — Concord."

The Fitchburg Railroad touches the pond about a hundred rods south of where I dwell. I usually go to the village along its causeway, and am, as it were, related to society by this link. The men on the freight trains, who go over the whole length of the road, bow to me as to an old acquaintance, they pass me so often, and apparently they take me for an employee; and so I am. I too would fain be a track-repairer somewhere in the orbit of the earth.

The whistle of the locomotive penetrates my woods summer and winter, sounding like the scream of a hawk sailing over some farmer's yard, informing me that many restless city merchants are arriving within the circle of the town, or adventurous country traders from the other side. As they come under one horizon, they shout their warning to get off the track to the other, heard sometimes through the circles of two towns. Here come your groceries, country; your rations, countrymen! Nor is there any man so independent on his farm that he can say them nay. And here's your pay for them! screams the countryman's whistle; timber like long battering rams going twenty miles an hour against the city's walls, and chairs enough to seat all the weary and heavy laden that dwell within them. With such huge and lumbering civility the country hands a chair to the city. All the Indian huckleberry hills are stripped, all the cranberry meadows are raked into the city. Up comes the cotton, down goes the woven cloth; up comes the silk, down goes the woollen; up come the books, but down goes the wit that writes them.

When I meet the engine with its train of cars moving off with planetary motion, — or, rather, like a comet, for the beholder knows not if with that velocity and with that direction it will ever revisit this system, since its orbit does not look like a returning curve, — with its steam cloud like a banner streaming behind in golden and silver wreaths, like many a downy cloud which I have seen, high in the heavens, unfolding its masses to the light, — as if this travelling demigod, this cloud-compeller, would ere long take the sunset sky for the livery of his train; when I hear the iron horse make the hills echo with his snort like thunder, shaking the earth with his feet, and breathing fire and smoke from his nostrils, (what kind of winged horse or fiery dragon they will put into the new Mythology I don't know,) it seems as if the earth had got a race now worthy to inhabit it. If all were as it seems, and men made the elements their servants for noble ends! If the cloud that hangs over the engine were the perspiration of heroic deeds, or as beneficent as that which floats over the farmer's fields, then the elements and Nature herself would cheerfully accompany men on their errands and be their escort.

I watch the passage of the morning cars with the same feeling that I do the rising of the sun, which is hardly more regular. Their train of clouds stretching far behind and rising higher and higher, going to heaven while the cars are going to Boston, conceals the sun for a minute and casts my distant field into the shade, a celestial train beside which the petty train of cars which hugs the earth is but the barb of the spear. The stabler of the iron horse was up early this winter morning by the light of the stars amid the mountains, to fodder and harness his steed. Fire, too, was awakened thus early to put the vital heat in him and get him off. If the enterprise were as innocent as it is early! If the snow lies deep, they strap on his snow-shoes, and with the giant plough plough a furrow from the mountains to the seaboard, in which the cars, like a following drill-barrow, sprinkle all the restless men and floating merchandise in the country for seed. All day the fire-steed flies over the country, stopping only that his master may rest, and I am awakened by his tramp and defiant snort at midnight, when in some remote glen in the woods he fronts the elements incased in ice and snow; and he will reach his stall only with the morning star, to start once more on his travels without rest or slumber. Or perchance, at evening, I hear him in his stable blowing off the superfluous energy of the day, that he may calm his nerves and cool his liver and brain for a few hours of iron slumber. If the enterprise were as heroic and commanding as it is protracted and unwearied!

Far through unfrequented woods on the confines of towns, where once only the hunter penetrated by day, in the darkest night dart these bright saloons without the knowledge of their inhabitants; this moment stopping at some brilliant station-house in town or city, where a social crowd is gathered, the next in the Dismal Swamp, scaring the owl and fox. The startings and arrivals of the cars are now the epochs in the village day. They go and come with such regularity and precision, and their whistle can be heard so far, that the farmers set their clocks by them, and thus one well conducted institution regulates a whole country. Have not men improved somewhat in punctuality since the railroad was invented? Do they not talk and think faster in the depot than they did in the stage-office? There is something electrifying in the atmosphere of the former place. I have been astonished at the miracles it has wrought; that some of my neighbors, who, I should have prophesied, once for all, would never get to Boston by so prompt a conveyance, are on hand when the bell rings. To do things "railroad fashion" is now the byword; and it is worth the while to be warned so often and so sincerely by any power to get off its track. There is no stopping to read the riot act, no firing over the heads of the mob, in this case. We have constructed a fate, an *Atropos*, that never turns aside. (Let that be the name of your engine.) Men are advertised that at a certain hour and minute these bolts will be shot toward particular points of the compass; yet it interferes with no man's business, and the children go to school on the other track. We live the steadier for it. We are all educated thus to be sons of Tell. The air is full of invisible bolts. Every path but your own is the path of fate. Keep on your own track, then.

V

SOCIAL CLASSES IN INDUSTRIAL SOCIETY

As industrialism began to dominate the economies of Europe and America in the mid-nineteenth century, thinkers on either side of the Atlantic attempted to appraise the social effects of accelerated economic expansion. Henry C. Carey (1793–1879), probably the most influential American economist of the early nineteenth century, spent a lifetime arguing that capital, if allowed to grow without government interference, would shower prosperity on all. Carey thus devoted his career to refuting the classical economists after Thomas Malthus and David Ricardo, who held that economic growth was matched by population growth and that men must therefore continue to compete for scarce resources. In Carey's scheme, the benefits of freely expanding capital reduced the harmful effects of competition and promoted harmony between social classes — in particular, between capitalists and laborers.

For Karl Marx (1818–1883), industrialism intensified the historical conflict between classes, pitting the increasingly exploited proletariat against the bourgeoisie. Marx agreed with Carey that capital would expand; he even appeared to concede that the expansion of capital would bring more material goods to the working man. But that greater prosperity was not so important to Marx as the question of power, a question largely ignored in Carey's analysis. Though it might increase in wealth, the proletariat saw its relative position in society continually eroded as capitalists gained more and more power. Between capital and labor, therefore, there could only be conflict. Marx considered Carey's work proof that the notion of class struggle was still incomprehensible in America. When Carey argued that economic conditions promoted harmony, rather than struggle, he only showed, Marx wrote in 1852, "that he is taking the 'undeveloped' conditions of the United States for 'normal conditions.'" [1]

[1] Karl Marx to Joseph Weydemeyer, March 5, 1852, quoted in Lewis S. Feuer, ed., *Marx and Engels: Basic Writings on Politics and Philosophy* (Garden City: Doubleday, 1959), 456–457.

Capital and Labor
(1837–1840, 1858, 1873)

HENRY C. CAREY

Of all the unsettled questions of the day there is no one of higher moment; none deserving of more serious and earnest consideration. For many years it has, more and more, taken the form, as it now bears the name, of a war between capital and labor. The parties to the contest seem themselves to understand it; and it behooves all who are in authority, either as leaders of public opinion or as makers of public law, to take thought in time and look for the means of establishing peace through justice, for only righteousness and peace can travel hand in hand, just as wrong and war are ever joined together.

Labor, at wages, goes daily to the auction block, its forces to be there knocked down to the lowest bidder. In our system of industrial disorder the laborer's lowest reward is the employer's highest profit. He has no capital on which to rely for effectual resistance. His necessities are continuous; his employment and its remuneration fluctuate with all the changes in the markets of the time, whether that in which the interest of money is determined, or that in which corn or cotton, hats or shoes, are sold. His own market is therefore but a troubled sea, subject to high and low tides, to storms and calms, and to it he cannot say, "thus far shalt thou come and no further, and here shall thy wild waves be stayed." He cannot command the public movements by which his fortunes are to be governed. Seeing the unequal distribution of the world's goods, and regarding them all as the product of that labor which receives so small a share, he looks for means or measures by which to compel an equitable distribution. He is clear as to the end to be obtained; clear as to its necessity; clear as to its justice. From the purpose to the end, however, in all societary, social, moral, or even divine purposes, the distance is great; and under the laws that rule in the lives of men, results, however desirable and just, are to be brought about by a system that may not be forced. This, however, he does not see. Perhaps we might say that he will not see it. To recognize the steady and necessary operative *law* in that condition of

From *Debates of the Convention to Amend the Constitution of Pennsylvania* (Harrisburg: Benjamin Singerly, State Printer, 1873), 472–473; H. C. Carey, *Principles of Political Economy* (Philadelphia: Carey, Lea and Blanchard, 1837–40), part 3, 299–305, 310–315; H. C. Carey, *Principles of Social Science* (Philadelphia: J. B. Lippincott, 1888), vol. III, 131–134, 147–148, 153–154, 159–160.

things which so sorely oppresses him he is most unwilling, for this would command his submission. Seeing only wrong in the order of human affairs, he shuts his eyes and falls back upon his strength in assault on one hand, and resistance on the other. He calls upon the State to interpose, not in reference to causes, but to their effects, thus demanding the end, not the means by which that end might be attained. Legal pains and penalties are his chosen remedies, and in keeping with this impulse he enters into association with his fellow-toiler, surrendering his own liberties as largely as he would invade those of others of his fellow-men on whom he looks as his oppressors. Further even than this, he forbids the opportunities of labor to his brother, his son, his daughter, that he may thus, as he imagines, be enabled to secure himself against evils resulting from competition for the sale of labor.

Such measures are as useless as, to all the parties concerned, they are unjust. They are not remedies for the evils suffered and apprehended, for the reason that they are based upon radically erroneous notions of causes and effects. In the first place, it is assumed that labor and capital are naturally hostile to each other. This is not true. Laborers and capitalists may go to war, but labor and capital are joined in indissoluble partnership, with interests essentially identical and, with the progress of the industrial arts, ever becoming more closely interdependent. The remedy for the subsisting hostility of the parties and its evils is, therefore, not to be found in legal compulsion on the one hand or on the other. They must not fall out by the way, but in harmony search for the causes of existing evil, and by combined effort seek to perfect their connection. The societary system is governed by laws as absolute and persistent in operation as those of any other part of the creation. War among its elements constitutes no part of its system. Kindred to this primary mistake is the dreadful severity of the measures adopted by labor associations for limiting the number of apprentices in the productive arts. Beginning with a fear of the very capital by which they are aided, they fall now upon another fundamental error, to wit, fear of competition in their own class for the employment which they would monopolize, because, as they think, the market for labor may be over-crowded.

In the nature of things, however, there is no possibility that labor shall ever fail of its opportunities if its market be kept free and fairly balanced. There has never yet been a day in the world's history when the productive industries were at all adequate to the wants of consumers. In a true order of business not all the possible labor of muscle and mind, with all the appliances of machinery and natural agencies, can overpass the wants of the world. There is possibly a limit to the consumption of food, as there is to the area and fertility of the earth; but their respective limits are providentially adjusted to each other step by step through all the stages of their growth; whereas, with respect to all other industries, supply creates demand. Their market can, therefore, never be gorged, and the fear of competition in production is as baseless as the measures taken to repress it are both cruel and unjust. To mechanics and manufacturers no measure applies, nor are there any limits needing to be feared. Fifty years ago stage coaches were seldom crowded. Since then the canal boat, the steamboat and the railroad car have been produced with thousands of times the capacity of former vehicles of transportation; yet are they constantly taxed to their utmost capacity for work. Fifty years ago weekly newspapers printed a few hundreds for their lean lists of subscribers; now tens of millions are being daily issued. Fifty years ago four or five yards of muslin per head was the meagre average annual consumption of our people; now they consume as much as would make a tent cover for the whole of the inhabited continent. Then, the women of the household, at their simple wheels and handlooms, in the leisure hours of their daily work, supplied the woollens that the country wore; now power-looms, yielding thousands of times more cloth and hosiery, are tasked to meet the demand. As well might education be restricted in the fear that men might become too intelligent, as to place restraints upon skilled industry for fear of glutting the market with its products.

We come now to inquire what is the effect produced upon the number of annuitants, or proprietors — of persons who consume without producing — by the increase of population and capital, causing increase of production, and doubt not we shall satisfy our readers that it is the same as upon the shopkeepers, viz. *an increase of number*, attended by a *diminution in the proportion* which they bear to the whole community.

We trust that they are already satisfied that with every increase in the productiveness of labor, the labourer is enabled to retain *an increased proportion* of the commodity produced, *leaving a diminished proportion to the capitalist*. Such being the case, we will see what would be the effect upon the capitalists, *were the proportions in the numbers of the two parties to remain the same*. Let us suppose that in a community of 1000 persons, *ten* are capitalists, and 990 are labourers; that the whole amount produced is 100,000 dollars — or bushels of wheat — and that, owing to the scarcity of capital, the owners thereof are enabled to demand one half, giving them 50,000 = 5,000 each, and leaving to the labourers a fraction over 50 bushels each.

The quality of labour being improved, 2,000 persons are enabled to produce 225,000 bushels of wheat, of which the landlords can now claim only two fifths, giving them 90,000, and leaving 135,000 to the labourers. If the proportions of the population remain the same, there will be 4,500 for each of the *twenty* capitalists, and 68 for each labourer.

With a further improvement, 3,000 persons produce 350,000 bushels, of which the *thirty* capitalists claim one third, giving them 116,667, or 3,888 to each, and nearly 80 to each labourer. Another period gives 4,000 persons, producing 480,000 bushels, of which the *forty* owners claim one fourth, or 120,000, giving 3,000 to each of the *forty* capitalists, and above 90 to each labourer. A further step onwards gives us 5,000 persons, producing 625,000 bushels, of which one fifth, or 125,000, goes to the capitalists, *fifty* in number, giving to each of them 2,500 bushels, and to each labourer above 100 bushels.

At another period, when 10,000 persons produce 2,000,000 of bushels, the proprietors, then *one hundred* in number, would receive one eighth, or 250,000 bushels, being 2,500 bushels, while each labourer would have 200 bushels.

We now give another scale of production and distribution, that the reader may see how it would operate.

Population	Production	Proportion of the capitalist	Quantity to each capitalist	Quantity to each labourer
1,000	100,000	½	5,000	50
2,000	300,000	⅖	6,000	90
3,000	600,000	⅓	6,667	133
4,000	1,000,000	¼	6,250	187
5,000	1,500,000	⅕	6,000	240
6,000	2,000,000	⅙	5,550	280

Here it will be observed, that the *quantity* allotted to the capitalist is somewhat increased, because we have assumed a more rapid improvement in the quality of labour, retaining, for the division, the same proportions as at first.

If we take a still more rapid improvement, we shall obtain the following results:

1,000	100,000	½	5,000	50
2,000	400,000	⅖	8,000	120
3,000	750,000	⅓	8,333	166
4,000	1,200,000	¼	7,500	225
5,000	2,000,000	⅕	8,000	320
6,000	3,000,000	⅙	8,333	416

COMPARATIVE VIEW

First		*Second*		*Third*	
Capitalist	Labourer	Capitalist	Labourer	Capitalist	Labourer
5,000	50	5,000	50	5,000	50
4,500	68	6,000	90	8,000	120
3,888	80	6,667	133	8,333	166
3,000	90	6,250	187	7,500	225
2,500	100	6,000	240	8,000	320
2,500	200	5,550	280	8,333	416

The reader will here remark, in every case, an approximation of the condition of the labourer and capitalist. In the first it is accompanied with a diminution in the quantity falling to the share of each owner of capital, but in the last it is accompanied with an increase of 66⅔ per cent., while the quantity of the labourer has increased 832 per cent.

On a former occasion we showed the change that has taken place in the last five hundred years, in the condition of both labourer and capitalist. In the reign of Henry VII., the whole sum allowed to the daughter of Edward IV., for the maintenance of her establishment, was little more than £ 100; and at a subsequent period the Duke of Northumberland, one of the most powerful nobles of England, when changing his residence from one palace to another, always removed his furniture, the whole of which was, we think, transported in one or two wagons.

The change that has taken place in the condition of the mere labourer, is great, but not greater than in that of the capitalist, if so great. The former has it in his power to obtain 8, 10, or 12 times as much of the necessaries and comforts of life, but the latter may now obtain perhaps 15, 20, or 25 times the quantity that he could then. Such could not be the case, if the *proportion* in the number of capitalists and labourers remained the same.

Every improvement in the quality of labour is attended with a diminution in the quantity required for obtaining any given result. The quality of labour improves with the increase of population and of capital, attended by constant diminution in its severity, and a constant increase in its reward. The *employer* of capital obtains a *constantly increasing proportion*, and the *owner* therof a *constantly decreasing one*. The value of skill or talent is constantly rising, when compared with that of the commodities, or things which constitute capital. If the owners of the latter did not exert themselves, by bringing their talents into activity in aid of their capital, they would find themselves unable to maintain their position in society. To do so they are compelled to exertion, and thus every improvement in the quality of labour — every increase in its return — every improvement in the mode of living — produces *new necessity* for the exertion of whatever powers an individual may possess, while he finds *new inducements* thereto in the constant *diminution* in the severity of labour, and equally constant *increase* in its reward; and thus *the proportion* which those who live upon the income of capital, and without bodily or mental exertion, bear to the whole population, must be constantly decreasing.

In the United States, there has been a steady improvement in the condition of both labourer and capitalist. The extent of the change that has taken place in that of the former, we have already shown. In regard to the latter the change has been far greater.

If we examine the several parts of the American Union, we shall find, with improvement in the quality of labour, a diminution in the disposition to *inactivity*. In Massachusetts, where capital most abounds, and where the largest fortunes are found, it exists in the smallest degree. Such likewise is the case as we trace the course of improvement in England for centuries. We think the reader will now agree with us that it may be admitted *as a law*, that with the increase of population, and of capital, there is a constant *diminution in the proportion* which shopkeepers and merchants, lawyers, and physicians — and annuitants, or persons living on their own capital, and without personal or mental exertion yielding them *wages* — must bear to the whole number.

It is possible, however, to prevent this from taking place, and even to increase the number of those classes, as we see has been the case in England within the last twenty years. *Restraints upon the employment of capital* may compel the owner thereof to send it to the United States, to South America, or to New Holland, or to invest it in foreign loans, in which case he becomes an annuitant. The people around him who would, under other circumstances, have been benefited by the use of his capital, may emigrate to those places, and thus restore the proportion, but in the mean time they must have experienced the inconvenience resulting from an increase of population without a corresponding increase of capital.

After the proportion of traders, annuitants, etc., shall have been reduced, it is possible to increase it again, by the adoption of measures tending to diminish the ratio which the growth of capital bears to that of population. In a war like that waged with France from 1793 to 1815, and requiring large expenditure, those who accumulate capital lend it to the government, and are paid for the use therefor out of the taxes imposed upon the labouring classes. Every such loan tends to diminish the inducement for the application of talent to production, and to increase the tendency towards becoming annuitants, because with every one the *capitalist's proportion rises, and that of the labourer falls.*

In both of these cases, the effect in reducing the amount of commodities produced is the same. Both are, therefore, injurious to labourer and capitalist. In the latter, however, the burthen falls most heavily upon the labourer. Capital is rendered scarce, and he is compelled to give to the owner thereof a large proportion for its use, *retaining for himself a small proportion of the diminished product*. In the former, capital is rendered superabundant, and its owner seeks in vain for the means of employing it. The general production is diminished, and *he retains a small proportion*, leaving to the labourer, or employer of capital, *a large proportion of a small product*.

At the present time, England offers to us the extraordinary spectacle of a superabundance of capital, and a great deal of poverty. By restraints of various kinds she limits the field for employment of capital, and forces vast numbers to engage in occupations in which their labour is *compar-*

atively unproductive. The shopkeepers produce the commodities at the place at which they are wanted; the physician and the lawyer produce their services, and the proprietor produces his houses. Shops, medical and legal services, and houses abound, and the proprietor and the owners are willing to take a very small remuneration as profit for the capital employed, and as wages for their attention in supplying them. *The proportion which they bear to the whole population is increasing instead of decreasing.*

The difficulty of employing capital is so great that it wanders in every direction seeking employment. The owner of it is glad to open a shop, if by so doing he can add a small amount to his income, whereas, the whole sum would not, under other circumstances, be a compensation for his services, were he without capital. The student of law or of medicine expends a large capital upon his education, that he may obtain ordinary wages, and the capitalist erects houses that he may, by giving his attention thereto, obtain some compensation for his time. Every employment that yields reasonable wages, whether in the army, the church, or trade, is a subject of purchase and sale, and the owner of a few hundred pounds is glad to give it to secure himself a clerkship for life, yielding him moderate wages for his time and attention. An established stand for business is never deserted; a connexion in trade is the object coveted by those who possess capital, and even the instruction acquired by an apprentice is obtained at the cost of a large amount of it. In every pursuit capital is used as a means to enable its possessor to obtain ordinary wages for the employment of his time. The obvious effect of this is to give to those who occupy established stands, or who have been in any way so fortunate as to obtain the eye or ear of the public, the opportunity of making large fortunes, while thousands of equal talent can obtain no employment, and thus, while the incomes of established lawyers, doctors, and merchants are immense, vast numbers find it exceedingly difficult to obtain the means of existence. *Every measure that tends to diminish production, tends to continue and to increase the inequality of fortune, while every measure that tends to increase production, tends to diminish inequality, while raising the standard of living of both labourer and capitalist.*

Here we have a state of things differing entirely from that which exists in France. *There* the labourer gives a high price for a small amount of capital, to enable him to obtain an increase of wages; *here* capital is seeking employment and the owner grants to the labourer its use, reserving a small proportion of the proceeds; *there* the landlord retains three sevenths as his *fonciere*, or rent; *here* the proportion is from one fifth to one fourth of the proceeds; *there* the persons possessing capital sufficient to establish shops or places of exchange, are few in number, and they demand *a large proportion* of the commodities as their commission; *here* the owners of capital are seeking employment for it, and shops are so numerous, that the owner is willing to accept *a very small proportion;* and *there* the owner of manufacturing machinery takes one half of the product, while *here* he has but one tenth or perhaps less. *In the first* labour is thrown in, as the article of least value, to unite with capital, while *in the last* capital is added to labour, in the hopes of obtaining wages. . . .

The proposition in regard to the distribution of wealth, that we have submitted to the reader, is, that with every improvement in the quality of labour there is an increase of production; that with every increase of production the labourer takes an increased proportion of the product, leaving to the capitalist a *diminished proportion,* but that with this diminution of proportion there is a constant *increase in the quantity* allotted to him, and that consequently the wages of the labourer and the profits of the capitalist increase with the augmentation of capital and improvement in the quality of labour. Such, precisely, will be found to be the case, if we confine ourselves to the examination of India, France, and the United States; but in England we find that the capitalist has a *lower proportion and a lower quantity than in the United States.*

The field for the employment of British capital is not *permitted* to increase, and the effect is that the quality of labour does not improve with the rapidity that it would otherwise do — the amount of production is restrained — and the capitalist has a small proportion of a comparatively small product; whereas, were the restraints removed, the demand for capital would increase, the quality of labour would be improved, production would be increased, and the capitalist would have a larger proportion of a larger product, while the labourer, taking a smaller proportion, would have an increased quantity of commodities in return for his labour. A removal of the existing restraints would speedily cause the production of England to rise to £ 350,000,000, 27½ per cent. of which would give to the capitalists 96 millions, instead of 65 or 70, which they now receive. We should then find them receiving the *smallest proportion,* and dividing among themselves the *largest quantity.*

In India and France, similar restraints exist, but in neither of them is to be found that security which is necessary to the productiveness of labour and the augmentation of capital. England possesses all the requisites for the rapid increase of capital and improvement in the quality of labour except one, that of permitting the field of employment to increase with the increase in quantity. The labourer and the capitalist are both sufferers.

In the United States, we find security. Capital grows rapidly, while the field of employment extends with it. Production is large; the share of the labourer is large; that of the capitalist is small; but both labourer and capitalist are more abundantly rewarded than in any other country. Nevertheless, the field of employment has been restrained by interferences with *the right* which every individual possesses to use his capital and to apply his labour in such manner as he deems likely to contribute most to the improvement of his condition. The consequence has been felt by the capitalists in a reduction of profits, and by the labourer in a reduction of wages. At no period in the history of the United States was the profit of capital so low, or its waste so great, as in the period from 1820 to 1830, when interferences were greatest.

In comparing the different portions of the several countries, we find abundant evidence that the proposition above referred to is universally true. Commencing in Massachusetts, with a population of 80 to a square mile, we find labour most productive, and the capitalist receiving the smallest portion of the proceeds, yet in no part of the Union does wealth so much abound. Passing thence to the south and west, with the diminution in the density of population there is a constant increase in the proportion of the capitalist, who obtains ten or fifteen per cent. in Mississippi, and twenty per cent. in Arkansas, while in Massachusetts he is content with five per cent. The same difference of distribution is to be found in all cases. In Illinois, and in Wisconsin, to which the tide of emigration is rapid, the price of wheat is far lower, when compared with flour, than is the case in New York or Pennsylvania, because the owner of capital in the form of a mill must have a large proportion of the grain which he grinds. The shopkeeper must have a large advance, and the owner of land upon which a house is built, obtains a large proportion of the product.

If we look to England, we shall find a similar state of things. In the portions of the kingdom in which the population is dense, as in Lancashire, or in Middlesex, capital may be obtained on payment of a smaller proportion of the product than in Cumberland or Westmoreland, where it is more scattered. The farmer and the labourer can exchange their products more advantageously where shops are plenty, as in Lancashire, or Yorkshire, than among the mountains of Cumberland, where they are few and widely scattered.

If we look to France, we shall find that the proportion taken by the proprietor of capital in the north, is less than in the south, or in the west, and that the labourer of the department of the north, retains a much larger proportion than does the labourer of the Limousin, or of Brittany.

M. Dupin says that each agricultural labourer in the north produces commodities worth 257 francs and 69 centimes, of which 103 francs are taken by the capitalist; and that in the south he produces 200 francs 93 centimes, and capital takes only 69 francs. In the former case he allows above 40 per cent., whereas, in the latter, it is little more than one third. Were this view correct, it would disprove the proposition which we have offered to the reader, but it is not so. M. Dupin considers only the rent of the land, and he does not take into consideration the quantity that is taken as profit by the shopkeeper, and by the various persons through whose hands the products of the south must pass, before they reach the market. The owner of the land has expended less, and therefore *his share* must be small, but the owners of all other capital must take their shares also; and thus the amount is increased until the proportion becomes largest.

A man who settled in the neighbourhood of the Rocky Mountains, or in Texas, would pay no rent, because no capital had been applied to the improvement of the land, but the proportion of his product that he would allow to the owners of wagons and horses, to carry it to market, would be so great, that it would be better for him to take land near New York or Philadelphia, that would yield only half the quantity, of which one half would be claimed by the owner. Such is the case in the south and west of France. Capital is small: production is limited; the owners of capital have a large share; the labourer has a small one; wages are low; the whole amount received by the owners of capital is small: they and the labourers are miserable.

In those parts of India in which the permanent settlement exists, production is much greater than in southern and western India, yet the capitalist takes a *larger proportion* in the former than in the latter. The great landholder, the Company, fixes in southern and western India, what shall be the rate of wages, and the Zemindars, or landholders of Bengal, to whom it has assigned its claims upon the labourers, take nearly all that is produced above the amount of wages so fixed, and have consequently a large proportion. Were the permanent settlement established throughout India, production would be greatly increased, capital would accumulate with rapidity, and *the proportion* of the capitalist would fall, while *the amount* distributed as profits would be greatly increased — the proportion of the labourer would be increased, wages would rise, and the condition of the whole people would be greatly improved.

In comparing the densely peopled portions of the United States, France, and England, with those in which population is scattered, we find one general law, viz. that with the extension of cultivation over inferior soils there is a diminished proportion retained by the owner of capital, leaving an increased proportion in the hands of the labourer, and enabling him to command a larger quantity of the comforts of life; yet in comparing Massachusetts, with a population of 80 to a square mile, with India, having 300, and with France, which has 160, we do not find such to be the case. The cause of this is to be found in the slower growth of capital, consequent upon the greater expenditure by the government, to which we have already briefly referred, but which we shall now examine more at length, first, however, embodying in the form of propositions, the conclusions at which we have arrived, which are,

I. That with the increase of production there is a diminution in *the proportion* assigned to the capitalist.

II. That this diminution of proportion is accompanied by an increase in the facility with which both labourer and capitalist obtain the necessaries, conveniences, comforts, and luxuries of life, and by an improvement in the mode of living.

III. That increase of production being attended by a *diminution* in the proportion of the product obtained by their *owners* for the use of commodities or things, and *an increase* in the proportion retained by the *employers* of them, there is a *tendency* to a more rapid improvement in the condition of the latter than of the former.

IV. That this tendency can be counteracted only by the exertion of skill or talent on the part of the former, so that increase of production has a direct tendency to stimulate the owner of capital to the exertion of his powers in order that he may maintain his position in relation to other portions of society.

V. That, therefore, with the increase of production there is a tendency to reduction in the proportion which the unproductive bear to the productive classes.

VI. That with this *diminution in proportion* there is a constant increase in the facility of obtaining intellectual and material capital, and a constant *increase in the amount of reward* obtained for its use.

VII. That thus with improvement in the condition of the labourer there is a constant improvement in the condition of the landholder and capitalist, the man of science, the painter, and the teacher.

VIII. That this improvement of condition is in the exact ratio of the increase of production, and that every measure tending to augment the rapidity of its increase, tends equally to produce further and more rapid improvement of condition, while every one that tends to retard it tends equally to retard improvement.

IX. That increase of production results from improvement in the quality of labour, produced by the increased application of capital.

X. That every measure tending to prevent the increase of capital, or to interfere with its free application, tends to prevent increase of production — to produce *an increase in the landlord's or capitalist's proportion* — to produce an *increase in the proportion* which the unproductive bear to the productive classes — to produce *a diminution in the labourer's proportion,* with *a diminution in the quantity of both labourer and capitalist* — and thus to prevent improvement in the condition of all classes of society.

XI. That it is, therefore, contrary to the interest of both labourer and capitalist to adopt any measure tending to restrain the growth of capital, or its free circulation and application in aid of production.

Thus far, in our examination of the great natural laws to which man and matter are subjected, they have proved equally true, whether considered in relation to the earth itself, or to the axes, canoes, ships, or clothing, into which man converts the materials by which he is surrounded. His course, in all communities that increase in wealth and population, is ever onward — passing from the knife of stone to that of steel — from the skin he has torn from an animal's back to a woollen coat — from the canoe to the ship — from the Indian path to the railroad — and from the poor lands of the hills and slopes to the fertile soils of the valleys, whose occupation in the earlier day had been prevented by the moisture with which they had been saturated, and the heavy timber with which they had been covered. Wealth is power — the more the richer soils are cultivated, and the more numerous the people who can draw support from a given surface, the greater being the facility of association, and the tendency towards combination for overcoming the yet remaining resistance of nature.

Here, as everywhere, the first step is the most costly and the least productive. At each succeeding stage, less effort is demanded, while the returns to labor as steadily increase. The cost of reproducing instruments, equal in power with those in use, gradually declining, the value of the latter, too, declines — the early land and the early axe being generally abandoned.

Rent, too, declines — the owner of land being required to content himself with a diminished proportion of the product as compensation for its use. Had the owner of the first little farm been asked for permission to cultivate it, his answer would have been: "Obtaining with this as much food in return to the labor of a day, as without it you could have in a week, you can well afford to give me three-fourths of the product of land and labor. This will, it is true, leave you but a small proportion of the things produced, but — your quantity being so much increased — your wages will be one-half greater then than now. You must, therefore, be content."

The contract made, both parties find their powers increased — enabling them to devote both time and mind to the construction of machinery required for effecting further economies of labor. The little farm had cost years of almost ceaseless effort; and yet was capable of yielding only 100 bushels, in return to a given amount of labor devoted to its cultivation. Mental power gradually combining with that which is purely physical, a farm of 200 bushels may now be produced at diminished cost. So, too, with others — the one of 300 being obtained in return for less labor than had, at the first, been given for one of 100; and one of 400 becoming, subsequently, the reward of much less effort. With each successive stage of improvement, the value of man increases, as compared with capital — present labor acquiring power at the expense of past accumulations, and rent diminishing in its proportions, though increasing in its quantity. The first proprietor could compel the laborer to rest content with a fourth of the product of his toil; but, when the second came to measure the power of his accumulations against those of the men around him, he found the relative position of man and matter had greatly changed. His own powers had increased, but so had theirs. He could obtain a farm of 200 bushels a-year at the cost of far less labor than before had been given for one of 100; but so might they. Instead, then, of demanding three-fourths, he now extracts but three-fifths — receiving 120, in lieu of the 75 of his predecessor, and leaving to the laborer 80 — being more than thrice the quantity at first allowed.

At the third stage, the same phenomena present themselves for consideration, and in yet greater force. A farm capable of yielding 300 bushels being now obtainable at the cost of far less labor than before had been expended in obtaining one of 200, its owner treats with laborers of greater power — with men who are themselves accumulating capital. Demanding now but half the product, he receives 150 — leaving to the laborer 150, where his immediate predecessor had left but 80. Wages have now risen to 150 bushels — greatly facilitating the further increase of capital. Moving with constantly accelerated force, the progress towards the creation of still improved machinery becomes far more rapid than it before had been; and now a farm capable of yielding 400 bushels is obtained at the cost of far less effort, than had been required for producing the one of 300. The cost of *reproduction* having thus fallen, its owner is forced to content himself with 45 *per cent.* — taking 180, and leaving to the laborer 220.

At the fifth stage, the proportion of the capitalist falls to two-fifths — the power of the community to command the services of nature having so much increased, that a farm of 600 bushels may be obtained in return to half the effort that had been required for any of its predecessors. So, too, with the next, yielding 1000 bushels. Wages having grown in a corresponding degree, the laborer, measuring his powers against the labor for which the new farm could be exchanged, finds himself entitled to claim two-thirds — leaving to the owner but a single third, where his early predecessor had claimed and received three-fourths.

In all the distribution thus effected, the capitalist profits by obtaining a *constantly increased quantity* resulting from a *constantly diminished proportion* of a constantly augmenting product; but the laborer profits still more largely — retaining for himself a constantly increasing proportion of that augmented quantity, as here is shown: —

	Total	Share of capital	Share of labor
First	100	75	25
Second	200	120	80
Third	300	150	150
Fourth	400	180	220
Fifth	600	240	360
Sixth	1000	333	667

The power of capital has, thus, little more than quadrupled, while that of labor has increased more than six-and-twenty times. The more rapid the reduction of the capitalist's share, the greater is the tendency towards increase in the proportion of fixed to floating capital, and to further decrease in the share that can be claimed as rent. With the growth of the power of man over matter, there is, therefore, a steady tendency to decline in the power of man over his fellow-man, and to the establishment of equality among the various portions of the human race. That the weak may find themselves on a level with the strong, and that the woman may take her place by the side of the being who everywhere has been her master, all that is required is that wealth be permitted to grow — that association be allowed to increase — and that individuality be developed, by means of that diversification of employments which is indispensable to rapidity in the circulation, and to the power of further progress. . . .

Such is the course of things in every country in which wealth and population are permitted to increase, and commerce is allowed to extend itself — all existing commodities then necessarily declining in their value as compared with labor, and labor rising as compared with them, because of constant diminution in the cost of reproduction. In Prussia, forty years since, a third of the product was regarded as the share to which the tenant might equitably be entitled. Since then — labor having become greatly more productive — the laborer's proportion has rapidly increased. So, too, is it in Russia and in Spain; whereas, in Ireland, India, Mexico, and Turkey, it has steadily declined — wealth, in all those countries, tending downwards, instead of upwards.

Wealth *should* grow more rapidly than population. Its growth, however, being in the direct ratio of the rapidity of circulation, it is necessarily slow in all the countries of advancing centralization — that being the certain road towards slavery, and political and moral death. Every increase in the ratio of wealth to population, is attended with an augmentation of the power of the laborer, as compared with that of landed or other capital. We all see, that when ships are more numerous than cargoes, freights are low; and, *vice versâ*, that when cargoes are more abundant than ships, freights are high. When ploughs and horses more abound than ploughmen, the latter fix the wages; but when ploughmen are more abundant than ploughs, the owners of the latter determine the distribution of the product. Wealth increasing rapidly, new soils are brought into cultivation, and more ploughmen are required. The demand for ploughs producing a demand for more men to mine the coal and smelt the ore, the iron-master becomes a competitor for the laborer, who obtains a larger proportion of the constantly increasing return to labor. He, in turn, becoming a better purchaser of cloth, the manufacturer becomes a competitor with the iron-master and the farmer for his services. His proportion being again increased, he now requires sugar, and tea, and coffee; and next, the ship-master competes with the manufacturer, the iron-master, and the farmer. With the growth of wealth and population, there is, thus, a constant increase in the demand for mental and physical effort — the increased productiveness of which, and the consequently increased facility of accumulating wealth, are followed necessarily, and certainly, by an increase of the laborer's proportion. His wages rising, the *proportion* of the capitalist falls; yet now the latter accumulates fortune more rapidly than ever — his interest, and that of the laborer, being in perfect harmony with each other. Seeking evidence of this, we find it in the constantly increasing amount of the rental of France and England, derived from the appropriation of a constantly decreasing proportion of the product of the land; as well as in the enormous amount of railroad tolls, derived from a charge for transportation that sinks into insignificance, when compared with those of the wagoner and the turnpike owner. The highest evidence of increasing wealth, is to be found in the reduction of the capitalist's proportion; and yet, the cardinal principle of the Ricardo-Malthusian doctrine is found in the assertion, that, with the growth of wealth and population, that proportion must increase. . . .

How stands it with the laborer? Seeing that, with every increase in the number and quality of spades and ploughs, engines and roads, mills and factories, his labor becomes more productive — that, with every increase in the ratio which spades and ploughs, engines and mills, bear to the men by whom they are to be employed, he is enabled to retain an increased proportion of the larger product — and that, whereas, when the land in cultivation yielded a net product of only six bushels to the acre, the owner took two-thirds, leaving him but two, now, when it yields forty bushels, he takes but a fifth, leaving him thirty-two — he *feels* that his interests are, like those of the rent receiver, directly advanced by every measure tending to the augmentation of wealth, and to the promotion of improvement in the modes of cultivation.

The harmony of all the permanent interests of man being perfect, it would seem to be required, only, that men should be persuaded of its existence — appreciating fully the advantages of co-operation over antagonism, and seeing that, like mercy —

> "It droppeth as the gentle rain from heaven,
> Upon the place beneath" ——

blessing both "him that gives, and him that takes," to induce all honest and enlightened men to an effort for enabling their fellowmen, everywhere, to indulge their natural desire for association and combination — the husbandman and the artisan taking their places by each other's side. The necessity for this, and the advantages to be derived from it by all — Gaul and Briton — Russian and American — Turk and Christian — being more fully understood, peace and commerce would take the place of trading jealousy and universal discord. The harmony of classes thus begetting a harmony of nations, the love of peace would diffuse itself throughout the earth. All would then become satisfied that, in the laws which govern the relations of man with his fellow-man, there reign the same beautiful simplicity and harmony everywhere else so abundantly evident; all, by degrees, would learn, that their own interests would be best promoted by respecting, in others, those rights of person and property they desired to have respected in themselves; and all become, at length, convinced that the whole of social science is embraced in the brief words of the great founder of Christianity: "Do unto others as ye would that others should do unto you."

Mr. [David] Ricardo's system is one of discords. Its parts not agreeing with each other, its whole tends to the promotion of war among both classes and nations. Professing an admiration for freedom of commerce, he teaches that a monopoly of the land is in accordance with a great law of nature. Believing in freedom of action, he teaches that if men and women *will* unite in marriage — thus doing that which most stimulates to exertion, and most tends to improve both heart and mind — starvation is to be their probable reward. Thoroughly admiring sound morality, he enforces the advantages of celibacy — thus affording countenance to the many restrictions by which marriage is prevented, and profligacy promoted. Professing a desire for free trade in corn, he teaches the landlord, that his interests will be injuriously affected by it. Anxious to improve the condition of the people, he assures the land-owner, that all wealth appropriated to improvement in the modes of cultivation, must diminish the progress of rent. Desiring that the rights of property may be respected, he instructs the laborer, that the interests of the land-owner are to be promoted by every measure tending to produce a scarcity of food — rent being paid because of an exercise of power on the part of the few, who have appropriated to themselves, that which a beneficent Deity intended for the common good of all. His book is the true manual of the demagogue — seeking power by means of agrarianism, war, and plunder. Its lessons being inconsistent with those afforded by the study of all well-observed facts, and inconsistent even with themselves, the sooner they shall come to be discarded the better will it be, for the interests of landlord and tenant, manufacturer and mechanic, and mankind at large. . . .

All the facts thus far laid before to the reader, in relation to wages, profits, and rents, and all those presented by the history of the world, now range themselves under the following propositions: —

That, in the early periods of society, population being small, and widely scattered, the possession of a small amount of capital gives to its owner a great amount of power — enabling him to hold the laborer dependent on his will, as serf or slave:

That, with growth of wealth and numbers, the power of combination increases, with great increase in the productiveness of labor, and in the power of accumulation — every step in that direction, being attended by decline in the power of the already existing capital to command the services of the laborer, and by increase of power on the part of the latter to command the aid of capital:

That the *proportion* of the increased product of labor assigned to the laborer tends, thus, steadily to increase, while that of the capitalist tends, as regularly, to decline:

That the *quantity* assigned to both, increases — that of the laborer growing, however, far more rapidly than that retained by the capitalist — the latter having a smaller proportion of the augmented quantity, while the former has a constantly increasing proportion of the rapidly increasing quantity:

That the tendency to equality is, therefore, in the direct ratio of the growth of wealth, and consequent productiveness of labor:

That wealth grows in the ratio of the rapidity of circulation:

That the circulation increases in rapidity, as individuality is more and more developed — with growing power for the diversification of employments among those who labor:

That, the more rapid the circulation, the larger must be the proportion of the laborer, and the greater must be the tendency towards equality, elevation, and freedom, among the people — and the greater strength of the State.

Wage-Labor and Capital
(1849)

KARL MARX

What is it that takes place in the exchange between the capitalist and the wage-labor?

The laborer receives means of subsistence in exchange for his labor-power; but the capitalist receives, in exchange for his means of subsistence, labor, the productive activity of the laborer, the creative force by which the worker not only replaces what he consumes, but also *gives to the accumulated labor a greater value than it previously possessed.* The laborer gets from the capitalist a portion of the existing means of subsistence. For what purpose do these *means of subsistence* serve him? For immediate consumption. But as soon as I consume means of subsistence, they are irrevocably lost to me, unless I employ the time during which these means sustain my life in producing new means of subsistence, in creating by my labor new values in place of the values lost in consumption. But it is just this noble reproductive power that the laborer surrenders to the capitalist in exchange for means of subsistence received. Consequently, he has lost it for himself.

Let us take an example. For one dollar a laborer works all day long in the fields of a farmer, to whom he thus secures a return of two dollars. The farmer not only receives the replaced value which he has given to the day-laborer; he has doubled it. Therefore he has consumed the one dollar that he gave to the day-laborer in a fruitful, productive manner. For the one dollar he has bought the labor-power of the day-laborer, which creates products of the soil of twice the value, and out of one dollar makes two. The day-laborer, on the contrary, receives in the place of his productive force, whose results he has just surrendered to the farmer, one dollar, which he exchanges for *means of subsistence*, which he consumes more or less quickly. The one dollar has therefore been consumed in a double manner — *reproductively* for the capitalist, for it has been exchanged for labor-power, which brought forth two dollars; *unproductively* for the worker, for it has been exchanged for means of subsistence which are lost for ever, and whose value he can obtain again only by repeating the same exchange with the farmer. *Capital therefore presupposes wage-*

From Karl Marx, *Wage-Labor and Capital* (New York: New York Labor News Company, 1902), 39–60. Friedrich Engels revised Marx's text in 1891. The revised version is printed here.

labor; wage-labor presupposes capital. They condition each other; each brings the other into existence.

Does a worker in a cotton factory produce only cotton goods? No. He produces capital. He produces values which serve anew to command his work and to create by means of its new values.

Capital can multiply itself only by exchanging itself for labor-power, by calling wage-labor into life. The labor-power of the wage-laborer can exchange itself for capital only by increasing capital, by strengthening that very power whose slave it is. *Increase of capital, therefore, is increase of the proletariat, i.e., of the working class.*

And so, the bourgeoisie and its economists maintain that the interest of the capitalist and of the laborer is the same. And in fact, so they are! The worker perishes if capital does not keep him busy. Capital perishes if it does not exploit labor-power, which, in order to exploit, it must buy. The more quickly the capital destined for production — the productive capital — increases, the more prosperous industry is, the more the bourgeoisie enriches itself, the better business gets, so many more workers does the capitalist need, so much the dearer does the worker sell himself.

The fastest possible growth of productive capital is, therefore, the indispensable condition for a tolerable life to the laborer.

But what is growth of productive capital? Growth of the power of accumulated labor over living labor; growth of the rule of the bourgeoisie over the working class. When wage-labor produces the alien wealth of dominating it, the power hostile to it, capital, there flow back to it its means of employment, *i.e.*, its means of subsistence, under the condition that it again become a part of capital, that it become again the lever whereby capital is to be forced into an accelerated expansive movement.

To say that the interests of capital and the interests of the workers are identical, signifies only this, that capital and wage labor are two sides of one and the same relation. The one conditions the other in the same way that the usurer and the borrower condition each other.

As long as the wage-laborer remains a wage-laborer, his lot is dependent upon capital. That is what the boasted community of interests between worker and capitalists amounts to.

If capital grows, the mass of wage-labor grows, the number of wage-workers increases; in a word, the sway of capital extends over a greater mass of individuals.

Let us suppose the most favorable case: if productive capital grows, the demand for labor grows. It therefore increases the price of labor-power, wages.

A house may be large or small; as long as the neighboring houses are likewise small, it satisfies all social requirements for a residence. But let there arise next to the little house a palace, and the little house shrinks into a hut. The little house now makes it clear that its inmate has no social position at all to maintain, or but a very insignificant one; and however high it may shoot up in the course of civilisation, if the neighboring palace rises in equal or even in greater measure, the occupant of the relatively little house will always find himself more uncomfortable, more dissatisfied, more cramped within his four walls.

An appreciable rise in wages presupposes a rapid growth of productive capital. Rapid growth of productive capital calls forth just as rapid a growth of wealth, of luxury, of social needs and social pleasures. Therefore, although the pleasures of the laborer have increased, the social gratification which they afford has fallen in comparison with the increased pleasures of the capitalist, which are inaccessible to the worker, in comparison with the stage of development of society in general. Our wants and pleasures have their origin in society; we therefore measure them in relation to society; we do not measure them in relation to the objects which serve for their gratification. Since they are of a social nature, they are of a relative nature. . . .

Wages are determined above all by their relations to the gain, the profit, of the capitalist. In other words, wages are a proportionate, relative quantity.

Real wages express the price of labor-power in relation to the price of other commodities; *relative wages*, on the other hand, express the share of immediate labor in the value newly created by it, in relation to the share of it which falls to accumulated labor, to capital.

We have said: "Wages are not a share of the worker in the commodities produced by him. Wages are that part of already existing commodities with which the capitalist buys a certain amount of productive labor-power." But the capitalist must replace these wages out of the price for which he sells the product made by the worker; he must so replace it that, as a rule, there remains to him a surplus above the cost of production expended by him, that is, he must get a profit. The selling price of the commodities produced by the worker is divided, from the point of view of the capitalist, into three parts: *First*, the replacement of the price of the raw materials advanced by him, in addition to the replacement of the wear and tear of the tools, machines, and other instruments of labor likewise advanced by him; *second*, the replacement of the wages advanced; and *third*, the surplus left over, i.e., the profit of the capitalist. While the first part merely replaces *previously existing values*, it is evident that the replacement of the wages and the surplus (the profit of capital) are as a whole taken out of the *new value*, which is *produced by the labor of the worker* and added to the raw materials. And *in this sense* we can view wages as well as profit, for the purpose of comparing them with each other, as shares in the product of the worker.

Real wages may remain the same, they may even rise, nevertheless the relative wages may fall. Let us suppose, for instance, that all means of subsistence have fallen two-thirds in price, while the day's wages have fallen but one-third; for example, from three to two dollars. Although the worker can now get a greater amount of commodities with these two dollars than he formerly did with three dollars, yet his wages have decreased in proportion to the gain of the capitalist. The profit of the capitalist — the manufacturer's for instance — has increased by one dollar, which means that for a smaller amount of exchange values, which he pays to the worker, the latter must produce a greater amount of exchange values than before. The share of capital in proportion to the share of labor has risen. The distribution of social wealth between capital and labor has become still more unequal. The capitalist commands a greater amount of labor with the same capital. The power of the capitalist class over the working class has grown, the social position of the worker has become worse, has been forced down still another degree below that of the capitalist.

What, then, is the general law that determines the rise and fall of wages and profit in their reciprocal relation?

They stand in inverse proportion to each other. The share of (profit) increases in the same proportion in which the share of labor (wages) falls, and vice versa. Profit rises in the same degree in which wages fall; it falls in the same degree in which wages rise. . . .

We thus see *that, even if we keep ourselves within the relation of capital and wage-labor, the interests of capital and the interests of wage-labor are diametrically opposed to each other.*

A rapid growth of capital is synonymous with a rapid growth of profits. Profits can grow rapidly only when the price of labor — the relative wages — decrease just as rapidly. Relative wages may fall, although real wages rise simultaneously with nominal wages, with the money value of labor, provided only that the real wage does not rise in the same proportion as the profit. If, for instance, in good business years wages rise 5 per cent. while profits rise 30 per cent., the proportional, the relative wage has not *increased*, but *decreased*.

If, therefore, the income of the worker increases with the rapid growth of capital, there is at the same time a widening of the social chasm that divides the worker from the capitalist, an increase in the power of capital over labor, a great dependence of labor upon capital.

To say that "the worker has an interest in the rapid growth of capital," means only this; that the more speedily the worker augments the wealth of the capitalist, the larger will be the crumbs which fall to him, the greater will be the number of workers that can be called into existence, the more can the mass of slaves dependent upon capital be increased.

We have thus seen that even the *most favorable situation* for the working class, namely, the most rapid growth of capital, however much it may improve the material life of the worker, does not abolish the antagonism between his interests and the interests of the capitalist. *Profit and wages* remain as before, *in inverse proportion.*

If capital grows rapidly, wages may rise, but the profit of capital rises disproportionately faster. The material position of the worker has improved, but at the cost of his social position. The social chasm that separates him from the capitalist has widened.

Finally, to say that "the most favorable condition for wage-labor is the fastest possible growth of productive capital," is the same as to say: the quicker the working class multiplies and augments the power inimical to it — the wealth of another which lords it over that class — the more favorable will be the conditions under which it will be permitted to toil anew at the multiplication of bourgeois wealth, at the enlargement of the power of capital, content thus to forge for itself the golden chains by which the bourgeoisie drags it in its train.

Growth of productive capital and rise of wages, are they really so indissolubly united as the bourgeois economists maintain? We must not believe their mere words. We dare not believe them even when they claim that the fatter capital is the more will its slave be pampered. The bourgeoisie is too much enlightened, it keeps its accounts much too carefully, to share the prejudices of the feudal lord, who makes an ostentatious display of the magnificence of his retinue. The conditions of existence of the bourgeoisie compel it to attend carefully to its bookkeeping. We must therefore examine more closely into the following question:

In what manner does the growth of productive capital affect wages?

If as a whole, the productive capital of bourgeois society grows, there takes place a more many-sided accumulation of labor. The individual capitals increase in number and in magnitude. The multiplications of individual capitals *increases the competition among capitalists.* The *increasing magnitude* of individual capitals provides the means for *leading more powerful armies of workers with more gigantic instruments of war upon the industrial battlefield.*

The one capitalist can drive the other from the field and carry off his capital only by selling more cheaply. In order to sell more cheaply without ruining himself, he must produce more cheaply, *i.e.*, increase the productive force of labor as much as possible. But the productive power of labor is increased above all by a *greater division of labor* and by a more general introduction and constant improvement of *machinery*. The larger the army of workers among whom the labor is subdivided, the more gigantic the scale upon which machinery is introduced, the more in proportion does the cost of production decrease, the more fruitful is the labor. And so there arises among the capitalists a universal rivalry for the increase of the division of labor and of machinery and for their exploitation upon the greatest possible scale. If, now, by a greater division of labor, by the application and improvement of new machines, by a more advantageous exploitation of the forces of nature on a larger scale, a capitalist has found the means of producing with the same amount of labor (whether it be direct or accumulated labor) a larger amount of products of commodities than his competitors — if, for instance, he can produce a whole yard of linen in the same labor-time in which his competitors weave half a yard — how will this capitalist act?

He could keep on selling half a yard of linen at the old market price; but this would not have the effect of driving his opponents from the field and enlarging his own market. But his need of a market has increased in the same measure in which his productive power has extended. The more powerful and costly means of production that he has called into existence *enable* him, it is true, to sell his wares more cheaply, but they *compel* him at the same time *to sell more wares*, to get control of a very much *greater* market for his commodities; consequently, this capitalist will sell his half yard of linen more cheaply than his competitors.

But the capitalist will not sell the whole yard so cheaply as his competitors sell the half yard, although the production of the whole yard costs no more to him than does that of the half yard to the others. Otherwise he would make no extra profit, and would get back in exchange only the cost of production. He might obtain a greater income from having set in motion a larger capital, but not from having made a greater profit on his capital than the others. Moreover, he attains the object he is aiming at if he prices his goods only a small percentage lower than his competitors. He drives them off the field, he wrests from them at least a part of their market, by *underselling* them.

And finally, let us remember that the current price always stands either *above or below the cost of production*, according as the sale of a commodity take place in the favorable or unfavorable period of the industry. According as the market price of the yard of linen stands above or below its former cost of production, will the percentage vary at which the capitalist who has made use of the new and more fruitful means of production sell above his real cost of production.

But the *privilege* of our capitalist is not of long duration. Other competing capitalists introduce the same machines, the same division of labor, and introduce them upon the same or even upon a greater scale. And finally this introduction becomes so universal that the price of the linen is lowered not only below its old, but even below its new cost of production.

The capitalists therefore find themselves, in their mutual relations, in the same situation in which they were before the introduction of the new means of production; and if they are by these means enabled to offer double the product at the old price, they are now forced to furnish double the product for less than the old price. Having arrived at the new point, the new cost of production, the battle for supremacy in the market has to be fought out anew. Given more division of labor and more machinery, and there results a greater scale upon which division of labor and machinery are exploited. And competition again brings the same reaction against this result.

We thus see how the method of production and the means of production are constantly enlarged, revolutionised, how *division of labor necessarily draws after it greater division of labor, the employment of machinery greater employment of machinery, work upon a large scale work upon a still greater scale.* This is the law that continually throws capitalist production out of its old ruts and compels capital to strain ever more the productive forces of labor *for the very reason* that it has already strained them — the law that grants it no respite, and constantly shouts in its ear: March! march!

This is no other law than that which, within the periodical fluctuations of commerce, necessarily *adjusts the price of a commodity to its cost of production.*

No matter how powerful the means of production which a capitalist may bring into the field, competition will make their adoption general; and from the moment that they have been generally adopted, the sole result of the greater productiveness of his capital will be that he must furnish *at the same price,* ten, twenty, one hundred times as much as before. But since he must find a market for, perhaps, a thousand times as much, in order to outweigh the lower selling price by the greater quantity of the sales; since now a more extensive sale is necessary not only to gain a greater profit, but also in order to replace the cost of production (the instrument of production itself grows always more costly, as we have seen), and since this more extensive sale has become a question of life and death not only for him, but also for his rivals, the old struggle must begin again, and it is all the more violent the more powerful the means of production already invented are. *The division of labor and the application of machinery will therefore take a fresh start, and upon an even greater scale.*

Whatever be the power of the means of production which are employed, competition seeks to rob capital of the golden fruits of this power by reducing the price of commodities to the cost of production; in the same measure in which production is cheapened, *i.e.*, in the same measure in which more can be produced with the same amount of labor, it compels by a law which is irresistible a still greater cheapening of production, the sale of ever greater masses of product for smaller prices. Thus the capitalist will have gained nothing more by his efforts than the obligation to furnish a greater product in the same labor-time; in a word, more difficult conditions for the profitable employment of his capital. While competition, therefore, constantly pursues him with its law of the cost of production and turns against himself every weapon that he forges against his rivals, the capitalist continually seeks to get the best of competition by restlessly introducing further subdivision of labor and new machines, which, though more expensive, enable him to produce more cheaply, instead of waiting until the new machines shall have been rendered obsolete by competition.

If we now conceive this feverish agitation as it operates in the *market of the whole world,* we shall be in a position to comprehend how the growth, accumulation, and concentration of capital bring in their train an ever more detailed subdivision of labor, an ever greater improvement of old machines, and a constant application of new machines — a process which goes on uninterruptedly, with feverish haste, and upon an ever more gigantic scale.

But what effect do these conditions, which are inseparable from the growth of productive capital, have upon the determination of wages?

The greater *division of labor* enables one laborer to accomplish the work of five, ten, or twenty laborers; it therefore increases competition among the laborers fivefold, tenfold, or twentyfold. The laborers compete not only by selling themselves one cheaper than the other, but also by one doing the work of five, then ten, or twenty; and they are forced to compete in this manner by the division of labor, which is introduced and steadily improved by capital.

Furthermore, to the same degree in which the division of labor increases, is the labor simplified. The special skill of the laborer becomes worthless. He becomes transformed into a simple monotonous force of production, with neither physical nor mental elasticity. His work becomes accessible to all; therefore competitors press upon him from all sides. Moreover, it must be remembered that the more simple, the more easily learned the work is, so much the less is its cost of production, the expense of its acquisition, and so much the lower must the wages sink — for, like the price of any other commodity, they are determined by the cost of production. Therefore, *in the same measure in which labor becomes more unsatisfactory, more repulsive, do competition increase and wages decrease*. The laborer seeks to maintain the total of his wages for a given time by performing more labor, either by working a greater number of hours, or by accomplishing more in the same number of hours. Thus, urged on by want, he himself multiplies the disastrous effects of division of labor. The result is: *the more he works, the less wages he receives*. And for this simple reason: the more he works, the more he competes against his fellow workmen, the more he compels them to compete against him, and to offer themselves on the same wretched conditions as he does; so that, in the last analysis, *he competes against himself as a member of the working class.*

Machinery produces the same effects, but upon a much larger scale. It supplants skilled laborers by unskilled, men by women, adults by children; where newly introduced, it throws workers upon the streets in great masses; and as it becomes more highly developed and more productive it discards them in additional though smaller numbers.

We have hastily sketched in broad outlines the *industrial war of capitalists among themselves. This war has the peculiarity that the battles in it are won less by recruiting than by discharging the army of workers. The generals (the capitalists) vie with one another as to who can discharge the greatest number of industrial soldiers.*

The economists tell us, to be sure, that those laborers who have been rendered superfluous by machinery find new avenues of employment. They dare not assert directly that the same laborers that have been discharged find situations in new branches of labor. Facts cry out too loudly against this lie. Strictly speaking, they only maintain that new means of employment will be found *for other sections of the working class;* for example, for that portion of the young generation of laborers who were about to enter upon that branch of industry which had just been abolished. Of course, this is a great satisfaction to the disabled laborers. There will be no lack of fresh exploitable blood and muscle for the Messrs. Capitalists — the dead may bury their dead. This consolation seems to be intended more for the comfort of the capitalists themselves than of their laborers. If the whole class of the wage-laborer were to be annihilated by machinery, how terrible that would be for capital, *which, without wage-labor, ceases to be capital!*

But even if we assume that all who are directly forced out of employment by machinery, as well as all of the rising generation who were waiting for a chance of employment in the same branch of industry, do actually find some new employment — are we to believe that this new employment will pay as high wages as did the one they have lost? If it did, *it would be in contradiction to all the laws of political economy.* We have seen how modern industry always tends to the substitution of the simpler and more subordinate employments for the higher and more complex ones. How, then, could a mass of workers thrown out of one branch of industry by machinery find refuge in another branch, unless they were to be paid more poorly?

An exception to the law has been adduced, namely, the workers who are employed in the manufacture of machinery itself. As soon as there is in industry a greater demand for and a greater consumption of machinery, it is said that the number of machines must necessarily increase; consequently, also, the manufacture of machines; consequently, also, the employment of workers in machine manufacture; — and the workers employed in this branch of industry are skilled, even educated, workers.

Since the year 1840 this assertion, which even before that date was only half true, has lost all semblance of truth; for the most diverse machines are now applied to the manufacture of the machines themselves on quite as extensive a scale as in the manufacture of cotton yarn, and the laborers employed in machine factories can but play the rôle of very stupid machines alongside of the highly ingenious machines.

But in place of the man who has been dismissed by the machine, the factory may employ, perhaps, three children and one woman! And must not the wages of the man have previously sufficed for the three children and one woman? Must not the minimum wages have sufficed for the preservation and propagation of the race? What, then, do these beloved bourgeois phrases prove? Nothing more than that now four times as many workers' lives are used up as there were previously, in order to obtain the livelihood of one working family.

To sum up: *the more productive capital grows, the more it extends the division of labor and the application of machinery; the more the division of labor and the application of machinery extend, the more does competition extend among the workers, the more do their wages shrink together*.

In addition, the working class is also recruited from the *higher strata* of society; a mass of small business men and of people living upon the interest of their capitals is precipitated into the ranks of the working class, and they will have nothing else to do than to stretch out their arms alongside of the arms of the workers. Thus the forest of outstretched arms, begging for work, grows ever thicker, while the arms themselves grow ever leaner.

It is evident that the small manufacturer cannot survive in a struggle in which the first condition of success is production upon an ever greater scale. It is evident that the small manufacturer cannot at the same time be a big manufacturer.

That the interest on capital decreases in the same ratio in which the mass and number of capitals increase, that it diminishes with the growth of capital, that therefore the small capitalist can no longer live on his interest, but must consequently throw himself upon industry by joining the ranks of the small manufacturers and thereby increasing the number of candidates for the proletariat — all this requires no further elucidation.

Finally, in the same measure in which the capitalists are compelled, by the movement described above, to exploit the already existing gigantic means of production on an ever-increasing scale, and for this purpose to set in motion all the mainsprings of credit, in the same measure do they increase the industrial earthquakes, in the midst of which the commercial world can preserve itself only by sacrificing a portion of its wealth, its products, and even its forces of production, to the gods of the lower world — in short, the *crises* increase. They become more frequent and more violent, if for no other reason, than for this alone, that in the same measure in which the mass of products grows, and therefore the needs for extensive markets, in the same measure does the world market shrink ever more, and ever fewer markets remain to be exploited, since every previous crisis has subjected to the commerce of the world a hitherto unconquered or but superficially exploited market. But capital not only lives upon labor. Like a master, at once distinguished and barbarous, it drags with it into its grave the corpses of its slaves, whole hecatombs of workers, who perish in the crises. We thus see that *if capital grows rapidly, competition among the workers grows with even greater rapidity, i.e., the means of employment and subsistence for the working class decrease in proportion even more rapidly; but, this notwithstanding, the rapid growth of capital is the most favorable condition for wage-labor.*

VI

DARWINISM

Herbert Spencer (1820–1903) published his first work, Social Statics, *in 1851, eight years before the publication of Charles Darwin's* On the Origin of Species. *In* Social Statics, *Spencer set out the anti-reformist, anti-statist doctrines that were later to be collectively described as Social Darwinism. To Spencer's claim that attempts to influence social development violated immutable natural laws, Darwin added the clinching argument that nature had, in any case, provided its own mechanism for development: natural selection. Darwin's ideas thus did not initiate, but strongly reinforced, a developing body of social thought whose outstanding characteristic was the application of principles derived from science, especially biological science, to social analysis. The Social Darwinists' monistic premise that the same laws governed nature and society led to the familiar arguments of late nineteenth-century conservatives in favor of laissez-faire and in opposition to collective endeavor.*

This phase of conservative thought departed significantly from the tradition of Edmund Burke and John Adams. Earlier conservatives, particularly in Europe, had stressed authority, tradition, and the collective sentiments of the community as the determining elements of social life. But the Social Darwinists were individualistic to the point of being virtually anarchic; their system was founded on a theory of transformation, drawing support from biological discoveries that shattered existing conventions. Most important, the Social Darwinists eschewed any appeal to sentiment and instead grounded their ideas in supposedly dispassionate, objective science. But in spite of these modifications, Social Darwinism still stood within the conservative tradition. Darwinian ideas served the usual conservative purposes of justifying the status quo and opposing rapid social change.

Spencer, an accomplished dilettante, probably had the greatest influence of any Victorian thinker on both European and American social thought. From him William Graham Sumner (1840–1910), professor of political and social science at Yale, derived many of his ideas. Yet Sumner could never accept Spencer's optimistic conclusions about the course of evolution; he remained profoundly — and perhaps uncharacteristically for an American thinker — pessimistic about human society. The democratic social order that he praised he regarded as only a passing phase in the development of civilization, doomed to extinction when growing populations began to exhaust the available supply of land. But he shared with Spencer the notions that the individual, not the group, was the basic social component, that only the fittest individuals should survive in the struggle against nature and other men, and that the state should refrain from interfering in that struggle.

The ideas of Spencer and Sumner were well fitted to a burgeoning capitalist economy that required the services of freewheeling entrepreneurs. But when the industrial conditions those entrepreneurs fostered began to threaten the welfare and freedom of other men, a different social analysis emerged — though one still grounded in Darwinian principles. The English biologist Thomas Henry Huxley (1825–1895) and the American sociologist Lester Frank Ward (1841–1913) were leading proponents of that analysis, which the historian Eric Goldman has called Reform Darwinism.

Where thinkers like Spencer and Sumner had emphasized the essential unity of the natural and social orders, the Reform Darwinists insisted on the difference between society and nature. Man was indeed, they said, the highest product of evolution and natural selection. But with his appearance a fundamentally new element had been introduced into the evolutionary scheme: man had an active intelligence and could thus shape his environment to his will, rather than simply adapt to it. The Reform Darwinists also departed from the system of Spencer and Sumner on a moral level when they denied that ethical principles could be derived from observed scientific facts. Finally, they rejected the individualistic ideas of the conservative Social Darwinists and pointed to the possibility and benefit of collective human effort. In particular, they argued that the most logical instrumentality of collective endeavor was the state, that bogey of laissez-faire conservatives. Corporate pursuit of the general welfare through the state, they held, was the next logical and necessary step in the evolution of human society. Thus, thinkers like Huxley and Ward stayed within the general framework of Darwinian ideas, but came to conclusions nearly opposite those of Spencer and Sumner. In so doing they set the stage for the development of a general theory of the welfare state that preoccupied many European and American intellectuals in the early twentieth century.

The Coming Slavery
(1884)

HERBERT SPENCER

Laws to check intemperance, beginning in early times and coming down to our own times, when further restraints on the sale of intoxicating liquors occupy nights every session, not having done what was expected, there come demands for more thorough-going laws, locally preventing the sale altogether; and here, as in America, these will doubtless be followed by demands that prevention shall be made universal. All the many appliances for "stamping out" epidemic diseases not having succeeded in preventing outbreaks of small-pox, fevers, and the like, a further remedy is applied for in the shape of police-power to search houses for diseased persons, and authority for medical officers to examine any one they think fit, to see whether he or she is suffering from an infectious or contagious malady. Habits of improvidence having for generations been cultivated by the Poor-Law, and the improvident enabled to multiply, the evils produced by compulsory charity are now proposed to be met by compulsory insurance.

The extension of this policy, causing extension of corresponding ideas, fosters everywhere the tacit assumption that Government should step in whenever anything is not going right. "Surely you would not have this misery continue!" exclaims some one, if you hint a demurrer to much that is now being said and done. Observe what is implied by this exclamation. It takes for granted, first, that all suffering ought to be prevented, which is not true: much suffering is curative, and prevention of it is prevention of a remedy. In the second place, it takes for granted that every evil can be removed: the truth being that with the existing defects of human nature, many evils can only be thrust out of one place or form into another place or form — often being increased by the change. The exclamation also implies the unhesitating belief, here especially concerning us, that evils of all kinds should be dealt with by the State. There does not occur the inquiry whether there are at work other agencies capable of dealing with evils, and whether the evils in question may not be among those which are best dealt with by these other agencies. (And obviously, the more numerous governmental interventions become, the more confirmed does this habit of thought grow, and the more loud and perpetual the demands for intervention.)

From Herbert Spencer, *The Man Versus the State* (New York: D. Appleton, 1891), 27–43.

Every extension of the regulative policy involves an addition to the regulative agents — a further growth of officialism and an increasing power of the organization formed of officials. Take a pair of scales with many shot in the one and a few in the other. Lift shot after shot out of the loaded scale and put it into the unloaded scale. Presently you will produce a balance; and if you go on, the position of the scales will be reversed. Suppose the beam to be unequally divided, and let the lightly loaded scale be at the end of a very long arm; then the transfer of each shot, producing a much greater effect, will far sooner bring about a change of position. I use the figure to illustrate what results from transferring one individual after another from the regulated mass of the community to the regulating structures. The transfer weakens the one and strengthens the other in a far greater degree than is implied by the relative change of numbers. A comparatively small body of officials, coherent, having common interests, and acting under central authority, has an immense advantage over an incoherent public which has no settled policy, and can be brought to act unitedly only under strong provocation. Hence an organization of officials, once passing a certain stage of growth, becomes less and less resistible; as we see in the bureaucracies of the Continent.

Not only does the power of resistance of the regulated part decrease in a geometrical ratio as the regulating part increases, but the private interests of many in the regulated part itself, make the change of ratio still more rapid. In every circle conversations show that now, when the passing of competitive examinations renders them eligible for the public service, youths are being educated in such ways that they may pass them and get employment under Government. One consequence is that men who might otherwise reprobate some further growth of officialism, are led to look on it with tolerance, if not favourably, as offering possible careers for those dependent on them and those related to them. Any one who remembers the numbers of upper-class and middle-class families anxious to place their children, will see that no small encouragement to the spread of legislative control is now coming from those who, but for the personal interests thus arising, would be hostile to it.

This pressing desire for careers is enforced by the preference for careers which are thought respectable. "Even if his salary is small, his occupation will be that of a gentleman," thinks the father, who wants to get a Government-clerkship for his son. And this relative dignity of State-servants as compared with those occupied in business, increases as the administrative organization becomes a larger and more powerful element in society, and tends more and more to fix the standard of honour. The prevalent ambition with a young Frenchman is to get some small official post in his locality, to rise thence to a place in the local centre of government, and finally to reach some head office in Paris. And in Russia, where that universality of State-regulation which characterizes the militant type of society has been carried furthest, we see this ambition pushed to its extreme. Says Mr. Wallace, quoting a passage from a play: — "All men, even shopkeepers and cobblers, aim at becoming officers, and the man who has passed his whole life without official rank seems to be not a human being."

These various influences working from above downwards meet with an increasing response of expectations and solicitations proceeding from below upwards. The hard-worked and over-burdened who form the great majority, and still more the incapables perpetually helped who are ever led to look for more help, are ready supporters of schemes which promise them this or the other benefit by State agency, and ready believers of those who tell them that such benefits can be given, and ought to be given. They listen with eager faith to all builders of political air-castles, from Oxford graduates down to Irish irreconcilables; and every additional tax-supported appliance for their welfare raises hopes of further ones. Indeed the more numerous public instrumentalities become, the more is there generated in citizens the notion that everything is to be done for them, and nothing by them. Each generation is made less familiar with the attainment of desired ends by individual actions or private combinations, and more familiar with the attainment of them by governmental agencies; until, eventually, governmental agencies come to be thought of as the only available agencies. This result was well shown in the recent Trades-Unions Congress at Paris. The English delegates, reporting to their constituents, said that between themselves and their foreign colleagues "the point of difference was the extent to which the State should be asked to protect labour": reference being thus made to the fact, conspicuous in the reports of the proceedings, that the French delegates always invoked governmental power as the only means of satisfying their wishes.

The diffusion of education has worked, and will work still more, in the same direction. "We must educate our masters," is the well-known saying of a Liberal who opposed the last extension of the franchise. Yes, if the education were worthy to be so called, and were relevant to the political enlightenment needed, much might be hoped from it. But knowing rules of syntax, being able to add up correctly, having geographical information, and a memory stocked with the dates of kings' accessions and generals' victories, no more implies fitness to form political conclusions than acquirement of skill in drawing implies expertness in telegraphing, or than ability to play cricket implies proficiency on the violin. "Surely," rejoins some one, "facility in reading opens the way to political knowledge." Doubtless; but will the way be followed? Table-talk proves that nine out of ten people read what amuses them or interests them rather than what instructs them; and that the last thing they read is something which tells them disagreeable truths or dispels groundless hopes. That popular education results in an extensive reading of publications which foster pleasant illusions rather than of those which insist on hard realities, is beyond question. Says "A Mechanic," writing in the *Pall Mall Gazette* of December 3, 1883: —

> Improved education instils the desire for culture — culture instils the desire for many things as yet quite beyond working men's reach . . . . in the furious competition to which the present age is given up they are utterly impossible to the poorer classes; hence they are discontented with things as they are, and the more educated the more discontented. Hence, too, Mr. Ruskin and Mr. Morris are regarded as true prophets by many of us.

And that the connexion of cause and effect here alleged is a real one, we may see clearly enough in the present state of Germany.

Being possessed of electoral power, as are now the mass of those who are thus led to nurture sanguine anticipations of benefits to be obtained by social reorganization, it results that whoever seeks their votes must at least refrain from exposing their mistaken beliefs; even if he does not yield to the temptation to express agreement with them. Every candidate for Parliament is prompted to propose or support some new piece of *ad captandum* legislation. Nay, even the chiefs of parties — these anxious to retain office and those to wrest it from them — severally aim to get adherents by outbidding one another. Each seeks popularity by promising more than his opponent has promised, as we have lately seen. And then, as divisions in Parliament show us, the traditional loyalty to leaders overrides questions concerning the intrinsic propriety of proposed measures. Representatives are unconscientious enough to vote for Bills which they believe to be wrong in principle, because party-needs and regard for the next election demand it. And thus a vicious policy is strengthened even by those who see its viciousness.

Meanwhile there goes on out-of-doors an active propaganda to which all these influences are ancillary. Communistic theories, partially indorsed by one Act of Parliament after another, and tacitly if not avowedly favoured by numerous public men seeking supporters, are being advocated more and more vociferously under one or other form by popular leaders, and urged on by organized societies. There is the movement for land-nationalization which, aiming at a system of land-tenure equitable in the abstract, is, as all the world knows, pressed by Mr. George and his friends with avowed disregard for the just claims of existing owners, and as the basis of a scheme going more than half-way to State-socialism. And then there is the thorough-going Democratic Federation of Mr. Hyndman and his adherents. We are told by them that "the handful of marauders who now hold possession [of the land] have and can have no right save brute force against the tens of millions whom they wrong." They exclaim against "the shareholders who have been allowed to lay hands upon (!) our great railway communications." They condemn "above all, the active capitalist class, the loan-mongers, the farmers, the mine exploiters, the contractors, the middle-men, the factory-lords — these, the modern slave drivers" who exact "more and yet more surplus value out of the wage-slaves whom they employ." And they think it "high time" that trade should be "removed from the control of individual greed."

It remains to point out that the tendencies thus variously displayed, are being strengthened by press-advocacy, daily more pronounced. Journalists, always chary of saying that which is distasteful to their readers, are some of them going with the stream and adding to its force. Legislative meddlings which they would once have condemned they now pass in silence, if they do not advocate them; and they speak of *laissez-faire* as an exploded doctrine. "People are no longer frightened at the thought of socialism," is the statement which meets us one day. On another day, a town which does not adopt the Free Libraries Act is sneered at as being alarmed by a measure so moderately communistic. And then, along with editorial assertions that this economic evolution is coming and must be accepted, there is prominence given to the contributions of its advocates. Meanwhile those who regard the recent course of legislation as disastrous, and see that its future course is likely to be still more disastrous, are being reduced to silence by the belief that it is useless to reason with people in a state of political intoxication.

See, then, the many concurrent causes which threaten continually to accelerate the transformation now going on. There is that spread of regulation caused by following precedents, which become the more authoritative the further the policy is carried. There is that increasing need for administrative compulsions and restraints, which results from the unforeseen evils and shortcomings of preceding compulsions and restraints. Moreover, every additional State-interference strengthens the tacit assumption that it is the duty of the State to deal with all evils and secure all benefits. Increasing power of a growing administrative organization is accompanied by decreasing power of the rest of the society to resist its further growth and control. The multiplication of careers opened by a developing bureaucracy, tempts members of the classes regulated by it to favour its extension, as adding to the chances of safe and respectable places for their relatives. The people at large, led to look on benefits received through public agencies as gratis benefits, have their hopes continually excited by the prospects of more. A spreading education, furthering the diffusion of pleasing errors rather than of stern truths, renders such hopes both stronger and more general. Worse still, such hopes are ministered to by candidates for public choice, to augment their chances of success; and leading statesmen, in pursuit of party ends, bid for popular favour by countenancing them. Getting repeated justifications from new laws harmonizing with their doctrines, political enthusiasts and unwise philanthropists push their agitations with growing confidence and success. Journalism, ever responsive to popular opinion, daily strengthens it by giving it voice; while counter-opinion, more and more discouraged, finds little utterance.

Thus influences of various kinds conspire to increase corporate action and decrease individual action. And the change is being on all sides aided by schemers, each of whom thinks only of his pet project and not at all of the general re-organization which his, joined with others such, are working out. It is said that the French Revolution devoured its own children. Here an analogous catastrophe seems not unlikely. The numerous socialistic changes made by Act of Parliament, joined with the numerous others presently to be made, will by-and-by be all merged in State Socialism — swallowed in the vast wave which they have little by little raised.

"But why is this change described as 'the coming slavery'?" is a question which many will still ask. The reply is simple. All socialism involves slavery.

What is essential to the idea of a slave? We primarily think of him as one who is owned by another. To be more than nominal, however, the ownership must be shown by control of the slave's actions — a control which is habitually for the benefit of the controller. That which fundamentally distinguishes the slave is that he labours under coercion to satisfy another's desires. The relation admits of sundry gradations. Remembering that originally the slave is a prisoner whose life is at the mercy of his captor, it suffices here to note that there is a harsh form of slavery in which, treated as an animal, he has to expend his entire effort for his owner's advantage. Under a system less harsh, though occupied chiefly in working for his owner, he is allowed a short time in which to work for himself, and some ground on which to grow extra food. A further amelioration gives him power to sell the produce of his plot and keep the proceeds. Then we come to the still more moderated form which commonly arises where, having been a free man working on his own land, conquest turns him into what we distinguish as a serf; and he has to give to his owner each year a fixed amount of labour or produce, or both: retaining the rest himself. Finally, in some cases, as in Russia until recently, he is allowed to leave his owner's estate and work or trade for himself elsewhere, under the condition that he shall pay an annual sum. What is it which, in these cases, leads us to qualify our conception of the slavery as more or less severe? Evidently the greater or smaller extent to which effort is compulsorily expended for the benefit of another instead of for self-benefit. If all the slave's labour is for his owner the slavery is heavy, and if but little it is light. Take now a further step. Suppose an owner dies, and his estate with its slaves comes into the hands of trustees; or suppose the estate and everything on it to be bought by a company; is the condition of the slave any the better if the amount of his compulsory labour remains the same? Suppose that for a company we substitute the community; does it make any difference to the slave if the time he has to work for others is as great, and the time left for himself is as small, as before? The essential question is — How much is he compelled to labour for other benefit than his own, and how much can he labour for his own benefit? The degree of his slavery varies according to the ratio between that which he is forced to yield up and that which he is allowed to retain; and it matters not whether his master is a single person or a society. If, without option, he has to labour for the society, and receives from the general stock such portion as the society awards him, he becomes a slave to the society. Socialistic arrangements necessitate an enslavement of this kind; and towards such an enslavement many recent measures, and still more the measures advocated, are carrying us. Let us observe, first, their proximate effects, and then their ultimate effects.

The policy initiated by the Industrial Dwellings Acts admits of development, and will develop. Where municipal bodies turn housebuilders, they inevitably lower the values of houses otherwise built, and check the supply of more. Every dictation respecting modes of building and conveniences to be provided, diminishes the builder's profit, and prompts him to use his capital where the profit is not thus diminished. So, too, the owner, already finding that small houses entail much labour and many losses — already subject to troubles of inspection and interference, and to consequent costs, and having his property daily rendered a more undesirable investment, is prompted to sell; and as buyers are for like reasons deterred, he has to sell at a loss. And now these still-multiplying regulations, ending, it may be, as Lord Grey proposes, in one requiring the owner to maintain the salubrity of his houses by evicting dirty tenants, and thus adding to his other responsibilities that of inspector of nuisances, must further prompt sales and further deter purchasers: so necessitating greater depreciation. What must happen? The multiplication of houses, and especially small houses, being increasingly checked, there must come an increasing demand upon the local authority to make up for the deficient supply. More and more the municipal or kindred body will have to build houses, or to purchase houses rendered unsaleable to private persons in the way shown — houses which, greatly lowered in value as they must become, it will, in many cases, pay to buy rather than to build new ones. Nay, this process must work in a double way; since every entailed increase of local taxation still further depreciates property.[1] And then, when in towns this process has gone so far as to make the local authority the chief owner of houses, there will be a good precedent for publicly providing houses for the rural population, as proposed in the Radical programme, and as urged by the Democratic Federation; which insists on "the compulsory construction of healthy artisans' and agricultural labourers' dwellings in proportion to the population." Manifestly, the tendency of that which has been done, is being done, and is presently to be done, is to approach the socialistic ideal in which the community is sole house-proprietor.

Such, too, must be the effect of the daily-growing policy on the tenure and utilization of the land. More numerous public benefits, to be achieved by more numerous public agencies, at the cost of augmented public burdens, must increasingly deduct from the returns on land; until, as the depreciation in value becomes greater and greater, the resistance to change of tenure becomes less and less. Already, as every one knows, there is in many places difficulty in obtaining tenants, even at greatly reduced rents; and land of inferior fertility in some cases lies idle, or when farmed by the owner is often farmed at a loss. Clearly the profit on capital invested in land is not such that taxes, local and general, can be greatly raised to support extended public administrations, without an absorption of it which will prompt owners to sell, and make the best of what reduced price they can get by emigrating and buying land not subject to heavy burdens; as, indeed, some are now doing. This process, carried far, must have the result of throwing inferior land out of cultivation; after which there will be raised more generally the demand made by Mr. Arch, who, addressing the Radical Association of Brighton lately, and contending that existing landlords do not make their land adequately productive for the public benefit, said "he should like the present Government to pass a Compulsory Cultivation Bill": an applauded proposal which he justified by instancing compulsory vaccination (thus illustrating the influence of precedent). And this demand will be pressed, not only by the need for making the land productive, but also by the need for employing the rural population. After the Government has extended the practice of hiring the unemployed to work on deserted lands,

[1] If any one thinks such fears are groundless, let him contemplate the fact that from 1867–8 to 1880–1, our annual local expenditure for the United Kingdom has grown from £36,132,834 to £63,276,283; and that during the same 13 years, the municipal expenditure in England and Wales alone, has grown from 13 millions to 30 millions a year! How the increase of public burdens will join with other causes in bringing about public ownership, is shown by a statement made by Mr. W. Rathbone, M.P., to which my attention has been drawn since the above paragraph was in type. He says, "within my own experience, local taxation in New York has risen from 12*s.* 6*d.* per cent. to £2 12*s.* 6*d.* per cent. on the capital of its citizens — a charge which would more than absorb the whole income of an average English landlord." — *Nineteenth Century*, February, 1883.

or lands acquired at nominal prices, there will be reached a stage whence there is but a small further step to that arrangement which, in the programme of the Democratic Federation, is to follow nationalization of the land — the "organization of agricultural and industrial armies under State control on co-operative principles."

To one who doubts whether such a revolution may be so reached, facts may be cited showing its likelihood. In Gaul, during the decline of the Roman Empire, "so numerous were the receivers in comparison with the payers, and so enormous the weight of taxation, that the labourer broke down, the plains became deserts, and woods grew where the plough had been." In like manner, when the French Revolution was approaching, the public burdens had become such, that many farms remained uncultivated and many were deserted: one quarter of the soil was absolutely lying waste; and in some provinces one-half was in heath. Nor have we been without incidents of a kindred nature at home. Besides the facts that under the old Poor Law the rates had in some parishes risen to half the rental, and that in various places farms were lying idle, there is the fact that in one case the rates had absorbed the whole proceeds of the soil.

> At Cholesbury, in Buckinghamshire, in 1832, the poor-rate "suddenly ceased in consequence of the impossibility to continue its collection, the landlords having given up their rents, the farmers their tenancies, and the clergyman his glebe and his tithes. The clergyman, Mr. Jeston, states that in October, 1832, the parish officers threw up their books, and the poor assembled in a body before his door while he was in bed, asking for advice and food. Partly from his own small means, partly from the charity of neighbours, and partly by rates in aid, imposed on the neighbouring parishes, they were for some time supported."

And the Commissioners add that "the benevolent rector recommends that the whole of the land should be divided among the able-bodied paupers": hoping that after help afforded for two years, they might be able to maintain themselves. These facts, giving colour to the prophecy made in Parliament that continuance of the old Poor Law for another thirty years would throw the land out of cultivation, clearly show that increase of public burdens may end in forced cultivation under public control.

Then, again, comes State-ownership of railways. Already this exists to a large extent on the Continent. Already we have had here a few years ago loud advocacy of it. And now the cry, which was raised by sundry politicians and publicists, is taken up afresh by the Democratic Federation; which proposes "State-appropriation of railways, with or without compensation." Evidently, pressure from above joined by pressure from below, is likely to affect this change dictated by the policy everywhere spreading; and with it must come many attendant changes.

For railway-proprietors, at first owners and workers of railways only, have become masters of numerous businesses directly or indirectly connected with railways; and these will have to be purchased by Government when the railways are purchased. Already exclusive letter-carrier, exclusive transmitter of telegrams, and on the way to become exclusive carrier of parcels, the State will not only be exclusive carrier of passengers, goods, and minerals, but will add to its present various trades many other trades. Even now, besides erecting its naval and military establishments and building harbours, docks, breakwaters, etc., it does the work of shipbuilder, cannon-founder, small-arms maker, manufacturer of ammunition, army-clothier and bootmaker; and when the railways have been appropriated "with or without compensation," as the Democratic Federationists say, it will have to become locomotive-engine-builder, carriage-maker, tarpaulin and grease manufacturer, passenger-vessel owner, coal-miner, stone-quarrier, omnibus proprietor, etc. Meanwhile its local lieutenants, the municipal governments, already in many places suppliers of water, gas-makers, owners and workers of tramways, proprietors of baths, will doubtless have undertaken various other businesses. And when the State, directly or by proxy, has thus come into possession of, or has established, numerous concerns for wholesale production and for wholesale distribution, there will be good precedents for extending its function to retail distribution: following such an example, say, as is offered by the French Government, which has long been a retail tobacconist.

Evidently then, the changes made, the changes in progress, and the changes urged, will carry us not only towards State-ownership of land and dwellings and means of communication, all to be administered and worked by State-agents, but towards State-usurpation of all industries: the private forms of which, disadvantaged more and more in competition with the State, which can arrange everything for its own convenience, will more and more die away; just as many voluntary schools have, in presence of Board-schools. And so will be brought about the desired ideal of the socialists.

And now when there has been compassed this desired ideal, which "practical" politicians are helping socialists to reach, and which is so tempting on that bright side which socialists contemplate, what must be the accompanying shady side which they do not contemplate? It is a matter of common remark, often made when a marriage is impending, that those possessed by strong hopes habitually dwell on the promised pleasures and think nothing of the accompanying pains. A further exemplification of this truth is supplied by these political enthusiasts and fanatical revolutionists. Impressed with the miseries existing under our present social arrangements, and not regarding these miseries as caused by the ill-working of a human nature but partially adapted to the social state, they imagine them to be forthwith curable by this or that rearrangement. Yet, even did their plans succeed it could only be by substituting one kind of evil for another. A little deliberate thought would show that under their proposed arrangements, their liberties must be surrendered in proportion as their material welfares were cared for.

For no form of co-operation, small or great, can be carried on without regulation, and an implied submission to the regulating agencies. Even one of their own organizations for effecting social changes yields them proof. It is compelled to have its councils, its local and general officers, its authoritative leaders, who must be obeyed under penalty of confusion and failure. And the experience of those who are loudest in their advocacy of a new social order under the paternal control of a Government, shows that even in private voluntarily-formed societies, the power of the regulative organization becomes great, if not irresistible: often, indeed, causing grumbling and restiveness among those controlled. Trades Unions' which carry on a kind of industrial war in defence of workers' interests *versus* employers' interests, find that subordination almost military in its strictness is needful to secure efficient action; for divided councils prove fatal to success. And even in bodies of co-operators, formed for carrying on manufacturing or distributing businesses, and not needing that obedience to leaders which is required where the aims are offensive or defensive, it is still found that the administrative agency gains such supremacy that there arise complaints about "the tyranny of organization." Judge then what must happen when, instead of relatively small combinations, to which men may belong or not as they please, we have a national combination in which each citizen finds himself incorporated, and from which he cannot separate himself without leaving the country. Judge what must under such conditions become the despotism of a graduated and centralized officialism, holding in its hands the resources of the community, and having behind it whatever amount of force it finds requisite to carry out its decrees and maintain what it calls order. Well may Prince Bismarck display leanings towards State-socialism.

And then after recognizing, as they must if they think out their scheme, the power possessed by the regulative agency in the new social system so temptingly pictured, let its advocates ask themselves to what end this power must be used. Not dwelling exclusively, as they habitually do, on the material well-being and the mental gratifications to be provided for them by a beneficent administration, let them dwell a little on the price to be paid. The officials cannot create the needful supplies: they can but distribute among individuals that which the individuals have joined to produce. If the public agency is required to provide for them, it must reciprocally require them to furnish the means. There cannot be, as under our existing system, agreement between employer and employed — this the scheme excludes. There must in place of it be command by local authorities over workers, and acceptance by the workers of that which the authorities assign to them. And this, indeed, is the arrangement distinctly, but as it would seem inadvertently, pointed to by the members of the Democratic Federation. For they propose that production should be carried on by "agricultural and industrial *armies* under State-control": apparently not remembering that armies pre-suppose grades of officers, by whom obedience would have to be insisted upon; since otherwise neither order nor efficient work could be ensured. So that each would stand toward the governing agency in the relation of slave to master.

"But the governing agency would be a master which he and others made and kept constantly in check; and one which therefore would not control him or others more than was needful for the benefit of each and all."

To which reply the first rejoinder is that, even if so, each member of the community as an individual would be a slave to the community as a whole. Such a relation has habitually existed in militant communities, even under quasi-popular forms of government. In ancient Greece the accepted principle was that the citizen belonged neither to himself nor to his family, but belonged to his city — the city being with the Greek equivalent to the community. And this doctrine, proper to a state of constant warfare, is a doctrine which socialism unawares re-introduces into a state intended to be purely industrial. The services of each will belong to the aggregate of all; and for these services, such returns will be given as the authorities think proper. So that even if the administration is of the beneficent kind intended to be secured, slavery, however mild, must be the outcome of the arrangement.

A second rejoinder is that the administration will presently become not of the intended kind, and that the slavery will not be mild. The socialist speculation is vitiated by an asumption like that which vitiates the speculations of the "practical" politician. It is assumed that officialism will work as it is intended to work, which it never does. The machinery of Communism-like existing social machinery, has to be framed out of existing human nature; and the defects of existing human nature will generate in the one the same evils as in the other. The love of power, the selfishness, the injustice, the untruthfulness, which often in comparatively short times bring private organisations to disaster will inevitably, where their effects accumulate from generation to generation, work evils far greater and less remediable; since, vast and complex and possessed of all the resources, the administrative organization once developed and consolidated, must become irresistible. And if there needs proof that the periodic exercise of electoral power would fail to prevent this, it suffices to instance the French Government, which, purely popular in origin, and subject at short intervals to popular judgment, nevertheless tramples on the freedom of citizens to an extent which the English delegates to the late Trades Unions Congress say "is a disgrace to, and an anomaly in, a Republican nation."

The final result would be a revival of despotism. A disciplined army of civil officials, like an army of military officials, gives supreme power to its head — a power which has often led to usurpation, as in mediæval Europe and still more in Japan — nay, has thus so led among our neighbours, within our own times. The recent confessions of M. de Maupas have shown how readily a constitutional head, elected and trusted by the whole people, may, with the aid of a few unscrupulous confederates, paralyze the representative body and make himself autocrat. That those who rose to power in a socialistic organization would not scruple to carry out their aims at all costs, we have good reason for concluding. When we find that shareholders who, sometimes gaining but often losing, have made that railway-system by which national prosperity has been so greatly increased, are spoken of by the council of the Democratic Federation as having "laid hands" on the means of communication, we may infer that those who directed a socialistic administration might interpret with extreme perversity the claims of individuals and classes under their control. And when, further, we find members of this same council urging that the State should take possession of the railways, "with or without compensation," we may suspect that the heads of the ideal society desired, would be but little deterred by considerations of equity from pursuing whatever policy they thought needful: a policy which would always be one identified with their own supremacy. It would need but a war with an adjacent society, or some internal discontent demanding forcible suppression, to at once transform a socialistic administration into a grinding tyranny like that of ancient Peru; under which the mass of the people, controlled by grades of officials, and leading lives that were inspected out-of-doors and in-doors, laboured for the support of the organisation which regulated them, and were left with but a bare subsistence for themselves. And then would be completely revived, under a different form, that *régime* of status — that system of compulsory co-operation, the decaying tradition of which is represented by the old Toryism, and towards which the new Toryism is carrying us back.

"But we shall be on our guard against all that — we shall take precautions to ward off such disasters," will doubtless say the enthusiasts. Be they "practical" politicians with their new regulative measures, or communists with their schemes for re-organizing labour, their reply is ever the same: — "It is true that plans of kindred nature have, from unforeseen causes or adverse accidents, or the misdeeds of those concerned, been brought to failure; but this time we shall profit by past experiences and succeed." There seems no getting people to accept the truth, which nevertheless is conspicuous enough, that the welfare of a society and the justice of its arrangements are at bottom dependent on the characters of its members; and that improvement in neither can take place without that improvement in character which results from carrying on peaceful industry under the restraints imposed by an orderly social life. The belief, not only of the socialists but also of those so-called Liberals who are diligently preparing the way for them, is that by due skill an ill-working humanity may be framed into well-working institutions. It is a delusion. The defective natures of citizens will show themselves in the bad acting of whatever social structure they are arranged into. There is no political alchemy by which you can get golden conduct out of leaden instincts.

Socialism

(1880's)

WILLIAM GRAHAM SUMNER

Socialism is no new thing. In one form or another it is to be found throughout all history. It arises from an observation of certain harsh facts in the lot of man on earth, the concrete expression of which is poverty and misery. These facts challenge us. It is folly to try to shut our eyes to them. We have first to notice what they are, and then to face them squarely.

Man is born under the necessity of sustaining the existence he has received by an onerous struggle against nature, both to win what is essential to his life and to ward off what is prejudicial to it. He is born under a burden and a necessity. Nature holds what is essential to him, but she offers nothing gratuitously. He may win for his use what she holds, if he can. Only the most meager and inadequate supply for human needs can be obtained directly from nature. There are trees which may be used for fuel and for dwellings, but labor is required to fit them for this use. There are ores in the ground, but labor is necessary to get

From Albert Galloway Keller, ed., *The Challenge of Facts and Other Essays* (New Haven: Yale University Press, 1914), 17, 20–27, 35–52. Keller, who edited Sumner's papers for publication after Sumner's death, titled this essay "The Challenge of Facts." We have restored Sumner's original title, while accepting Keller's guess about the date of composition.

out the metals and make tools or weapons. For any real satisfaction, labor is necessary to fit the products of nature for human use. In this struggle every individual is under the pressure of the necessities for food, clothing, shelter, fuel, and every individual brings with him more or less energy for the conflict necessary to supply his needs. The relation, therefore, between each man's needs and each man's energy, or "individualism," is the first fact of human life. . . .

The next great fact we have to notice in regard to the struggle of human life is that labor which is spent in a direct struggle with nature is severe in the extreme and is but slightly productive. To subjugate nature, man needs weapons and tools. These, however, cannot be won unless the food and clothing and other prime and direct necessities are supplied in such amount that they can be consumed while tools and weapons are being made, for the tools and weapons themselves satisfy no needs directly. A man who tills the ground with his fingers or with a pointed stick picked up without labor will get a small crop. To fashion even the rudest spade or hoe will cost time, during which the laborer must still eat and drink and wear, but the tool, when obtained, will multiply immensely the power to produce. Such products of labor, used to assist production, have a function so peculiar in the nature of things that we need to distinguish them. We call them capital. A lever is capital, and the advantage of lifting a weight with a lever over lifting it by direct exertion is only a feeble illustration of the power of capital in production. The origin of capital lies in the darkness before history, and it is probably impossible for us to imagine the slow and painful steps by which the race began the formation of it. Since then it has gone on rising to higher and higher powers by a ceaseless involution, if I may use a mathematical expression. Capital is labor raised to a higher power by being constantly multiplied into itself. Nature has been more and more subjugated by the human race through the power of capital, and every human being now living shares the improved status of the race to a degree which neither he nor any one else can measure, and for which he pays nothing.

Let us understand this point, because our subject will require future reference to it. It is the most shortsighted ignorance not to see that, in a civilized community, all the advantage of capital except a small fraction is gratuitously enjoyed by the community. For instance, suppose the case of a man utterly destitute of tools, who is trying to till the ground with a pointed stick. He could get something out of it. If now he should obtain a spade with which to till the ground, let us suppose, for illustration, that he could get twenty times as great a product. Could, then, the owner of a spade in a civilized state demand, as its price, from the man who had no spade, nineteen-twentieths of the product which could be produced by the use of it? Certainly not. The price of a spade is fixed by the supply and demand of products in the community. A spade is bought for a dollar and the gain from the use of it is an inheritance of knowledge, experience, and skill which every man who lives in a civilized state gets for nothing. What we pay for steam transportation is no trifle, but imagine, if you can, eastern Massachusetts cut off from steam connection with the rest of the world, turnpikes and sailing vessels remaining. The cost of food would rise so high that a quarter of the population would starve to death and another quarter would have to emigrate. To-day every man here gets an enormous advantage from the status of a society on a level of steam transportation, telegraph, and machinery, for which he pays nothing.

So far as I have yet spoken, we have before us the struggle of man with nature, but the social problems, strictly speaking, arise at the next step. Each man carries on the struggle to win his support for himself, but there are others by his side engaged in the same struggle. If the stores of nature were unlimited, or if the last unit of the supply she offers could be won as easily as the first, there would be no social problem. If a square mile of land could support an indefinite number of human beings, or if it cost only twice as much labor to get forty bushels of wheat from an acre as to get twenty, we should have no social problem. If a square mile of land could support millions, no one would ever emigrate and there would be no trade or commerce. If it cost only twice as much labor to get forty bushels as twenty, there would be no advance in the arts. The fact is far otherwise. So long as the population is low in proportion to the amount of land, on a given stage of the arts, life is easy and the competition of man with man is weak. When more persons are trying to live on a square mile than it can support, on the existing stage of the arts, life is hard and the competition of man with man is intense. In the former case, industry and prudence may be on a low grade; the penalties are not severe, or certain, or speedy. In the latter case, each individual needs to exert on his own behalf every force, original or acquired, which he can command. In the former case, the average condition will be one of comfort and the population will be all nearly on the average. In the latter case, the average condition will not be one of comfort, but the population will cover wide extremes of comfort and misery. Each will find his place according to his ability and his effort. The former society will be democratic; the latter will be aristocratic.

The constant tendency of population to outstrip the means of subsistence is the force which has distributed population over the world, and produced all advance in civilization. To this day the two means of escape for an overpopulated country are emigration and an advance in the arts. The former wins more land for the same people; the latter makes the same land support more persons. If, however, either of these means opens a chance for an increase of population, it is evident that the advantage so won may be speedily exhausted if the increase takes place. The social difficulty has only undergone a temporary amelioration, and when the conditions of pressure and competition are renewed, misery and poverty reappear. The victims of them are those who have inherited disease and depraved appetites, or have been brought up in vice and ignorance, or have themselves yielded to vice, extravagance, idleness, and imprudence. In the last analysis, therefore, we come back to vice, in its original and hereditary forms, as the correlative of misery and poverty.

The condition for the complete and regular action of the force of competition is liberty. Liberty means the security given to each man that, if he employs his energies to sustain the struggle on behalf of himself and those he cares for, he shall dispose of the product exclusively as he chooses. It is impossible to know whence any definition or criterion of justice can be derived, if it is not deducted from this view of things; or if it is not the definition of justice that each shall enjoy the fruit of his own labor and self-denial, and of injustice that the idle and the industrious, the self-indulgent and the self-denying, shall share equally in the product. Aside from the *a priori* speculations of philosophers who have tried to make equality an essential element in justice, the human race has recognized, from the earliest times, the above conception of justice as the true one, and has founded upon it the right of property. The right of property, with marriage and the family, gives the right of bequest.

Monogamic marriage, however, is the most exclusive of social institutions. It contains, as essential principles, preference, superiority, selection, devotion. It would not be at all what it is if it were not for these characteristic traits, and it always degenerates when these traits are not present. For instance, if a man should not have a distinct preference for the woman he married, and if he did not select her as superior to others, the marriage would be an imperfect one according to the standard of true monogamic marriage. The family under monogamy, also, is a closed group, having special interests and estimating privacy and reserve as valuable advantages for family development. We grant high prerogatives, in our society, to parents, although our observation teaches us that thousands of human beings are unfit to be parents or to be entrusted with the care of children. It follows, therefore, from the organization of marriage and the family, under monogamy, that great inequalities must exist in a society based on those institutions. The son of wise parents cannot start on a level with the son of foolish ones, and the man who has had no home discipline cannot be equal to the man who has had home discipline. If the contrary were true, we could rid ourselves at once of the wearing labor of inculcating sound morals and manners in our children.

Private property, also, which we have seen to be a feature of society organized in accordance with the natural conditions of the struggle for existence produces inequalities between men. The struggle for existence is aimed against nature. It is from her niggardly hand that we have to wrest the satisfactions for our needs, but our fellow-men are our competitors for the meager supply. Competition, therefore, is a law of nature. Nature is entirely neutral; she submits to him who most energetically and resolutely assails her. She grants her rewards to the fittest, therefore, without regard to other considerations of any kind. If, then, there be liberty, men get from her just in proportion to their works, and their having and enjoying are just in proportion to their being and their doing. Such is the system of nature. If we do not like it, and if we try to amend it, there is only one way in which we can do it. We can take from the better and give to the worse. We can deflect the penalties of those who have done ill and throw them on those who have done better. We can take the rewards from those who have done better and give them to those who have done worse. We shall thus lessen the inequalities. We shall favor the survival of the unfittest, and we shall accomplish this by destroying liberty. Let it be understood that we cannot go outside of this alternative: liberty, inequality, survival of the fittest; not-liberty, equality, survival of the unfittest. The former carries society forward and favors all its best members; the latter carries society downwards and favors all its worst members.

For three hundred years now men have been trying to understand and realize liberty. Liberty is not the right or chance to do what we choose; there is no such liberty as that on earth. No man can do as he chooses: the autocrat of Russia or the King of Dahomey has limits to his arbitrary will; the savage in the wilderness, whom some people think free, is the slave of routine, tradition, and superstitious fears; the civilized man must earn his living, or take care of his property, or concede his own will to the rights and claims of his parents, his wife, his children, and all the persons with whom he is connected by the ties and contracts of civilized life.

What we mean by liberty is civil liberty, or liberty under law; and this means the guarantees of law that a man shall not be interfered with while using his own powers for his own welfare. It is, therefore, a civil and political status; and that nation has the freest institutions in which the guarantees of peace for the laborer and security for the capitalist are the highest. Liberty, therefore, does not by any means do away with the struggle for existence. We might as well try to do away with the need of eating, for that would, in effect, be the same thing. What civil liberty does is to turn the competition of man with man from violence and brute force into an industrial competition under which men vie with one another for the acquisition of material goods by industry, energy, skill, frugality, prudence, temperance, and other industrial virtues. Under this changed order of things the inequalities are not done away with. Nature still grants her rewards of having and enjoying, according to our being and doing, but it is now the man of the highest training and not the man of the heaviest fist who gains the highest reward. It is impossible that the man with capital and the man without capital should be equal. To affirm that they are equal would be to say that a man who has no tool can get as much food out of the ground as the man who has a spade or a plough; or that the man who has no weapon can defend himself as well against hostile beasts or hostile men as the man who has a weapon. If that were so, none of us would work any more. We work and deny ourselves to get capital just because, other things being equal, the man who has it is superior, for attaining all the ends of life, to the man who has it not. Considering the eagerness with which we all seek capital and the estimate we put upon it, either in cherishing it if we have it, or envying others who have it while we have it not, it is very strange what platitudes pass current about it in our society so soon as we begin to generalize about it. If our young people really believed some of the teachings they hear, it would not be amiss to preach them a sermon once in a while to reassure them, setting forth that it is not wicked to be rich, nay even, that it is not wicked to be richer than your neighbor.

It follows from what we have observed that it is the utmost folly to denounce capital. To do so is to undermine civilization, for capital is the first requisite of every social gain, educational, ecclesiastical, political, æsthetic, or other. . . .

A century ago there were very few wealthy men except owners of land. The extension of commerce, manufactures, and mining, the introduction of the factory system and machinery, the opening of new countries, and the great discoveries and inventions have created a new middle class, based on wealth, and developed out of the peasants, artisans, unskilled laborers, and small shop-keepers of a century ago. The consequence has been that the chance of acquiring capital and all which depends on capital has opened before classes which formerly passed their lives in a dull round of ignorance and drudgery. This chance has brought with it the same alternative which accompanies every other opportunity offered to mortals. Those who were wise and able to profit by the chance succeeded grandly; those who were negligent or unable to profit by it suffered proportionately. The result has been wide inequalities of wealth within the industrial classes. The net result, however, for all, has been the cheapening of luxuries and a vast extension of physical enjoyment. The appetite for enjoyment has been awakened and nourished in classes which formerly never missed what they never thought of, and it has produced eagerness for material good, discontent, and impatient ambition. This is the reverse side of that eager uprising of the industrial classes which is such a great force in modern life. The chance is opened to advance, by industry, prudence, economy, and emigration, to the possession of capital; but the way is long and tedious. The impatience for enjoyment and the thirst for luxury whch we have mentioned are the greatest foes to the accumulation of capital; and there is a still darker side to the picture when we come to notice that those who yield to the impatience to enjoy, but who see others outstrip them, are led to malice and envy. Mobs arise which manifest the most savage and senseless disposition to burn and destroy what they cannot enjoy. We have already had evidence, in more than one country, that such a wild disposition exists and needs only opportunity to burst into activity.

The origin of socialism, which is the extreme development of the sentimental philosophy, lies in the undisputed facts which I described at the outset. The socialist regards this misery as the fault of society. He thinks that we can organize society as we like and that an organization can be devised in which poverty and misery shall disappear. He goes further even than this. He assumes that men have artificially organized society as it now exists. Hence if anything is disagreeable or hard in the present state of society it follows, on that view, that the task of organizing society has been imperfectly and badly performed, and that it needs to be done over again. These are the assumptions with which the socialist starts, and many socialists seem also to believe that if they can destroy belief in an Almighty God who is supposed to have made the world such as it is, they will then have overthrown the belief that there is a fixed order in human nature and human life which man can scarcely alter at all, and, if at all, only infinitesimally.

The truth is that the social order is fixed by laws of nature precisely analogous to those of the physical order. The most that man can do is by ignorance and self-conceit to mar the operation of social laws. The evils of society are to a great extent the result of the dogmatism and self-interest of statesmen, philosophers, and ecclesiastics who in past time have done just what the socialists now want to do. Instead of studying the natural laws of the social order, they assumed that they could organize society as they chose, they made up their minds what kind of a society they wanted to make, and they planned their little measures for the ends they had resolved upon. It will take centuries of scientific study of the facts of nature to eliminate from human society the mischievous institutions and traditions which the said statesmen, philosophers, and ecclesiastics have introduced into it. Let us not, however, even then delude ourselves with any impossible hopes. The hardships of life would not be eliminated if the laws of nature acted directly and without interference. The task of right living forever changes its form, but let us not imagine that that task will ever reach a final solution or that any race of men on this earth can ever be emancipated from the necessity of industry, prudence, continence, and temperance if they are to pass their lives prosperously. If you believe the contrary you must suppose that some men can come to exist who shall know nothing of old age, disease, and death.

The socialist enterprise of reorganizing society in order to change what is harsh and sad in it at present is therefore as impossible, from the outset, as a plan for changing the physical order. I read the other day a story in which a man dreamt that somebody had invented an application of electricity for eradicating certain facts from the memory. Just think of it! What an emancipation to the human race, if a man could so emancipate himself from all those incidents in his past life which he regrets! Let there no longer be such a thing as remorse or vain regret! It would be half as good as finding a fountain of eternal youth. Or invent us a world in which two and two could make five. Two two-dollar notes could then pay five dollars of debts. They say that political economy is a dismal science and that its doctrines are dark and cruel. I think the hardest fact in human life is that two and two cannot make five; but in sociology while people will agree that two and two cannot make five, yet they think that it might somehow be possible by adjusting two and two to one another in some way or other to make two and two equal to four and one-tenth.

I have shown how men emerge from barbarism only by the use of capital and why it is that, as soon as they begin to use capital, if there is liberty, there will be inequality. The socialist looking at these facts says that it is capital which produces the inequality. It is the inequality of men in what they get out of life which shocks the socialist. He finds enough to criticize in the products of past dogmatism and bad statesmanship to which I have alluded, and the program of reforms to be accomplished and abuses to be rectified which the socialists have set up have often been admirable. It is their analysis of the situation which is at fault. Their diagnosis of the social disease is founded on sectarian assumptions, not on the scientific study of the structure and functions of the social body. In attacking capital they are simply attacking the foundations of civilization, and every socialistic scheme which has ever been proposed, so far as it has lessened the motives to saving or the security of capital, is anti-social and anti-civilizing.

Rousseau, who is the great father of the modern socialism, laid accusation for the inequalities existing amongst men upon wheat and iron. What he meant was that wheat is a symbol of agriculture, and when men took to agriculture and wheat diet they broke up their old tribal relations, which were partly communistic, and developed individualism and private property. At the same time agriculture called for tools and machines, of which iron is a symbol; but these tools and machines are capital. Agriculture, individualism, tools, capital were, according to Rousseau's ideas, the causes of inequality. He was, in a certain way, correct, as we have already seen by our own analysis of the facts of the social order. When human society reached the agricultural stage machinery became necessary. Capital was far more important than on the hunting or pastoral stage, and the inequalities of men were developed with great rapidity, so that we have a Humboldt, a Newton, or a Shakespeare at one end of the scale and a Digger Indian at the other. The Humboldt or Newton is one of the highest products produced by the constant selection and advance of the best part of the human race, *viz.*, those who have seized every chance of advancing; and the Digger Indian is a specimen of that part of the race which withdrew from the competition clear back at the beginning and has consequently never made any advance beyond the first superiority of man to beasts. Rousseau, following the logic of his own explanation of the facts, offered distinctly as the cure for inequality a return to the hunting stage of life as practiced by the American Indians. In this he was plainly and distinctly right. If you want equality you must not look forward for it on the path of advancing civilization. You may go back to the mode of life of the American Indian, and, although you will not then reach equality, you will escape those glaring inequalities of wealth and poverty by coming down to a comparative equality, that is, to a status in which all are equally miserable. Even this, however, you cannot do without submitting to other conditions which are far more appalling than any sad facts in the existing order of society. The population of Massachusetts is about two hundred to the square mile; on the hunting stage Massachusetts could not probably support, at the utmost, five to the square mile; hence to get back to the hunting stage would cost the reduction of the population to two and a half where there are now one hundred. In Rousseau's day people did not even know that this question of the power of land to support population was to be taken into account.

Socialists find it necessary to alter the definition of capital in order to maintain their attacks upon it. Karl Marx, for instance, regards capital as an accumulation of the differences which a merchant makes between his buying price and his selling price. It is, according to him, an accumulation of the differences which the employer gains between what he pays to the employees for making the thing and what he obtains for it from the consumer. In this view of the matter the capitalist employer is a pure parasite, who has fastened on the wage-receiving employee without need or reason and is levying toll on industry. All socialistic writers follow, in different degrees, this conception of capital. If it is true, why do not I levy on some workers somewhere and steal this difference in the product of their labor? Is it because I am more honest or magnanimous than those who are capitalist-employers? I should not trust myself to resist the chance if I had it. Or again, let us ask why, if this conception of the origin of capital is correct, the workmen submit to a pure and unnecessary imposition. If this notion were true, co-operation in production would not need any effort to bring it about; it would take an army to keep it down. The reason why it is not possible for the first comer to start out as an employer of labor is that capital is a prerequisite to all industry. So soon as men pass beyond the stage of life in which they live, like beasts, on the spontaneous fruits of the earth, capital must precede every productive enterprise. It would lead me too far away from my present subject to elaborate this statement as it deserves and perhaps as it needs, but I may say that there is no sound political economy and especially no correct conception of wages which is not based on a complete recognition of the character of capital as necessarily going before every industrial operation. The reason why co-operation in production is exceedingly difficult, and indeed is not possible except in the highest and rarest conditions of education and culture amongst artisans, is that workmen cannot undertake an enterprise without capital, and that capital always means the fruits of prudence and self-denial already accomplished. The capitalist's profits, therefore, are only the reward for the contribution he has made to a joint enterprise which could not go on without him, and his share is as legitimate as that of the hand-worker.

The socialist assails particularly the institution of bequest or hereditary property, by which some men come into life with special protection and advantage. The right of bequest rests on no other grounds than those of expediency. The love of children is the strongest motive to frugality and to the accumulation of capital. The state guarantees the power of bequest only because it thereby encourages the accumulation of capital on which the welfare of society depends. It is true enough that inherited capital often proves a curse. Wealth is like health, physical strength, education, or anything else which enhances the power of the individual; it is only a chance; its moral character depends entirely upon the use which is made of it. Any force which, when well used, is capable of elevating a man, will, if abused, debase him in the same proportion. This is true of education, which is often and incorrectly vaunted as a positive and purely beneficent instrumentality. An education ill used makes a man only a more mischievous scoundrel, just as an education well used makes him a more efficient, good citizen and producer. So it is with wealth; it is a means to all the higher developments of intellectual and moral culture. A man of inherited wealth can gain in youth all the advantages which are essential to high culture, and which a man who must first earn the capital cannot attain until he is almost past the time of life for profiting by them. If one should believe the newspapers, one would be driven to a philosophy something like this: it is extremely praiseworthy for a man born in poverty to accumulate a fortune; the reason why he wants to secure a fortune is that he wants to secure the position of his children and start them with better advantages than he enjoyed himself; this is a noble desire on his part, but he really ought to doubt and hesitate about so doing because the chances are that he would do far better for his children to leave them poor. The children who inherit his wealth are put under suspicion by it; it creates a presumption against them in all the activities of citizenship.

Now it is no doubt true that the struggle to win a fortune gives strength of character and a practical judgment and efficiency which a man who inherits wealth rarely gets, but hereditary wealth transmitted from generation to generation is the strongest instrument by which we keep up a steadily advancing civilization. In the absence of laws of entail and perpetuity it is inevitable that capital should speedily slip from the hold of the man who is not fit to possess it, back into the great stream of capital, and so find its way into the hands of those who can use it for the benefit of society.

The love of children is an instinct which, as I have said before, grows stronger with advancing civilization. All attacks on capital have, up to this time, been shipwrecked on this instinct. Consequently the most rigorous and logical socialists have always been led sooner or later to attack the family. For, if bequest should be abolished, parents would give their property to their children in their own life-time; and so it becomes a logical necessity to substitute some sort of communistic or socialistic life for family life, and to educate children in masses without the tie of parentage. Every socialistic theory which has been pursued energetically has led out to this consequence. I will not follow up this topic, but it is plain to see that the only equality which could be reached on this course would be that men should be all equal to each other when they were all equal to swine.

Socialists are filled with the enthusiasm of equality. Every scheme of theirs for securing equality has destroyed liberty. The student of political philosophy has the antagonism of equality and liberty constantly forced upon him. Equality of possession or of rights and equality before the law are diametrically opposed to each other. The object of equality before the law is to make the state entirely neutral. The state, under that theory, takes no cognizance of persons. It surrounds all, without distinctions, with the same conditions and guarantees. If it educates one, it educates all — black, white, red, or yellow; Jew or Gentile; native or alien. If it taxes one, it taxes all, by the same system and under the same conditions. If it exempts one from police regulations in home, church, and occupation, it exempts all. From this statement it is at once evident that pure equality before the law is impossible. Some occupations must be subjected to police regulation. Not all can be made subject to militia duty even for the same limited period. The exceptions and special cases furnish the chance for abuse. Equality before the law, however, is one of the cardinal principles of civil liberty, because it leaves each man to run the race of life for himself as best he can. The state stands neutral but benevolent. It does not undertake to aid some and handicap others at the outset in order to offset hereditary advantages and disadvantages, or to make them start equally. Such a notion would belong to the false and spurious theory of equality which is socialistic. If the state should attempt this it would make itself the servant of envy. I am entitled to make the most I can of myself without hindrance from anybody, but I am not entitled to any guarantee that I shall make as much of myself as somebody else makes of himself.

The modern thirst for equality of rights is explained by its historical origin. The mediaeval notion of rights was that rights were special privileges, exemptions, franchises, and powers given to individuals by the king; hence each man had just so many as he and his ancestors had been able to buy or beg by force or favor, and if a man had obtained no grants he had no rights. Hence no two persons were equal in rights and the mass of the population had none. The theory of natural rights and of equal rights was a revolt against the mediaeval theory. It was asserted that men did not have to wait for a king to grant them rights; they have them by nature, or in the nature of things, because they are men and members of civil society. If rights come from nature, it is inferred that they fall like air and light on all equally. It was an immense step in advance for the human race when this new doctrine was promulgated. Its own limitations and errors need not now be pointed out. Its significance is plain, and its limits are to some extent defined when we note its historical origin.

I have already shown that where these guarantees exist and where there is liberty, the results cannot be equal, but with all liberty there must go responsibility. If I take my own way I must take my own consequences; if it proves that I have made a mistake, I cannot be allowed to throw the consequences on my neighbor. If my neighbor is a free man and resents interference from me he must not call on me to bear the consequences of his mistakes. Hence it is plain that liberty, equality before the law, responsibility, individualism, monogamy, and private property all hold together as consistent parts of the same structure of society, and that an assault on one part must sooner or later involve an assault on all the others.

To all this must be added the political element in socialism. The acquisition of some capital — the amount is of very subordinate importance — is the first and simplest proof that an individual possesses the industrial and civil virtues which make a good citizen and a useful member of society. Political power, a century ago, was associated more or less, even in the United States, with the possession of land. It has been gradually extended until the suffrage is to all intents and purposes universal in North and South America, in Australia, and in all Europe except Russia and Turkey. On this system political control belongs to the numerical majority, limited only by institutions. It may be doubted, if the terms are taken strictly and correctly, whether the non-capitalists outnumber the capitalists in any civilized country, but in many cities where capital is most collected they certainly do. The powers of government have been abused for ages by the classes who possessed them to enable kings, countiers, nobles, politicians, demagogues, and their friends to live in exemption from labor and self-denial, that is, from the universal lot of man. It is only a continuation of the same abuse if the new possessors of power attempt to employ it to secure for themselves the selfish advantages which all possessors of power have taken. Such a course would, however, overthrow all that we think has been won in the way of making government an organ of justice, peace, order, and security, without respect of persons; and if those gains are not to be lost they will have to be defended, before this century closes, against popular majorities, especially in cities, just as they had to be won in a struggle with kings and nobles in the centuries past.

The newest socialism is, in its method, political. The essential feature of its latest phases is the attempt to use the power of the state to realize its plans and to secure its objects. These objects are to do away with poverty and misery, and there are no socialistic schemes yet proposed, of any sort, which do not, upon analysis, turn out to be projects for curing poverty and misery by making those who have share with those who have not. Whether they are paper-money schemes, tariff schemes, subsidy schemes, internal improvement schemes, or usury laws, they all have this in common with the most vulgar of the communistic projects, and the errors of this sort in the past which have been committed in the interest of the capitalist class now furnish precedents, illustration, and encouragement for the new category of demands. The latest socialism divides into two phases: one which aims at centralization and despotism — believing that political form more available for its purposes; the other, the anarchical, which prefers to split up the state into townships, or "communes," to the same end. The latter furnishes the true etymology and meaning of "communism" in its present use, but all socialism, in its second stage, merges into a division of property according to the old sense of communism.

It is impossible to notice socialism as it presents itself at the present moment without pointing out the immense mischief which has been done by sentimental economists and social philosophers who have thought it their professional duty, not to investigate and teach the truth, but to dabble in philanthropy. It is in Germany that this development has been most marked, and as a consequence of it the judgment and sense of the whole people in regard to political and social questions have been corrupted. It is remarkable that the country whose learned men have wrought so much for every other science, especially by virtue of their scientific method and rigorous critical processes, should have furnished a body of social philosophers without method, discipline, or severity of scholarship, who have led the nation in pursuit of whims and dreams and impossible desires. Amongst us there has been less of it, for our people still possess enough sterling sense to reject sentimental rubbish in its grosser forms, but we have had and still have abundance of the more subtle forms of socialistic doctrine, and these open the way to the others. We may already see the two developments forming a congenial alliance. We have also our writers and teachers who seem to think that "the weak" and "the poor" are terms of exact definition; that government exists, in some especial sense, for the sake of the classes so designated; and that the same classes (whoever they are) have some especial claim on the interest and attention of the economist and social philosopher. It may be believed that, in the opinion of these persons, the training of men is the only branch of human effort in which the labor and care should be spent, not on the best specimens but on the poorest.

It is a matter of course that a reactionary party should arise to declare that universal suffrage, popular education, machinery, free trade, and all the other innovations of the last hundred years are all a mistake. If any one ever believed that these innovations were so many clear strides towards the millennium, that they involve no evils or abuses of their own, that they tend to emancipate mankind from the need for prudence, caution, forethought, vigilance — in short, from the eternal struggle against evil — it is not strange that he should be disappointed. If any one ever believed that some "form of government" could be found which would run itself and turn out the pure results of abstract peace, justice, and righteousness without any trouble to anybody, he may be dissatisfied. To talk of turning back, however, is only to enhance still further the confusion and danger of our position. The world cannot go back. Its destiny is to go forward and to meet the new problems which are continually arising. Under our so-called progress evil only alters its forms, and we must esteem it a grand advance if we can believe that, on the whole, and over a wide view of human affairs, good has gained a hair's breadth over evil in a century. Popular institutions have their own abuses and dangers just as much as monarchical or aristocratic institutions. We are only just finding out what they are. All the institutions which we have inherited were invented to guard liberty against the encroachments of a powerful monarch or aristocracy, when these classes possessed land and the possession of land was the greatest social power. Institutions must now be devised to guard civil liberty against popular majorities, and this necessity arises first in regard to the protection of property, the first and greatest function of government and element in civil liberty. There is no escape from any dangers involved in this or any other social struggle save in going forward and working out the development. It will cost a struggle and will demand the highest wisdom of this and the next generation. It is very probable that some nations — those, namely, which come up to this problem with the least preparation, with the least intelligent comprehension of the problem, and under the most inefficient leadership — will suffer a severe check in their development and prosperity; it is very probable that in some nations the development may lead through revolution and bloodshed; it is very probable that in some nations the consequence may be a reaction towards arbitrary power. In every view we take of it, it is clear that the general abolition of slavery has only cleared the way for a new social problem of far wider scope and far greater difficulty. It seems to me, in fact, that this must always be the case. The conquest of one difficulty will only open the way to another; the solution of one problem will only bring man face to face with another. Man wins by the fight, not by the victory, and therefore the possibilities of growth are unlimited, for the fight has no end.

The progress which men have made in developing the possibilities of human existence has never been made by jumps and strides. It has never resulted from the schemes of philosophers and reformers. It has never been guided through a set program by the wisdom of any sages, statesmen, or philanthropists. The progress which has been made has been won in minute stages by men who had a definite task before them, and who have dealt with it in detail, as it presented itself, without referring to general principles, or attempting to bring it into logical relations to an *a priori* system. In most cases the agents are unknown and cannot be found. New and better arrangements have grown up imperceptibly by the natural effort of all to make the best of actual circumstances. In this way, no doubt, the new problems arising in our modern society must be solved or must solve themselves. The chief safeguard and hope of such a development is in the sound instincts and strong sense of the people, which, although it may not reason closely, can reject instinctively. If there are laws — and there certainly are such — which permit the acquisition of property without industry, by cunning, force, gambling, swindling, favoritism, or corruption, such laws transfer property from those who have earned it to those who have not. Such laws contain the radical vice of socialism. They demand correction and offer an open field for reform because reform would lie in the direction of greater purity and security of the right of property. Whatever assails that right, or goes in the direction of making it still more uncertain whether the industrious man can dispose of the fruits of his industry for his own interests exclusively, tends directly towards violence, bloodshed, poverty, and misery. If any large section of modern society should rise against the rest for the purpose of attempting any such spoliation, either by violence or through the forms of law, it would destroy civilization as it was destroyed by the irruption of the barbarians into the Roman Empire.

The sound student of sociology can hold out to mankind, as individuals or as a race, only one hope of better and happier living. That hope lies in an enhancement of the industrial virtues and of the moral forces which thence arise. Industry, self-denial, and temperance are the laws of prosperity for men and states; without them advance in the arts and in wealth means only corruption and decay through luxury and vice. With them progress in the arts and increasing wealth are the prime conditions of an advancing civilization which is sound enough to endure. The power of the human race to-day over the conditions of prosperous and happy living are sufficient to banish poverty and misery if it were not for folly and vice. The earth does not begin to be populated up to its power to support population on the present stage of the arts; if the United States were as densely populated as the British Islands, we should have 1,000,000,000 people here. If, therefore, men were willing to set to work with energy and courage to subdue the outlying parts of the earth, all might live in plenty and prosperity. But if they insist on remaining in the slums of great cities or on the borders of an old society, and on a comparatively exhausted soil, there is no device of economist or statesman which can prevent them from falling victims to poverty and misery or from succumbing in the competition of life to those who have greater command of capital. The socialist or philanthropist who nourishes them in their situation and saves them from the distress of it is only cultivating the distress which he pretends to cure.

The Struggle for Existence in Human Society (1888, 1893)

THOMAS H. HUXLEY

There is another fallacy which appears to me to pervade the so-called "ethics of evolution." It is the notion that because, on the whole, animals and plants have advanced in perfection of organization by means of the struggle for existence and the consequent 'survival of the fittest'; therefore men in society, men as ethical beings, must look to the same process to help them towards perfection. I suspect that this fallacy has arisen out of the unfortunate ambiguity of the phrase 'survival of the fittest.' 'Fittest' has a connotation of 'best'; and about 'best' there hangs

From Thomas H. Huxley, *Evolution and Ethics and Other Essays* (New York: D. Appleton, 1898), 80–85, 226–231. The first portion of this selection is taken from Huxley's essay "Evolution and Ethics" (1893), the second from "The Struggle for Existence in Human Society" (1888).

a moral flavour. In cosmic nature, however, what is 'fittest' depends upon the conditions. Long since, I ventured to point out that if our hemisphere were to cool again, the survival of the fittest might bring about, in the vegetable kingdom, a population of more and more stunted and humbler and humbler organisms, until the 'fittest' that survived might be nothing but lichens, diatoms, and such microscopic organisms as those which give red snow its colour; while, if it becomes hotter, the pleasant valleys of the Thames and Isis might be uninhabitable by any animated beings save those that flourish in a tropical jungle. They, as the fitttest, the best adapted to the changed conditions, would survive.

Men in society are undoubtedly subject to the cosmic process. As among other animals, multiplication goes on without cessation, and involves severe competition for the means of support. The struggle for existence tends to eliminate those less fitted to adapt themselves to the circumstances of their existence. The strongest, the most self-assertive, tend to tread down the weaker. But the influence of the cosmic process on the evolution of society is the greater the more rudimentary its civilization. Social progress means a checking of the cosmic process at every step and the substitution for it of another, which may be called the ethical process; the end of which is not the survival of those who may happen to be the fittest, in respect of the whole of the conditions which obtain, but of those who are ethically the best.

As I have already urged, the practice of that which is ethically best — what we call goodness or virtue — involves a course of conduct which, in all respects, is opposed to that which leads to success in the cosmic struggle for existence. In place of ruthless self-assertion it demands self-restraint; in place of thrusting aside, or treading down, all competitors, it requires that the individual shall not merely respect, but shall help his fellows; its influence is directed, not so much to the survival of the fittest, as to the fitting of as many as possible to survive. It repudiates the gladiatorial theory of existence. It demands that each man who enters into the enjoyment of the advantages of a polity shall be mindful of his debt to those who have laboriously constructed it; and shall take heed that no act of his weakens the fabric in which he has been permitted to live. Laws and moral precepts are directed to the end of curbing the cosmic process and reminding the individual of his duty to the community, to the protection and influence of which he owes, if not existence itself, at least the life of something better than a brutal savage.

It is from neglect of these plain considerations that the fanatical individualism of our time attempts to apply the analogy of cosmic nature to society. Once more we have a misapplication of the stoical injunction to follow nature; the duties of the individual to the state are forgotten, and his tendencies to self-assertion are dignified by the name of rights. It is seriously debated whether the members of a community are justified in using their combined strength to constrain one of their number to contribute his share to the maintenance of it; or even to prevent him from doing his best to destroy it. The struggle for existence, which has done such admirable work in cosmic nature, must, it appears, be equally beneficent in the ethical sphere. Yet if that which I have insisted upon is true; if the cosmic process has no sort of relation to moral ends; if the imitation of it by man is inconsistent with the first principles of ethics; what becomes of this surprising theory?

Let us understand, once for all, that the ethical progress of society depends, not on imitating the cosmic process, still less in running away from it, but in combating it. It may seem an audacious proposal thus to pit the microcosm against the macrocosm and to set man to subdue nature to his higher ends; but I venture to think that the great intellectual difference between the ancient times with which we have been occupied and our day, lies in the solid foundation we have acquired for the hope that such an enterprise may meet with a certain measure of success.

The history of civilization details the steps by which men have succeeded in building up an artificial world within the cosmos. Fragile reed as he may be, man, as Pascal says, is a thinking reed: there lies within him a fund of energy, operating intelligently and so far akin to that which pervades the universe, that it is competent to influence and modify the cosmic process. In virtue of his intelligence, the dwarf bends the Titan to his will. In every family, in every polity that has been established, the cosmic process in man has been restrained and otherwise modified by law and custom; in surrounding nature, it has been similarly influenced by the art of the shepherd, the agriculturist, the artisan. As civilization has advanced, so has the extent of this interference increased; until the organized and highly developed sciences and arts of the present day have endowed man with a command over the course of non-human nature greater than that once attributed to the magicians. The most impressive, I might say startling, of these changes have been brought about in the course of the last two centuries; while a right comprehension of the process of life and of the means of influencing its manifestations is only just dawning upon us. We do not yet see our way beyond generalities; and we are befogged by the obtrusion of false analogies and crude anticipations. But Astronomy, Physics, Chemistry, have all had to pass through similar phases, before they reached the stage at which their influence became an important factor in human affairs. Physiology, Psychology, Ethics, Political Science, must submit to the same ordeal. Yet it seems to me irrational to doubt that, at no distant period, they will work as great a revolution in the sphere of practice.

The theory of evolution encourages no millennial anticipations. If, for millions of years, our globe has taken the upward road, yet, some time, the summit will be reached and the downward route will be commenced.

The most daring imagination will hardly venture upon the suggestion that the power and the intelligence of man can ever arrest the procession of the great year.

Moreover, the cosmic nature born with us and, to a large extent, necessary for our maintenance, is the outcome of millions of years of severe training, and it would be folly to imagine that a few centuries will suffice to subdue its masterfulness to purely ethical ends. Ethical nature may count upon having to reckon with a tenacious and powerful enemy as long as the world lasts. But, on the other hand, I see no limit to the extent to which intelligence and will, guided by sound principles of investigation, and organized in common effort, may modify the conditions of existence, for a period longer than that now covered by history. And much may be done to change the nature of man himself. The intelligence which has converted the brother of the wolf into the faithful guardian of the flock ought to be able to do something towards curbing the instincts of savagery in civilized men. . . .

We are here, as in all other questions of social organization, met by two diametrically opposed views. On the one hand, the methods pursued in foreign countries are held up as our example. The state is exhorted to take the matter in hand, and establish a great system of technical education. On the other hand, many economists of the individualist school exhaust the resources of language in condemning and repudiating, not merely the interference of the general government in such matters, but the application of a farthing of the funds raised by local taxation to these purposes. I entertain a strong conviction that, in this country, at any rate, the State had much better leave purely technical and trade instruction alone. But, although my personal leanings are decidedly towards the individualists, I have arrived at that conclusion on merely practical grounds. In fact, my individualism is rather of a sentimental sort, and I sometimes think I should be stronger in the faith if it were less vehemently advocated. I am unable to see that civil society is anything but a corporation established for a moral object — namely, the good of its members — and therefore that it may take such measures as seem fitting for the attainment of that which the general voice decides to be the general good. That the suffrage of the majority is by no means a scientific test of social good and evil is unfortunately too true; but, in practice, it is the only test we can apply, and the refusal to abide by it means anarchy. The purest despotism that ever existed is as much based upon that will of the majority (which is usually submission to the will of a small minority) as the freest republic. Law is the expression of the opinion of the majority; and it is law, and not mere opinion, because the many are strong enough to enforce it.

I am as strongly convinced as the most pronounced individualist can be, that it is desirable that every man should be free to act in every way which does not limit the corresponding freedom of his fellow-man. But

I fail to connect that great induction of political science with the practical corollary which is frequently drawn from it: that the State — that is, the people in their corporate capacity — has no business to meddle with anything but the administration of justice and external defence. It appears to me that the amount of freedom which incorporate society may fitly leave to its members is not a fixed quantity, to be determined *a priori* by deduction from the fiction called "natural rights"; but that it must be determined by, and vary with, circumstances. I conceive it to be demonstrable that the higher and the more complex the organization of the social body, the more closely is the life of each member bound up with that of the whole; and the larger becomes the category of acts which cease to be merely self-regarding, and which interfere with the freedom of others more or less seriously.

If a squatter, living ten miles away from any neighbour, chooses to burn his house down to get rid of vermin, there may be no necessity (in the absence of insurance offices) that the law should interfere with his freedom of action; his act can hurt nobody but himself. But, if the dweller in a street chooses to do the same thing, the State very properly makes such a proceeding a crime, and punishes it as such. He does meddle with his neighbour's freedom, and that seriously. So it might, perhaps, be a tenable doctrine, that it would be needless, and even tyrannous, to make education compulsory in a sparse agricultural population, living in abundance on the produce of its own soil; but, in a densely populated manufacturing country, struggling for existence with competitors, every ignorant person tends to become a burden upon, and, so far, an infringer of the liberty of, his fellows, and an obstacle to their success. Under such circumstances an education rate is, in fact, a war tax, levied for purposes of defence.

That State action always has been more or less misdirected, and always will be so, is, I believe, perfectly true. But I am not aware that it is more true of the action of men in their corporate capacity than it is of the doings of individuals. The wisest and most dispassionate man in existence, merely wishing to go from one stile in a field to the opposite, will not walk quite straight — he is always going a little wrong, and always correcting himself; and I can only congratulate the individualist who is able to say that his general course of life has been of a less undulatory character. To abolish State action, because its direction is never more than approximately correct, appears to me to be much the same thing as abolishing the man at the wheel altogether, because, do what he will, the ship yaws more or less. "Why should I be robbed of my property to pay for teaching another man's children?" is an individualist question, which is not unfrequently put as if it settled the whole business. Perhaps it does, but I find difficulties in seeing why it should. The parish in which I live makes me pay my share for the paving and lighting of a great many streets that I never pass through; and I might plead that I am robbed to smooth the way and lighten the darkness of other people. But I am afraid the parochial authorities would not let me off on this plea; and I must confess I do not see why they should.

I cannot speak of my own knowledge, but I have every reason to believe that I came into this world a small reddish person, certainly without a gold spoon in my mouth, and in fact with no discernible abstract or concrete "rights" or property of any description. If a foot was not set upon me, at once, as a squalling nuisance, it was either the natural affection of those about me, which I certainly had done nothing to deserve, or the fear of the law which, ages before my birth, was painfully built up by the society into which I intruded, that prevented that catastrophe. If I was nourished, cared for, taught, saved from the vagabondage of a wastrel, I certainly am not aware that I did anything to deserve those advantages. And, if I possess anything now, it strikes me that, though I may have fairly earned my day's wages for my day's work, and may justly call them my property — yet, without that organization of society, created out of the toil and blood of long generations before my time, I should probably have had nothing but a flint axe and an indifferent hut to call my own; and even those would be mine only so long as no stronger savage came my way.

So that if society, having, quite gratuitously, done all these things for me, asks me in turn to do something towards its preservation — even if that something is to contribute to the teaching of other men's children — I really, in spite of all my individualist leanings, feel rather ashamed to say no. And if I were not ashamed, I cannot say that I think that society would be dealing unjustly with me in converting the moral obligation into a legal one. There is a manifest unfairness in letting all the burden be borne by the willing horse.

Mind as a Social Factor

(1884)

LESTER FRANK WARD

Just as the metaphysicians lost their bearings by an empty worship of mind and made philosophy a plaything, so the modern evolutionists have missed their mark by degrading mind to a level with mechanical force.

From Lester F. Ward, *Glimpses of the Cosmos* (New York: Knickerbocker Press, 1913–18), vol. 3, 367–377.

They seem thus about to fling away the grand results that the doctrine of evolution cannot otherwise fail to achieve. Far be it from me to appeal to the prejudices of the enemies of science by casting opprobrium upon scientific deductions, but when I consider the tendencies which are now so unmistakable, and which are so certainly the consequence of the protracted study, on the part of leading scientists, of the unquestionable methods of nature, I think I can, though holding precisely opposite opinions, fully sympathise with Carlyle in characterising the philosophy of evolution as a "gospel of dirt."

But I need not longer dwell upon the blighting influence of this construction of the known laws of nature. Let us approach the kernel of the problem.

The *laissez faire* doctrine fails to recognise that, in the development of mind, a virtually *new power* was introduced into the world. To say that this has been done is no startling announcement. It is no more than has taken place many times in the course of the evolution of living and feeling beings out of the tenuous nebulæ of space. For, while it is true that nature makes no leaps, while, so long as we consider their beginning, all the great steps in evolution are due to minute increments repeated through vast periods, still, when we survey the whole field, as we must do to comprehend the scheme, and contrast the extremes, we find that nature has been making a series of enormous strides, and reaching from one plane of development to another. It is these independent achievements of evolution that the true philosopher must study.

Not to mention the great steps in the cosmical history of the solar system and of the earth, we must regard the evolution of protoplasm, the "physical basis of life," as one of those gigantic strides which thenceforth completely revolutionised the surface of our planet. The development of the cell as the unit of organisation was another such stride. The origin of vertebrate life introduced a new element, and the birth of man wrought still another transformation. These are only a few of nature's revolutions. Many more will suggest themselves. And although, in no single one of these cases can it be said at what exact point the new essence commenced to exist, although the development of all these several expressions of Nature's method of concentrating her hitherto diffused forces was accomplished through an unbroken series of minute transitional increments continued through eons of time, still, it is not a whit less true that each of these grand products of evolution, when at length fully formed, constituted a new cosmic energy, and proceeded to stamp all future products and processes with a character hitherto wholly unknown upon the globe.

It is in this sense, and in this only, that I claim the development of mind — of the thinking, reasoning, inventing faculty of the human brain — as another, and one of the best marked, of the great cosmic strides that have characterised the course of evolution and belong to the legitimate methods of nature.

It is, for example, only to limited extent and in the most general way that we can apply the same canons to the organic as to the inorganic world. It is usually, but falsely, supposed that the student of biology need know nothing of physics, the assumption being that they have nothing in common. While this error is fatal to all fundamental acquaintance with the laws of life, it well illustrates the immensity of the advance from one realm to the other. The same could be said, in varying degrees of obviousness, of every one of the ascending steps to which reference has been made. I freely admit that the theologians and metaphysicians commit the most fatal error in treating the soul, or mind, as independent of the body, but this enormous fallacy is scarcely greater than that of the modern evolutionist, who, finding out their dependence, ignores the *magnitude* of the step by which mind was made a property of body, and proceeds as though no new factor had entered into the world.

But all this may be regarded as mere generality. Let us come to something more specific.

It has always been a marvel to my comprehension that wise men and philosophers, when smitten with the specious logic of the *laissez faire* school, can close their eyes to the most obtrusive fact that civilisation presents. In spite of the influence of philosophy, all forms of which have thus far been negative and nihilistic, the human animal, with his growing intellect, has still ever realised the power that is vouchsafed through mind, and has ever exercised that power. Philosophy would have long since robbed him of it and caused his early extermination from the earth but for the persistence, through heredity, of the impulse to exercise in self-preservation every power in his possession; by which practice alone he first gained his ascendancy ages before philosophy began.

The great fact, then, to which I allude is that, in spite of all philosophy, whether mythologic, metaphysical, or naturalistic, declaring that man must and can do nothing, he *has*, from the very dawn of his intelligence, been transforming the entire surface of the planet he inhabits. No other animal performs anything comparable to what man performs. This is solely because no other possesses the developed psychic faculty.

If we analyse mind into its two departments, sense and intellect, we shall see that it is through this latter faculty that these results are accomplished. If we inquire more closely into the mode by which intellect operates, we shall find that it serves as a guiding power to those natural forces with which it is acquainted (and no others), directing them into channels of human advantage. If we seek for a single term by which to characterise with precision the nature of this process, we find this in

Invention. The essential characteristic of all intellectual action is invention.

Glancing now at the *ensemble* of human achievement, which may be collectively called civilisation, we readily see that it is all the result of this inventive process. All practical art is merely the product of successful invention, and it requires no undue expansion of the term, nor extraordinary power of generalisation, to see in all human institutions only modified forms of arts, and true products of the intellectual, or inventive, faculty.

But what is the general result of all this? An entirely new dispensation has been given to the world. All the materials and forces of nature have been thus placed completely under the control of one of the otherwise least powerful of the creatures inhabiting the earth. He has only to know them in order to become their master. Nature has thus been made the servant of man. Thus only has man succeeded in peopling the entire globe while all other animals are restricted to narrow faunal areas. He has also peopled certain portions far more densely than any other species could have done, and he seems destined to continue multiplying his numbers for a long time yet in the future. But this quantitative proof is even less telling than the qualitative. When we confine our attention to the *élite* of mankind we do not need to have the ways specified in detail by which the powers of mind have exalted the intellectual being above all other products of creation. At the present moment the most dense and the most enlightened populations of the globe occupy what are termed temperate latitudes, which mean latitudes in which for from three to five months each year vegetation ceases entirely, the waters are locked in ice, and the temperature frequently sinks far below the zero of the Fahrenheit thermometer. Imagine the thin-skinned, furless animal man subsisting in such a climate. Extinguish his fires, banish his clothing, blot out the habitations that deck the civilised landscape. How long would the puny race survive? But these are not products of nature, they are products of *art*, the wages of thought — fruits of the intellect.

When a well-clothed philosopher on a bitter winter's night sits in a warm room well lighted for his purpose and writes on paper with pen and ink in the arbitrary characters of a highly developed language the statement that civilisation is the result of natural laws, and that man's duty is to let nature alone so that untrammeled it may work out a higher civilisation, he simply ignores every circumstance of his existence and deliberately closes his eyes to every fact within the range of his faculties. If man had acted upon his theory there would have been no civilisation, and our philosopher would have remained a troglodyte.

But how shall we distinguish this human, or anthropic, method from the method of nature? Simply by reversing all the definitions. Art is the antithesis of nature. If we call one the natural method we must call the other the artificial method. If nature's process is rightly named natural selection, man's process is artificial selection. The survival of the fittest is simply the survival of the strong, which implies, and might as well be called, the destruction of the weak. And if nature progresses through the destruction of the weak, man progresses through the *protection* of the weak. This is the essential distinction.

In human society the psychic power has operated to secure the protection of the weak in two distinct ways: first, by increasing the supply of the necessities of life, and, secondly, by preventing the destruction of life through the enemies of man. The immediate instrumentality through which the first of these processes is carried on is art, the product of invention. The second process takes place through the establishment of positive institutions.

It is difficult to say which of these agencies has been most effective. Both were always indispensable, and therefore all comparison is unprofitable.

Art operates to protect the weak against adverse surroundings. It is directed against natural forces, chiefly physical. By thus defeating the destructive influences of the elements and hostile forms of life, and by forcing nature to yield an unnatural supply of man's necessities, many who would have succumbed from inability to resist these adverse agencies — the feebler members of society — were able to survive, and population increased and expanded. While no one openly denies this, there is a tendency either to ignore it in politico-economic discussions, or to deny its application to them as an answer to naturalistic arguments.

If, on the other hand, we inquire into the nature of human institutions, we shall perceive that they are of three kinds, tending to protect the weak in three ways, or ascending degrees. These three successively higher means through which this end is attained are, first, Justice, second, Morality, and third, Charity. These forms of action have been reached through the development, respectively, of the three corresponding sentiments: Equity, Beneficence, and Benevolence.

All of these altruistic sentiments are wholly unknown, or known only in the merest embryo, to all animals below man, and therefore no such means of protection exist among them. They are strictly human, or anthropic. Many evolutionists fail to recognise this. Some sociologists refuse to admit it. They look about and see so much injustice, immorality and rapacity that they are led to suppose that only natural methods are in operation in society. This is a great mistake. In point of fact, the keener the sense of justice the more conspicuous the diminishing number of violations of it come to appear, and conversely, the obviousness of injustice proves the general prevalence of justice. It is the same with morality and philanthropy.

If we consider the effect of these three codes of human conduct in the direction of enabling the weaker ones to survive we shall see that it has been immense. Out of the first has arisen government, the chief value and function of which has always been and still is such protection. Great systems of jurisprudence have been elaborated, engrossing the attention of a large portion of the population of enlightened as well as of barbaric states. To say that these have been failures because often weighted with grave defects is to misinterpret history and misunderstand society. No one could probably be found to gainsay that the moral law of society has exerted a salutary influence, yet its aim is strictly altruistic, opposed to the law of the survival of the fittest, and wholly in the direction of enabling those to survive who would not survive without its protection. Finally, the last sentiment to be developed, and doubtless the highest, is so universally recognised as peculiar to man that his very name has been given to it — the sentiment of *humanity*. Yet the mode of protecting the weak arising out of this sentiment is the one that has been most seriously called in question by the naturalistic school. It must be admitted that humanitarian institutions have done far less good than either juridical or ethical institutions. The sentiment itself is of recent origin, the product only of highly developed and greatly refined mental organisation. It exists to an appreciable degree only in a minute fraction of the most enlightened populations. It is rarely directed with judgment; no fixed, self-enforcing code of conduct, as in the other cases, having had time to take shape. The institutions established to enforce it are for the most part poorly supported, badly managed, and often founded on a total misconception of human nature and of the true mode of attaining the end in view. Hence they are specially open to attack. But if ever humanitarian sentiments become diffused throughout the body politic, become the object of deep study, as have those of justice and right, it may be confidently predicted that society will prove itself capable of caring for the most unfortunate of its members in a manner that shall not work demoralisation.

In all these ways man, through his intelligence, has laboured successfully to resist the law of nature. His success is conclusively demonstrated by a comparison of his condition with that of other species of animals. No other cause can be assigned for his superiority. How can the naturalistic philosophers shut their eyes to such obvious facts? Yet, what is their attitude? They condemn all attempts to protect the weak, whether by private or public methods. They claim that it deteriorates the race by enabling the unfit to survive and transmit their inferiority. This is true only in certain cases of hereditary diseases or mental deficiencies, which should be taken account of by man because they are not by nature. Nothing is easier than to show that the unrestricted competition of nature does not secure the survival of the fittest possible, but only of the actually fittest, and in every attempt man makes to obtain something fitter than this actual fittest he succeeds, as witness improved breeds of animals and grafts of fruits. Now, the human method of protecting the weak deals in some such way with men. It not only increases the number but improves the quality.

But "government," at least, must *laisser faire*. It must not "meddle" with natural laws. The laws of trade, business, social intercourse, are natural laws, immutable and indestructible. All interference with them is vain. The fallacy here is a *non sequitur*. It may be readily granted that these laws are immutable and indestructible. Were this not the case it would certainly be hopeless to interfere with their action. But every mechanical invention proves that nothing is easier than to interfere successfully with the operation of these uniform natural forces. They have only to be first thoroughly understood and then they are easily *controlled*. To *destroy* a force is one thing, to control its action is quite another. Those who talk in this way involve themselves in the most palpable inconsistency. They must not be allowed to stop where they do. They must go on and carry their strictures to a logical conclusion. They must deny to government the right to protect its citizens from injustice. This is a clear interference with the natural laws of society. They must deny to society the right to enforce its code of morals. Nothing is more unnatural. They must suppress the healing art which keeps the sick from dying as they do among animals. Nor is this all. They must condemn all interference with physical laws and natural forces. To dam a stream must be characterised as a "vain" attempt to overcome a natural law. The wind must be left free to blow where it will, and not be forced against the fan of a wind-mill. The vapour of heated water must be allowed to float off naturally into the air and not be pent up in a steam-boiler and thence conducted into the cylinder of a steam-engine. All these things and every other device of inventive man are so many attempts to "violate" the laws of nature, which is declared impossible.

What then remains of the *laissez faire* doctrine? Nothing but this: That it is useless, and may be dangerous, to attempt to control natural forces until their character is first well understood. This is a proposition which is true for every department of force, and does not involve the surrender of the whole domain of sociology after it has been demonstrated that society is a theatre of forces.

The truth thus comes forth from a rational study of nature and human society that social progress has been due only in very slight degree to natural evolution as accomplished through the survival of the fittest, and its chief success has resulted from the reduction of competition in the struggle for existence and the protection of the weaker members. Such competition, in so far as it has been permitted to operate, has tended to lower the standard of the fittest and to check advancement. It is not, of course, claimed that the natural method has ever been fully overcome. It has always operated, and still operates, powerfully in many ways. It has been chiefly in the simpler departments of physical and mechanical phenomena that the psychic, or anthropic, method has superseded it. The inventive arts have been the result. Vital forces have yielded to some extent to the influence of mind in bringing about improved stocks of animals and vegetables, and even certain social laws have come under rational control through the establishment of institutions. Still, every step in this progress has been contested. It was not enough that the intellect was feeble and ill-fitted to grapple with such problems. It was not enough that ignorance of nature's laws should cause unnumbered failures. A still stronger barrier was presented by the intellect itself in the form of positive error embodied in philosophy. As already remarked, philosophy has always been negative and nihilistic, and has steadily antagonised the common sense of mankind. It is only quite recently that there has come into existence anything like a truly *positive* philosophy, *i.e.*, a philosophy of *action*. The intellectual power of enlightened man has at length become sufficient to grasp the problems of social life. A large body of truth has been accumulated by which to be guided in their solution. Positive error in the drawing of false conclusions from established facts is now the chief obstacle. Rational interpretation has come to prevail in all the lower departments of phenomena. It is chiefly in the complex departments of psychic and social action that error still holds sway. Nothing remains to be done but to apply the established canons of science to these higher fields of activity. Here there is still competition. Here the weaker still go to the wall. Here the strong are still the fittest to survive. Here Nature still practises her costly selection which always involves the destruction of the defenceless. The demand is for still further reduction of competition, still greater interference with the operations of natural forces, still more complete control of the laws of nature, and still more absolute supremacy of the psychic over the natural method of evolution.

These ends will be secured in proportion as the true nature of mind is understood. When nature comes to be regarded as passive and man as active, instead of the reverse as now, when human action is recognized as the most important of all forms of action, and when the power of the human intellect over vital, psychic and social phenomena is practically conceded, then, and then only, can man justly claim to have risen out of the animal and fully to have entered the human stage of development.

VII

THE REVOLT AGAINST POSITIVISM AND FORMALISM: FICTIONALISM

The decade of the 1890's marked an important watershed in both European and American intellectual life. Moreover, the changes in intellectual orientation experienced by Europeans and Americans at the turn of the century, while not identical, exhibited important similarities. Two American scholars have examined the underlying presuppositions of the European and American intellectual revolutions of the 1890's, and a brief account of their analyses should serve to guide the student through this and the following two groups of readings.

In Consciousness and Society: The Reorientation of European Social Thought 1890–1930, *H. Stuart Hughes argues that the unifying theme of early twentieth-century European thought was a "revolt against positivism." By positivism, Hughes means, first of all, the endeavor of late nineteenth-century thinkers to develop a social science modeled on the natural sciences. The Darwinian social theories that the reader encountered in Section VI can serve as a prime example of that endeavor. Positivist social theory entailed a search for fixed social laws, which eventually would permit the kind of predictability in social life that the physicist or chemist demonstrated in the natural world. In more general terms, according to Hughes, positivism implied an intellectual atmosphere receptive to philosophical materialism and to mechanistic and deterministic psychological conceptions, while insensitive to the imagination, to the arts, and to the complexities and irrationality of much social and psychological behavior.*

The intellectuals of the generation of 1890, Hughes argues, reacted against both the specific tenets and the underlying assumptions of positivism. Led by such giants as Sigmund Freud, Max Weber, Emile Durkheim, and Benedetto Croce, they abandoned the notion that social and psychological theory could be constructed on the model of physics, chemistry, or biology. Indeed, even the natural scientists of this generation, whom Hughes does not treat expressly in his book, came to reject the methodological presuppositions of their predecessors, especially after Max Plank's quantum theory and Albert Einstein's great work on relativity had substantially undermined the certainties of Newtonian physics. Similarly, the psychologists and sociologists of the generation of 1890 — as Sections VII, VIII, and IX demonstrate — discarded many of the substantive prejudices of positivism, preferring subjective, even spiritual, explanations to the materialistic and mechanistic formulations favored by the previous generation.

Morton White has found an analogous pattern among American intellectuals at the turn of the century. In *Social Thought in America: The Revolt against Formalism*, White treats the work of five American social theorists: Charles A. Beard, John Dewey, Oliver Wendell Holmes, Jr., James Harvey Robinson, and Thorstein Veblen. He suggests that the characteristic motif in the writings of all these men was a reaction against the formalistic nature of nineteenth-century philosophy, economic theory, political science, and jurisprudence. All were convinced, says White, that "logic, abstraction, deduction, mathematics, and mechanics were inadequate to social research and incapable of containing the rich, moving, living current of social life." [1] Accordingly, they emphasized empirical, interdisciplinary, and historical approaches to problems of social analysis. Veblen, for example, sought to replace the formalistic methodology of classical political economy (the tradition of Adam Smith and David Ricardo, which deduced the laws of economic behavior from an imagined world of perfect competition) with empirical studies of actual economic behavior in America, Germany, and other countries.

The affinities between the intellectual revolution described by White and that described by Hughes are immediately apparent. Both groups of intellectuals were rebelling against a style of thought that was incapable, in White's phrase, of "coming to grips with life, experience, process, growth, context, function." [2] But there were differences as well. Most important, the European critics of positivism were not necessarily hostile to intellectual abstraction. What they disliked in positivism, in other words, was not the use of abstractions as such, but the use of abstractions, drawn from the natural sciences, that were inappropriate to the study of man and society.

[1] Morton White, *Social Thought in America: The Revolt against Formalism* (Boston: Beacon Press, 1957), 11.
[2] *Ibid.*, 13.

The readings in this section introduce the characteristic epistemological concerns of the early twentieth century. We have entitled the section "Fictionalism," a concept that Hans Vaihinger defines at some length below, because the thinkers represented here shared a common dissatisfaction with the conceptual realism of their predecessors, whether positivist social scientists, idealist philosophers, or classical economists. The American variant of fictionalism, pragmatism, actually preceded and to some extent determined the development of fictionalist thinking in Europe, thus revenging the capture of American intellectuals by European Darwinism in the previous generation. The pragmatist movement in American philosophy traces its origins to Charles Peirce's essay "How to Make Our Ideas Clear," written in 1878, although, as William James points out in "What Pragmatism Means," Peirce's ideas exerted little influence until James revived them in 1898. Both Peirce (1839–1914) and James (1842–1910) argue that the truth of a belief is a function of its practical significance; that is, its truth is not independent of the individual who holds it, but is in fact relative to the human action that issues from it. James is consistently more radical in his relativism and subjectivism than Peirce. Indeed, when James went to the extreme of claiming, admittedly with tongue partially in cheek, that ideas become *true if one believes them, Peirce was sufficiently scandalized to dissociate himself from the pragmatist school, renaming his own position "pragmaticism."*

Hans Vaihinger (1852–1933) wrote his Philosophy of 'as If' *with much the same sense of paradox that informs the work of Peirce and James. Fictions, Vaihinger tells us, are ideas "which are known to be false, but which are employed because of their utility."* [3] *However, a subtle difference of purpose distinguishes Vaihinger's fictionalism from the pragmatism of his American counterparts. The usefulness of fictions, according to Vaihinger, is measured not by their practical significance, but in purely intellectual terms. Like Max Weber's concept of ideal types — the sociological analogue of Vaihinger's fictions — a fiction serves to facilitate understanding. Where Peirce and, to a lesser extent, James seem preoccupied with eliminating redundant or meaningless distinctions, Vaihinger, and Weber as well, are interested in enriching our conceptual universe. One might legitimately ask whether this differences of emphasis reflects an anti-intellectual strain in pragmatism perhaps characteristic of the American intellectual tradition as a whole.*

The final selection from Georges Sorel (1847–1922) illustrates the uses of fictional thinking — or, as Sorel would have it, mythical

[3] Hans Vaihinger, *The Philosophy of 'as If,'* tr. C. K. Ogden (London: Routledge and Kegan Paul, 1924), XLII.

thinking — for radical social criticism. Sorel, like all Marxist intellectuals of his generation, was concerned with what has been called the failure of polarization. Marx's Capital *had predicted that, preceding the socialist revolution, capitalist society would divide into two antagonistic camps: a small class of extraordinarily wealthy capitalists and a vast, dispossessed army of proletarians. However, as the nineteenth century gave way to the twentieth, it became increasingly evident that no such polarization was taking place. Rather, a growing class of white collar workers, neither capitalist nor proletarian, had interposed itself between the traditional Marxian antagonists. Moreover, the proletariat itself, instead of experiencing the progressive impoverishment forecast by Marx, was enjoying a considerable improvement of its lot. Most of the theoretical and tactical controversies that divided the ranks of socialists at the turn of the century resulted from the effort to cope with this unexpected turn of events. In particular, the emergence of both revisionist, or democratic, socialism and Leninist communism can be traced directly to the failure of polarization.*

In Reflections on Violence *Sorel propounds his own rather idiosyncratic solution to this dilemma. He suggests that a mythical conception, the idea of the general strike, might serve to recreate, at least psychologically, the conditions that Marx's theory had predicted. Sorel, it should be noted, was significantly influenced by William James, both directly and through the mediation of Henri Bergson, also an admirer and correspondent of James's. In fact, Sorel's theory of the general strike ingeniously combines Bergson's intuitionism (the notion that the mind grasps reality immediately as a totality, rather than piecemeal by means of analysis) and James's theory that the truth of a belief is a function of its effectiveness.*

How to Make Our Ideas Clear

(1878)

CHARLES SANDERS PEIRCE

The principles set forth in the first of these papers lead, at once, to a method of reaching a clearness of thought of a far higher grade than the "distinctness" of the logicians. We have there found that the action of

From *Popular Science Monthly*, XII (January, 1878), 289–295, 297–301.

thought is excited by the irritation of doubt, and ceases when belief is attained; so that the production of belief is the sole function of thought. All these words, however, are too strong for my purpose. It is as if I had described the phenomena as they appear under a mental microscope. Doubt and Belief, as the words are commonly employed, relate to religious or other grave discussions. But here I use them to designate the starting of any question, no matter how small or how great, and the resolution of it. If, for instance, in a horse-car, I pull out my purse and find a five-cent nickel and five coppers, I decide, while my hand is going to the purse, in which way I will pay my fare. To call such a question Doubt, and my decision Belief, is certainly to use words very disproportionate to the occasion. To speak of such a doubt as causing an irritation which needs to be appeased, suggests a temper which is uncomfortable to the verge of insanity. Yet, looking at the matter minutely, it must be admitted that, if there is the least hesitation as to whether I shall pay the five coppers or the nickel (as there will be sure to be, unless I act from some previously contracted habit in the matter), though irritation is too strong a word, yet I am excited to such small mental activity as may be necessary to deciding how I shall act. Most frequently doubts arise from some indecision, however momentary, in our action. Sometimes it is not so. I have, for example, to wait in a railway-station, and to pass the time I read the advertisements on the walls, I compare the advantages of different trains and different routes which I never expect to take, merely fancying myself to be in a state of hesitancy, because I am bored with having nothing to trouble me. Feigned hesitancy, whether feigned for mere amusement or with a lofty purpose, plays a great part in the production of scientific inquiry. However the doubt may originate, it stimulates the mind to an activity which may be slight or energetic, calm or turbulent. Images pass rapidly through consciousness, one incessantly melting into another, until at last, when all is over — it may be in a fraction of a second, in an hour, or after long years — we find ourselves decided as to how we should act under such circumstances as those which occasioned our hesitation. In other words, we have attained belief.

In this process we observe two sorts of elements of consciousness, the distinction between which may best be made clear by means of an illustration. In a piece of music there are the separate notes, and there is the air. A single tone may be prolonged for an hour or a day, and it exists as perfectly in each second of that time as in the whole taken together; so that, as long as it is sounding, it might be present to a sense from which everything in the past was as completely absent as the future itself. But it is different with the air, the performance of which occupies a certain time, during the portions of which only portions of it are played. It consists in an orderliness in the succession of sounds which strike the ear at different times; and to perceive it there must be some continuity of consciousness which makes the events of a lapse of time present to us. We certainly only perceive the air by hearing the separate notes; yet we cannot be said to directly hear it, for we hear only what is present at the instant, and an orderliness of succession cannot exist in an instant. These two sorts of objects, what we are *immediately* conscious of and what we are *mediately* conscious of, are found in all consciousness. Some elements (the sensations) are completely present at every instant so long as they last, while others (like thought) are actions having beginning, middle, and end, and consist in a congruence in the succession of sensations which flow through the mind. They cannot be immediately present to us, but must cover some portion of the past or future. Thought is a thread of melody running through the succession of our sensations.

We may add that just as a piece of music may be written in parts, each part having its own air, so various systems of relationship of succession subsist together between the same sensations. These different systems are distinguished by having different motives, ideas, or functions. Thought is only one such system, for its sole motive, idea, and function, is to produce belief, and whatever does not concern that purpose belongs to some other system of relations. The action of thinking may incidentally have other results; it may serve to amuse us, for example, and among *dilettanti* it is not rare to find those who have so perverted thought to the purposes of pleasure that it seems to vex them to think that the questions upon which they delight to exercise it may ever get finally settled; and a positive discovery which takes a favorite subject out of the arena of literary debate is met with ill-concealed dislike. This disposition is the very debauchery of thought. But the soul and meaning of thought, abstracted from the other elements which accompany it, though it may be voluntarily thwarted, can never be made to direct itself toward anything but the production of belief. Thought in action has for its only possible motive the attainment of thought at rest; and whatever does not refer to belief is no part of the thought itself.

And what, then, is belief? It is the demi-cadence which closes a musical phrase in the symphony of our intellectual life. We have seen that it has just three properties: First, it is something that we are aware of; second, it appeases the irritation of doubt; and, third, it involves the establishment in our nature of a rule of action, or, say for short, a *habit*. As it appeases the irritation of doubt, which is the motive for thinking, thought relaxes, and comes to rest for a moment when belief is reached. But, since belief is a rule for action, the application of which involves further doubt and further thought, at the same time that it is a stopping-place, it is also a new starting-place for thought. That is why I have permitted myself to call it thought at rest, although thought is essentially an action. The *final* upshot of thinking is the exercise of volition, and of this thought no longer forms a part; but belief is only a stadium of mental action, an effect upon our nature due to thought, which will influence future thinking.

The essence of belief is the establishment of a habit, and different beliefs are distinguished by the different modes of action to which they give rise. If beliefs do not differ in this respect, if they appease the same doubt by producing the same rule of action, then no mere differences in the manner of consciousness of them can make them different beliefs, any more than playing a tune in different keys is playing different tunes. Imaginary distinctions are often drawn between beliefs which differ only in their mode of expression; — the wrangling which ensues is real enough, however. . . . Such false distinctions do as much harm as the confusion of beliefs really different, and are among the pitfalls of which we ought constantly to beware, especially when we are upon metaphysical ground. One singular deception of that sort, which often occurs, is to mistake the sensation produced by our own unclearness of thought for a character of the object we are thinking. Instead of perceiving that the obscurity is purely subjective, we fancy that we contemplate a quality of the object which is essentially mysterious; and if our conception be afterward presented to us in a clear form we do not recognize it as the same, owing to the absence of the feeling of unintelligibility. So long as this deception lasts, it obviously puts an impassable barrier in the way of perspicuous thinking; so that it equally interests the opponents of rational thought to perpetuate it, and its adherents to guard against it.

Another such deception is to mistake a mere difference in the grammatical construction of two words for a distinction between the ideas they express. In this pedantic age, when the general mob of writers attend so much more to words than to things, this error is common enough. When I just said that thought is an *action*, and that it consists in a *relation*, although a person performs an action but not a relation, which can only be the result of an action, yet there was no inconsistency in what I said, but only a grammatical vagueness.

From all these sophisms we shall be perfectly safe so long as we reflect that the whole function of thought is to produce habits of action; and that whatever there is connected with a thought, but irrelevant to its purpose, is an accretion to it, but no part of it. If there be a unity among our sensations which has no reference to how we shall act on a given occasion, as when we listen to a piece of music, why we do not call that thinking. To develop its meaning, we have, therefore, simply to determine what habits it produces, for what a thing means is simply what habits it involves. Now, the identity of a habit depends on how it might lead us to act, not merely under such circumstances as are likely to arise, but under such as might possibly occur, no matter how improbable they may be. What the habit is depends on *when* and *how* it causes us to act. As for the *when*, every stimulus to action is derived from perception; as for the *how*, every purpose of action is to produce some sensible result. Thus, we come down to what is tangible and practical, as the root of every real distinction of thought, no matter how subtile it may be; and there is no distinction of meaning so fine as to consist in anything but a possible difference of practice.

To see what this principle leads to, consider in the light of it such a doctrine as that of transubstantiation. The Protestant churches generally hold that the elements of the sacrament are flesh and blood only in a tropical sense; they nourish our souls as meat and the juice of it would our bodies. But the Catholics maintain that they are literally just that; although they possess all the sensible qualities of wafer-cakes and diluted wine. But we can have no conception of wine except what may enter into a belief, either —

1. That this, that, or the other, is wine; or,
2. That wine possesses certain properties.

Such beliefs are nothing but self-notifications that we should, upon occasion, act in regard to such things as we believe to be wine according to the qualities which we believe wine to possess. The occasion of such action would be some sensible perception, the motive of it to produce some sensible result. Thus our action has exclusive reference to what affects the senses, our habit has the same bearing as our action, our belief the same as our habit, our conception the same as our belief; and we can consequently mean nothing by wine but what has certain effects, direct or indirect, upon our senses; and to talk of something as having all the sensible characters of wine, yet being in reality blood, is senseless jargon. Now, it is not my object to pursue the theological question; and having used it as a logical example I drop it, without caring to anticipate the theologian's reply. I only desire to point out how impossible it is that we should have an idea in our minds which relates to anything but conceived sensible effects of things. Our idea of anything *is* our idea of its sensible effects; and if we fancy that we have any other we deceive ourselves, and mistake a mere sensation accompanying the thought for a part of the thought itself. It is absurd to say that thought has any meaning unrelated to its only function. It is foolish for Catholics and Protestants to fancy themselves in disagreement about the elements of the sacrament, if they agree in regard to all their sensible effects, here or hereafter.

It appears, then, that the rule for attaining the third grade of clearness of apprehension is as follows: Consider what effects, which might conceivably have practical bearings, we conceive the object of our conception to have. Then, our conception of these effects is the whole of our conception of the object.

Let us illustrate this rule by some examples; and, to begin with the simplest one possible, let us ask what we mean by calling a thing *hard*. Evidently that it will not be scratched by many other substances. The whole conception of this quality, as of every other, lies in its conceived effects. There is absolutely no difference between a hard thing and a soft thing so long as they are not brought to the test. Suppose, then, that a diamond could be crystallized in the midst of a cushion of soft cotton, and should remain there until it was finally burned up. Would it be false to say that that diamond was soft? This seems a foolish question, and would be so, in fact, except in the realm of logic. There such questions are often of the greatest utility as serving to bring logical principles into sharper relief than real discussions ever could. In studying logic we must not put them aside with hasty answers, but must consider them with attentive care, in order to make out the principles involved. We may, in the present case, modify our question, and ask what prevents us from saying that all hard bodies remain perfectly soft until they are touched, when their hardness increases with the pressure until they are scratched. Reflection will show that the reply is this: there would be no *falsity* in such modes of speech. They would involve a modification of our present usage of speech with regard to the words hard and soft, but not of their meanings. For they represent no fact to be different from what it is; only they involve arrangements of facts which would be exceedingly maladroit. This leads us to remark that the question of what would occur under circumstances which do not actually arise is not a question of fact, but only of the most perspicuous arrangement of them. For example, the question of free-will and fate in its simplest form, stripped of verbiage, is something like this: I have done something of which I am ashamed; could I, by an effort of the will, have resisted the temptation, and done otherwise? The philosophical reply is, that this is not a question of fact, but only of the arrangement of facts. Arranging them so as to exhibit what is particularly pertinent to my question — namely, that I ought to blame myself for having done wrong — it is perfectly true to say that, if I had willed to do otherwise than I did, I should have done otherwise. On the other hand, arranging the facts so as to exhibit another important consideration, it is equally true that, when a temptation has once been allowed to work, it will, if it has a certain force, produce its effect, let me struggle how I may. There is no objection to a contradiction in what would result from a false supposition. The *reductio ad absurdum* consists in showing that contradictory results would follow from a hypothesis which is consequently judged to be false. Many questions are involved in the free-will discussion, and I am far from desiring to say that both sides are equally right. On the contrary, I am of opinion that one side denies important facts, and that the other does not. But what I do say is, that the above single question was the origin of the whole doubt; that, had it not been for this question, the controversy would never have arisen; and that this question is perfectly solved in the manner which I have indicated. . . .

Let us now approach the subject of logic, and consider a conception which particularly concerns it, that of *reality*. Taking clearness in the sense of familiarity, no idea could be clearer than this. Every child uses it with perfect confidence, never dreaming that he does not understand it. As for clearness in its second grade, however, it would probably puzzle most men, even among those of a reflective turn of mind, to give an abstract definition of the real. Yet such a definition may perhaps be reached by considering the points of difference between reality and its opposite, fiction. A figment is a product of somebody's imagination; it has such characters as his thought impresses upon it. That whose characters are independent of how you or I think is an external reality. There are, however, phenomena within our own minds, dependent upon our thought, which are at the same time real in the sense that we really think them. But though their characters depend on how we think, they do not depend on what we think those characters to be. Thus, a dream has a real existence as a mental phenomenon, if somebody has really dreamt it; that he dreamt so and so, does not depend on what anybody thinks was dreamt, but is completely independent of all opinion on the subject. On the other hand, considering, not the fact of dreaming, but the thing dreamt, it retains its peculiarities by virtue of no other fact than that it was dreamt to possess them. Thus we may define the real as that whose characters are independent of what anybody may think them to be.

But, however satisfactory such a definition may be found, it would be a great mistake to suppose that it makes the idea of reality perfectly clear. Here, then, let us apply our rules. According to them, reality, like every other quality, consists in the peculiar sensible effects which things partaking of it produce. The only effect which real things have is to cause belief, for all the sensations which they excite emerge into consciousness in the form of beliefs. The question therefore is, how is true belief (or belief in the real) distinguished from false belief (or belief in fiction). Now, as we have seen in the former paper, the ideas of truth and falsehood, in their full development, appertain exclusively to the scientific method of settling opinion. A person who arbitrarily chooses the propositions which he will adopt can use the word truth only to emphasize the expression of his determination to hold on to his choice. Of course, the method of tenacity never prevailed exclusively; reason is to natural to men for that. But in the literature of the dark ages we find some fine examples of it. When Scotus Erigena is commenting upon a poetical passage in which hellebore is spoken of as having caused the death of Socrates, he does not hesitate to inform the inquiring reader that Helleborus and Socrates were two eminent Greek philosophers, and that the latter having been overcome in argument by the former took the matter to heart and died of it! What sort of an idea of truth could a man have who could adopt and teach, without the qualification of a perhaps, an opinion taken so entirely at random? The real spirit of Socrates, who I hope would have been delighted to have been "overcome in argument," because he would have learned something by it, is in curious contrast with the naïve idea of the glossist, for whom discussion would seem to have been simply a struggle. When philosophy began to awake from its long slumber, and before theology completely dominated it, the practice seems to have been for each professor to seize upon any philosophical position he found unoccupied and which seemed a strong one, to intrench himself in it, and to sally forth from time to time to give battle to the others. Thus, even the scanty records we possess of those disputes enable us to make out a dozen or more opinions held by different teachers at one time concerning the question of nominalism and realism. Read the opening part of the "Historia Calamitatum" of Abelard, who was certainly as philosophical as any of his contemporaries, and see the spirit of combat which it breathes. For him, the truth is simply his particular stronghold. When the method of authority prevailed, the truth meant little more than the Catholic faith. All the efforts of the scholastic doctors are directed toward harmonizing their faith in Aristotle and their faith in the Church, and one may search their ponderous folios through without finding an argument which goes any further. It is noticeable that where different faiths flourish side by side, renegades are looked upon with contempt even by the party whose belief they adopt; so completely has the idea of loyalty replaced that of truth-seeking. Since the time of Descartes, the defect in the conception of truth has been less apparent. Still, it will sometimes strike a scientific man that the philosophers have been less intent on finding out what the facts are, than on inquiring what belief is most in harmony with their system. It is hard to convince a follower of the *a priori* method by adducing facts; but show him that an opinion he is defending is inconsistent with what he has laid down elsewhere, and he will be very apt to retract it. These minds do not seem to believe that disputation is ever to cease; they seem to think that the opinion which is natural for one man is not so for another, and that belief will, consequently, never be settled. In contenting themselves with fixing their own opinions by a method which would lead another man to a different result, they betray their feeble hold of the conception of what truth is.

On the other hand, all the followers of science are fully persuaded that the processes of investigation, if only pushed far enough, will give one certain solution to every question to which they can be applied. One man may investigate the velocity of light by studying the transits of Venus and the aberration of the stars; another by the oppositions of Mars and the eclipses of Jupiter's satellites; a third by the method of Fizeau; a fourth by that of Foucault; a fifth by the motions of the curves of Lissajoux; a sixth, a seventh, an eighth, and a ninth, may follow the different methods of comparing the measures of statical and dynamical electricity. They may at first obtain different results, but, as each perfects his method and his processes, the results will move steadily together toward a destined centre. So with all scientific research. Different minds may set out with the most antagonistic views, but the progress of investigation carries them by a force outside of themselves to one and the same conclusion. This activity of thought by which we are carried, not where we wish, but to a foreordained goal, is like the operation of destiny. No modification of the point of view taken, no selection of other facts for study, no natural bent of mind even, can enable a man to escape the predestinate opinion. This great law is embodied in the conception of truth and reality. The opinion which is fated to be ultimately agreed to by all who investigate, is what we mean by the truth, and the object represented in this opinion is the real. That is the way I would explain reality.

But it may be said that this view is directly opposed to the abstract definition which we have given of reality, inasmuch as it makes the characters of the real to depend on what is ultimately thought about them. But the answer to this is that, on the one hand, reality is independent, not necessarily of thought in general, but only of what you or I or any finite number of men may think about it; and that, on the other hand, though the object of the final opinion depends on what that opinion is, yet what that opinion is does not depend on what you or I or any man thinks. Our perversity and that of others may indefinitely postpone the settlement of opinion; it might even conceivably cause an arbitrary proposition to be universally accepted as long as the human race should last. Yet even that would not change the nature of the belief, which alone could be the result of investigation carried sufficiently far; and if, after the extinction of our race, another should arise with faculties and disposition for investigation, that true opinion must be the one which they would ultimately come to. "Truth crushed to earth shall rise again," and the opinion which would finally result from investigation does not depend on how anybody may actually think. But the reality of that which is real does depend on the real fact that investigation is destined to lead, at last, if continued long enough, to a belief in it.

But I may be asked what I have to say to all the minute facts of history, forgotten never to be recovered, to the lost books of the ancients, to the buried secrets.

> "Full many a gem of purest ray serene
> The dark, unfathomed caves of ocean bear;
> Full many a flower is born to blush unseen,
> And waste its sweetness on the desert air."

Do these things not really exist because they are hopelessly beyond the reach of our knowledge? And then, after the universe is dead (according to the prediction of some scientists), and all life has ceased forever, will not the shock of atoms continue though there will be no mind to know it? To this I reply that, though in no possible state of knowledge can any number be great enough to express the relation between the amount of what rests unknown to the amount of the known, yet it is unphilosophical to suppose that, with regard to any given question (which has any clear meaning), investigation would not bring forth a solution of it, if it were carried far enough. Who would have said, a few years ago, that we could ever know of what substances stars are made whose light may have been longer in reaching us than the human race has existed? Who can be sure of what we shall not know in a few hundred years? Who can guess what would be the result of continuing the pursuit of science for ten thousand years, with the activity of the last hundred? And if it were to go on for a million, or a billion, or any number of years you please, how is it possible to say that there is any question which might not ultimately be solved?

But it may be objected, "Why make so much of these remote considerations, especially when it is your principle that only practical distinctions have a meaning?" Well, I must confess that it makes very little difference whether we say that a stone on the bottom of the ocean, in complete darkness, is brilliant or not — that is to say, that it *probably* makes no difference, remembering always that that stone *may* be fished up to-morrow. But that there are gems at the bottom of the sea, flowers in the untraveled desert, etc., are propositions which, like that about a diamond being hard when it is not pressed, concern much more the arrangement of our language than they do the meaning of our ideas.

What Pragmatism Means
(1907)

WILLIAM JAMES

. . . The pragmatic method is primarily a method of settling metaphysical disputes that otherwise might be interminable. Is the world one or many? — fated or free? — material or spiritual? — here are notions either of which may or may not hold good of the world; and disputes over such notions are unending. The pragmatic method in such cases

From William James, *Pragmatism* (New York: Longmans, Green, and Co., 1907), 45–81.

is to try to interpret each notion by tracing its respective practical consequences. What difference would it practically make to any one if this notion rather than that notion were true? If no practical difference whatever can be traced, then the alternatives mean practically the same thing, and all dispute is idle. Whenever a dispute is serious, we ought to be able to show some practical difference that must follow from one side or the other's being right.

A glance at the history of the idea will show you still better what pragmatism means. The term is derived from the same Greek word πράγμα, meaning action, from which our words 'practice' and 'practical' come. It was first introduced into philosophy by Mr. Charles Peirce in 1878. In an article entitled 'How to Make Our Ideas Clear,' in the 'Popular Science Monthly' for January of that year Mr. Peirce, after pointing out that our beliefs are really rules for action, said that, to develop a thought's meaning, we need only determine what conduct it is fitted to produce: that conduct is for us its sole significance. And the tangible fact at the root of all our thought-distinctions, however subtle, is that there is no one of them so fine as to consist in anything but a possible difference of practice. To attain perfect clearness in our thoughts of an object, then, we need only consider what conceivable effects of a practical kind the object may involve — what sensations we are to expect from it, and what reactions we must prepare. Our conception of these effects, whether immediate or remote, is then for us the whole of our conception of the object, so far as that conception has positive significance at all.

This is the principle of Peirce, the principle of pragmatism. It lay entirely unnoticed by any one for twenty years, until I, in an address before Professor Howison's philosophical union at the university of California, brought it forward again and made a special application of it to religion. By that date (1898) the times seemed ripe for its reception. The word 'pragmatism' spread, and at present it fairly spots the pages of the philosophic journals. On all hands we find the 'pragmatic movement' spoken of, sometimes with respect, sometimes with contumely, seldom with clear understanding. It is evident that the term applies itself conveniently to a number of tendencies that hitherto have lacked a collective name, and that it has 'come to stay.'

To take in the importance of Peirce's principle, one must get accustomed to applying it to concrete cases. I found a few years ago that Ostwald, the illustrious Leipzig chemist, had been making prefectly distinct use of the principle of pragmatism in his lectures on the philosophy of science, though he had not called it by that name.

"All realities influence our practice," he wrote me, "and that influence is their meaning for us. I am accustomed to put questions to my classes in this way: In what respects would the world be different if this alternative or that were true? If I can find nothing that would become different, then the alternative has no sense."

That is, the rival views mean practically the same thing, and meaning, other than practical, there is for us none. Ostwald in a published lecture gives this example of what he means. Chemists have long wrangled over the inner constitution of certain bodies called 'tautomerous.' Their properties seemed equally consistent with the notion that an instable hydrogen atom oscillates inside of them, or that they are instable mixtures of two bodies. Controversy raged, but never was decided. "It would never have begun," says Ostwald, "if the combatants had asked themselves what particular experimental fact could have been made different by one or the other view being correct. For it would then have appeared that no difference of fact could possibly ensue; and the quarrel was as unreal as if, theorizing in primitive times about the raising of dough by yeast, one party should have invoked a 'brownie,' while another insisted on an 'elf' as the true cause of the phenomenon."

It is astonishing to see how many philosophical disputes collapse into insignificance the moment you subject them to this simple test of tracing a concrete consequence. There can *be* no difference anywhere that does n't *make* a difference elsewhere — no difference in abstract truth that does n't express itself in a difference in concrete fact and in conduct consequent upon that fact, imposed on somebody, somehow, somewhere, and somewhen. The whole function of philosophy ought to be to find out what definite difference it will make to you and me, at definite instances of our life, if this world-formula or that world-formula be the true one. . . .

Pragmatism represents a perfectly familiar attitude in philosophy, the empiricist attitude, but it represents it, as it seems to me, both in a more radical and in a less objectionable form than it has ever yet assumed. A pragmatist turns his back resolutely and once for all upon a lot of inveterate habits dear to professional philosophers. He turns away from abstraction and insufficiency, from verbal solutions, from bad *a priori* reasons, from fixed principles, closed systems, and pretended absolutes and origins. He turns towards concreteness and adequacy, towards facts, towards action and towards power. That means the empiricist temper regnant and the rationalist temper sincerely given up. It means the open air and possibilities of nature, as against dogma, artificiality, and the pretence of finality in truth.

At the same time it does not stand for any special results. It is a method only. But the general triumph of that method would mean an enormous change in what I called in my last lecture the 'temperament' of philosophy. Teachers of the ultra-rationalistic type would be frozen out, much as the courtier type is frozen out in republics, as the ultramontane type of priest is frozen out in protestant lands. Science and metaphysics would come much nearer together, would in fact work absolutely hand in hand.

Metaphysics has usually followed a very primitive kind of quest. You know how men have always hankered after unlawful magic, and you know what a great part in magic *words* have always played. If you have his name, or the formula of incantation that binds him, you can control the spirit, genie, afrite, or whatever the power may be. Solomon knew the names of all the spirits, and having their names, he held them subject to his will. So the universe has always appeared to the natural mind as a kind of enigma, of which the key must be sought in the shape of some illuminating or power-bringing word or name. That word names the universe's *principle*, and to possess it is after a fashion to possess the universe itself. 'God,' 'Matter,' 'Reason,' 'the Absolute,' 'Energy,' are so many solving names. You can rest when you have them. You are at the end of your metaphysical quest.

But if you follow the pragmatic method, you cannot look on any such word as closing your quest. You must bring out of each word its practical cash-value, set it at work within the stream of your experience. It appears less as a solution, then, than as a program for more work, and more particularly as an indication of the ways in which existing realities may be *changed*.

Theories thus become instruments, not answers to enigmas, in which we can rest. We don't lie back upon them, we move forward, and, on occasion, make nature over again by their aid. Pragmatism unstiffens all our theories, limbers them up and sets each one at work. Being nothing essentially new, it harmonizes with many ancient philosophic tendencies. It agrees with nominalism for instance, in always appealing to particulars; with utilitarianism in emphasizing practical aspects; with positivism in its disdain for verbal solutions, useless questions and metaphysical abstractions.

All these, you see, are *anti-intellectualist* tendencies. Against rationalism as a pretension and a method pragmatism is fully armed and militant. But, at the outset, at least, it stands for no particular results. It has no dogmas, and no doctrines save its method. As the young Italian pragmatist Papini has well said, it lies in the midst of our theories, like a corridor in a hotel. Innumerable chambers open out of it. In one you may find a man writing an atheistic volume; in the next some one on his knees praying for faith and strength; in a third a chemist investigating a body's properties. In a fourth a system of idealistic metaphysics is being excogitated; in a fifth the impossibility of metaphysics is being shown. But they all own the corridor, and all must pass through it if they want a practicable way of getting into or out of their respective rooms.

No particular results then, so far, but only an attitude of orientation, is what the pragmatic method means. *The attitude of looking away from first things, principles, 'categories,' supposed necessities; and of looking towards last things, fruits, consequences, facts.*

So much for the pragmatic method! You may say that I have been praising it rather than explaining it to you, but I shall presently explain it abundantly enough by showing how it works on some familiar problems. Meanwhile the word pragmatism has come to be used in a still wider sense, as meaning also a certain *theory of truth.* I mean to give a whole lecture to the statement of that theory, after first paving the way, so I can be very brief now. But brevity is hard to follow, so I ask for your redoubled attention for a quarter of an hour. . . .

One of the most successfully cultivated branches of philosophy in our time is what is called inductive logic, the study of the conditions under which our sciences have evolved. Writers on this subject have begun to show a singular unanimity as to what the laws of nature and elements of fact mean, when formulated by mathematicians, physicists and chemists. When the first mathematical, logical, and natural uniformities, the first *laws,* were discovered, men were so carried away by the clearness, beauty and simplification that resulted, that they believed themselves to have deciphered authentically the eternal thoughts of the Almighty. His mind also thundered and reverberated in syllogisms. He also thought in conic sections, squares and roots and ratios, and geometrized like Euclid. He made Kepler's laws for the planets to follow; he made velocity increase proportionally to the time in falling bodies; he made the law of the sines for light to obey when refracted; he established the classes, orders, families and genera of plants and animals, and fixed the distances between them. He thought the archetypes of all things, and devised their variations; and when we rediscover any one of these his wondrous institutions, we seize his mind in its very literal intention.

But as the sciences have developed farther, the notion has gained ground that most, perhaps all, of our laws are only approximations. The laws themselves, moreover, have grown so numerous that there is no counting them; and so many rival formulations are proposed in all the branches of science that investigators have become accustomed to the notion that no theory is absolutely a transcript of reality, but that any one of them may from some point of view be useful. Their great use is to summarize old facts and to lead to new ones. They are only a man-made language, a conceptual shorthand, as some one calls them, in which we write our reports of nature; and languages, as is well known, tolerate much choice of expression and many dialects. . . .

Riding now on the front of this wave of scientific logic Messrs. Schiller and Dewey appear with their pragmatistic account of what truth everywhere signifies. Everywhere, these teachers say, 'truth' in our ideas and beliefs means the same thing that it means in science. It means, they say, nothing but this, *that ideas (which themselves are but parts of our experience*) *become true just in so far as they help us to get into satisfactory relation with other parts of our experience*, to summarize them and get about among them by conceptual short-cuts instead of following the interminable succession of particular phenomena. Any idea upon which we can ride, so to speak; any idea that will carry us prosperously from any one part of our experience to any other part, linking things satisfactorily, working securely, simplifying, saving labor; is true for just so much, true in so far forth, true *instrumentally*. This is the 'instrumental' view of truth taught so successfully at Chicago, the view that truth in our ideas means their power to 'work,' promulgated so brilliantly at Oxford.

Messrs. Dewey, Schiller and their allies, in reaching this general conception of all truth, have only followed the example of geologists, biologists and philologists. In the establishment of these other sciences, the successful stroke was always to take some simple process actually observable in operation — as denudation by weather, say, or variation from parental type, or change of dialect by incorporation of new words and pronunciations — and then to generalize it, making it apply to all times, and produce great results by summating its effects through the ages.

The observable process which Schiller and Dewey particularly singled out for generalization is the familiar one by which any individual settles into *new opinions*. The process here is always the same. The individual has a stock of old opinions already, but he meets a new experience that puts them to a strain. Somebody contradicts them; or in a reflective moment he discovers that they contradict each other; or he hears of facts with which they are incompatible; or desires arise in him which they cease to satisfy. The result is an inward trouble to which his mind till then had been a stranger, and from which he seeks to escape by modifying his previous mass of opinions. He saves as much of it as he can, for in this matter of belief we are all extreme conservatives. So he tries to change first this opinion, and then that (for they resist change very variously), until at last some new idea comes up which he can graft upon the ancient stock with a minimum of disturbance of the latter, some idea that mediates between the stock and the new experience and runs them into one another most felicitously and expediently.

This new idea is then adopted as the true one. It preserves the older stock of truths with a minimum of modification, stretching them just enough to make them admit the novelty, but conceiving that in ways as familiar as the case leaves possible. An *outrée* explanation, violating all our preconceptions, would never pass for a true account of a novelty. We should scratch round industriously till we found something less excentric. The most violent revolutions in an individual's beliefs leave most of his old order standing. Time and space, cause and effect, nature and history, and one's own biography remain untouched. New truth is always a go-between, a smoother-over of transitions. It marries old opinion to new fact so as ever to show a minimum of jolt, a maximum of continuity. We hold a theory true just in proportion to its successs in solving this 'problem of maxima and minima.' But success in solving this problem is eminently a matter of approximation. We say this theory solves it on the whole more satisfactorily than that theory; but that means more satisfactorily to ourselves, and individuals will emphasize their points of satisfaction differently. To a certain degree, therefore, everything here is plastic.

The point I now urge you to observe particularly is the part played by the older truths. Failure to take account of it is the source of much of the unjust criticism levelled against pragmatism. Their influence is absolutely controlling. Loyalty to them is the first principle — in most cases it is the only principle; for by far the most usual way of handling phenomena so novel that they would make for a serious rearrangement of our preconception is to ignore them altogether, or to abuse those who bear witness for them.

You doubtless wish examples of this process of truth's growth, and the only trouble is their superabundance. The simplest case of new truth is of course the mere numerical addition of new kinds of facts, or of new single facts of old kinds, to our experience — an addition that involves no alteration in the old beliefs. Day follows day, and its contents are simply added. The new contents themselves are not true, they simply *come* and *are*. Truth is *what we say about* them, and when we say that they have come, truth is satisfied by the plain additive formula.

But often the day's contents oblige a rearrangement. If I should now utter piercing shrieks and act like a maniac on this platform, it would make many of you revise your ideas as to the probable worth of my philosophy. 'Radium' came the other day as part of the day's content, and seemed for a moment to contradict our ideas of the whole order of nature, that order having come to be identified with what is called the conservation of energy. The mere sight of radium paying heat away indefinitely out of its own pocket seemed to violate that conservation. What to think? If the radiations from it were nothing but an escape of unsuspected 'potential' energy, pre-existent inside of the atoms, the principle of conservation would be saved. The discovery of 'helium' as the radiation's outcome, opened a way to this belief. So Ramsay's view is generally held to be true, because, although it extends our old ideas of energy, it causes a minimum of alteration in their nature.

I need not multiply instances. A new opinion counts as 'true' just in proportion as it gratifies the individual's desire to assimilate the novel in his experience to his beliefs in stock. It must both lean on old truth and grasp new fact; and its success (as I said a moment ago) in doing this, is a matter for the individual's appreciation. When old truth grows, then, by new truth's addition, it is for subjective reasons. We are in the process and obey the reasons. That new idea is truest which performs most felicitously its function of satisfying our double urgency. It makes itself true, gets itself classed as true, by the way it works; grafting itself then upon the ancient body of truth, which thus grows much as a tree grows by the activity of a new layer of cambium.

Now Dewey and Schiller proceed to generalize this observation and to apply it to the most ancient parts of truth. They also once were plastic. They also were called true for human reasons. They also mediated between still earlier truths and what in those days were novel observations. Purely objective truth, truth in whose establishment the function of giving human satisfaction in marrying previous parts of experience with newer parts played no rôle whatever, is nowhere to be found. The reasons why we call things true is the reason why they *are* true, for 'to be true' *means* only to perform this marriage-function.

The trail of the human serpent is thus over everything. Truth independent; truth that we *find* merely; truth no longer malleable to human need; truth incorrigible, in a word; such truth exists indeed superabundantly — or is supposed to exist by rationalistically minded thinkers; but then it means only the dead heart of the living tree, and its being there means only that truth also has its paleontology, and its 'prescription,' and may grow stiff with years of veteran service and petrified in men's regard by sheer antiquity. But how plastic even the oldest truths nevertheless really are has been vividly shown in our day by the transformation of logical and mathematical ideas, a transformation which seems even to be invading physics. The ancient formulas are reinterpreted as special expressions of much wider principles, principles that our ancestors never got a glimpse of in their present shape and formulation. . . .

You will probably be surprised to learn, then, that Messrs. Schiller's and Dewey's theories have suffered a hailstorm of contempt and ridicule. All rationalism has risen against them. In influential quarters Mr. Schiller, in particular, has been treated like an impudent schoolboy who deserves a spanking. I should not mention this, but for the fact that it throws so much sidelight upon that rationalistic temper to which I have opposed the temper of pragmatism. Pragmatism is uncomfortable away from facts. Rationalism is comfortable only in the presence of abstractions. This pragmatist talk about truths in the plural, about their utility and satisfactoriness, about the success with which they 'work,' etc., suggests to the typical intellectualist mind a sort of coarse lame second-rate makeshift article of truth. Such truths are not real truth. Such tests are merely subjective. As against this, objective truth must be something nonutilitarian, haughty, refined, remote, august, exalted. It must be an absolute correspondence of our thoughts with an equally absolute reality.

It must be what we *ought* to think unconditionally. The conditioned ways in which we *do* think are so much irrelevance and matter for psychology. Down with psychology, up with logic, in all this question!

See the exquisite contrast of the types of mind! The pragmatist clings to facts and concreteness, observes truth at its work in particular cases, and generalizes. Truth, for him, becomes a class-name for all sorts of definite working-values in experience. For the rationalist it remains a pure abstraction, to the bare name of which we must defer. When the pragmatist undertakes to show in detail just *why* we must defer, the rationalist is unable to recognize the concretes from which his own abstraction is taken. He accuses us of *denying* truth; whereas we have only sought to trace exactly why people follow it and always ought to follow it. Your typical ultra-abstractionist fairly shudders at concreteness: other things equal, he positively prefers the pale and spectral. If the two universes were offered, he would always choose the skinny outline rather than the rich thicket of reality. It is so much purer, clearer, nobler.

I hope that as these lectures go on, the concreteness and closeness to facts of the pragmatism which they advocate may be what approves itself to you as its most satisfactory peculiarity. It only follows here the example of the sister-sciences, interpreting the unobserved by the observed. It brings old and new harmoniously together. It converts the absolutely empty notion of a static relation of 'correspondence' (what that may mean we must ask later) between our minds and reality, into that of a rich and active commerce (that any one may follow in detail and understand) between particular thoughts of ours, and the great universe of other experiences in which they play their parts and have their uses.

But enough of this at present. The justification of what I say must be postponed. I wish now to add a word in further explanation of the claim I made at our last meeting, that pragmatism may be a happy harmonizer of empiricist ways of thinking with the more religious demands of human beings.

Men who are strongly of the fact-loving temperament, you may remember me to have said, are liable to be kept at a distance by the small sympathy with facts which that philosophy from the present-day fashion of idealism offers them. It is far too intellectualistic. Old fashioned theism was bad enough, with its notion of God as an exalted monarch, made up a lot of unintelligible or preposterous 'attributes'; but, so long as it held strongly by the argument from design, it kept some touch with concrete realities. Since, however, darwinism has once for all displaced design from the minds of the 'scientific,' theism has lost that foothold; and some kind of an immanent or pantheistic deity working *in* things rather than above them is, if any, the kind recommended to our contemporary imagination. Aspirants to a philosophic religion turn, as a rule, more hopefully nowadays towards idealistic pantheism than towards the older dualistic theism, in spite of the fact that the latter still counts able defenders.

But, as I said in my first lecture, the brand of pantheism offered is hard for them to assimilate if they are lovers of facts, or empirically minded. It is the absolutistic brand, spurning the dust and reared upon pure logic. It keeps no connexion whatever with concreteness. Affirming the Absolute Mind, which is its substitute for God, to be the rational presupposition of all particulars of fact, whatever they may be, it remains supremely indifferent to what the particular facts in our world actually are. Be they what they may, the Absolute will father them. . . .

Far be it from me to deny the majesty of this conception, or its capacity to yield religious comfort to a most respectable class of minds. But from the human point of view, no one can pretend that it does n't suffer from the faults of remoteness and abstractness. It is eminently a product of what I have ventured to call the rationalistic temper. It disdains empiricism's needs. It substitutes a pallid outline for the real world's richness. It is dapper, it is noble in the bad sense, in the sense in which to be noble is to be inapt for humble service. In this real world of sweat and dirt, it seems to me that when a view of things is 'noble,' that ought to count as a presumption against its truth, and as a philosophic disqualification. The prince of darkness may be a gentleman, as we are told he is, but whatever the God of earth and heaven is, he can surely be no gentleman. His menial services are needed in the dust of our human trials, even more than his dignity is needed in the empyrean.

Now pragmatism, devoted though she be to facts, has no such materialistic bias as ordinary empiricism labors under. Moreover, she has no objection whatever to the realizing of abstractions, so long as you get about among particulars with their aid and they actually carry you somewhere. Interested in no conclusions but those which our minds and our experiences work out together, she has no *a priori* prejudices against theology. *If theological ideas prove to have a value for concrete life, they will be true, for pragmatism, in the sense of being good for so much. For how much more they are true, will depend entirely on their relations to the other truths that also have to be acknowledged.* . . .

I am well aware how odd it must seem to some of you to hear me say that an idea is 'true' so long as to believe it is profitable to our lives. That it is *good*, for as much as it profits, you will gladly admit. If what we do by its aid is good, you will allow the idea itself to be good in so far forth, for we are the better for possessing it. But is it not a strange misuse of the word 'truth,' you will say, to call ideas also 'true' for this reason?

To answer this difficulty fully is impossible at this stage of my account. . . . Let me now say only this, that truth is *one species of good*, and not, as is usually supposed, a category distinct from good, and co-ordinate with it. *The true is the name of whatever proves itself to be good in the way of belief, and good, too, for definite, assignable reasons.* Surely you must admit this, that if there were *no* good for life in true ideas, or if the knowledge of them were positively disadvantageous and false ideas the only useful ones, then the current notion that truth is divine and precious, and its pursuit a duty, could never have grown up or become a dogma. In a world like that, our duty would be to *shun* truth, rather. But in this world, just as certain foods are not only agreeable to our taste, but good for our teeth, our stomach, and our tissues; so certain ideas are not only agreeable to think about, or agreeable as supporting other ideas that we are fond of, but they are also helpful in life's practical struggles. If there be any life that it is really better we should lead, and if there be any idea which, if believed in, would help us to lead that life, then it would be really *better for us* to believe in that idea, *unless, indeed, belief in it incidentally clashed with other greater vital benefits.*

'What would be better for us to believe'! This sounds very like a definition of truth. It comes very near to saying 'what we *ought* to believe': and in *that* definition none of you would find any oddity. Ought we ever not to believe what it is *better for us* to believe? And can we then keep the notion of what is better for us, and what is true for us, permanently apart?

Pragmatism says no, and I fully agree with her. Probably you also agree, so far as the abstract statement goes, but with a suspicion that if we practically did believe everything that made for good in our own personal lives, we should be found indulging all kinds of fancies about this world's affairs, and all kinds of sentimental superstitions about a world hereafter. Your suspicion here is undoubtedly well founded, and it is evident that something happens when you pass from the abstract to the concrete that complicates the situation.

I said just now that what is better for us to believe is true *unless the belief incidentally clashes with some other vital benefit.* Now in real life what vital benefits is any particular belief of ours most liable to clash with? What indeed except the vital benefits yielded by *other beliefs* when these prove incompatible with the first ones? In other words, the greatest enemy of any one of our truths may be the rest of our truths. Truths have once for all this desperate instinct of self-preservation and of desire to extinguish whatever contradicts them. My belief in the Absolute, based on the good it does me, must run the gauntlet of all my other beliefs. Grant that it may be true in giving me a moral holiday. Nevertheless, as I conceive it, — and let me speak now confidentially, as it were, and merely in my own private person, — it clashes with other truths of mine whose benefits I hate to give up on its account. It happens to be associated with a kind of logic of which I am the enemy, I find that it entangles me in metaphysical paradoxes that are inacceptable, etc., etc. But as I have enough trouble in life already without adding the trouble of carrying these intellectual inconsistencies, I personally just give up the Absolute. I just *take* my moral holidays; or else as a professional philosopher, I try to justify them by some other principle.

If I could restrict my notion of the Absolute to its bare holiday-giving value, it would n't clash with my other truths. But we can not easily thus restrict our hypotheses. They carry supernumerary features, and these it is that clash so. My disbelief in the Absolute means then disbelief in those other supernumerary features, for I fully believe in the legitimacy of taking moral holidays.

Yet see by this what I meant when I called pragmatism a mediator and reconciler and said, borrowing the word from Papini, that she 'unstiffens' our theories. She has in fact no prejudices whatever, no obstructive dogmas, no rigid canons of what shall count as proof. She is completely genial. She will entertain any hypothesis, she will consider any evidence. It follows that in the religious field she is at a great advantage both over positivistic empiricism, with its anti-theological bias, and over religious rationalism, with its exclusive interest in the remote, the noble, the simple, and the abstract in the way of conception.

In short, she widens the field of search for God. Rationalism sticks to logic and the empyrean. Empiricism sticks to the external senses. Pragmatism is willing to take anything, to follow either logic or the senses and to count the humblest and most personal experiences. She will count mystical experiences if they have practical consequences. She will take a God who lives in the very dirt of private fact — if that should seem a likely place to find him.

Her only test of probable truth is what works best in the way of leading us, what fits every part of life best and combines with the collectivity of experience's demands, nothing being omitted. If theological ideas should do this, if the notion of God, in particular, should prove to do it, how could pragmatism possibly deny God's existence? She could see no meaning in treating as 'not true' a notion that was pragmatically so successful. What other kind of truth could there be, for her, than all this agreement with concrete reality?

In my last lecture I shall return again to the relations of pragmatism with religion. But you see already how democratic she is. Her manners are as various and flexible, her resources as rich and endless, and her conclusions as friendly as those of mother nature.

The Philosophy of 'as If'

(1911)

HANS VAIHINGER

General Introductory Remarks on Fictional Constructs

The normal and most natural methods of thought always have as their primary object the formation of those particular apperceptions that are of a final and definitive character; and only such ideational constructs are formed as can be shown to correspond to some kind of reality. It is in fact the essential object of science to develop only such ideas as have an objective correlate and to eliminate all admixture of the subjective.

Such a task is, however, not easily accomplished, for many difficulties are encountered. The ideal, in which the world of ideas consists exclusively of congruous, well-ordered and noncontradictory constructs, is only to be attained slowly and with difficulty. The way to this ideal is through methodology.

The first and the natural task of methodology is to suggest in what direction representations possessed of real validity are to be sought.

Our natural tendency is to adjust all our representations, to test them by comparison with reality, and to render them free from contradiction. This is the most natural and obvious method, and it appears to be the only way of advancing a scientific theory of knowledge. This would hold true even if our mental constructs were direct reflections of reality. But the customary modes and results of thought already contain so many subjective and fictional elements that it is not surprising if thought also strikes out along other lines. It must be remembered that the object of the world of ideas as a whole is not the portrayal of reality — this would be an utterly impossible task — but rather to provide us with an *instrument for finding our way about more easily in this world.* Subjective processes of thought inhere in the entire structure of cosmic phenomena. They represent the highest and ultimate results of organic development, and the world of ideas is the fine flower of the whole cosmic process; but for that very reason it is not a copy of it in the ordinary sense. Logical processes are a part of the cosmic process and have as their more immediate object the preservation and enrichment of the life of organisms; they should serve as instruments for enabling them to attain to a more complete life; they serve as intermediaries between living beings. The

From Hans Vaihinger, *The Philosophy of 'as If,'* tr. C. K. Ogden (London: Routledge and Kegan Paul, 1924), 15–20, 22, 24–27, 85–90.

world of ideas is an edifice well calculated to fulfil this purpose; but to regard it for that reason as a copy is to indulge in a hasty and unjustifiable comparison. Not even elementary sensations are copies of reality; they are rather mere gauges for measuring the changes in reality.

Before entering on our task it is necessary to make a distinction that will subsequently assume considerable importance. Ideational constructs are in the strict sense of the term real fictions when they are not only in contradiction with reality but self-contradictory in themselves; the concept of the atom, for example, or the "Ding an sich."[1] To be distinguished from these are constructs which only contradict reality as given, or deviate from it, but are not in themselves self-contradictory (e.g. artificial classes). The latter might be called half-fictions or semi-fictions. These types are not sharply divided from one another but are connected by transitions. Thought begins with slight initial deviations from reality (half-fictions), and, becoming bolder and bolder, ends by operating with constructs that are not only opposed to the facts but are self-contradictory.

Artificial Classification

The most widely used of those "provisional methods" which we have called "semi-fictions" is *artificial classification*. The ultimately valid construct corresponding to it, and eventually to take its place, is the *natural system*. All cosmic objects present special forms which are theoretically expressed in some classification, and when this specification corresponds with reality in every respect then it is a natural system. The natural system is in itself one of the most complicated problems of philosophy and of natural science, and from it arises the vital question of the nature of species.

A natural system is one in which entities are arranged according to the principles apparently followed by nature in their development. To put it briefly, the natural system of classification must be a copy corresponding to the actual origins and the mutual relationship of all things. This is the goal of science and any direct method must work straight towards it.

It is at this point that all the considerations so far advanced are justified. The material at our disposal puts so many formidable obstacles in the direct path that the logical function strikes out along by-ways. It makes use of an artifice; it creates artificial classes. Now what does this mean? In our psychological terminology it means that it *provisionally substitutes for the correct constructs others which do not directly correspond to reality*. It then operates with these fictional classes as if they were real ones. We can here only draw attention to the well-known fact that the artificial and fictive classification always selects from a whole

[1] [Thing in itself. — Eds.]

group of characters some one that is particularly prominent, and bases its division upon this without paying any attention to the way in which these characters are naturally determined by one another. These provisional classificatory aids not only serve the practical purpose of permitting objects to be arranged and brought under definite rubrics, and provide at the same time a sort of mnemonic device, but they also possess a theoretical value, in so far as they perform a *heuristic* service by preparing for and facilitating the discovery of a natural system. Artificial systems are generally based on these concepts of species, which themselves only bring a superficial order provisionally into the confused mass of phenomena.

Heuristic methods based upon dichotomy, etc. are but special subdivisions of this artificial method of grouping. The artificial classifications, however, themselves follow in certain essential respects another theory than the natural one; i.e. the methodological rules which appertain to them and which determine their applicability are clearly of a different nature from those that hold for natural classification. These rules relate particularly to the prevention of the mistakes that necessarily spring from artificial divisions: mistakes which are due not only to the fact that the natural arrangement of phenomena cannot be forced into this artificial edifice and does not coincide with it, but also to the fact that through this artificial system impossible sub-divisions arise which cannot exist in actual reality.

As examples we have among others the Linnean system and many later classifications of animals, plants and men, all of which have been framed with a more or less conscious feeling of their artificiality. Lamarck, in particular, is to be praised in this respect. In the technical rules given in his *Philosophie Zoologique* concerning "Artificial devices" . . . he discusses this subject in detail. And with him may be mentioned Cuvier, Blumenbach, Kant and a large number of scientists who either applied these artificial classifications themselves or dealt with their theoretical basis.

This artificial classification is almost the only one of the accessories to thought which has had the good fortune to be thoroughly studied by logicians. It was, of course, quite obvious in this case that we were not directly and immediately dealing with reality but with *indirect and provisional ideational constructs and modes of thought*. The various features characteristic of all fictions are here already clearly manifested: the fact, in particular, that all such fictions in the last analysis lead to contradictions, is worthy of special consideration, and later on we shall emphasize it more specifically.

As long as such fictions are treated as hypotheses without a realization of their nature, they are *false hypotheses*. They derive real value only if it is realized that they have been deliberately constructed as provisional representations which at some future time are to make room for better and more natural systems.

Abstractive (Neglective) Fictions

I include under this term various methods in which the deviation from reality manifests itself specifically in the neglect of certain elements.

The factor common to all fictions in this class consists in a neglect of important elements of reality. As a rule the reason for the formation of these fictions is to be sought in the highly intricate character of the facts which make theoretical treatment exceedingly difficult owing to their unusual complexity. The logical functions are thus unable to perform their work undisturbed, because it is not possible here to keep the various threads out of which reality is woven, apart from one another.

Since, then, the material is too complicated and confused for thought to be able to break it up into its component elements, and since the causal factors sought are probably of too complicated a nature for them to be determined directly, thought makes use of an artifice by means of which it provisionally and temporarily neglects a number of characters and selects from them the more important phenomena.

A standard example is the well-known assumption of Adam Smith, according to which all human actions are dictated by egoism. We shall try to give an especially typical example of every variety of artifice, and to use it in order to study by the most thorough analysis both the scheme of the construct and the methodology of the artifice employed. As regards artificial classification, by far the most typical historical example is the botanical system of Linnæus; while of abstractive fictions based on the neglect of certain elements the best is Adam Smith's assumption, which was long regarded as an hypothesis.

Neither Adam Smith nor Linnæus regarded himself as dealing with more than a fiction. The proof of the statement that Adam Smith intended his assumption to be merely a provisional fiction was given by Buckle in the introduction to his *History of Civilization in England,* and this view has been expressly emphasized in Germany by F. A. Lange.

The empirical manifestations of human actions are so excessively complicated that they present almost insuperable obstacles when we try to understand them theoretically and to reduce them to causal factors. For the construction of his system of political economy it was essential for Adam Smith to interpret human activity causally. With unerring instinct he realized that the main cause lay in egoism and he formulated his assumption in such a way that all human actions, and particularly those of a business or politico-economical nature, could be looked upon *as if* their driving force lay in but one single factor — egoism. Thus all the subsidiary causes and partially conditional factors, such as good-will, habit and so forth, are here neglected. With the aid of this abstract cause

Adam Smith then succeeded in bringing the whole of political economy into an ordered system. He presented it as an axiom and deduced from it the relations involved in trade and commerce, which followed with systematic necessity. The assumption of a "harmony" of all individual interests is intimately bound up with this; and it is an assumption which, though of great value as fiction, is positively ruinous as hypothesis or dogma.

But these are only provisional assumptions, which, however rigorously applied, are to be sharply differentiated from hypotheses. They are, or at least should be, accompanied by the consciousness that they do not correspond to reality and that they *deliberately substitute a fraction of reality for the complete range of causes and facts.*

These artificial methods are applied wherever there are complex situations of this kind, particularly in the treatment of political economy and social and moral relations. . . .

A priori, no objection can be made to this procedure; indeed, it is very likely that something of real importance might be gained by it. Abstract mechanics is full of just such formulæ, obtained only by discarding a large number of empirical data, and events are always interpreted *as if* dependent upon these formulated laws. But at the same time it is clear that these fictions approximate closely to simple experiments, i.e. experiments where purely arbitrary values are provisionally assumed in the treatment of mathematical problems and then gradually "tested" one after another.

It is still often an open question whether such an assumption is an hypothesis or a fiction; but a regrettable lack of scientific understanding is apt to appear in the conclusion frequently drawn that because such constructs are devoid of *reality* they are to be regarded as devoid of *utility*. This is just as incorrect as the reverse inference — from their utility to their validity. Any true insight into the psychological setting and origin of knowledge proves that many things may be theoretically wrong and yet from a practical standpoint be fruitful in results, taking the term "practical," of course, in a wide sense. . . .

SCHEMATIC . . . FICTIONS

. . . This sub-group was already in evidence in the two types already described. Both in classification and in the abstractive fictions we have the postulation of schematic, general types conceived as absolutely bare and deprived of all those characters of reality that might interfere with the procedure. Nevertheless they quite legitimately form a sub-group by themselves. Whereas in the case of the abstractive fictions a certain portion of reality is cut off and set aside, and only the remainder taken into consideration, in the case of schematic fictions a scaffolding, that is to say, the skeleton of a definite complex is erected and thought proceeds in relation to this bare picture which is devoid of many of the features of reality. The distortion of reality has, however, progressed further here than in the preceding sub-groups. Here too a subjective and abstract representation is formed in order to base theoretical procedure upon it and not upon the far more complicated reality. To a certain extent the laws of nature are here studied by means of simpler models, containing, it is true, the essentials of reality but in a much simpler and purer form. The *schematic drawings* employed in many sciences give us an idea of this method which here finds extensive application. . . .

These forms might also be called the fiction of *the simple case*. A typical example is what is known as "Thünen's idea," a fiction which was introduced into economics at the beginning of the nineteenth century by Thünen and led to a reform of the subject. It is also the most famous historical example of this type of methodological expedient. It consists in postulating an imaginary city, in order the better to determine conditions of agriculture, transportation, etc. Around it in concentric zones are arranged the different spheres of activity from which the necessary means for supplying the requirements of the city are drawn. With the aid of this ingenious artifice all agricultural and economic laws are then systematically deduced. Fictions of this type are specially common in political economy. The schematic fiction of an isolated man, an isolated city (or island), an isolated state, etc., belongs to the same category. Similar schemata are employed in all the social sciences for the operation and deduction of theoretical laws. . . .

Another group, though one which may be treated as a variety of the schematic fiction, is formed by *Utopian* fictions. The name given to this group derives from the Utopias and fictions so prevalent in earlier times, such as those depicted by More and Campanella. Plato's ideal state may be mentioned here as historically the first example of this method. To the same category belongs the fiction of a primeval state, which was particularly popular in the eighteenth century and still played an important part in the writings of Fichte.

The idea of a primordial or world spirit also belongs here; such as that so happily employed, for instance, by Dubois-Reymond in his well-known address, for the elucidation and theoretical development of a strictly scientific train of thought. And here too we must place the Platonic idea of a (hermaphrodite) original man, and all those fictions of primordial laws, religions, pacts, traditions, and the like that once were or still are of importance. Indeed it is just in this field that scientific phantasy often manifests itself most freely. As long as such fictions are taken for what they are and not called hypotheses, they can frequently be of great service to science.

Another species of fiction closely bound up with the above is the *type-fiction* or the imaginary *original form*. Here a picture of a species or type is built up from a series of organisms, and then not merely are the laws governing particular organisms deduced from it, but all these organisms themselves are regarded as modifications of the type. In this group the interplay of fiction and hypothesis is often remarkable. The classical example is Goethe's idea of an original plant and an original animal, a question in which interest was revived in modern times through Darwinism. The first question is what Goethe understood by a "plant archetype," whether it was a fiction or an hypothesis; and we may also ask whether in the present state of our knowledge the historical existence of such an "archetype" can be assumed, or if the mere imaginary postulation of such an original form still serves any scientific purpose. Characteristic, and not without significance for the theory of this kind of fiction, is the well-known phrase of Schiller, "this original plant is merely an idea," whereby he stated in Kantian terminology that it was an ideal or typical fiction. . . .

The Difference between Fiction and Hypothesis

We have already shown that the fiction is generally treated as an hypothesis (although, methodologically, it is entirely different). The explanation for this lies in the fact that fiction and hypothesis are externally very similar; that they cannot always be strictly separated in actuality; and, finally, that a logical theory in general can really only take form some time after the development of a scientific precedure.

An hypothesis is directed towards reality,[2] i.c. the ideational construct contained in it claims, or hopes, to coincide with some perception in the future. It submits its reality to the test and demands *vertification,* i.e. it wants to be proved true, real, and an expression of a reality. Every hypothesis without exception endeavours to establish a reality, and even though we are still uncertain as to the actual occurrence of something hypothetically assumed, we yet entertain the hope that the assumption will eventually prove to be true. If, therefore, we put forward the hypothesis that Man is descended from the lower Mammals, we are definitely insisting upon the actual existence of direct and indirect ancestors of Man, we are expressing the *belief* that had we lived at that time — a fiction impossible from the practical standpoint but logically necessary — they would have presented themselves to perception, and the hope that the remains of these vanished links may still be discovered. We are compelled to frame this hypothesis by the law of causality. For according to this law, to which there has hitherto been no known exception, every phenomenon is to be explained by some other, unless it be an elementary

[2] That is why in the case of a number of hypotheses, all equally possible, the most probable one is always selected. On the other hand, in the case of a number of equally possible fictions, the most expedient is chosen. The difference between the two constructs is here clearly shown.

one. And since the human organism shows every indication of *not* being an elementary phenomenon, it must be regarded as the result of other phenomena. We therefore infer the existence of a still unknown link — the missing link — a necessary causal relation on the analogy of interconnections otherwise known to us. What we infer and hypothetically assume is the existence of an intermediate form from which the men of to-day are directly descended according to unalterable laws of sequence. This is an *hypothesis*.

We are now in a position to deal with the *fiction*. When Goethe introduced the idea of an animal archetype on the analogy of which all animals were to be treated and explained, and as modifications of which all known animal species were to be regarded, this invention of an animal archetype was a schematic fiction. For Goethe did not desire thereby to assert the actual existence of an animal archetype or to imply either that it would ever be perceived, or could ever have existed; he was merely stating that all animals should be regarded *as if* they were modifications of an archetype. The fictional element in a fiction of this kind is that we are invited to proceed *as if such an animal could have existed;* the hypothetical element — for it is a semi-fiction — being the statement that all animal forms are reducible to a single type. This is an assertion based upon observation, and its correctness would have to be demonstrated inductively by showing that all animal forms, as a whole and in particular, should be treated as modifications of such an ideal type.

The value of Goethe's fiction is quite clear. It suggests an entirely new classification of animal forms and also prepares the way heuristically for the truth. It was recognized, after a time, as a heuristic fiction, but it has now been given up because the correct view has taken its place in the Darwinian theory, which assumes that all animal forms develop from one another and that an animal archetype can at most be thought of as a unicellular organism. Thus Goethe's fiction prepared the way heuristically for the Darwinian hypothesis. Whereas Darwinism asserts the actual existence of such animal archetypes, Goethe definitely denied it.

Goethe wanted his idea to be regarded as a fiction. And this was not an error on his part, as might perhaps be supposed, for Goethe's animal archetype was a useful fiction, in that it included the protozoa and assumed an original form, an original type, for all forms, and regarded them as modifications of it. Whether this fiction is useful now is another question. The primitive animal of to-day (Monera, Bathybia) is very different from the animal archetype of Goethe, who did not understand thereby beings so formless as these, nor did he claim that it had actually existed. He had in mind a single form, a type (not an animal archetype, but *the* animal archetype, said Goethe). His fiction was not concerned to assert a real fact but something by means of which reality could be dealt with and grasped, and this is actually the case in the example given. This example also serves to show how readily fiction and hypothesis can be confused and how essential is a sharp, logical distinction here.

The function of an hypothesis is, of course, only provisional — but the goal which it has ultimately in view is to be theoretically tested and established by the facts of experience. The hypothesis has also to be discarded, but this is because the hypothetical idea has become fully qualified for admission into the circle of what is accepted as real. The provisional object of the fiction is quite different; for the fiction, in so far as we have termed it a provisional auxilliary construct, ought to drop out in the course of time and make way for its real function; but in so far as it is a pure fiction, it ought, at any rate logically, to disappear as soon as it has done its duty.

Closely related to this is the question how far, on occasion, it may be doubtful whether a given assumption is a fiction or an hypothesis — where, for instance, an hypothesis is of so general a character that, in the end, it cannot possibly coincide with actual reality, and where some modification, as well as a verification of its general part, is expected. Thus we may still call Adam Smith's assumption an hypothesis, in so far as it actually expresses, in part, a real fact and a modification of the general assumption by further conditions is expected. But it is always better in such cases to avoid all possibility of error by calling such an assumption a fiction. On the other hand, it may sometimes be advisable not to include a given assumption immediately under the category of fiction, especially where there is still some doubt as to the possibility of its corresponding to something real. We must be careful not to bar the road to verification by the use of the term *fiction*, and still less must we commit the more obvious mistake of labelling an assumption a fiction through sheer laziness, in order thereby to avoid the laborious task of verification. In particular instances it may be very questionable whether a given assumption is a fiction or an hypothesis, and in any given case we can adopt the *hypothesis that it is only a fiction*. The possibility of this interlacing is the best proof that fiction and hypothesis should be distinguished. If, then, there is some doubt as to whether a given assumption is a fiction or an hypothesis, a detailed and specific examination should be undertaken to decide the point.

Thus the real difference between the two is that the fiction is a mere auxiliary construct, a circuitous approach, a scaffolding afterwards to be demolished, while the hypothesis looks forward to being definitely established. The former is artificial, the latter natural. What is untenable as an hypothesis can often render excellent service as a fiction, and of this we have given many examples above. On the other hand, a fiction may become superfluous in the course of time, and we know that thought is always glad to throw aside its crutches. But the main types of true fictions are never repudiated by thought, for without them reflection and analysis would be quite impossible.

The hypothesis has ultimately only a theoretical object, that of connecting facts and filling up the gaps in the connection, which experience shows to be numerous; and of establishing what is ultimately the primarily unalterable. On the other hand every fiction has, strictly speaking, only a practical object in science, for it does not create real knowledge. The hypothesis endeavors to do away with actually observed contradictions, while the fiction calls logical contradictions into existence. For that reason both their tendency and their method of application are quite distinct. The hypothesis tries to discover, the fiction, to invent. The former is therefore often also called a *découverte;* whereas the differential calculus is generally (by d'Alembert for instance) called an *invention.* Thus natural laws are *discovered* but machines *invented.* Fictions, as scientific mental instruments without which a higher development of thought is impossible, are invented. It is, however, well known that discovery and invention cannot always be sharply differentiated, any more than can hypothesis and fiction. The atom is not a discovery of natural science but an invention.

We spoke above of the necessity that every hypothesis should be confirmed by verification. But must not something similar take place in the case of the fiction?

To the *verification* of the hypothesis corresponds the *justification* of the fiction. If the former must be confirmed by experience, the latter must be justified by the services it renders to the science of experience. If a fictional construct is formed, its excuse and justification must be that it is of service to discursive thought. This justification is always a matter of special proof, like verification. Fictions that do not justify themselves, i.e. cannot be proved to be useful and necessary, must be eliminated, no less than hypotheses that cannot be verified.

The construction of fictions is as justifiable and indispensable a means of scientific investigation as that of hypotheses. What A. Lange says of hypotheses holds, *mutatis mutandis,* also of fictions: "The wise man is not he who avoids hypotheses, but he who asserts the most probable, and who knows best how to estimate the degree of their probability." If we substitute here fictions for hypotheses, and expediency for probability, this holds absolutely for fictions. Indeed the very objection that is rightly urged against those who despise hypotheses, namely that even the most common assumptions of man are based upon hypotheses that have simply attained a high degree of probability and often not even that — this same objection can and must be urged against those who . . . disapprove of fictions. For it is unquestionable that not even the most ordinary assertion can be made without the creation of fictions, such, for example, as the very categories and general ideas without which no proposition can be asserted; though in the course of time they have become so matter-of-fact that their fictional nature is no longer recognized. In reality they are fictions that daily justify themselves anew by the services which they render.

It is quite natural that the fiction should have an entirely different methodology from that of the hypothesis. The methodology of the latter consists essentially in this, that the assumption is not merely possible for thought but also actually possible, and that the facts of experience agree with it. One single fact at variance with it can destroy an hypothesis. This does not hold at all in the case of the fiction: neither its contradiction of experience nor even logical objections can disturb it, or at any rate they disturb it quite differently from an hypothesis. The principle of the rules of hypothetical method is the *probability of the conceptual constructs*, that of fictional method is their *expediency*. The rules can be deducted from this general principle, but they can be better reached inductively from the observation of particular fiction and of the procedure by which they are successfully applied. Expediency not only determines the acceptance or rejection of a particular fiction but also its selection from among others. If a fiction has finally been accepted, the principal requirement is that of being careful not to transform it either into an hypothesis or into a dogma, and not to substitute for reality what has been deduced from the fiction, without having first made the necessary corrections. A far more important requirement, however, is that we should not permit ourselves to be misled or disturbed by the contradictions of the fiction with the world of experience or its inconsistency with itself, and that we should not infer so-called world-riddles from these contradictions. In other words, we must not become attached to these fictions as though they were the essential thing, but we must recognize them as fictions and be content with this knowledge, and refuse to allow ourselves to be enticed and confused by the illusory questions and illusory problems arising out of them.

To indulge in subtleties over these contradictions involves us in the most serious aberrations of thought and we must guard against losing ourselves in side-tracks and mazes of this kind. All this is very different from the rules which hold of the hypothesis. As Lotze well puts it (*Logik*, p. 399), "every hypothesis claims to be not only a figure of thought, or a means of making thought concrete, but a statement of fact." "Everyone who sets up an hypothesis believes that he has extended the series of real facts by a happy divination of facts not less real though falling outside the range of his observation." "The fact under consideration must be thought of as an existing actuality." "*Fictions*, on the other hand," he says . . . "are assumptions made with a full realization of impossibility of the thing assumed, whether because it is internally contradictory, or because on external grounds it cannot be a constituent of reality." Lotze here not only states quite correctly the distinction between fiction and hypothesis but also indicates the difference between the two kinds of fiction.

The Proletarian Strike
(1906)

GEORGES SOREL

Every time we attempt to obtain an exact conception of the ideas behind proletarian violence we are forced to go back to the notion of the general strike; and this same conception may render many other services, and throw an unexpected light on all the obscure parts of Socialism. In the last pages of the first chapter I compared the general strike to the Napoleonic battle which definitely crushes an adversary; this comparison will help us to understand the part played by the general strike in the world of ideas.

Military writers of to-day, when discussing the new methods of war necessitated by the employment of troops infinitely more numerous than those of Napoleon, equipped with arms much more deadly than those of his time, do not for all that imagine that wars will be decided in any other way than that of the Napoleonic battle. The new tactics proposed must fit into the drama Napoleon had conceived; the detailed development of the combat will doubtless be quite different from what it used to be, but the end must always be the catastrophic defeat of the enemy. The methods of military instruction are intended to prepare the soldier for this great and terrible action, in which everybody must be ready to take part at the first signal. From the highest to the lowest, the members of a really solid army have always in mind this catastrophic issue of international conflicts.

The revolutionary Syndicates argue about Socialist action exactly in the same manner as military writers argue about war; they restrict the whole of Socialism to the general strike; they look upon every combination as one that should culminate in this catastrophe; they see in each strike a reduced facsimile, an essay, a preparation for the great final upheaval.

From Georges Sorel, *Reflections on Violence*, tr. T. E. Hulme (Glencoe, Ill.: The Free Press, 1950), 136–137, 139–153, 157–159, 169–170. Reprinted by permission of The Macmillan Company, Copyright 1950 by The Free Press, a corporation.

The *new school*, which calls itself Marxist, Syndicalist, and revolutionary, declared in favour of the idea of the general strike as soon as it became clearly conscious of the true sense of its own doctrine, of the consequences of its activity, and of its own originality. It was thus led to leave the old official, Utopian, and political tabernacles, which hold the general strike in horror, and to launch itself into the true current of the proletarian revolutionary movement; for a long time past the proletariat had made adherence to the principle of the general strike the *test* by means of which the Socialism of the workers was distinguished from that of the amateur revolutionaries.

Parliamentary Socialists can only obtain great influence if they can manage, by the use of a very confused language, to impose themselves on very diverse groups; for example, they must have working-men constituents simple enough to allow themselves to be duped by high-sounding phrases about future collectivism; they are compelled to represent themselves as profound philosophers to stupid middle-class people who wish to appear to be well informed about social questions; it is very necessary also for them to be able to exploit rich people who think that they are earning the gratitude of humanity by taking shares in the enterprises of Socialist politicians. This influence is founded on balderdash, and our bigwigs endeavour — sometimes only too successfully — to spread confusion among the ideas of their readers; they detest the general strike because all propaganda carried on from that point of view is too socialistic to please philanthropists. . . .

Against this noisy, garrulous, and lying Socialism, which is exploited by ambitious people of every description, which amuses a few buffoons, and which is admired by decadents — revolutionary Syndicalism takes its stand, and endeavours, on the contrary, to leave nothing in a state of indecision; its ideas are honestly expressed, without trickery and without mental reservations; no attempt is made to dilute doctrines by a stream of confused commentaries. Syndicalism endeavours to employ methods of expression which throw a full light on things, which put them exactly in the place assigned to them by their nature, and which bring out the whole value of the forces in play. Oppositions, instead of being glozed over, must be thrown into sharp relief if we desire to obtain a clear idea of the Syndicalist movement; the groups which are struggling one against the other must be shown as separate and as compact as possible; in short, the movements of the revolted masses must be represented in such a way that the soul of the revolutionaries may receive a deep and lasting impression.

These results could not be produced in any very certain manner by the use of ordinary language; use must be made of a body of images which, *by intuition alone*, and before any considered analyses are made, is capable of evoking as an undivided whole the mass of sentiments which corresponds to the different manifestations of the war undertaken by Socialism against modern society. The Syndicalists solve this problem perfectly, by concentrating the whole of Socialism in the drama of the general strike; there is thus no longer any place for the reconciliation of contraries in the equivocations of the professors; everything is clearly mapped out, so that only one interpretation of Socialism is possible. This method has all the advantages which "integral" knowledge has over analysis, according to the doctrine of Bergson; and perhaps it would not be possible to cite another example which would so perfectly demonstrate the value of the famous professor's doctrines.

The possibility of the actual realisation of the general strike has been much discussed; it has been stated that the Socialist war could not be decided in one single battle. To the people who think themselves cautious, practical, and scientific the difficulty of setting great masses of the proletariat in motion at the same moment seems prodigious; they have analysed the difficulties of detail which such an enormous struggle would present. It is the opinion of the Socialist-sociologists, as also of the politicians, that the general strike is a popular dream, characteristic of the beginnings of a working-class movement; we have had quoted against us the authority of Sidney Webb,[1] who has decreed that the general strike is an illusion of youth, of which the English workers — whom the monopolists of sociology have so often presented to us as the depositaries of the true conception of the working-class movement — soon rid themselves.

That the general strike is not popular in contemporary England, is a poor argument to bring against the historical significance of the idea, for the English are distinguished by an extraordinary lack of understanding of the class war; their ideas have remained very much dominated by medieval influences: the guild, privileged, or at least protected by laws, still seems to them the ideal of working-class organisation; it is for England that the term *working-class aristocracy*, as a name for the trades unionists, was invented, and, as a matter of fact, trades unionism does pursue the acquisition of legal privileges. We might therefore say that the aversion felt by England for the general strike should be looked upon as strong presumptive evidence in favour of the latter by all those who look upon the class war as the essence of Socialism. . . .

Neither do I attach any importance to the objections made to the general strike based on considerations of a practical order. The attempt to construct hypotheses about the nature of the struggles of the future and the means of suppressing capitalism, on the model furnished by history, is a return to the old methods of the Utopists. There is no

[1] [Webb, along with his wife, Beatrice, George Bernard Shaw, and Graham Wallas, was a prominent figure in the Fabian Society, which hoped to introduce socialism in England without recourse to violence or the class struggle. — Eds.]

process by which the future can be predicted scientifically, nor even one which enables us to discuss whether one hypothesis about it is better than another; it has been proved by too many memorable examples that the greatest men have committed prodigious errors in thus desiring to make predictions about even the least distant future.

And yet without leaving the present, without reasoning about this future, which seems for ever condemned to escape our reason, we should be unable to act at all. Experience shows that the *framing of a future, in some indeterminate time,* may, when it is done in a certain way, be very effective, and have very few inconveniences; this happens when the anticipations of the future take the form of those myths, which enclose with them, all the strongest inclinations of a people, of a party or of a class, inclinations which recur to the mind with the insistence of instincts in all the circumstances of life; and which give an aspect of complete reality to the hopes of immediate action by which, more easily than by any other method, men can reform their desires, passions, and mental activity. We know, moreover, that these social myths in no way prevent a man profiting by the observations which he makes in the course of his life, and form no obstacle to the pursuit of his normal occupations.

The truth of this may be shown by numerous examples.

The first Christians expected the return of Christ and the total ruin of the pagan world, with the inauguration of the kingdom of the saints, at the end of the first generation. The catastrophe did not come to pass, but Christian thought profited so greatly from the apocalyptic myth that certain contemporary scholars maintain that the whole preaching of Christ referred solely to this one point. The hopes which Luther and Calvin had formed of the religious exaltation of Europe were by no means realised; these fathers of the Reformation very soon seemed men of a past era; for present-day Protestants they belong rather to the Middle Ages than to modern times, and the problems which troubled them most occupy very little place in contemporary Protestantism. Must we for that reason deny the immense result which came from their dreams of Christian renovation? It must be admitted that the real developments of the Revolution did not in any way resemble the enchanting pictures which created the enthusiasm at its first adepts; but without those pictures would the Revolution have been victorious? Many Utopias were mixed up with the Revolutionary myth, because it had been formed by a society passionately fond of imaginative literature, full of confidence in the "science," and very little acquainted with the economic history of the past. These Utopias came to nothing; but it may be asked whether the Revolution was not a much more profound transformation than those dreamed of by the people who in the eighteenth century had invented social Utopias. In our own times Mazzini pursued what the wiseacres of his time called a mad chimera; but it can no longer be denied that, without Mazzini, Italy would never have become a great power, and that he did more for Italian unity than Cavour and all the politicians of his school.

A knowledge of what the myths contain in the way of details which will actually form part of the history of the future is then of small importance; they are not astrological almanacs; it is even possible that nothing which they contain will ever come to pass, — as was the case with the catastrophe expected by the first Christians. In our own daily life, are we not familiar with the fact that what actually happens is very different from our preconceived notion of it? And that does not prevent us from continuing to make resolutions. Psychologists say that there is heterogeneity between the ends in view and the ends actually realised: the slightest experience of life reveals this law to us, with Spencer transferred into nature, to extract therefrom his theory of the multiplication of effects.

The myth must be judged as a means of acting on the present; any attempt to discuss how far it can be taken literally as future history is devoid of sense. *It is the myth in its entirety which is alone important:* its parts are only of interest in so far as they bring out the main idea. No useful purpose is served, therefore, in arguing about the incidents which may occur in the course of a social war, and about the decisive conflicts which may give victory to the proletariat; even supposing the revolutionaries to have been wholly and entirely deluded in setting up this imaginary picture of the general strike, this picture may yet have been, in the course of the preparation for the Revolution, a great element of strength, if it has embraced all the aspirations of Socialism, and if it has given to the whole body of Revolutionary thought a precision and a rigidity which no other method of thought could have given.

To estimate, then, the significance of the idea of the general strike, all the methods of discussion which are current among politicians, sociologists, or people with pretensions to political science, must be abandoned. Everything which its opponents endeavour to establish may be conceded to them, without reducing in any way the value of the theory which they think they have refuted. The question whether the general strike is a partial reality, or only a product of popular imagination, is of little importance. All that it is necessary to know is, whether the general strike contains everything that the Socialist doctrine expects of the revolutionary proletariat.

To solve this question we are no longer compelled to argue learnedly about the future; we are not obliged to indulge in lofty reflections about philosophy, history, or economics; we are not on the plane of theories, and we can remain on the level of observable facts. We have to question men who take a very active part in the real revolutionary movement amidst the proletariat, men who do not aspire to climb into the middle class and whose mind is not dominated by corporative prejudices. These men may be deceived about an infinite number of political, economical, or moral questions; but their testimony is decisive, sovereign, and irrefutable when it is a question of knowing what are the ideas which most powerfully move them and their comrades, which most appeal to them as being identical with their socialistic conceptions, and thanks to which their reason, their hopes, and their way of looking at particular facts seem to make but one indivisible unity.

Thanks to these men, we know that the general strike is indeed what I have said: the *myth* in which Socialism is wholly comprised, *i.e.* a body of images capable of evoking instinctively all the sentiments which correspond to the different manifestations of the war undertaken by Socialism against modern society. Strikes have engendered in the proletariat the noblest, deepest, and most moving sentiments that they possess; the general strike groups them all in a co-ordinated picture, and, by bringing them together, gives to each one of them its maximum of intensity; appealing to their painful memories of particular conflicts, it colours with an intense life all the details of the composition presented to consciousness. We thus obtain that intuition of Socialism which language cannot give us with perfect clearness — and we obtain it as a whole, perceived instantaneously.

We may urge yet another piece of evidence to prove the power of the idea of the general strike. If that idea were a pure chimera, as is so frequently said, Parliamentary Socialists would not attack it with such heat; I do not remember that they ever attacked the senseless hopes which the Utopists have always held up before the dazzled eyes of the people.[2] . . . But when it is a question of the general strike, it is quite another thing; our politicians are no longer content with complicated reservations; they speak violently, and endeavour to induce their listeners to abandon this conception. . . .

They struggle against the conception of the general strike, because they recognise, in the course of their propagandist rounds, that this conception is so admirably adapted to the working-class mind that there is a possibility of its dominating the latter in the most absolute manner, thus leaving no place for the desires which the Parliamentarians are able to satisfy. They perceive that this idea is so effective as a motive force that once it has entered the minds of the people they can no longer be controlled by leaders, and that thus the power of the deputies would be

[2] I do not remember that the official Socialists have ever shown up the *ridiculousness* of the novels of Bellamy, which have had so great a success. These novels needed criticism all the more, because they presented to the people an entirely middle-class ideal of life. They were a natural product of America, a country which is ignorant of the class war; but in Europe, would not the theorists of the class war have understood them?

reduced to nothing. In short, they feel in a vague way that the whole Socialist movement might easily be absorbed by the general strike, which would render useless all those compromises between political groups in view of which the Parliamentary régime has been built up.

The opposition it meets with from official Socialists, therefore, furnishes a confirmation of our first inquiry into the scope of the general strike.

We must now proceed further, and inquire whether the picture furnished by the general strike is really complete; that is to say, whether it comprises all those features of the struggle which are recognised by modern Socialism. But, first of all, we must state the problem more precisely; this will not be difficult if we start from the explanations given above on the nature of the conception. We have seen that the general strike must be considered as an undivided whole; consequently, no details about ways and means will be the slightest help to the understanding of Socialism; it must even be added that there is always a danger of losing something of this understanding, if an attempt is made to split up this whole into parts. We will now endeavour to show that there is a fundamental identity between the chief tenets of Marxism and the co-ordinated aspects furnished by the picture of the general strike.

This affirmation is certain to appear paradoxical to many who have read the publications of the most accredited Marxians; and, in fact, for a very long time a well-marked hostility to the general strike existed in Marxian circles. This tradition has done a good deal of harm to the progress of Marx's doctrine; and it is in fact a very good illustration of the way in which, as a rule, disciples tend to restrict the application of their master's ideas. The *new school* has had considerable difficulty in liberating itself from these influences; it was formed by people who had received the Marxian imprint in a very marked degree; and it was a long time before the school recognised that the objections brought against the general strike arose from the incapacity of the official representatives of Marxism rather than from the principles of the doctrine itself. . . .

A decided step towards reform was made when those Marxians who aspired to think for themselves began to study the syndicalist movement; they discovered that "the genuine trade unionists have more to teach us than they have to learn from us." This was the beginning of wisdom; it was a step towards the realistic method which had led Marx to his real discoveries; in this way a return might be made to those methods which alone merit the name philosophical, "for true and fruitful ideas are so many close contacts with currents of reality," and they "owe most of their clearness to the light which the facts, and the applications to which they led, have by reflection shed on them — the clearness of a concept being scarcely anything more at bottom than the certainty, at last obtained, of manipulating the concept profitably." [3] And yet another profound thought of Bergson may usefully be quoted: "For we do not obtain an intuition from reality — that is, an intellectual sympathy with the most intimate part of it — unless we have won its confidence by a long fellowship with its superficial manifestations. And it is not merely a question of assimilating the most conspicuous facts; so immense a mass of facts must be accumulated and fused together, that in this fusion all the preconceived and premature ideas which observers may unwittingly have put into their observations will be certain to neutralize each other. In this way only can the bare materiality of the known facts be exposed to view." Finally, what Bergson calls *an integral experience* is obtained.

Thanks to the new principle, people very soon came to recognise that the propositions which in their opinion contained a complete statement of Socialism were deplorably inadequate, so that they were often more dangerous than useful. It is the superstitious respect paid by social democracy to the mere text of its doctrines that nullified every attempt in Germany to perfect Marxism.

When thc *new school* had acquired a full understanding of the general strike, and had thus obtained a profound intuition of the working-class movement, it saw that all the Socialist theories, interpreted in the light of this powerful construction, took on a meaning which till then they had lacked; it perceived that the clumsy and rickety apparatus which had been manufactured in Germany to explain Marx's doctrines, must be rejected if the contemporary transformation of the proletarian idea was to be followed exactly; it discovered that the conception of the general strike enabled them to explore profitably the whole vast domain of Marxism, which until then had remained practically unknown to the big-wigs who professed to be guiding Socialism. Thus the fundamental principles of Marxism are perfectly intelligible only with the aid of the picture of the general strike, and, on the other hand, the full significance of this picture, it may be supposed, is apparent only to those who are deeply versed in the Marxian doctrine.

First of all, I shall speak of the class war, which is the point of departure for all Socialistic thought, and which stands in such great need of elucidation, since sophists have endeavoured to give a false idea of it.

(1) Marx speaks of society as if it were divided into two fundamentally antagonistic groups; observation, it has often been urged, does not justify this division, and it is true that a certain effort of will is necessary before we can find it verified in the phenomena of everyday life.

The organisation of a capitalistic workshop furnishes a first approximation, and piece-work plays an essential part in the formation of the class idea; in fact, it throws into relief the very clear opposition of interests about the price of commodities; the workers feel themselves under

[3] Bergson [*Introduction à la metaphysique*].

the thumb of the employers in the same way that peasants feel themselves in the power of the merchants and the money-lenders of the towns; history shows that no economic opposition has been more clearly felt than the latter; since civilisation has existed, country and town have formed two hostile camps. Piecework also shows that in the wage-earning world there is a group of men somewhat analogous to the retail shopkeepers, possessing the confidence of the employer, and not belonging to the proletariat class.

The strike throws a new light on all this; it separates the interests and the different ways of thinking of the two groups of wage-earners — the foremen clerks, engineers, etc., as contrasted with the workmen who alone go on strike — much better than the daily circumstances of life do; it then becomes clear that the administrative group has a natural tendency to become a little aristocracy; for these people, State Socialism would be advantageous, because they would go up one in the social hierarchy.

But all oppositions become extraordinarily clear when conflicts are supposed to be enlarged to the size of the general strike; then all parts of the economico-judicial structure, in so far as the latter is looked upon from the point of view of the class war, reach the summit of their perfection; society is plainly divided into two camps, and only into two, on a field of battle. No philosophical explanation of the facts observed in practical affairs could throw such vivid light on the situation as the extremely simple picture called up by the conception of the general strike.

(2) It would be impossible to conceive the disappearance of capitalistic dominance if we did not suppose an ardent sentiment of revolt, always present in the soul of the worker; but experience shows that very often the revolts of a day are far from possessing a really specifically socialistic character; more than once the most violent outbursts have depended on passions which could be satisfied inside the middle-class world; many revolutionaries have been seen to abandon their old irreconcilability when they found themselves on the road to fortune. It is not only satisfactions of a material kind which produce these frequent and scandalous conversions; vanity, much more than money, is the great motive force in transformation of the revolutionary into a burgeois. All that would be negligible if it were only a question of a few exceptional people, but it has often been maintained that the psychology of the working classes would so easily adapt itself to the capitalistic order of things that social peace would be rapidly obtained if employers on their part would make a few sacrifices of money and *amour propre*.

G. Le Bon says that the belief in the revolutionary instincts of crowds is a very great mistake, that their tendencies are conservative, that the whole power of Socialism lies in the rather muddled state of mind of the middle class; he is convinced that the masses will always flock to a

Cæsar. There is a good deal of truth in these judgments, which are founded on a very wide knowledge of history, but G. Le Bon's theories must be corrected in one respect: they are only valid for societies which lack the conception of the class war.

Observation shows that this last conception is maintained with an indestructible vitality in every circle which has been touched by the idea of the general strike: the day when the slightest incidents of daily life become symptoms of the state of war between the classes, when every conflict is an incident in the social war, when every strike begets the perspective of a total catastrophe, on that day there is no longer any possibility of social peace, of resignation to routine, or of enthusiasm for philanthropic or successful employers. The idea of the general strike has such power behind it that it drags into the revolutionary track everything it touches. In virtue of this idea, Socialism remains ever young; all attempts made to bring about social peace seem childish; desertions of comrades into the ranks of the middle class, far from discouraging the masses, only excite them still more to rebellion; in a word, the line of cleavage is never in danger of disappearing.

(3) The successes obtained by politicians in their attempts to make what they call the proletarian influence felt in middle-class institutions, constitute a very great obstacle to the maintenance of the notion of class war. The world has always been carried on by compromises between opposing parties, and order has always been provisional. No change, however considerable, can be looked upon as impossible in a time like ours, which has seen so many novelties introduced in an unexpected manner. Modern progress has been brought about by successive compromises; why not pursue the aims of Socialism by methods which have succeeded so well? Many means of satisfying the more pressing desires of the unfortunate classes can be thought of. For a long time these proposals for improvement were inspired by conservative, feudal, or Catholic spirit. We wish, said the inventors, to rescue the masses from the influence of the Radicals.[4] The latter, seeing their political influence assailed, not so much by their old enemies as by Socialist politicians, invent nowadays all kinds of projects of a progressive, democratic, free-thinking colour. We are beginning at last to be threatened with socialistic compromises! . . .

The idea of the general strike destroys all the theoretical consequences of every possible social policy; its partisans look upon even the most popular reforms as having a middle-class character; so far as they are concerned, nothing can weaken the fundamental opposition of the class war. The more the policy of social reforms becomes preponderant, the more will Socialists feel the need of placing against the picture of the progress

[4] [The Radicals, despite their name, were the petty bourgeois party of the Third Republic; they stood considerably to the right of the Socialists. — Eds.]

which it is the aim of this policy to bring about, this other picture of complete catastrophe furnished so perfectly by the general strike. . . .

Socialism has always inspired terror because of the enormous element of the unknown which it contains; people feel that a transformation of this kind would permit of no turning back. Utopists have used all their literary art in the endeavour to lull anxiety by pictures of the future, so enchanting that fear might be banished; but the more they accumulated fine promises, the more did thoughtful people suspect traps, and in this they were not altogether mistaken, for the Utopists would have led the world to disasters, tyranny, and stupidity, if they had been hearkened to.

Marx was firmly convinced that the social revolution of which he spoke would constitute an *irrevocable transformation,* and that it would mark an absolute separation between two historical eras; he often returned to this idea, and Engels has endeavoured to show, by means of images which were sometimes a little grandiose, how economic enfranchisement would be the point of departure of an era having no relationship with the past. Rejecting all Utopias, these two founders of modern Socialism renounced all the resources by which their predecessors had rendered the prospect of a great revolution less formidable; but however strong the expressions which they employed might have been, the effects which they produced are still very inferior to those produced by the evocation of the general strike. This conception makes it impossible for us to ignore the fact that a kind of irresistible wave will pass over the old civilisation.

There is something really terrifying in all this; but I believe that it is very essential that this feature of Socialism should be insisted on if the latter is to have its full educational value. Socialists must be convinced that the work to which they are devoting themselves is a *serious, formidable, and sublime work;* it is only on this condition that they will be able to bear the innumerable sacrifices imposed on them by a propaganda, which can procure them neither honours, profits, nor even immediate intellectual satisfaction. Even if the only result of the idea of the general strike was to make the Socialist conception more heroic, it should on that account alone be looked upon as having an incalculable value.

The resemblances which I have just established between Marxism and the general strike might be carried still further and deeper; if they have been overlooked hitherto, it is because we are much more struck by the form of things than by their content; a large number of people find great difficulty in believing that there can be any parallelism between a philosophy based on Hegelianism and the constructions made by men entirely devoid of higher culture. Marx had acquired in Germany a taste for very condensed formulas, and these formulas were so admirably suited to the conditions in the midst of which he worked that he naturally made great use of them. When he wrote, there had been none of the great and numerous strikes which would have enabled him to speak with a detailed knowledge of the means by which the proletariat may prepare itself for the revolution. This absence of knowledge gained from experience very much hampered Marx's thought; he avoided the use of too precise formulas which would have had this inconvenience of giving a kind of sanction to existing institutions, which seemed valueless to him; he was therefore happy to be able to find in German academic writing a habit of abstract language which allowed him to avoid all discussion of detail.

No better proof perhaps can be given of Marx's genius than the remarkable agreement which is found to exist between his views and the doctrine which revolutionary Syndicalism is to-day building up slowly and laboriously, keeping always strictly to strike tactics. . . .

We are perfectly well aware that the historians of the future are bound to discover that we laboured under many illusions, because they will see behind them a finished world. We, on the other hand, must act, and nobody can tell us to-day what these historians will know; nobody can furnish us with the means of modifying our motor images in such a way as to avoid their criticisms.

Our situation resembles somewhat that of the physicists who work at huge calculations based on theories which are not destined to endure for ever. We have nowadays abandoned all hopes of discovering a complete science of nature; the spectacle of modern scientific revolutions is not encouraging for scientists, and has no doubt led many people, naturally enough, to proclaim the bankruptcy of science, and yet we should be mad if we handed the management of industry over to sorcerers, mediums, and wonder-workers. The philosopher who *does not seek to make a practical application of his theories* may take up the point of view of the future historian of science, and then dispute the absolute character of present-day scientific theses; but he is as ignorant as the present-day physicist when he is asked how to correct the explanations given by the latter; must he therefore take refuge in scepticism?

Nowadays no philosophers worthy of consideration accept the sceptical position; their great aim, on the contrary, is to prove the legitimacy of a science which, however, makes no claim to know the real nature of things, and which confines itself to discovering relations which can be utilised for practical ends. It is because sociology is in the hands of people who are incapable of any philosophic reasoning that it is possible for us to be attacked (in the name of the *little science*) for being content with methods founded on the laws that a really thorough psychological analysis reveals as fundamental in the genesis of action, and which are revealed to us in all great historical movements.

To proceed scientifically means, first of all, to know what forces exist in the world, and then to take measures whereby we may utilise them, by reasoning from experience. That is why I say that, by accepting the idea of the general strike, although we know that it is a myth, we are proceeding exactly as a modern physicist does who has complete confidence in his science, although he knows that the future will look upon it as antiquated. It is we who really possess the scientific spirit, while our critics have lost touch both with modern science and modern philosophy; and having proved this, we are quite easy in our minds.

VIII

THE REVOLT AGAINST POSITIVISM AND FORMALISM: THE PSYCHOLOGY OF THE UNCONSCIOUS

Many psychologists in the closing years of the nineteenth century were attempting to establish psychology as a discipline in its own right, to remove it from its status as a branch of philosophy and make it a truly scientific area of inquiry. The American William James (1842–1910) and the Austrian Sigmund Freud (1856–1939) were among the principal figures in that development. They shared a common educational background as physicians (though James never practiced medicine), a similar desire to devise therapeutic approaches to mental problems, and a mutual interest in the abnormal, irrational activities of the mind.

James and Freud also shared in the effort to transcend the static psychological theory of the positivists, who depicted the mind as simply responding to stimuli from the environment. To supplant that mechanistic formula the newer scientific psychologists fashioned a portrait of the mind as a dynamic agent that interacted with the environment. The mind, they said, did not simply act reflexively; it contained within itself motives and purposes and sources of behavior.

In his master-work, Principles of Psychology, *published in 1890, James described the mind as an active organ whose principal functions consisted in selecting significant data from the welter of sense experience and prescribing the appropriate course of action. Those functions, said James, implied "consciousness," and he vigorously denied that "unconscious mental states" existed. To the growing body of evidence introduced to demonstrate the existence of such states — as, for example, the passage from one mental condition to another, with no awareness of a logically necessary transitional condition — James's usual rebuttal was that they could be accounted for in terms of periods of consciousness that the individual had simply forgotten. It was James's intention, in refuting the notion of unconscious mental states, to strengthen his case for the mind as a participating agent rather than an inert spectator or mechanical automaton in the life process. His argument here adumbrated in many significant ways the pragmatic theory of truth that he began to popularize at the end of the decade.*

Sigmund Freud did not "discover" the unconscious. But he looked favorably on the theories concerning its existence that James, at first, so forcefully rejected, and he assigned to the unconscious a paramount place in his brilliant and epoch making description of the topography of the mind. For Freud, the mind did not only select among stimuli in the external environment, as James had argued. Powerful forces within the mind itself, whose character was largely formed in infancy, and whose energy was closely associated with the sexual instinct, significantly determined human behavior. In the course of his clinical practice, Freud found that his patients were not conscious of those forces, or of their influence on the patients' health.

By the time James came to write The Varieties of Religious Experience, *from which the selection below is taken, he was much more amenable to the idea of an unconscious mental region than he had been in the* Principles. *Indeed, his opposition in the earlier work had been directed against a passive view of the mind, and when it seemed that Freud's theories did not necessarily relegate the mind to a passive role, James could make the step from opposition to substantial acceptance without really abandoning the essential logic of his earlier position. When Freud came to America in 1909, he had a brief meeting with James, who was only a few months away from death. Generously, James commented to Ernest Jones, Freud's colleague, "The future of psychology belongs to your work."* [1]

But though James moved in the direction of Freud's theory, he remained some distance from completely embracing it. He could not accept the sexual aspects of the theory. More important, a significant difference in general purpose separated James from Freud. Freud aimed to conquer sentimentality and religion with the weapons of science and to control emotions by the therapeutic application of reason. James, on the other hand, always deeply religious, hoped to use psychology to effect a reconciliation between science

[1] Quoted in Ernest Jones, *The Life and Work of Sigmund Freud,* ed. and abr. Lionel Trilling and Steven Marcus (Garden City, N.J.: Doubleday, 1963), 261.

and religion, and he maintained a more optimistic disposition toward the emotional life than Freud.

The selections below, which offer samples of Freud's and James's explanations for neurotic behavior, illustrate some of the points of contact and divergence between these two powerful thinkers.

The Theory of the Neuroses
(1917)

SIGMUND FREUD

Ladies and Gentlemen, — In the last lecture I explained to you that clinical psychiatry takes little notice of the outward form or content of individual symptoms, but that psycho-analysis takes matters up at precisely that point and has established in the first place the fact that symptoms have a sense and are related to the patient's experiences. The sense of neurotic symptoms was first discovered by Josef Breuer from his study and successful cure (between 1880 and 1882) of a case of hysteria which has since become famous. It is true that Pierre Janet brought forward the same evidence independently; indeed, the French worker can claim priority of publication, for it was only a decade later (in 1893 and 1895), while he was collaborating with me, that Breuer published his observation. In any case it may seem a matter of some indifference who made the discovery, for, as you know, every discovery is made more than once and none is made all at once. And, apart from this, success does not always go along with merit: America is not named after Columbus. The great psychiatrist Leuret gave it as his opinion, before Breuer and Janet, that even the delusional ideas of the insane would certainly be found to have a sense if only we understood how to translate them. I must admit that for a long time I was prepared to give Janet very great credit for throwing light on neurotic symptoms, because he regarded them as expressions of *idées inconscientes* which dominated the patients. But since then he has expressed himself with exaggerated reserve, as if he wanted to admit that the unconscious had been nothing more to him than a form of words, a makeshift, *une façon de parler* — that he had meant nothing real by it. Since then I have ceased to understand Janet's writings; but I think he has unnecessarily forfeited much credit.

Thus neurotic symptoms have a sense, like parapraxes and dreams, and, like them, have a connection with the life of those who produce them. I should now like to make this important discovery plainer to you by a few examples. I can indeed only assert, I cannot prove, that it is always and in every instance so. Anyone who looks for experiences himself, will find convincing evidence. But for certain reasons I shall choose these examples from cases not of hysteria but of another, highly remarkable neurosis which is fundamentally very much akin to it and about which I have a few introductory remarks to make.

This neurosis, known as 'obsessional neurosis,' is not so popular as the universally familiar hysteria. It is not, if I may express myself thus, so obtrusively noisy, it behaves more like a private affair of the patient's, it dispenses almost entirely with somatic phenomena, and creates all its symptoms in the mental sphere. Obsessional neurosis and hysteria are the forms of neurotic illness upon the study of which psycho-analysis was first built, and in the treatment of which, too, our therapy celebrates its triumphs. But obsessional neurosis, in which the puzzling leap from the mental to the physical plays no part, has actually, through the efforts of psycho-analysis, become more perspicuous and familiar to us than hysteria, and we have learnt that it displays certain extreme characteristics of the nature of neurosis far more glaringly.

Obsessional neurosis is shown in the patient's being occupied with thoughts in which he is in fact not interested, in his being aware of impulses in himself which appear very strange to him and in his being led to actions the performance of which give him no enjoyment, but which it is quite impossible for him to omit. The thoughts (obsessions) may be senseless in themselves, or merely a matter of indifference to the subject; often they are completely silly, and invariably they are the starting-point of a strenuous mental activity, which exhausts the patient and to which he only surrenders himself most unwillingly. He is obliged against his will to brood and speculate as though it were a question of his most important vital problems. The impulses which the patient is aware of in himself may also make a childish and senseless impression; but as a rule they have a content of the most frightful kind, tempting him, for instance, to commit serious crimes, so that he not merely disavows them as alien to himself, but flies from them in horror and protects himself from carrying them out by prohibitions, renunciations and restrictions upon his freedom. At the same time, these impulses never — literally never — force their way through to performance, the outcome lies always in victory for the flight and the precautions. What the patient actually carries out — his so-called obsessional actions — are very harmless and certainly trivial things, for the most part repetitions or ceremonial elaborations of the activities of ordinary life. But these necessary activities (such as going to bed, washing, dressing or going for a walk) become extremely tedious and almost insoluble tasks. In different forms and cases of obsessional neurosis the pathological ideas, impulses and actions are not combined in equal proportions; it is the rule, rather, that one or other of these factors dominates the picture and gives its name to the illness, but the common element in all these forms is sufficiently unmistakable. . . .

I shall give you only two examples of the analysis of an obsessional symptom: one an old observation which I cannot find a better one to replace, and another recently met with. I limit myself to this small number, because it is impossible in such reports to avoid being very diffuse and entering into every detail.

A lady, nearly thirty years of age, who suffered from the most severe obsessional manifestations and whom I might perhaps have helped if a malicious chance had not brought my work to nothing — I may be able to tell you more about this later on — performed (among others) the following remarkable obsessional action many times a day. She ran from her room into another neighbouring one, took up a particular position there beside a table that stood in the middle, rang the bell for her housemaid, sent her on some indifferent errand or let her go without one, and then ran back into her own room. This was certainly not a very distressing symptom, but was nevertheless calculated to excite curiosity. The explanation was reached in the most unequivocal and unobjectionable manner, free from any possible contribution on the doctor's part. I cannot see how I could possibly have formed any suspicion of the sense of this obsessional action or could have offered any suggestion on how it was to be interpreted. Whenever I asked the patient 'Why do you do that? What sense has it?' she answered: 'I don't know.' But one day, after I had succeeded in defeating a major, fundamental doubt of hers, she suddenly knew the answer and told me what it was that was connected with the obsessional action. More than ten years before, she had married a man very much older than herself, and on the wedding-night he was impotent. Many times during the night he had come running from his room into hers to try once more, but every time without success. Next morning he had said angrily: 'I should feel ashamed in front of the housemaid when she makes the bed,' took up a bottle of red ink that happened to be in the room and poured its contents over the sheet, but not on the exact place where a stain would have been appropriate. I could not understand at first what this recollection had to do with the obsessional action in question; the only resemblance I could find was in the repeated running from one room into the other, and perhaps also in the entrance of the housemaid. My patient then led me up to the table in the second room and showed me a big stain on the tablecloth. She further explained that she took up her position in relation to the table in such a way that the maid who had been sent for could not fail to see the stain. There could no longer be any doubt of the intimate connection between the scene on her wedding-night and her present obsessional action, though all kinds of other things remained to be learnt.

It was clear, in the first place, that the patient was identifying herself with her husband; she was playing his part by imitating his running from one room into the other. Further, to carry on the analogy, we must agree that the bed and the sheet were replaced by the table and the tablecloth. This might seem arbitrary, but surely we have not studied dream-symbolism to no purpose. In dreams too we often find a table which has to be interpreted as a bed. Table and bed together stand for marriage, so that the one can easily take the place of the other.

It already seems proved that the obsessional action had a sense; it appears to have been a representation, a repetition, of the significant scene. But we are not obliged to come to a halt here. If we examine the relation between the two more closely, we shall probably obtain information about something that goes further — about the intention of the obsessional action. Its kernel was obviously the summoning of the housemaid, before whose eyes the patient displayed the stain, in contrast to her husband's remark that he would feel ashamed in front of the maid. Thus he, whose part she was playing, did not feel ashamed in front of the maid; accordingly the stain was in the right place. We see, therefore, that she was not simply repeating the scene, she was continuing and at the same time correcting it; she was putting it right. But by this she was also correcting the other thing, which had been so distressing that night and had made the expedient with the red ink necessary — his impotence. So the obsessional action was saying: 'No, it's not true. He had no need to feel ashamed in front of the housemaid; he was not impotent.' It represented this wish, in the manner of a dream, as fulfilled in a present-day action; it served the purpose of making her husband superior to his past mishap.

Everything I could tell you about this woman fits in with this. Or, more correctly speaking, everything else we know about her points the way to this interpretation of what was in itself an unintelligible obsessional action. The woman had been living apart from her husband for years and was struggling with an intention to obtain a legal divorce. But there was no question of her being free of him; she was forced to remain faithful to him; she withdrew from the world so as not to be tempted; she exculpated and magnified his nature in her imagination. Indeed, the deepest secret of her illness was that by means of it she protected her husband from malicious gossip, justified her separation from him and enabled him to lead a comfortable separate life. Thus the analysis of a harmless obsessional action led directly to the inmost core of an illness, but at the same time betrayed to us no small part of the secret of obsessional neurosis in general. I am glad to let you dwell a little on this example because it combines conditions which we could not fairly expect to find in every case. Here the interpretation of the symptom was discovered by the patient herself at a single blow, without any prompting or intervention on the analyst's part; and it resulted from a connection with an event which did not (as is usually the case) belong to a forgotten period of childhood, but which had happened in the patient's adult life and had remained undimmed in her memory. All the objections which criticism is normally in the habit of raising against our interpretation of symptoms fall to the ground in this particular case. We cannot hope always to have such good luck.

And one thing more. Were you not struck by the way in which this unobtrusive obsessional action has led us into the intimacies of the patient's life? A woman cannot have anything much more intimate to tell than the story of her wedding-night. Is it a matter of chance and of no further significance that we have arrived precisely at the intimacies of sexual life? No doubt it might be the result of the choice I have made on this occasion. Do not let us be too hasty in forming our judgment, and let us turn to my second example, which is of quite a different kind — a sample of a very common species, a sleep-ceremonial.

A nineteen-year-old girl, well developed and gifted, was the only child of parents to whom she was superior in education and intellectual liveliness. As a child she had been wild and high-spirited, and in the course of the last few years had changed, without any visible cause, into a neurotic. She was very irritable, particularly towards her mother, always dissatisfied and depressed, and inclined to indecisiveness and doubt; finally she admitted that she was no longer able to walk by herself across squares or along comparatively wide streets. We will not concern ourselves much with her complicated illness, which called for at least two diagnoses — agoraphobia and obsessional neurosis — but will dwell only on the fact that she also developed a sleep-ceremonial, with which she tormented her parents. In a certain sense it may be said that every normal person has his sleep-ceremonial or that he has established certain necessary conditions the non-fulfilment of which interferes with his going to sleep; he has imposed certain forms on the transition from the waking to the sleeping state and repeats them in the same manner every evening. But everything that a healthy person requires as a necessary condition for sleep can be understood rationally, and if external circumstances call for a change he will comply easily and without waste of time. A pathological ceremonial, however, is unyielding and insists on being carried through, even at the cost of great sacrifices; it too is screened by having a rational basis and at a superficial glance seems to diverge from the normal only by a certain exaggerated meticulousness. On closer examination, nevertheless, we can see that the screen is insufficient, that the ceremonial comprises some stipulations which go far beyond its rational basis and others which positively run counter to it. Our present patient put forward as a pretext for her nightly precautions that she needed quiet in order to sleep and must exclude every source of noise. With that end in view she did two kinds of things. The big clock in her room was stopped, all the other clocks or watches in the room were removed, and her tiny wrist-watch was not allowed even to be inside her bedside table. Flower-pots and vases were collected on the writing-table so that they might not fall over in the night and break, and disturb her in her sleep. She was aware that these measures could find only an *ostensible* justification in the rule in favor of quiet: the ticking of the little watch would not have been audible even if it had been left lying on the top of the bedside table, and we have all had experience of the fact that the regular ticking of a pendulum-clock never disturbs sleep but acts, rather, as a soporific. She admitted too that her fear that flower-pots and vases, if they were left in their places, might fall over and break of their own accord lacked all plausibility. In the case of other stipulations made by the ceremonial the need for quiet was dropped as a basis. Indeed, the requirement that the door between her room and her parents' bedroom should stay half-open — the fulfilment of which she ensured by placing various objects in the open doorway — seemed on the contrary to act as a source of disturbing noises. But the most important stipulations related to the bed itself. The pillow at the top end of the bed must not touch the wooden back of the bedstead. The small top-pillow must lie on this large pillow in one specific way only — namely, so as to form a diamond shape. Her head had then to lie exactly along the long diameter of the diamond. The eiderdown (or '*Duchent*' as we call it in Austria) had to be shaken before being laid on the bed so that its bottom end became very thick; afterwards, however, she never failed to even out this accumulation of feathers by pressing them apart.

With your leave I will pass over the remaining, often very trivial, details of the ceremonial; they would teach us nothing new, and would lead us too far afield from our aims. But you must not overlook the fact that all this was not carried out smoothly. There was always an apprehension that things might not have been done properly. Everything must be checked and repeated, doubts assailed first one and then another of the safety measures, and the result was that one or two hours were spent, during which the girl herself could not sleep and would not allow her intimidated parents to sleep either.

The analysis of these torments did not proceed so simply as that of our earlier patient's obsessional action. I was obliged to give the girl hints and propose interpretations, which were always rejected with a decided 'no' or accepted with contemptuous doubt. But after this first reaction of rejection there followed a time during which she occupied herself with the possibilities put before her, collected associations to them, produced recollections and made connections, until by her own work she had accepted all the interpretations. In proportion as this happened, she relaxed the performance of her obsessional measures, and even before the end of the treatment she had given up the whole ceremonial. You must understand, too, that the work of analysis as we carry it out to-day quite excludes the systematic treatment of any individual symptom till it has been entirely cleared up. We are, on the contrary, obliged to keep on leaving any particular topic, in the certain expectation of coming back to it again in other connections. The interpretation of her symptoms which I am about to give you is accordingly a synthesis of findings which were arrived at, interrupted by other work, over a period of weeks and months.

Our patient gradually came to learn that it was as symbols of the female genitals that clocks were banished from her equipment for the night. Clocks and watches — though elsewhere we have found other symbolic interpretations for them — have arrived at a genital role owing to their relation to periodic processes and equal intervals of time. A woman may boast that her menstruation behaves with the regularity of clockwork. Our patient's anxiety, however, was directed in particular against being disturbed in her sleep by the ticking of a clock. The ticking of a clock may be compared with the knocking or throbbing in the clitoris during sexual excitement. She had in fact been repeatedly woken from her sleep by this sensation, which had now become distressing to her; and she gave expression to this fear of an erection in the rule that all clocks and watches that were going should be removed from her neighbourhood at night. Flower-pots and vases, like all vessels, are also female symbols. Taking precautions against their falling and being broken at night was thus not without its good sense. We know the widespread custom of breaking a vessel or plate at betrothal ceremonies. Each man present gets hold of a fragment, and we may regard this as a sign of his resigning the claims he had upon the bride in virtue of a marriage-regulation dating from before the establishment of monogamy. In connection with this part of her ceremonial the girl produced a recollection and several associations. Once when she was a child she had fallen down while she was carrying a glass or china vase and had cut her finger and bled profusely. When she grew up and came to know the facts about sexual intercourse she formed an anxious idea that on her wedding-night she would not bleed and would thus fail to show that she was a virgin. Her precautions against vases being broken thus meant a repudiation of the whole complex concerned with virginity and bleeding at the first intercourse — a repudiation equally of the fear of bleeding and of the contrary fear of not bleeding. These precautions, which she subsumed under her avoidance of noise, had only a remote connection with it.

She found out the central meaning of her ceremonial one day when she suddenly understood the meaning of the rule that the pillow must not touch the back of the bedstead. The pillow, she said, had always been a woman to her and the upright wooden back a man. Thus she wanted — by magic, we must interpolate — to keep the man and woman apart — that is, to separate her parents from each other, not to allow them to have sexual intercourse. In earlier years, before she had established the ceremonial, she had tried to achieve the same aim in a more direct way. She had simulated fear (or had exploited a tendency to fear which was already present) in order that the connecting doors between her parents' bedroom and the nursery should not be shut. This rule had, indeed, been retained in her present ceremonial. In that way she gave herself the opportunity of listening to her parents, but in making use of it she brought on an insomnia which lasted for months. Not satisfied with disturbing her parents by this means, she contrived to be allowed from time to time to sleep in her parents' bed between them. The 'pillow' and the 'wooden back' were thus really unable to come together. Finally, when she was so big that it became physically uncomfortable for her to find room in the bed between her parents, she managed, by a conscious simulation of anxiety, to arrange for her mother to exchange places with her for the night and to leave her own place so that the patient could sleep beside her father. This situation no doubt became the starting-point of phantasies whose after-effect was to be seen in the ceremonial.

If a pillow was a woman, than the shaking of the eiderdown till all the feathers were at the bottom and caused a swelling there had a sense as well. It meant making a woman pregnant; but she never failed to smooth away the pregnancy again, for she had for years been afraid that her parents' intercourse would result in another child and so present her with a competitor. On the other hand, if the big pillow was a woman, the mother, then the small top-pillow could only stand for the daughter. Why did this pillow have to be placed diamond-wise and her head precisely along its centre line? It was easy to recall to her that this diamond shape is the inscription scribbled on every wall to represent the open female genitals. If so, she herself was playing the man and replacing the male organ by her head. (Cf. the symbolism of beheading for castrating.)

Wild thoughts, you will say, to be running through an unmarried girl's head. I admit that is so. But you must not forget that I did not make these things but only interpreted them. A sleep-ceremonial like this is a strange thing too, and you will not fail to see how the ceremonial corresponds to the phantasies which are revealed by the interpretation. But I attach more importance to your noticing that what was seen in the ceremonial was a precipitate not of a *single* phantasy but of a number of them, though they had a nodal point somewhere, and, further, that the rules laid down by the ceremonial reproduced the patient's sexual wishes at one point positively and at another negatively — in part they represented them, but in part they served as a defence against them.

More could be made, too, of the analysis of this ceremonial if it could be properly linked up with the patient's other symptoms. But our path does not lead in that direction. You must be content with a hint that the girl was in the grip of an erotic attachment to her father whose beginnings went back to her childhood. Perhaps that was why she behaved in such an unfriendly way to her mother. Nor can we overlook the fact that the analysis of this symptom has once again taken us back to a patient's sexual life. We shall perhaps be less surprised at this the more often we gain an insight into the sense and intention of neurotic symptoms. . . .

Ladies and Gentlemen, — In my last lecture I expressed a desire that our work should go forward on the basis not of our doubts but of our discoveries. We have not yet had any discussion of two of the most interesting implications that follow from our two sample analyses.

To take the first of these. Both patients give us an impression of having been 'fixated' to a particular portion of their past, as though they could not manage to free themselves from it and were for that reason alienated from the present and the future. They then remained lodged in their illness in the sort of way in which in earlier days people retreated into a monastery in order to bear the burden there of their ill-fated lives. What had brought this fate upon our first patient was the marriage which she had in real life abandoned. By means of her symptoms she continued to carry on her dealings with her husband. We learnt to understand the voices that pleaded for him, that excused him, that put him on a pedestal and that lamented his loss. Although she was young and desirable to other men, she had taken every precaution, real and imaginary (magical), to remain faithful to him. She did not show herself to strangers and she neglected her personal appearance; furthermore, once she had sat down in a chair she was unable to get out of it quickly, she refused to sign her name, and she could not make any presents, on the ground that no one ought to receive anything from her.

The same effect was produced on the life of our second patient, the young girl, by an erotic attachment to her father which had started during the years before her puberty. The conclusion she herself drew was that she could not marry as long as she was so ill. We, however, may suspect that she had become so ill in order not to have to marry and in order to remain with her father.

We cannot dismiss the question of why, in what way and for what motive a person can arrive at such a remarkable attitude to life and one that is so inexpedient — assuming that this attitude is a general characteristic of neuroses and not a special peculiarity of these two patients. And in fact it is a general feature, of great practical importance, in every neurosis. Breuer's first hysterical patient was similarly fixated to the period when she was nursing her father in a serious illness. In spite of her recovery, in a certain respect she remained cut off from life; she remained healthy and efficient but avoided the normal course of a woman's life. In every one of our patients, analysis shows us that they have been carried back to some particular period of their past by the symptoms of their illness or their consequences. In the majority of cases, indeed, a very early phase of life is chosen for the purpose — a period of their childhood or even, laughable as this may sound, of their existence as an infant at the breast.

The closest analogy to this behaviour of our neurotics is afforded by illnesses which are being produced with special frequency precisely at the present time by the war — what are described as traumatic neuroses. Similar cases, of course, appeared before the war as well, after railway collisions and other alarming accidents involving fatal risks. Traumatic neuroses are not in their essence the same thing as the spontaneous neuroses which we are in the habit of investigating and treating by analysis; nor have we yet succeeded in bringing them into harmony with our views, and I hope I shall be able at some time to explain to you the reason for this limitation. But in one respect we may insist that there is a complete agreement between them. The traumatic neuroses give a clear indication that a fixation to the moment of the traumatic accident lies at their root. These patients regularly repeat the traumatic situation in their dreams; where hysteriform attacks occur that admit of an analysis, we find that the attack corresponds to a complete transplanting of the patient into the traumatic situation. It is as though these patients had not finished with the traumatic situation, as though they were still faced by it as an immediate task which has not been dealt with; and we take this view quite seriously. It shows us the way to what we may call an *economic* view of mental processes. Indeed, the term 'traumatic' has no other sense than an economic one. We apply it to an experience which within a short period of time presents the mind with an increase of stimulus too powerful to be dealt with or worked off in the normal way, and this must result in permanent disturbances of the manner in which the energy operates.

This analogy is bound to tempt us to describe as traumatic those experiences too to which our neurotic patients seem to be fixated. This would promise to offer us a simple determinant for the onset of neurosis. Neurosis could then be equated with a traumatic illness and would come about owing to inability to deal with an experience whose affective colouring was excessively powerful. And this indeed was actually the first formula in which (in 1893 and 1895) Breuer and I accounted theoretically for our new observations. A case like that of the first of the two patients in my last lecture — the young married woman separated from her husband — fits in very well with this view. She had not got over the failure of her marriage and remained attached to that trauma. But our second case — that of the girl with a fixation upon her father — shows us already that the formula is not sufficiently comprehensive. On the one hand, a little girl's being in love like this with her father is something so common and so frequently surmounted that the term 'traumatic' applied to it would lose all its meaning; and, on the other hand, the patient's history showed us that in the first instance her erotic fixation appeared to have passed off without doing any damage, and it was only several years later that it reappeared in the symptoms of the obsessional neurosis. Here, then, we foresee complications, a greater wealth of determinants for the onset of illness; but we may also suspect that there is no need to abandon the traumatic line of approach as being erroneous: it must be possible to fit it in and subsume it somewhere else.

Here once more, then, we must break off the course we have started on. For the moment it leads no further and we shall have to learn all kinds of other things before we can find its proper continuation. But on the subject of fixation to a particular phase in the past we may add that such behaviour is far more widespread than neurosis. Every neurosis includes a fixation of that kind, but not every fixation leads to a neurosis, coincides with a neurosis or arises owing to a neurosis. A perfect model of an affective fixation to something that is past is provided by mourning, which actually involves the most complete alienation from the present and the future. But even the judgement of a layman will distinguish sharply between mourning and neurosis. There are, on the other hand, neuroses which may be described as a pathological form of mourning.

It may happen, too, that a person is brought so completely to a stop by a traumatic event which shatters the foundations of his life that he abandons all interest in the present and future and remains permanently absorbed in mental concentration upon the past. But an unfortunate such as this need not on that account become a neurotic. We will not attach too much value to this one feature, therefore, in characterizing neurosis, however regularly present and however important it may usually be.

Let us turn now to the second of the discoveries which follow from our analyses; in its case we need not fear having to make a subsequent qualification of our views. I have described to you how our first patient carried out a senseless obsessional action and how she reported an intimate memory from her past life as having some connection with it: and how afterwards I examined the connection between the two and discovered the intention of the obsessional action from its relation to the memory. But there is one factor which I have entirely neglected, though it deserves our fullest attention. However often the patient repeated her obsessional action, she knew nothing of its being derived from the experience she had had. The connection between the two was hidden from her; she could only quite truthfully reply that she did not know what it was that was making her carry out her action. Then suddenly one day, under the influence of the treatment, she succeeded in discovering the connection and reported it to me. But she still knew nothing of the intention with which she was performing the obsessional action — the intention of correcting a distressing portion of the past and of putting her beloved husband in a better light. It took a fairly long time and called for much labour before she understood and admitted to me that such a motive alone could have been the driving force of her obsessional action.

The link with the scene after her unhappy wedding-night and the patient's affectionate motive constituted, taken together, what we have called the 'sense' of the obsessional action. But while she was carrying out the obsessional action this sense had been unknown to her in both directions — both its 'whence' and its 'whither.' Mental processes had therefore been at work in her and the obsessional action was the effect of them; she had been aware of this effect in a normal mental fashion, but none of the mental predeterminants of this effect came to the knowledge of her consciousness. She behaved in precisely the same way as a hypnotized subject whom Bernheim had ordered to open an umbrella in the hospital ward five minutes after he woke up. The man carried out this instruction when he was awake, but he could produce no motive for his action. It is a state of affairs of this sort that we have before our eyes when we speak of the existence of *unconscious mental processes*. We can challenge anyone in the world to give a more correct scientific account of this state of affairs, and if he does we will gladly renounce our hypothesis of unconscious mental processes. Till that happens, however, we will hold fast to the hypothesis; and if someone objects that here the unconscious is nothing real in a scientific sense, is a makeshift, *une façon de parler*, we can only shrug our shoulders resignedly and dismiss what he says as unintelligible. Something not real, which produces effects of such tangible reality as an obsessional action!

And we meet with what is in essence the same thing in our second patient. She had made a rule that the pillow must not touch the back of the bedstead, and she had to obey this rule though she did not know where it came from, what it meant or to what motives it owed its power. Whether she herself regarded the rule as a matter of indifference, or whether she struggled against it or raged against it or decided to transgress it — none of this made any difference to her carrying it out. It had to be obeyed, and she asked herself vainly why. We must recognize, however, that these symptoms of obsessional neurosis, these ideas and impulses which emerge one knows not whence, which prove so resistant to every influence from an otherwise normal mind, which give the patient himself the impression of being all-powerful guests from an alien world, immortal beings intruding into the turmoil of mortal life — these symptoms offer the plainest indication of there being a special region of the mind, shut off from the rest. They lead, by a path that cannot be missed, to a conviction of the existence of the unconscious in the mind; and that is precisely why clinical psychiatry, which is acquainted only with a psychology of consciousness, can deal with these symptoms in no other way than by declaring them to be signs of a special sort of degeneracy. Obsessional ideas and obsessional impulses are not, of course, themselves unconscious, any more than the performance of obsessional actions escapes conscious perception. They would not have become symptoms if they had not forced their way into consciousness. But their psychical predeterminants which we infer by means of analysis, the connections into which we insert them by interpretation, are unconscious, at least until we have made them conscious to the patient by the work of analysis.

If, now, you consider further that the state of affairs which we have established in our two cases is confirmed for every symptom of every neurotic illness — that always and everywhere the sense of the symptoms is unknown to the patient and that analysis regularly shows that these symptoms are derivatives of unconscious processes but can, subject to a variety of favourable circumstances, be made conscious — if you consider this, you will understand that in psycho-analysis we cannot do without what is at the same time unconscious and mental, and are accustomed to operate with it as though it were something palpable to the senses. But you will understand as well, perhaps, how incapable of forming a judgement on this question are all those other people, who are only acquainted with the unconscious as a concept, who have never carried out an analysis and have never interpreted dreams or found a sense and intention in neurotic symptoms. To say it for our ends once again: the possibility of giving a sense to neurotic symptoms by analytic interpretation is an unshakeable proof of the existence — or, if you prefer it, of the necessity for the hypothesis — of unconscious mental processes.

But that is not all. Thanks to a second discovery of Breuer's, which seems to me even more significant than the other and which he shared with no one, we learn still more of the connection between neurotic symptoms and the unconscious. Not only is the sense of the symptoms regularly unconscious, but there is an inseparable relation between this fact of the symptoms being unconscious and the possibility of their existing. You will understand me in a moment. I follow Breuer in asserting that every time we come upon a symptom we can infer that there are certain definite unconscious processes in the patient which contain the sense of the symptom. But it is also necessary for that sense to be unconscious in order that the symptom can come about. Symptoms are never constructed from conscious processes; as soon as the unconscious processes concerned have become conscious, the symptom must disappear. Here you will at once perceive a means of approach to therapy, a way of making symptoms disappear. And in this way Breuer did in fact restore his hysterical patient — that is, freed her from her symptoms; he found a technique for bringing to her consciousness the unconscious processes which contained the sense of the symptoms, and the symptoms disappeared.

This discovery of Breuer's was not the result of speculation but of a fortunate observation made possible by the patient's co-operation. Nor should you torment yourselves with attempts at understanding it by tracing it back to something already known; you should recognize in it a new fundamental fact, by whose help much else will become explicable. Allow me, therefore, to repeat the same thing to you in another way.

The construction of a symptom is a substitute for something else that did not happen. Some particular mental processes should normally have developed to a point at which consciousness received information of them. This, however, did not take place, and instead — out of the interrupted processes, which had been somehow disturbed and were obliged to remain unconscious — the symptom emerged. Thus something in the nature of an exchange has taken place; if this can be reversed the therapy of the neurotic symptoms will have achieved its task.

This discovery of Breuer's is still the foundation of psychoanalytic therapy. The thesis that symptoms disappear when we have made their unconscious predeterminants conscious has been confirmed by all subsequent research, although we meet with the strangest and most unexpected complications when we attempt to carry it through in practice. Our therapy works by transforming what is unconscious into what is conscious, and it works only in so far as it is in a position to effect that transformation.

And now I must quickly make a short digression, to avoid the risk of your imagining that this therapeutic work is accomplished too easily. From what I have so far said a neurosis would seem to be the result of a kind of ignorance — a not knowing about mental events that one ought to know of. This would be a close approximation to some well-known Socratic doctrines, according to which even vices are based on ignorance. Now it would as a rule be very easy for a doctor experienced in analysis to guess what mental impulses had remained unconscious in a particular patient. So it ought not to be very difficult, either, for him to restore the patient by communicating his knowledge to him and so remedying his ignorance. One part at least of the symptom's unconscious sense could be easily dealt with in this way, though it is true that the doctor cannot guess much about the other part — the connection between the symptoms and the patient's experiences —, since he himself does not know those experiences but must wait till the patient remembers them and tells them to him. But even for this a substitute can in some instances be found. One can make enquiries about these experiences from the patient's relatives and they will often be able to recognize which of them had a traumatic effect, and they can even sometimes report experiences of which the patient himself knows nothing because they occurred at a very early period of his life. Thus, by combining these two methods, we should have a prospect of relieving the patient of his pathogenic ignorance with little expense of time or trouble.

If only that was how things happened! We came upon discoveries in this connection for which we were at first unprepared. Knowledge is not always the same as knowledge: there are different sorts of knowledge, which are far from equivalent psychologically. 'Il y a fagots et fagots,' as Molière has said. The doctor's knowledge is not the same as the patient's and cannot produce the same effects. If the doctor transfers his knowledge to the patient as a piece of information, it has no result. No, it would be wrong to say that. It does not have the result of removing the symptoms, but it has another one — of setting the analysis in motion, of which the first signs are often expressions of denial. The patient knows after this what he did not know before — the sense of his symptom; yet he knows it just as little as he did. Thus we learn that there is more than one kind of ignorance. We shall need to have a somewhat deeper understanding of psychology to show us in what these differences consist. But our thesis that the symptoms vanish when their sense is known remains true in spite of this. All we have to add is that the knowledge must rest on an internal change in the patient such as can only be brought about by a piece of psychical work with a particular aim. We are faced here by problems which will presently be brought together into the *dynamics* of the construction of symptoms.

I must ask now, Gentlemen, whether what I am saying to you is not too obscure and complicated. Am I not confusing you by so often taking back what I have said or qualifying it — by starting up trains of thought and then dropping them? I should be sorry if that were so. But I have a strong dislike of simplifying things at the expense of truthfulness. I have no objection to your receiving the full impact of the many-sidedness and complexity of our subject; and I think, too, that it does no harm if I tell you more on every point than you can at the moment make use of. I am aware, after all, that every listener or reader puts what is presented to him into shape in his mind, shortens it and simplifies it, and selects from it what he would like to retain. Up to a certain point it is no doubt true that the more there is at one's disposal the more one is left with. Permit me to hope that, in spite of all the trimmings, you have clearly grasped the essential part of what I have told you — about the sense of symptoms, about the unconscious and about the relation between them. No doubt you have also understood that our further efforts will lead in two directions: first towards discovering how people fall ill and how they can come to adopt the neurotic attitude to life — which is a clinical problem; and secondly towards learning how the pathological symptoms develop from the determinants of the neurosis — which remains a problem of mental dynamics. There must moreover be a point somewhere at which the two problems converge.

Religion and Neurology

(1901–1902)

WILLIAM JAMES

There can be no doubt that as a matter of fact a religious life, exclusively pursued, does tend to make the person exceptional and eccentric. I speak not now of your ordinary religious believer, who follows the conventional observances of his country, whether it be Buddhist, Christian, or Mohammedan. His religion has been made for him by others, communicated to him by tradition, determined to fixed forms by imitation, and retained by habit. It would profit us little to study this second-hand religious life. We must make search rather for the original experiences which were the pattern-setters to all this mass of suggested feeling and

From William James, *The Varieties of Religious Experience* (New York: Longmans, Green, 1903), 6–12, 230–243. James originally made these remarks in the Gifford Lectures at the University of Edinburgh in 1901–1902.

imitated conduct. These experiences we can only find in individuals for whom religion exists not as a dull habit, but as an acute fever rather. But such individuals are 'geniuses' in the religious line; and like many other geniuses who have brought forth fruits effective enough for commemoration in the pages of biography, such religious geniuses have often shown symptoms of nervous instability. Even more perhaps than other kinds of genius, religious leaders have been subject to abnormal psychical visitations. Invariably they have been creatures of exalted emotional sensibility. Often they have led a discordant inner life, and had melancholy during a part of their career. They have known no measure, been liable to obsessions and fixed ideas; and frequently they have fallen into trances, heard voices, seen visions, and presented all sorts of peculiarities which are ordinarily classed as pathological. Often, moreover, these pathological features in their career have helped to give them their religious authority and influence.

If you ask for a concrete example, there can be no better one than is furnished by the person of George Fox. The Quaker religion which he founded is something which it is impossible to overpraise. In a day of shams, it was a religion of veracity rooted in spiritual inwardness, and a return to something more like the original gospel truth than men had ever known in England. So far as our Christian sects to-day are evolving into liberality, they are simply reverting in essence to the position which Fox and the early Quakers so long ago assumed. No one can pretend for a moment that in point of spiritual sagacity and capacity, Fox's mind was unsound. Every one who confronted him personally, from Oliver Cromwell down to county magistrates and jailers, seems to have acknowledged his superior power. Yet from the point of view of his nervous constitution, Fox was a psychopath or *détraqué* of the deepest dye. His Journal abounds in entries of this sort: —

> As I was walking with several friends, I lifted up my head, and saw three steeple-house spires, and they struck at my life. I asked them what place that was? They said, Lichfield. Immediately the word of the Lord came to me, that I must go thither. Being come to the house we were going to, I wished the friends to walk into the house, saying nothing to them of whither I was to go. As soon as they were gone I stept away, and went by my eye over hedge and ditch till I came within a mile of Lichfield; where, in a great field, shepherds were keeping their sheep. Then was I commanded by the Lord to pull off my shoes. I stood still, for it was winter: but the word of the Lord was like a fire in me. So I put off my shoes, and left them with the shepherds; and the poor shepherds trembled, and were astonished. Then I walked on about a mile, and as soon as I was got within the city, the word of the Lord came to me again, saying: Cry, "Wo to the bloody city of Lichfield!" So I went up and down the streets, crying with a loud voice, Wo to the bloody city of Lichfield! It being market day, I went into the market-place, and to and

> fro in the several parts of it, and made stands, crying as before, Wo to the bloody city of Lichfield! And no one laid hands on me. As I went thus crying through the streets, there seemed to me to be a channel of blood running down the streets, and the market-place appeared like a pool of blood. When I had declared what was upon me, and felt myself clear, I went out of the town in peace; and returning to the shepherds gave them some money, and took my shoes of them again. But the fire of the Lord was so on my feet, and all over me, that I did not matter to put on my shoes again, and was at a stand whether I should or no, till I felt freedom from the Lord so to do: then, after I had washed my feet, I put on my shoes again. After this a deep consideration came upon me, for what reason I should be sent to cry against that city, and call it The bloody city! For though the parliament had the minister one while, and the king another, and much blood had been shed in the town during the wars between them, yet there was no more than had befallen many other places. But afterwards I came to understand, that in the Emperor Diocletian's time a thousand Christians were martyr'd in Lichfield. So I was to go, without my shoes, through the channel of their blood, and into the pool of their blood in the market-place, that I might raise up the memorial of the blood of those martyrs, which had been shed above a thousand years before, and lay cold in their streets. So the sense of this blood was upon me, and I obeyed the word of the Lord.

Bent as we are on studying religion's existential conditions, we cannot possibly ignore these pathological aspects of the subject. We must describe and name them just as if they occurred in non-religious men. It is true that we instinctively recoil from seeing an object to which our emotions and affections are committed handled by the intellect as any other object is handled. The first thing the intellect does with an object is to class it along with something else. But any object that is infinitely important to us and awakens our devotion feels to us also as if it must be *sui generis* and unique. Probably a crab would be filled with a sense of personal outrage if it could hear us class it without ado or apology as a crustacean, and thus dispose of it. "I am no such thing," it would say; "I am MYSELF, MYSELF alone."

The next thing the intellect does is to lay bare the causes in which the thing originates. Spinoza says: "I will analyze the actions and appetites of men as if it were a question of lines, of planes, and of solids." And elsewhere he remarks that he will consider our passions and their properties with the same eye with which he looks on all other natural things, since the consequences of our affections flow from their nature with the same necessity as it results from the nature of a triangle that its three angles should be equal to two right angles. Similarly M. Taine, in the introduction to his history of English literature, has written: "Whether facts be moral or physical, it makes no matter. They always have their causes. There are causes for ambition, courage, veracity, just as there are for digestion, muscular movement, animal heat. Vice and virtue are products like vitriol and sugar." When we read such proclamations of the intellect bent on showing the existential conditions of absolutely everything, we feel — quite apart from our legitimate impatience at the somewhat ridiculous swagger of the program, in view of what the authors are actually able to perform — menaced and negated in the springs of our innermost life. Such cold-blooded assimilations threaten, we think, to undo our soul's vital secrets, as if the same breath which should succeed in explaining their origin would simultaneously explain away their significance, and make them appear of no more preciousness, either, than the useful groceries of which M. Taine speaks.

Perhaps the commonest expression of this assumption that spiritual value is undone if lowly origin be asserted is seen in those comments which unsentimental people so often pass on their more sentimental acquaintances. Alfred believes in immortality so strongly because his temperament is so emotional. Fanny's extraordinary conscientiousness is merely a matter of over-instigated nerves. William's melancholy about the universe is due to bad digestion — probably his liver is torpid. Eliza's delight in her church is a symptom of her hysterical constitution. Peter would be less troubled about his soul if he would take more exercise in the open air, etc. A more fully developed example of the same kind of reasoning is the fashion, quite common nowadays among certain writers, of criticising the religious emotions by showing a connection between them and the sexual life. Conversion is a crisis of puberty and adolescence. The macerations of saints, and the devotion of missionaries, are only instances of the parental instinct of self-sacrifice gone astray. For the hysterical nun, starving for natural life, Christ is but an imaginary substitute for a more earthly object of affection. And the like.[1] . . .

[1] As with many ideas that float in the air of one's time, this notion shrinks from dogmatic general statement and expresses itself only partially and by innuendo. It seems to me that few conceptions are less instructive than this re-interpretation of religion as perverted sexuality. It reminds one, so crudely is it often employed, of the famous Catholic taunt, that the Reformation may be best understood by remembering that its *fons et origo* was Luther's wish to marry a nun: — the effects are infinitely wider than the alleged causes, and for the most part opposite in nature. It is true that in the vast collection of religious phenomena, some are undisguisedly amatory — e. g., sex-deities and obscene rites in polytheism, and ecstatic feelings of union with the Saviour in a few Christian mystics. But then why not equally call religion an aberration of the digestive function, and prove one's point by the worship of Bacchus and Ceres, or by the ecstatic feelings of some other saints about the Eucharist? Religious language clothes itself in such poor symbols as our life affords, and the whole organism gives overtones of comment whenever the mind is strongly stirred to expression. Language drawn from eating and drinking is probably as common in religious literature as is language drawn from the sexual life. We 'hunger and thirst' after righteousness; we 'find the Lord a sweet savor'; we 'taste and see that he is good.'

. . . Is an instantaneous conversion a miracle in which God is present as he is present in no change of heart less strikingly abrupt? Are there two classes of human beings, even among the apparently regenerate, of which the one class really partakes of Christ's nature while the other merely seems to do so? Or, on the contrary, may the whole phenomenon of regeneration, even in these startling instantaneous examples, possibly be a strictly natural process, divine in its fruits, of course, but in one case more and in another less so, and neither more nor less divine in its mere causation and mechanism than any other process, high or low, of man's interior life?

Before proceeding to answer this question, I must ask you to listen to some more psychological remarks. At our last lecture, I explained the shifting of men's centres of personal energy within them and the lighting up of new crises of emotion. I explained the phenomena as partly due to explicitly conscious processes of thought and will, but as due largely also to the subconscious incubation and maturing of motives deposited by the experiences of life. When ripe, the results hatch out, or burst into flower. I have now to speak of the subconscious region, in which such processes of flowering may occur, in a somewhat less vague way. I only regret that my limits of time here force me to be so short.

The expression 'field of consciousness' has but recently come into vogue in the psychology books. Until quite lately the unit of mental life which figured most was the single 'idea,' supposed to be a definitely outlined thing. But at present psychologists are tending, first, to admit that the actual unit is more probably the total mental state, the entire wave

---

'Spiritual milk for American babes, drawn from the breasts of both testaments,' is a sub-title of the once famous New England Primer, and Christian devotional literature indeed quite floats in milk, thought of from the point of view, not of the mother, but of the greedy babe. . . .

In fact, one might almost as well interpret religion as a perversion of the respiratory function. The Bible is full of the language of respiratory oppression: "Hide not thine ear at my breathing; my groaning is not hid from thee; my heart panteth, my strength faileth me; my bones are hot with my roaring all the night long; as the hart panteth after the water-brooks, so my soul panteth after thee, O my God." *God's Breath in Man* is the title of the chief work of our best known American mystic (Thomas Lake Harris); and in certain non-Christian countries the foundation of all religious discipline consists in regulation of the inspiration and expiration.

These arguments are as good as much of the reasoning one hears in favor of the sexual theory. But the champions of the latter will then say that their chief argument has no analogue elsewhere. The two main phenomena of religion, namely, melancholy and conversion, they will say, are essentially phenomena of adolescence, and therefore synchronous with the development of sexual life. To which the retort again is easy. Even were the asserted synchrony unrestrictedly true as a fact (which it is not), it is not only the sexual life, but the entire higher mental life which awakens during adolescence. One might then as well set up the thesis that the interest in mechanics, physics, chemistry, logic, philosof consciousness or field of objects present to the thought at any time; and, second, to see that it is impossible to outline this wave, this field, with any definiteness.

As our mental fields succeed one another, each has its centre of interest, around which the objects of which we are less and less attentively conscious fade to a margin so faint that its limits are unassignable. Some fields are narrow fields and some are wide fields. Usually when we have a wide field we rejoice, for we then see masses of truth together, and often get glimpses of relations which we divine rather than see, for they shoot beyond the field into still remoter regions of objectivity, regions which we seem rather to be about to perceive than to perceive actually. At other times, of drowsiness, illness, or fatigue, our fields may narrow almost to a point, and we find ourselves correspondingly oppressed and contracted.

Different individuals present constitutional differences in this matter of width of field. Your great organizing geniuses are men with habitually vast fields of mental vision, in which a whole programme of future operations will appear dotted out at once, the rays shooting far ahead into definite directions of advance. In common people there is never this magnificent inclusive view of a topic. They stumble along, feeling their way, as it were, from point to point, and often stop entirely. In certain diseased conditions consciousness is a mere spark, without memory of the past or thought of the future, and with the present narrowed down to some one simple emotion or sensation of the body.

The important fact which this 'field' formula commemorates is the indetermination of the margin. Inattentively realized as is the matter

---

ophy, and sociology, which springs up during adolescent years along with that in poetry and religion, is also a perversion of the sexual instinct: — but that would be too absurd. Moreover, if the argument from synchrony is to decide, what is to be done with the fact that the religious age *par excellence* would seem to be old age, when the uproar of the sexual life is past?

The plain truth is that to interpret religion one must in the end look at the immediate content of the religious consciousness. The moment one does this, one sees how wholly disconnected it is in the main from the content of the sexual consciousness. Everything about the two things differs, objects, moods, faculties concerned, and acts impelled to. Any *general* assimilation is simply impossible: what we find most often is complete hostility and contrast. If now the defenders of the sex-theory say that this makes no difference to their thesis; that without the chemical contributions which the sex-organs make to the blood, the brain would not be nourished so as to carry on religious activities, this final proposition may be true or not true; but at any rate it has become profoundly uninstructive: we can deduce no consequences from it which help us to interpret religion's meaning or value. In this sense the religious life depends just as much upon the spleen, the pancreas, and the kidneys as on the sexual apparatus, and the whole theory has lost its point in evaporating into a vague general assertion of the dependence, *somehow,* of the mind upon the body.

which the margin contains, it is nevertheless there, and helps both to guide our behavior and to determine the next movement of our attention. It lies around us like a 'magnetic field,' inside of which our centre of energy turns like a compass-needle, as the present phase of consciousness alters into its successor. Our whole past store of memories floats beyond this margin, ready at a touch to come in; and the entire mass of residual powers, impulses, and knowledges that constitute our empirical self stretches continuously beyond it. So vaguely drawn are the outlines between what is actual and what is only potential at any moment of our conscious life, that it is always hard to say of certain mental elements whether we are conscious of them or not.

The ordinary psychology, admitting fully the difficulty of tracing the marginal outline, has nevertheless taken for granted, first, that all the consciousness the person now has, be the same focal or marginal, inattentive or attentive, is there in the 'field' of the moment, all dim and impossible to assign as the latter's outline may be; and, second, that what is absolutely extra-marginal is absolutely non-existent, and cannot be a fact of consciousness at all.

And having reached this point, I must now ask you to recall what I said in my last lecture about the subconscious life. I said, as you may recollect, that those who first laid stress upon these phenomena could not know the facts as we now know them. My first duty now is to tell you what I meant by such a statement.

I cannot but think that the most important step forward that has occurred in psychology since I have been a student of that science is the discovery, first made in 1886, that, in certain subjects at least, there is not only the consciousness of the ordinary field, with its usual centre and margin, but an addition thereto in the shape of a set of memories, thoughts, and feelings which are extra-marginal and outside of the primary consciousness altogether, but yet must be classed as conscious facts of some sort, able to reveal their presence by unmistakable signs. I call this the most important step forward because, unlike the other advances which psychology has made, this discovery has revealed to us an entirely unsuspected peculiarity in the constitution of human nature. No other step forward which psychology has made can proffer any such claim as this.

In particular this discovery of a consciousness existing beyond the field, or subliminally as Mr. Myers terms it, casts light on many phenomena of religious biography. That is why I have to avert to it now, although it is naturally impossible for me in this place to give you any account of the evidence on which the admission of such a consciousness is based. You will find it set forth in many recent books, Binet's Alterations of Personality being perhaps as good a one as any to recommend.

The human material on which the demonstration has been made has so far been rather limited and, in part at least, eccentric, consisting of unusually suggestible hypnotic subects, and of hysteric patients. Yet the elementary mechanisms of our life are presumably so uniform that what is shown to be true in a marked degree of some persons is probably true in some degree of all, and may in a few be true in an extraordinarily high degree.

The most important consequence of having a strongly developed ultra-marginal life of this sort is that one's ordinary fields of consciousness are liable to incursions from it of which the subject does not guess the source, and which, therefore, take for him the form of unaccountable impulses to act, or inhibitions of action, of obsessive ideas, or even of hallucinations of sight or hearing. The impulses may take the direction of automatic speech or writing, the meaning of which the subject himself may not understand even while he utters it; and generalizing this phenomenon, Mr. Myers has given the name of *automatism*, sensory or motor, emotional or intellectual, to this whole sphere of effects, due to 'uprushes' into the ordinary consciousness of energies originating in the subliminal parts of the mind.

The simplest instance of an automatism is the phenomenon of post-hypnotic suggestion, so-called. You give to a hypnotized subject, adequately susceptible, an order to perform some designated act — usual or eccentric, it makes no difference — after he wakes from his hypnotic sleep. Punctually, when the signal comes or the time elapses upon which you have told him that the act must ensue, he performs it; — but in so doing he has no recollection of your suggestion, and he always trumps up an improvised pretext for his behavior if the act be of an eccentric kind. It may even be suggested to a subject to have a vision or to hear a voice at a certain interval after waking, and when the time comes the vision is seen or the voice heard, and no inkling on the subject's part of its source. In the wonderful explorations by Binet, Janet, Breuer, Freud, Mason, Prince, and others, of the subliminal consciousness of patients with hysteria, we have revealed to us whole systems of underground life, in the shape of memories of a painful sort which lead a parasitic existence, buried outside of the primary fields of consciousness, and making irruptions thereinto with hallucinations, pains, convulsions, paralyses of feeling and of motion, and the whole procession of symptoms of hysteric disease of body and of mind. Alter or abolish by suggestion these subconscious memories, and the patient immediately gets well. His symptoms were automatisms, in Mr. Myers's sense of the word. These clinical records sound like fairy-tales when one first reads them, yet it is impossible to doubt their accuracy; and, the path having been once opened by these first observers, similar observations have been made elsewhere. They throw, as I said, a wholly new light upon our natural constitution.

And it seems to me that they make a farther step inevitable. Interpreting the unknown after the analogy of the known, it seems to me that hereafter, wherever we meet with a phenomenon of automatism, be it motor impulses, or obsessive idea, or unaccountable caprice, or delusion, or hallucination, we are bound first of all to make search whether it be not an explosion, into the fields of ordinary consciousness, of ideas elaborated outside of those fields in subliminal regions of the mind. We should look, therefore, for its source in the Subject's subconscious life. In the hypnotic cases, we ourselves create the source by our suggestion, so we know it directly. In the hysteric cases, the lost memories which are the source have to be extracted from the patient's Subliminal by a number of ingenious methods, for an account of which you must consult the books. In other pathological cases, insane delusions, for example, or psychopathic obsessions, the source is yet to seek, but by analogy it also should be a subliminal regions which improvements in our methods may yet conceivably put on tap. There lies the mechanism logically to be assumed, — but the assumption involves a vast program of work to be done in the way of vertification, in which the religious experiences of man must play their part.[2]

And thus I return to our own specific subject of instantaneous conversions. You remember the cases of Alline, Bradley, Brainerd, and the graduate of Oxford converted at three in the afternoon. Similar occurrences abound, some with and some without luminous visions, all with a

[2] The reader will here please notice that in my exclusive reliance . . . on the subconscious 'incubation' of motives deposited by a growing experience, I followed the method of employing accepted principles of explanation as far as one can. The subliminal region, whatever else it may be, is at any rate a place now admitted by psychologists to exist for the accumulation of vestiges of sensible experience (whether inattentively or attentively registered), and for their elaboration according to ordinary psychological or logical laws into results that end by attaining such a 'tension' that they may at times enter consciousness with something like a burst. It thus is 'scientific' to interpret all otherwise unaccountable invasive alterations of consciousness as results of the tension of subliminal memories reaching the bursting-point. But candor obliges me to confess that there are occasional bursts into consciousness of results of which it is not easy to demonstrate any prolonged subconscious incubation. . . . The case of Mr. Bradley, that of M. Ratisbonne, possibly that of Colonel Gardiner, possibly that of Saint Paul, might not be so easily explained in this simple way. The result, then, would have to be ascribed either to a merely physiological nerve storm, a 'discharging lesion' like that of epilepsy; or, in case it were useful and rational, as in the two latter cases named, to some more mystical or theological hypothesis. I make this remark in order that the reader may realize that the subject is really complex. But I shall keep myself as far as possible at present to the more 'scientific' view; and only as the plot thickens in subsequent lectures shall I consider the question of its absolute sufficiency as an explanation of all the facts. That subconscious incubation explains a great number of them, there can be no doubt.

sense of astonished happiness, and of being wrought on by a higher control. If, abstracting altogether from the question of their value for the future spiritual life of the individual, we take them on their psychological side exclusively, so many peculiarities in them remind us of what we find outside of conversion that we are tempted to class them along with other automatisms, and to suspect that what makes the difference between a sudden and a gradual convert is not necessarily the presence of divine miracle in the case of one and of something less divine in that of the other, but rather a simple psychological peculiarity, the fact, namely, that in the recipient of the more instantaneous grace we have one of those Subjects who are in possession of a large region in which mental work can go on subliminally, and from which invasive experiences, abruptly upsetting the equilibrium of the primary consciousness, may come.

I do not see why Methodists need object to such a view. Pray go back and recollect one of the conclusions to which I sought to lead you in my first lecture. You may remember how I there argued against the notion that the worth of a thing can be decided by its origin. Our spiritual judgment, I said, our opinion of the significance and value of a human event or condition, must be decided on empirical grounds exclusively. If the *fruits for life* of the state of conversion are good, we ought to idealize and venerate it, even though it be a piece of natural psychology; if not, we ought to make short work with it, no matter what supernatural being may have infused it.

Well, how is it with these fruits? If we except the class of preëminent saints of whom the names illumine history, and consider only the usual run of 'saints,' the shopkeeping church-members and ordinary youthful or middle-aged recipients of instantaneous conversion, whether at revivals or in the spontaneous course of methodistic growth, you will probably agree that no splendor worthy of a wholly supernatural creature fulgurates from them, or sets them apart from the mortals who have never experienced that favor. Were it true that a suddenly converted man as such is, as Edwards says, of an entirely different kind from a natural man, partaking as he does directly of Christ's substance, there surely ought to be some exquisite class-mark, some distinctive radiance attaching even to the lowliest specimen of this genus, to which no one of us could remain insensible, and which, so far as it went, would prove him more excellent than ever the most highly gifted among mere natural men. But notoriously there is no such radiance. Converted men as a class are indistinguishable from natural men; some natural men even excel some converted men in their fruits; and no one ignorant of doctrinal theology could guess by mere every-day inspection of the 'accidents' of the two groups of persons before him, that their substance differed as much as divine differs from human substance.

The believers in the non-natural character of sudden conversion have had practically to admit that there is no unmistakable class-mark distinctive of all true converts. The super-normal incidents, such as voices and visions and overpowering impressions of the meaning of suddenly presented scripture texts, the melting emotions and tumultuous affections connected with the crisis of change, may all come by way of nature, or worse still, be counterfeited by Satan. The real witness of the spirit to the second birth is to be found only in the disposition of the genuine child of God, the permanently patient heart, the love of self eradicated. And this, it has to be admitted, is also found in those who pass no crisis, and may even be found outside of Christianity altogether.

Throughout Jonathan Edwards's admirably rich and delicate description of the supernaturally infused condition, in his Treatise on Religious Affections, there is not one decisive trait, not one mark, that unmistakably parts it off from what may possibly be only an exceptionally high degree of natural goodness. In fact, one could hardly read a clearer argument than this book unwittingly offers in favor of the thesis that no chasm exists between the orders of human excellence, but that here as elsewhere, nature shows continuous differences, and generation and regeneration are matters of degree.

All which denial of two objective classes of human beings separated by a chasm must not leave us blind to the extraordinary momentousness of the fact of his conversion to the individual himself who gets converted. There are higher and lower limits of possibility set to each personal life. If a flood but goes above one's head, its absolute elevation becomes a matter of small importance; and when we touch our own upper limit and live in our own highest centre of energy, we may call ourselves saved, no matter how much higher some one else's centre may be. A small man's salvation will always be a great salvation and the greatest of all facts *for him,* and we should remember this when the fruits of our ordinary evangelicism look discouraging. Who knows how much less ideal still the lives of these spiritual grubs and earthworms, these Crumps and Stigginses, might have been, if such poor grace as they have received had never touched them at all?

If we roughly arrange human beings in classes, each class standing for a grade of spiritual excellence, I believe we shall find natural men and converts both sudden and gradual in all the classes. The forms which regenerative change effects have, then, no general spiritual significance, but only a psychological significance. We have seen how Starbuck's laborious statistical studies tend to assimilate conversion to ordinary spiritual growth. Another American psychologist, Professor A. Coe, has analyzed the cases of seventy-seven converts or ex-candidates for conversion, known to him, and the results strikingly confirm the view that sudden conversion is connected with the possession of an active subliminal self. Examining his subjects with reference to their hypnotic sensibility and to such automatisms as hypnagogic hallucinations, odd impulses, religious dreams about the time of their conversion, etc., he found these relatively much more frequent in the group of converts whose transformation had been 'striking,' 'striking' transformation being defined as "a change which, though not necessarily instantaneous, seems to the subject of it to be distinctly different from a process of growth, however rapid." Candidates for conversion at revivals are, as you know, often disappointed: they experience nothing striking. Professor Coe had a number of persons of this class among his seventy-seven subjects, and they almost all, when tested by hypnotism, proved to belong to a subclass which he calls 'spontaneous,' that is, fertile in self-suggestions, as distinguished from a 'passive' subclass, to which most of the subjects of striking transformation belonged. His inference is that self-suggestion of impossibility had prevented the influence upon these persons of an environment which, on the more 'passive' subjects, had easily brought forth the effects they looked for. Sharp distinctions are difficult in these regions, and Professor Coe's numbers are small. But his methods were careful, and the results tally with what one might expect; and they seem, on the whole, to justify his practical conclusion, which is that if you should expose to a converting influence a subject in whom three factors unite: first, pronounced emotional sensibility; second, tendency to automatisms; and third, suggestibility of the passive type; you might then safely predict the result: there would be a sudden conversion, a transformation of the striking kind.

Does this temperamental origin diminish the significance of the sudden conversion when it has occurred? Not in the least, as Professor Coe well says; for "the ultimate test of religious values is nothing psychological, nothing definable in terms of *how it happens*, but something ethical, definable only in terms of *what is attained*."

As we proceed farther in our inquiry we shall see that what is attained is often an altogether new level of spiritual vitality, a relatively heroic level, in which impossible things have become possible, and new energies and endurances are shown. The personality is changed, the man *is* born anew, whether or not his psychological idiosyncrasies are what give the particular shape to his metamorphosis. 'Sanctification' is the technical name of this result; and erelong examples of it shall be brought before you. In this lecture I have still only to add a few remarks on the assurance and peace which fill the hour of change itself.

One word more, though, before proceeding to that point, lest the final purpose of my explanation of suddenness by subliminal activity be misunderstood. I do indeed believe that if the Subject have no liability to such subconscious activity, or if his conscious fields have a hard rind of a margin that resists incursions from beyond it, his conversion must be gradual if it occur, and must resemble any simple growth into new habits. His possession of a developed subliminal self, and of a leaky or pervious margin, is thus a *conditio sine qua non* of the Subject's becoming converted in the instantaneous way. But if you, being orthodox Christians, ask me as a psychologist whether the reference of a phenomenon to a subliminal self does not exclude the notion of the direct presence of the Deity altogether, I have to say frankly that as a psychologist I do not see why it necessarily should. The lower manifestations of the Subliminal, indeed, fall within the resources of the personal subject: his ordinary sense-material, inattentively taken in and subconsciously remembered and combined, will account for all his usual automatisms. But just as our primary wide-awake consciousness throws open our senses to the touch of things material, so it is logically conceivable that *if there be* higher spiritual agencies that can directly touch us, the psychological condition of their doing so *might be* our possession of a subconscious region which alone should yield access to them. The hubbub of the waking life might close a door which in the dreamy Subliminal might remain ajar or open.

Thus that perception of external control which is so essential a feature in conversion might, in some cases at any rate, be interpreted as the orthodox interpret it: forces transcending the finite individual might impress him, on condition of his being what we may call a subliminal human specimen. But in any case the *value* of these forces would have to be determined by their effects, and the mere fact of their transcendency would of itself establish no presumption that they were more divine than diabolical.

IX

THE REVOLT AGAINST POSITIVISM AND FORMALISM: NEW APPROACHES IN THE SOCIAL SCIENCES

The anti-positivist, anti-formalist movements in European and American social science perhaps had no better representatives than the German sociologist Max Weber (1864–1920) and the American economist Thorstein Veblen (1857–1929). Both men matched their interests in an extraordinarily broad range of subject matter with a correspondingly expansive methodology. Both were also, not accidentally, active political critics. The selections in Section IX illustrate some of the characteristics of their methodology and some of the implications it carried for the content of social theory.

Weber was dissatisfied with the tidy categories of Marxian social analysis, as was Veblen with the static models of classical economics. Both also opposed any monistic theory of social action. Accordingly, abandoning all forms of determinism and substituting the new irrational psychology for the utilitarian psychological theories of the nineteenth century, they set out to explain social and economic behavior with reference to a wide variety of factors. Weber argued that psychological considerations of status and prestige conditioned men's social behavior in ways that Marx had ignored. Similarly, Veblen insisted that the "economic man" of classical economic theory was a useless abstraction. Economic behavior, he held, derived neither from rational calculations of profit and loss nor from reflex responses to pleasure and pain, but owed much of its character to the influence of vestigial institutions, habits, and customs that survived beyond the time of their original utility. Pecuniary emulation, as Veblen described it, was such a phenomenon.

The work of these two intellectuals pointed to an integrated so-

cial science appropriate to the study as well as to the direction of complex industrial societies. The tendencies they represented can also be seen in the writings of such figures as Vilfredo Pareto *and* Emile Durkheim *in Europe and* Charles Beard, George Herbert Mead, *and* Charles Horton Cooley *in America, all of whom were committed to a multifold, empirical social analysis capable of providing guidelines for public policy.*

Class, Status, Party

(1922)

MAX WEBER

1: Economically Determined Power and the Social Order

Law exists when there is a probability that an order will be upheld by a specific staff of men who will use physical or psychical compulsion with the intention of obtaining conformity with the order, or of inflicting sanctions for infringement of it. The structure of every legal order directly influences the distribution of power, economic or otherwise, within its respective community. This is true of all legal orders and not only that of the state. In general, we understand by 'power' the chance of a man or of a number of men to realize their own will in a communal action even against the resistance of others who are participating in the action.

'Economically conditioned' power is not, of course, identical with 'power' as such. On the contrary, the emergence of economic power may be the consequence of power existing on other grounds. Man does not strive for power only in order to enrich himself economically. Power, including economic power, may be valued 'for its own sake.' Very frequently the striving for power is also conditioned by the social 'honor' it entails. Not all power, however, entails social honor: The typical American Boss, as well as the typical big speculator, deliberately relinquishes social honor. Quite generally, 'mere economic' power, and especially 'naked' money power, is by no means a recognized basis of social honor. Nor is power the only basis of social honor. Indeed, social honor,

From H. H. Gerth and C. Wright Mills, eds. and trs., *From Max Weber: Essays in Sociology* (New York: Oxford University Press, 1946), 180–195. Reprinted by permission.

or prestige, may even be the basis of political or economic power, and very frequently has been. Power, as well as honor, may be guaranteed by the legal order, but, at least normally, it is not their primary source. The legal order is rather an additional factor that enhances the chance to hold power or honor; but it cannot always secure them.

The way in which social honor is distributed in a community between typical groups participating in this distribution we may call the 'social order.' The social order and the economic order are, of course, similarly related to the 'legal order.' However, the social and the economic order are not identical. The economic order is for us merely the way in which economic goods and services are distributed and used. The social order is of course conditioned by the economic order to a high degree, and in its turn reacts upon it.

Now: 'classes,' 'status groups,' and 'parties' are phenomena of the distribution of power within a community.

2: Determination of Class-Situation by Market-Situation

In our terminology, 'classes' are not communities; they merely represent possible, and frequent, bases for communal action. We may speak of a 'class' when (1) a number of people have in common a specific causal component of their life chances, in so far as (2) this component is represented exclusively by economic interests in the possession of goods and opportunities for income, and (3) is represented under the conditions of the commodity or labor markets. [These points refer to 'class situation,' which we may express more briefly as the typical chance for a supply of goods, external living conditions, and personal life experiences, in so far as this chance is determined by the amount and kind of power, or lack of such, to dispose of goods or skills for the sake of income in a given economic order. The term 'class' refers to any group of people that is found in the same class situation.]

It is the most elemental economic fact that the way in which the disposition over material property is distributed among a plurality of people, meeting competitively in the market for the purpose of exchange, in itself creates specific life chances. According to the law of marginal utility this mode of distribution excludes the non-owners from competing for highly valued goods; it favors the owners and, in fact, gives to them a monopoly to acquire such goods. Other things being equal, this mode of distribution monopolizes the opportunities for profitable deals for all those who, provided with goods, do not necessarily have to exchange them. It increases, at least generally, their power in price wars with those who, being propertyless, have nothing to offer but their services in native form or goods in a form constituted through their own labor, and who above all are compelled to get rid of these products in order barely to subsist. This mode of distribution gives to the propertied a monopoly on the possibility of transferring property from the sphere of use as a 'fortune,' to the sphere of 'capital goods'; that is, it gives them the entrepreneurial function and all chances to share directly or indirectly in returns on capital. All this holds true within the area in which pure market conditions prevail. 'Property' and 'lack of property' are, therefore, the basic categories of all class situations. It does not matter whether these two categories become effective in price wars or in competitive struggles.

Within these categories, however, class situations are further differentiated: on the one hand, according to the kind of property that is usable for returns; and, on the other hand, according to the kind of services that can be offered in the market. Ownership of domestic buildings; productive establishments; warehouses; stores; agriculturally usable land, large and small holdings — quantitative differences with possibly qualitative consequences —; ownership of mines; cattle; men (slaves); disposition over mobile instruments of production, or capital goods of all sorts, especially money or objects that can be exchanged for money easily and at any time; disposition over products of one's own labor or of others' labor differing according to their various distances from consumability; disposition over transferable monopolies of any kind — all these distinctions differentiate the class situations of the propertied just as does the 'meaning' which they can and do give to the utilization of property, especially to property which has money equivalence. Accordingly, the propertied, for instance, may belong to the class of rentiers or to the class of entrepreneurs.

Those who have no property but who offer services are differentiated just as much according to their kinds of services as according to the way in which they make use of these services, in a continuous or discontinuous relation to a recipient. But always this is the generic connotation of the concept of class: that the kind of chance in the *market* is the decisive moment which presents a common condition for the individual's fate. 'Class situation' is, in this sense, ultimately 'market situation.' The effect of naked possession *per se*, which among cattle breeders gives the non-owning slave or serf into the power of the cattle owner, is only a forerunner of real 'class' formation. However, in the cattle loan and in the naked severity of the law of debts in such communities, for the first time mere 'possession' as such emerges as decisive for the fate of the individual. This is very much in contrast to the agricultural communities based on labor. The creditor-debtor relation becomes the basis of 'class situations' only in those cities where a 'credit market,' however primitive, with rates of interest increasing according to the extent of dearth and a factual monopolization of credits, is developed by a plutocracy. Therewith 'class struggles' begin.

Those men whose fate is not determined by the chance of using goods or services for themselves on the market, e.g. slaves, are not, however, a 'class' in the technical sense of the term. They are, rather, a 'status group.'

3: Communal Action Flowing from Class Interest

According to our terminology, the factor that creates 'class' is unambiguously economic interest, and indeed, only those interests involved in the existence of the 'market.' Nevertheless, the concept of 'class-interest' is an ambiguous one: even as an empirical concept it is ambiguous as soon as one understands by it something other than the factual direction of interests following with a certain probability from the class situation for a certain 'average' of those people subjected to the class situation. The class situation and other circumstances remaining the same, the direction in which the individual worker, for instance, is likely to pursue his interests may vary widely, according to whether he is constitutionally qualified for the task at hand to a high, to an average, or to a low degree. In the same way, the direction of interests may vary according to whether or not a *communal* action of a larger or smaller portion of those commonly affected by the 'class situation,' or even an association among them, e.g. a 'trade union,' has grown out of the class situation from which the individual may or may not expect promising results. [Communal action refers to that action which is oriented to the feeling of the actors that they belong together. Societal action, on the other hand, is oriented to a rationally motivated adjustment of interests.] The rise of societal or even of communal action from a common class situation is by no means a universal phenomenon.

The class situation may be restricted in its effects to the generation of essentially *similar* reactions, that is to say, within our terminology, of 'mass actions.' However, it may not have even this result. Furthermore, often merely an amorphous communal action emerges. For example, the 'murmuring' of the workers known in ancient oriental ethics: the moral disapproval of the work-master's conduct, which in its practical significance was probably equivalent to an increasingly typical phenomenon of precisely the latest industrial development, namely, the 'slow down' (the deliberate limiting of work effort) of laborers by virtue of tacit agreement. The degree in which 'communal action' and possibly 'societal action,' emerges from the 'mass actions' of the members of a class is linked to general cultural conditions, especially to those of an intellectual sort. It is also linked to the extent of the contrasts that have already evolved, and is especially linked to the *transparency* of the connections between the causes and the consequences of the 'class situation.' For however different life chances may be, this fact in itself, according to all experience, by no means gives birth to 'class action' (communal action by the members of a class). The fact of being conditioned and the results of the class situation must be distinctly recognizable. For only then the contrast of life chances can be felt not as an absolutely given fact to be accepted, but as a resultant from either (1) the given distribution of property, or (2) the structure of the concrete economic order. It is only then that people may react against the class structure not only through acts of an intermittent and irrational protest, but in the form of rational association. There have been 'class situations' of the first category (1), of a specifically naked and transparent sort, in the urban centers of Antiquity and during the Middle Ages; especially then, when great fortunes were accumulated by factually monopolized trading in industrial products of these localities or in foodstuffs. Furthermore, under certain circumstances, in the rural economy of the most diverse periods, when agriculture was increasingly exploited in a profit-making manner. The most important historical example of the second category (2) is the class situation of the modern 'proletariat.'

4: Types of 'Class Struggle'

Thus every class may be the carrier of any one of the possibly innumerable forms of 'class action,' but this is not necessarily so. In any case, a class does not in itself constitute a community. To treat 'class' conceptually as having the same value as 'community' leads to distortion. That men in the same class situation regularly react in mass actions to such tangible situations as economic ones in the direction of those interests that are most adequate to their average number is an important and after all simple fact for the understanding of historical events. Above all, this fact must not lead to that kind of pseudo-scientific operation with the concepts of 'class' and 'class interests' so frequently found these days, and which has found its most classic expression in the statement of a talented author, that the individual may be in error concerning his interests but that the 'class' is 'infallible' about its interests. Yet, if classes as such are not communities, nevertheless class situations emerge only on the basis of communalization. The communal action that brings forth class situations, however, is not basically action between members of the identical class; it is an action between members of different classes. Communal actions that directly determine the class situation of the worker and the entrepreneur are: the labor market, the commodities market, and the capitalistic enterprise. But, in its turn, the existence of a capitalistic enterprise presupposes that a very specific communal action exists and that it is specifically structured to protect the possession of goods *per se*, and especially the power of individuals to dispose, in principle freely, over the means of production. The existence of a capitalistic enterprise is preconditioned by a specific kind of 'legal order.' Each kind of class situation, and above all when it rests upon the power of property *per se*, will become most clearly efficacious when all other determinants of reciprocal relations are, as far as possible, eliminated in their significance. It is in this way that the utilization of the power of property in the market obtains its most sovereign importance.

Now 'status groups' hinder the strict carrying through of the sheer market principle. In the present context they are of interest to us only from this one point of view. Before we briefly consider them, note that not much of a general nature can be said about the more specific kinds of antagonism between 'classes' (in our meaning of the term). The great shift, which has been going on continuously in the past, and up to our times, may be summarized, although at the cost of some precision: the struggle in which class situations are effective has progressively shifted from consumption credit toward, first, competitive struggles in the commodity market and, then, toward price wars on the labor market. The 'class struggles' of antiquity — to the extent that they were genuine class struggles and not struggles between status groups — were initially carried on by indebted peasants, and perhaps also by artisans threatened by debt bondage and struggling against urban creditors. For debt bondage is the normal result of the differentiation of wealth in commercial cities, especially in seaport cities. A similar situation has existed among cattle breeders. Debt relationships as such produced class action up to the time of Cataline. Along with this, and with an increase in provision of grain for the city by transporting it from the outside, the struggle over the means of sustenance emerged. It centered in the first place around the provision of bread and the determination of the price of bread. It lasted throughout antiquity and the entire Middle Ages. The propertyless as such flocked together against those who actually and supposedly were interested in the dearth of bread. This fight spread until it involved all those commodities essential to the way of life and to handicraft production. There were only incipient discussions of wage disputes in antiquity and in the Middle Ages. But they have been slowly increasing up into modern times. In the earlier periods they were completely secondary to slave rebellions as well as to fights in the commodity market.

The propertyless of antiquity and of the Middle Ages protested against monopolies, pre-emption, forestalling, and the withholding of goods from the market in order to raise prices. Today the central issue is the determination of the price of labor.

This transition is represented by the fight for access to the market and for the determination of the price of products. Such fights went on between merchants and workers in the putting-out system of domestic handicraft during the transition to modern times. Since it is quite a general phenomenon we must mention here that the class antagonisms that are conditioned through the market situation are usually most bitter between those who actually and directly participate as opponents in price wars. It is not the rentier, the share-holder, and the banker who suffer the ill will of the worker, but almost exclusively the manufacturer and the business executives who are the direct opponents of workers in price wars. This is so in spite of the fact that it is precisely the cash boxes of the rentier, the share-holder, and the banker into which the more or less 'unearned' gains flow, rather than into the pockets of the manufacturers or of the business executives. This simple state of affairs has very frequently been decisive for the role the class situation has played in the formation of political parties. For example, it has made possible the varieties of patriarchal socialism and the frequent attempts — formerly, at least — of threatened status groups to form alliances with the proletariat against the 'bourgeoisie.'

5: Status Honor

In contrast to classes, *status groups* are normally communities. They are, however, often of an amorphous kind. In contrast to the purely economically determined 'class situation' we wish to designate as 'status situation' every typical component of the life fate of men that is determined by a specific, positive or negative, social estimation of *honor*. This honor may be connected with any quality shared by a plurality, and, of course, it can be knit to a class situation: class distinctions are linked in the most varied ways with status distinctions. Property as such is not always recognized as a status qualification, but in the long run it is, and with extraordinary regularity. In the subsistence economy of the organized neighborhood, very often the richest man is simply the chieftain. However, this often means only an honorific preference. For example, in the so-called pure modern 'democracy,' that is, one devoid of any expressly ordered status privileges for individuals, it may be that only the families coming under approximately the same tax class dance with one another. This example is reported of certain smaller Swiss cities. But status honor need not necessarily be linked with a 'class situation.' On the contrary, it normally stands in sharp opposition to the pretensions of sheer property.

Both propertied and propertyless people can belong to the same status group, and frequently they do with very tangible consequences. This 'equality' of social esteem may, however, in the long run become quite precarious. The 'equality' of status among the American 'gentlemen,' for instance, is expressed by the fact that outside the subordination determined by the different functions of 'business,' it would be considered strictly repugnant — wherever the old tradition still prevails — if even the richest 'chief,' while playing billiards or cards in his club in the evening, would not treat his 'clerk' as in every sense fully his equal in birthright. It would be repugnant if the American 'chief' would bestow upon his 'clerk' the condescending 'benevolence' marking a distinction of 'position,' which the German chief can never dissever from his attitude. This is one of the most important reasons why in America the German 'clubby-ness' has never been able to attain the attraction that the American clubs have.

6: Guarantees of Status Stratification

In content, status honor is normally expressed by the fact that above all else a specific *style of life* can be expected from all those who wish to belong to the circle. Linked with this expectation are restrictions on 'social' intercourse (that is, intercourse which is not subservient to economic or any other of business's 'functional' purposes). These restrictions may confine normal marriages to within the status circle and may lead to complete endogamous closure. As soon as there is not a mere individual and socially irrelevant imitation of another style of life, but an agreed-upon communal action of this closing character, the 'status' development is under way.

In its characteristic form, stratification by 'status groups' on the basis of conventional styles of life evolves at the present time in the United States out of the traditional democracy. For example, only the resident of a certain street ('the street') is considered as belonging to 'society,' is qualified for social intercourse, and is visited and invited. Above all, this differentiation evolves in such a way as to make for strict submission to the fashion that is dominant at a given time in society. This submission to fashion also exists among men in America to a degree unknown in Germany. Such submission is considered to be an indication of the fact that a given man *pretends* to qualify as a gentleman. This submission decides, at least *prima facie*, that he will be treated as such. And this recognition becomes just as important for his employment chances in 'swank' establishments, and above all, for social intercourse and marriage with 'esteemed' families, as the qualification for dueling among Germans in the Kaiser's day. As for the rest: certain families resident for a long time, and, of course, correspondingly wealthy, e.g. 'F. F. V., i.e. First Families of Virginia,' or the actual or alleged descendants of the 'Indian Princess' Pocahontas, of the Pilgrim fathers, or of the Knickerbockers, the members of almost inaccessible sects and all sorts of circles setting themselves apart by means of any other characteristics and badges . . . all these elements usurp 'status' honor. The development of status is essentially a question of stratification resting upon usurpation. Such usurpation is the normal origin of almost all status honor. But the road from this purely conventional situation to legal privilege, positive or negative, is easily traveled as soon as a certain stratification of the social order has in fact been 'lived in' and has achieved stability by virtue of a stable distribution of economic power.

7: 'Ethnic' Segregation and 'Caste'

Where the consequences have been realized to their full extent, the status group evolves into a closed 'caste.' Status distinctions are then guaranteed not merely by conventions and laws, but also by *rituals*. This occurs in such a way that every physical contact with a member of any caste that is considered to be 'lower' by the members of a 'higher' caste is considered as making for a ritualistic impurity and to be a stigma which must be expiated by a religious act. Individual castes develop quite distinct cults and gods.

In general, however, the status structure reaches such extreme consequences only where there are underlying differences which are held to be 'ethnic.' The 'caste' is, indeed, the normal form in which ethnic communities usually live side by side in a 'societalized' manner. These ethnic communities believe in blood relationship and exclude exogamous marriage and social intercourse. Such a caste situation is part of the phenomenon of 'pariah' peoples and is found all over the world. These people form communities, acquire specific occupational traditions of handicrafts or of other arts, and cultivate a belief in their ethnic community. They live in a 'diaspora' strictly segregated from all personal intercourse, except that of an unavoidable sort, and their situation is legally precarious. Yet, by virtue of their economic indispensability, they are tolerated, indeed, frequently privileged, and they live in interspersed political communities. The Jews are the most impressive historical example.

A 'status' segregation grown into a 'caste' differs in its structure from a mere 'ethnic' segregation: the caste structure transforms the horizontal and unconnected coexistences of ethnically segregated groups into a vertical social system of super- and subordination. Correctly formulated: a comprehensive societalization integrates the ethnically divided communities into specific political and communal action. In their consequences they differ precisely in this way: ethnic coexistences condition a mutual repulsion and disdain but allow each ethnic community to consider its own honor as the highest one; the caste structure brings about a social subordination and an acknowledgment of 'more honor' in favor of the privileged caste and status groups. This is due to the fact that in the caste structure ethnic distinctions as such have become 'functional' distinctions within the political societalization (warriors, priests, artisans that are politically important for war and for building, and so on). But even pariah people who are most despised are usually apt to continue cultivating in some manner that which is equally peculiar to ethnic and to status communities: the belief in their own specific 'honor.' This is the case with the Jews.

Only with the negatively privileged status groups does the 'sense of dignity' take a specific deviation. A sense of dignity is the precipitation in individuals of social honor and of conventional demands which a positively privileged status group raises for the deportment of its members. The sense of dignity that characterizes positively privileged status groups is naturally related to their 'being' which does not transcend itself, that is, it is to their 'beauty and excellence' (καλο-κἀγαθια). Their kingdom is 'of this world.' They live for the present and by exploiting their great past. The sense of dignity of the negatively privileged strata naturally refers to a future lying beyond the present, whether it is of this life or of another. In other words, it must be nurtured by the belief in a providential 'mission' and by a belief in a specific honor before God. The 'chosen people's' dignity is nurtured by a belief either that in the beyond 'the last will be the first,' or that in this life a Messiah will appear to bring forth into the light of the world which has cast them out the hidden honor of the pariah people. This simple state of affairs, and not the 'resentment' which is so strongly emphasized in Nietzsche's much admired construction in the *Genealogy of Morals*, is the source of the religiosity cultivated by pariah status groups. In passing, we may note that resentment may be accurately applied only to a limited extent; for one of Nietzsche's main examples, Buddhism, it is not at all applicable.

Incidentally, the development of status groups from ethnic segregations is by no means the normal phenomenon. On the contrary, since objective 'racial differences' are by no means basic to every subjective sentiment of an ethnic community, the ultimately racial foundation of status structure is rightly and absolutely a question of the concrete individual case. Very frequently a status group is instrumental in the production of a thoroughbred anthropological type. Certainly a status group is to a high degree effective in producing extreme types, for they select personally qualified individuals (e.g. the Knighthood selects those who are fit for warfare, physically and psychically). But selection is far from being the only, or the predominant, way in which status groups are formed: Political membership or class situation has at all times been at least as frequently decisive. And today the class situation is by far the predominant factor, for of course the possibility of a style of life expected for members of a status group is usually conditioned economically.

8: Status Privileges

For all practical purposes, stratification by status goes hand in hand with a monopolization of ideal and material goods or opportunities, in a manner we have come to know as typical. Besides the specific status honor, which always rests upon distance and exclusiveness, we find all sorts of material monopolies. Such honorific preferences may consist of the privilege of wearing special costumes, of eating special dishes taboo to others, of carrying arms — which is most obvious in its consequences — the right to pursue certain non-professional dilettante artistic practices, e.g. to play certain musical instruments. Of course, material monopolies provide the most effective motives for the exclusiveness of a status group; although, in themselves, they are rarely sufficient, almost always they come into play to some extent. Within a status circle there is the question of intermarriage: the interest of the families in the monopolization of potential bridegrooms is at least of equal importance and is parallel to the interest in the monopolization of daughters. The daughters of the circle must be provided for. With an increased inclosure of the status group, the conventional preferential opportunities for special employment grow into a legal monopoly of special offices for the members. Certain goods become objects for monopolization by status groups. In the typical fashion these include 'entailed estates' and frequently also the possessions of serfs or bondsmen and, finally, special trades. This monopolization occurs positively when the status group is exclusively entitled to own and to manage them; and negatively when, in order to maintain its specific way of life, the status group must *not* own and manage them.

The decisive role of a 'style of life' in status 'honor' means that status groups are the specific bearers of all 'conventions.' In whatever way it may be manifest, all 'stylization' of life either originates in status groups or is at least conserved by them. Even if the principles of status conventions differ greatly, they reveal certain typical traits, especially among those strata which are most privileged. Quite generally, among privileged status groups there is a status disqualification that operates against the performance of common physical labor. This disqualification is now 'setting in' in America against the old tradition of esteem for labor. Very frequently every rational economic pursuit, and especially 'entrepreneurial activity,' is looked upon as a disqualification of status. Artistic and literary activity is also considered as degrading work as soon as it is exploited for income, or at least when it is connected with hard physical exertion. An example is the sculptor working like a mason in his dusty smock as over against the painter in his salon-like 'studio' and those forms of musical practice that are acceptable to the status group.

9: Economic Conditions and Effects of Status Stratification

The frequent disqualification of the gainfully employed as such is a direct result of the principle of status stratification peculiar to the social order, and of course, of this principle's opposition to a distribution of power which is regulated exclusively through the market. These two factors operate along with various individual ones, which will be touched upon below.

We have seen above that the market and its processes 'knows no personal distinctions'; 'functional' interests dominate it. It knows nothing of 'honor.' The status order means precisely the reverse, viz.: stratification in terms of 'honor' and of styles of life peculiar to status groups as such. If mere economic acquisition and naked economic power still bearing the stigma of its extra-status origin could bestow upon anyone who has won it the same honor as those who are interested in status by virtue of style of life claim for themselves, the status order would be threatened at its very root. This is the more so as, given equality of status honor, property *per se* represents an addition even if it is not overtly acknowledged to be such. Yet if such economic acquisition and power gave the agent any honor at all, his wealth would result in his attaining more honor than those who successfully claim honor by virtue of style of life. Therefore all groups having interests in the status order react with special sharpness precisely against the pretensions of purely economic acquisition. In most cases they react the more vigorously the more they feel themselves threatened. Calderon's respectful treatment of the peasant, for instance, as opposed to Shakespeare's simultaneous and ostensible disdain of the *canaille* illustrates the different way in which a firmly structured status order reacts as compared with a status order that has become economically precarious. This is an example of a state of affairs that recurs everywhere. Precisely because of the rigorous reactions against the claims of property *per se*, the 'parvenu' is never accepted, personally and without reservation, by the privileged status groups, no matter how completely his style of life has been adjusted to theirs. They will only accept his descendants who have been educated in the conventions of their status group and who have never besmirched its honor by their own economic labor.

As to the general *effect* of the status order, only one consequence can be stated, but it is a very important one: the hindrance of the free development of the market occurs first for those goods which status groups directly withheld from free exchange by monopolization. This monopolization may be effected either legally or conventionally. For example, in many Hellenic cities during the epoch of status groups, and also originally in Rome, the inherited estate (as is shown by the old formula for indiction against spendthrifts) was monopolized just as were the estates of knights, peasants, priests, and especially the clientele of the craft and merchant guilds. The market is restricted, and the power of naked property *per se*, which gives its stamp to 'class formation,' is pushed into the background. The results of this process can be most varied. Of course, they do not necessarily weaken the contrasts in the economic situation. Frequently they strengthen these contrasts, and in any case, where stratification by status permeates a community as strongly as was the case in all political communities of antiquity and of the Middle Ages, one can never speak of a genuinely free market competition as we understand it today. There are wider effects than this direct exclusion of special goods from the market. From the contrariety between the status order and the purely economic order mentioned above, it follows that in most instances the notion of honor peculiar to status absolutely abhors that which is essential to the market: higgling. Honor abhors higgling among peers and occasionally it taboos higgling for the members of a status group in general. Therefore, everywhere some status groups, and usually the most influential, consider almost any kind of overt participation in economic acquisition as absolutely stigmatizing.

With some over-simplification, one might thus say that 'classes' are stratified according to their relations to the production and acquisition of goods; whereas 'status groups' are stratified according to the principles of their *consumption* of goods as represented by special 'styles of life.'

An 'occupational group' is also a status group. For normally, it successfully claims social honor only by virtue of the special style of life which may be determined by it. The differences between classes and status groups frequently overlap. It is precisely those status communities most strictly segregated in terms of honor (viz. the Indian castes) who today show, although within very rigid limits, a relatively high degree of indifference to pecuniary income. However, the Brahmins seek such income in many different ways.

As to the general economic conditions making for the predominance of stratification by 'status,' only very little can be said. When the bases of the acquisition and distribution of goods are relatively stable, stratification by status is favored. Every technological repercussion and economic transformation threatens stratification by status and pushes the class situation into the foreground. Epochs and countries in which the naked class situation is of predominant significance are regularly the periods of technical and economic transformations. And every slowing down of the shifting of economic stratifications leads, in due course, to the growth of status structures and makes for a resuscitation of the important role of social honor.

10: Parties

Whereas the genuine place of 'classes' is within the economic order, the place of 'status groups' is within the social order, that is, within the sphere of the distribution of 'honor.' From within these spheres, classes and status groups influence one another and they influence the legal order and are in turn influenced by it. But 'parties' live in a house of 'power.'

Their action is oriented toward the acquisition of social 'power,' that is to say, toward influencing a communal action no matter what its content may be. In principle, parties may exist in a social 'club' as well as in a 'state.' As over against the actions of classes and status groups, for which this is not necessarily the case, the communal actions of 'parties' always mean a societalization. For party actions are always directed toward a goal which is striven for in planned manner. This goal may be a 'cause' (the party may aim at realizing a program for ideal or material purposes), or the goal may be 'personal' (sinecures, power, and from these, honor for the leader and the followers of the party). Usually the party action aims at all these simultaneously. Parties are, therefore, only possible within communities that are societalized, that is, which have some rational order and a staff of persons available who are ready to enforce it. For parties aim precisely at influencing this staff, and if possible, to recruit it from party followers.

In any individual case, parties may represent interests determined through 'class situation' or 'status situation,' and they may recruit their following respectively from one or the other. But they need be neither purely 'class' nor purely 'status' parties. In most cases they are partly class parties and partly status parties, but sometimes they are neither. They may represent ephemeral or enduring structures. Their means of attaining power may be quite varied, ranging from naked violence of any sort to canvassing for votes with coarse or subtle means: money, social influence, the force of speech, suggestion, clumsy hoax, and so on to the rougher or more artful tactics of obstruction in parliamentary bodies.

The sociological structure of parties differs in a basic way according to the kind of communal action which they struggle to influence. Parties also differ according to whether or not the community is stratified by status or by classes. Above all else, they vary according to the structure of domination within the community. For their leaders normally deal with the conquest of a community. They are, in the general concept which is maintained here, not only products of specially modern forms of domination. We shall also designate as parties the ancient and medieval 'parties,' despite the fact that their structure differs basically from the structure of modern parties. By virtue of these structural differences of domination it is impossible to say anything about the structure of parties without discussing the structural forms of social domination *per se*. Parties, which are always structures struggling for domination, are very frequently organized in a very strict 'authoritarian' fashion. . . .

Concerning 'classes,' 'status groups,' and 'parties,' it must be said in general that they necessarily presuppose a comprehensive societalization, and especially a political framework of communal action, within which they operate. This does not mean that parties would be confined by the frontiers of any individual political community. On the contrary, at all times it has been the order of the day that the societalization (even when it aims at the use of military force in common) reaches beyond the frontiers of politics. This has been the case in the solidarity of interests among the Oligarchs and among the democrats in Hellas, among the Guelfs and among Ghibellines in the Middle Ages, and within the Calvinist party during the period of religious struggles. It has been the case up to the solidarity of the landlords (international congress of agrarian landlords), and has continued among princes (holy alliance, Karlsbad decrees), socialist workers, conservatives (the longing of Prussian conservatives for Russian intervention in 1850). But their aim is not necessarily the establishment of new international political, i.e. *territorial,* dominion. In the main they aim to influence the existing dominion.

Pecuniary Emulation

(1899)

THORSTEIN VEBLEN

In the sequence of cultural evolution the emergence of a leisure class coincides with beginning of ownership. This is necessarily the case, for these two institutions result from the same set of economic forces. In the inchoate phase of their development they are but different aspects of the same general facts of social structure.

It is as elements of social structure — conventional facts — that leisure and ownership are matters of interest for the purpose in hand. An habitual neglect of work does not constitute a leisure class; neither does the mechanical fact of use and consumption constitute ownership. The present inquiry, therefore, is not concerned with the beginning of indolence, nor with the beginning of the appropriation of useful articles to individual consumption. The point in question is the origin and nature of a conventional leisure class on the one hand and the beginnings of individual ownership as a conventional right or equitable claim on the other hand.

The early differentiation out of which the distinction between a leisure and a working class arises is a division maintained between men's and women's work in the lower stages of barbarism. Likewise the earliest

From Thorstein Veblen, *The Theory of the Leisure Class* (New York: Macmillan, 1899), 22–34.

form of ownership is an ownership of the women by the ablebodied men of the community. The facts may be expressed in more general terms, and truer to the import of the barbarian theory of life, by saying that it is an ownership of the woman by the man.

There was undoubtedly some appropriation of useful articles before the custom of appropriating women arose. The usages of existing archaic communities in which there is no ownership of women is warrant for such a view. In all communities the members, both male and female, habitually appropriate to their individual use a variety of useful things; but these useful things are not thought of as owned by the person who appropriates and consumes them. The habitual appropriation and consumption of certain slight personal effects goes on without raising the question of ownership; that is to say, the question of a conventional, equitable claim to extraneous things.

The ownership of women begins in the lower barbarian stages of culture, apparently with the seizure of female captives. The original reason for the seizure and appropriation of women seems to have been their usefulness as trophies. The practice of seizing women from the enemy as trophies, gave rise to a form of ownership-marriage, resulting in a household with a male head. This was followed by an extension of slavery to other captives and inferiors, besides women, and by an extension of ownership-marriage to other women than those seized from the enemy. The outcome of emulation under the circumstances of a predatory life, therefore, has been on the one hand a form of marriage resting on coercion, and on the other hand the custom of ownership. The two institutions are not distinguishable in the initial phase of their development; both arise from the desire of the successful men to put their prowess in evidence by exhibiting some durable result of their exploits. Both also minister to that propensity for mastery which prevades all predatory communities. From the ownership of women the concept of ownership extends itself to include the products of their industry, and so there arises the ownership of things as well as of persons.

In this way a consistent system of property in goods is gradually installed. And although in the latest stages of the development, the serviceability of goods for consumption has come to be the most obtrusive element of their value, still, wealth has by no means yet lost its utility as a honorific evidence of the owner's prepotence.

Wherever the institution of private property is found, even in a slightly developed form, the economic process bears the character of a struggle between men for the possession of goods. It has been customary in economic theory, and especially among those economists who adhere with least faltering to the body of modernised classical doctrines, to construe this struggle for wealth as being substantially a struggle for subsistence. Such is, no doubt, its character in large part during the earlier and less efficient phases of industry. Such is also its character in all cases where the "niggardiness of nature" is so strict as to afford but a scanty livelihood to the community in return for strenuous and unremitting application to the business of getting the means of subsistence. But in all progressing communities an advance is presently made beyond this early stage of technological development. Industrial efficiency is presently carried to such a pitch as to afford something appreciably more than a bare livelihood to those engaged in the industrial process. It has not been unusual for economic theory to speak of the further struggle for wealth on this new industrial basis as a competition for an increase of the comforts of life, — primarily for an increase of the physical comforts which the consumption of goods affords.

The end of acquisition and accumulation is conventionally held to be the consumption of the goods accumulated — whether it is consumption directly by the owner of the goods or by the household attached to him and for this purpose identified with him in theory. This is at least felt to be the economically legitimate end of acquisition, which alone it is incumbent on the theory to take account of. Such consumption may of course be conceived to serve the consumer's physical wants — his physical comfort — or his so-called higher wants — spiritual, æsthetic, intellectual, or what not; the latter class of wants being served indirectly by an expenditure of goods, after the fashion familiar to all economic readers.

But it is only when taken in a sense far removed from its naïve meaning that consumption of goods can be said to afford the incentive from which accumulation invariably proceeds. The motive that lies at the root of ownership is emulation; and the same motive of emulation continues active in the further development of the institution to which it has given rise and in the development of all those features of the social structure which this institution of ownership touches. The possession of wealth confers honour; it is an invidious distinction. Nothing equally cogent can be said for the consumption of goods, nor for any other conceivable incentive to acquisition, and especially not for any incentive to the accumulation of wealth.

It is of course not to be overlooked that in a community where nearly all goods are private property the necessity of earning a livelihood is a powerful and everpresent incentive for the poorer members of the community. The need of subsistence and of an increase of physical comfort may for a time be the dominant motive of acquisition for those classes who are habitually employed at manual labour, whose subsistence is on a precarious footing, who possess little and ordinarily accumulate little; but it will appear in the course of the discussion that even in the case of these impecunious classes the predominance of the motive of physical want is not so decided as has sometimes been assumed. On the other hand, so far as regards those members and classes of the community who are chiefly concerned in the accumulation of wealth, the incentive of subsistence or of physical comfort never plays a considerable part. Ownership began and grew into a human institution on grounds unrelated to the subsistence minimum. The dominant incentive was from the outset the invidious distinction attaching to wealth, and, save temporarily and by exception, no other motive has usurped the primacy at any later stage of the development.

Property set out with being booty held as trophies of the successful raid. So long as the group had departed but little from the primitive communal organisation, and so long as it still stood in close contact with other hostile groups, the utility of things or persons owned lay chiefly in an invidious comparison between their possessor and the enemy from whom they were taken. The habit of distinguishing between the interests of the individual and those of the group to which he belongs is apparently a later growth. Invidious comparison between the possessor of the honorific booty and his less successful neighbours within the group was no doubt present early as an element of the utility of the things possessed, though this was not at the outset the chief element of their value. The man's prowess was still primarily the group's prowess, and the possessor of the booty felt himself to be primarily the keeper of the honour of his group. This appreciation of exploit from the communal point of view is met with also at later stages of social growth, especially as regards the laurels of war.

But so soon as the custom of individual ownership begins to gain consistency, the point of view taken in making the invidious comparison on which private property rests will begin to change. Indeed, the one change is but the reflex of the other. The initial phase of ownership, the phase of acquisition by naïve seizure and conversion, begins to pass into the subsequent stage of an incipient organisation of industry on the basis of private property (in slaves); the horde develops into a more or less self-sufficing industrial community; possessions then come to be valued not so much as evidence of successful foray, but rather as evidence of the prepotence of the possessor of these goods over other individuals within the community. The invidious comparison now becomes primarily a comparison of the owner with the other members of the group. Property is still of the nature of trophy, but, with the cultural advance, it becomes more and more a trophy of successes scored in the game of ownership carried on between the members of the group under the quasi-peaceable methods of nomadic life.

Gradually, as industrial activity further displaces predatory activity in the community's everyday life and in men's habits of thought, accumulated property more and more replaces trophies of predatory exploit as the conventional exponent of prepotence and success. With the growth of settled industry, therefore, the possession of wealth gains in relative importance and effectiveness as a customary basis of repute and esteem. Not that esteem ceases to be awarded on the basis of other, more direct evidence of prowess; not that successful predatory aggression of warlike exploit ceases to call out the approval and admiration of the crowd, or to stir the envy of the less successful competitors; but the opportunities for gaining distinction by means of this direct manifestation of superior force grow less available both in scope and frequency. At the same time opportunities for industrial aggression, and for the accumulation of property by the quasi-peaceable methods of nomadic industry, increase in scope and availability. And it is even more to the point that property now becomes the most easily recognised evidence of a reputable degree of success as distinguished from heroic or signal achievement. It therefore becomes the conventional basis of esteem. Its possession in some amount becomes necessary in order to [achieve] any reputable standing in the community. It becomes indispensable to accumulate, to acquire property, in order to retain one's good name. When accumulated goods have in this way once become the accepted badge of efficiency, the possession of wealth presently assumes the character of an independent and definitive basis of esteem. The possession of goods, whether acquired aggressively by one's own exertion or passively by transmission through inheritance from others, becomes a conventional basis of reputability. The possession of wealth, which was at the outset valued simply as an evidence of efficiency, becomes, in popular apprehension, itself a meritorious act. Wealth is now itself intrinsically honourable and confers honour on its possessor. By a further refinement, wealth acquired passively by transmission from ancestors or other antecedents presently becomes even more honorific than wealth acquired by the possessor's own effort; but this distinction belongs at a later stage in the evolution of the pecuniary culture and will be spoken of in its place.

Prowess and exploit may still remain the basis of award of the highest popular esteem, although the possession of wealth has become the basis of commonplace reputability and of a blameless social standing. The predatory instinct and the consequent approbation of predatory efficiency are deeply ingrained in the habits of thought of those peoples who have passed under the discipline of a protracted predatory culture. According to popular award, the highest honours within human reach may, even yet, be those gained by an unfolding of extraordinary predatory efficiency in war, or by a quasi-predatory efficiency in statecraft; but for the purposes of a commonplace decent standing in the community these means of repute have been replaced by the acquisition and accumulation of goods. In order to stand well in the eyes of the community, it is necessary to come up to a certain, somewhat indefinite, conventional standard of wealth; just as in the earlier predatory stage it is necessary for the barbarian man to come up to the tribe's standard of physical endurance, cunning, and skill at arms. A certain standard of wealth in the one case, and of prowess in the other, is a necessary condition of reputability, and anything in excess of this normal amount is meritorious.

Those members of the community who fall short of this, somewhat indefinite, normal degree of prowess or of property suffer in the esteem of their fellow-men; and consequently they suffer also in their own esteem, since the usual basis of self-respect is the respect accorded by one's neighbours. Only individuals with an aberrant temperament can in the long run retain their self-esteem in the face of the disesteem of their fellows. Apparent exceptions to the rule are met with, especially among people with strong religious convictions. But these apparent exceptions are scarcely real exceptions, since such persons commonly fall back on the putative approbation of some supernatural witness of their deeds.

So soon as the possession of property becomes the basis of popular esteem, therefore, it becomes also a requisite to that complacency which we call self-respect. In any community where goods are held in severalty it is necessary, in order to his own peace of mind, that an individual should possess as large a portion of goods as others with whom he is accustomed to class himself; and it is extremely gratifying to possess something more than others. But as fast as a person makes new acquisitions, and becomes accustomed to the resulting new standard of wealth, the new standard forthwith ceases to afford appreciably greater satisfaction than the earlier standard did. The tendency in any case is constantly to make the present pecuniary standard the point of departure for a fresh increase of wealth; and this in turn gives rise to a new standard of sufficiency and a new pecuniary classification of one's self as compared with one's neighbours. So far as concerns the present question, the end sought by accumulation is to rank high in comparison with the rest of the community in point of pecuniary strength. So long as the comparison is distinctly unfavourable to himself, the normal, average individual will live in chronic dissatisfaction with his present lot; and when he has reached what may be called the normal pecuniary standard of the community, or of his class in the community, this chronic dissatisfaction will give place to a restless straining to place a wider and ever-widening pecuniary interval between himself and this average standard. The invidious comparison can never become so favourable to the individual making it that he would not gladly rate himself still higher relatively to his competitors in the struggle for pecuniary reputability.

In the nature of the case, the desire for wealth can scarcely be satiated in any individual instance, and evidently a satiation of the average or general desire for wealth is out of the question. However widely, or equally, or "fairly," it may be distributed, no general increase of the community's wealth can make any approach to satiating this need, the ground of which is the desire of every one to excel every one else in the accumulation of goods. If, as is sometimes assumed, the incentive to accumulation were the want of subsistence or of physical comfort, then the aggregate economic wants of a community might conceivably be satisfied at some point in the advance of industrial efficiency; but since the struggle is substantially a race for reputability on the basis of an invidious comparison, no approach to a definitive attainment is possible.

What has just been said must not be taken to mean that there are no other incentives to acquisition and accumulation than this desire to excel in pecuniary standing and so gain the esteem and envy of one's fellow-men. The desire for added comfort and security from want is present as a motive at every stage of the process of accumulation in a modern industrial community; although the standard of sufficiency in these respects is in turn greatly affected by the habit of pecuniary emulation. To a great extent this emulation shapes the methods and selects the objects of expenditure for personal comfort and decent livelihood.

Besides this, the power conferred by wealth also affords a motive to accumulation. That propensity for purposeful activity and that repugnance to all futility of effort which belong to man by virtue of his character as an agent do not desert him when he emerges from the naïve communal culture where the dominant note of life is the unanalysed and undifferentiated solidarity of the individual with the group with which his life is bound up. When he enters upon the predatory stage, where self-seeking in the narrower sense becomes the dominant note, this propensity goes with him still, as the pervasive trait that shapes his scheme of life. The propensity for achievement and the repugnance to futility remain the underlying economic motive. The propensity changes only in the form of its expression and in the proximate objects to which it directs the man's activity. Under the régime of individual ownership the most available means of visibly achieving a purpose is that afforded by the acquisition and accumulation of goods; and as the self-regarding antithesis between man and man reaches fuller consciousness, the propensity for achievement — the instinct of workmanship — tends more and more to shape itself into a straining to excel others in pecuniary achievement. Relative success, tested by an invidious pecuniary comparison with other men, becomes the conventional end of action. The currently accepted legitimate end of effort becomes the achievement of a favourable comparison with other men; and therefore the repugnance to futility to a good extent coalesces with the incentive of emulation. It acts to accentuate the struggle for pecuniary reputability by visiting with a sharper disapproval all shortcoming and all evidence of shortcoming in point of pecuniary success. Purposeful effort comes to mean, primarily, effort directed to or resulting in a more creditable showing of accumulated wealth. Among the motives which lead men to accumulate wealth, the primacy, both in scope and intensity, therefore, continues to belong to this motive of pecuniary emulation.

In making use of the term "invidious," it may perhaps be unnecessary to remark, there is no intention to extol or depreciate, or to commend or deplore any of the phenomena which the word is used to characterise. The term is used in a technical sense as describing a comparison of persons with a view to rating and grading them in respect of relative worth or value — in an æsthetic or moral sense — and so awarding and defining the relative degrees of complacency with which they may legitimately be contemplated by themselves and by others. An invidious comparison is a process of valuation of persons in respect of worth.

X

WORLD WAR I AND THE CRISIS OF LIBERALISM

World War I was a far greater trauma for European intellectuals, and European society, than it was for Americans, yet on both continents a similar cleavage among social critics developed between those who supported or acquiesced in the war for nationalistic reasons and those who opposed it as inhumane and subversive of the liberal tradition. And in America as in Europe, the dissenters were in the minority. The French philosopher Julien Benda (1867–1956) and the American journalist Randolph Bourne (1886–1918) therefore represented minor though significant themes in their respective intellectual traditions. They stood as lonely critics of the statist doctrines that stemmed from the Reform Darwinist and pragmatic ideas of the late nineteenth century. Selections from their works are included here both because of their intrinsic importance and because they illuminate, through their opposition, the affect on liberalism of nationalist ideas in the early decades of the twentieth century, especially during World War I.

Benda first publicly defined his philosophy in the Dreyfus controversy and until his death departed from it but little. Essentially, he upheld the classical values of Western philosophy as a search for the good and the beautiful. He condemned the descent of intellectuals into the partisan political marketplace; it was their exclusive function, he believed, to serve as the conscience of society, to define its values and articulate its highest aspirations. They had no business justifying or helping to prosecute war, yet the Great War had drawn them into just such reprehensible activities. That unfortunate development, thought Benda, was a logical outgrowth of the generally relativist and pragmatic course of European thought since the late nineteenth century. It especially reflected, to him, the pernicious emphasis on the irrational and the repudiation of the values of the Enlightenment characteristic of turn-of-the-century European social thought.

Randolph Bourne did not have such a well-defined philosophical base as did Benda, but he condemned American intellectuals for their support of the war, just as Benda condemned Europeans. Similarly, he attributed that support to the absence of an ethical standard in the pragmatic philosophy. In their concern for instrumentalism, said Bourne, American pragmatists, particularly John Dewey, had abandoned the responsibility to create and define values. Hence they uncritically supported the war, justified the augmented power of the state — Bourne wrote elsewhere that "war is the health of the state" — and subverted many of the liberal values pragmatism had been thought to serve.

The Great Betrayal

(1927)

JULIEN BENDA

In all that I have said hitherto I have been considering only masses, whether bourgeois or proletarian, kings, ministers, political leaders, all that portion of the human species which I shall call "the laymen," whose whole function consists essentially in the pursuit of material interests, and who, by becoming more and more solely and systematically realist, have in fact only done what might be expected of them.

Side by side with this humanity whom the poet has described in a phrase — "O curvae in terram animae et celestium inanes" — there existed until the last half century another, essentially distinct humanity, which to a certain extent acted as a check upon the former. I mean that class of men whom I shall designate "*the clerks*," by which term I mean all those whose activity essentially is *not* the pursuit of practical aims, all those who seek their joy in the practice of an art or a science or metaphysical speculation, in short in the possession of non-material advantages, and hence in a certain manner say: "My kingdom is not of this world." Indeed, throughout history, for more than two thousand years until modern times, I see an uninterrupted series of philosophers, men of religion, men of literature, artists, men of learning (one might say almost all during this period), whose influence, whose life, were in direct opposition to the realism of the multitudes. To come down specifically to the political passions — the "clerks" were in opposition to them in two ways. They were either entirely indifferent to these passions, and, like Leonardo da Vinci, Malebranche, Goethe, set an example of attachment to the purely disinterested activity of the mind and created a belief in the supreme value of this form of existence; or, gazing as moralists upon the conflict of human egotisms, like Erasmus, Kant, Renan, they preached, in the name of humanity or justice, the adoption of an abstract principle superior to and directly opposed to these passions. Although these "clerks" founded the modern State to the extent that it dominates individual egotisms, their activity undoubtedly was chiefly theoretical, and they were unable to prevent the laymen from filling all history with the noise of their hatreds and their slaughters; *but the "clerks" did prevent the laymen from setting up their actions as a religion, they did prevent them from thinking themselves great men as they carried out these activities*. It may be said that, thanks to the "clerks," humanity did evil for two thousand years, but honored good. This contradiction was an honor to the human species, and formed the rift whereby civilization slipped into the world.

Now, at the end of the nineteenth century a fundamental change occurred: *the "clerks" began to play the game of political passions*. The men who had acted as a check on the realism of the people began to act as its stimulators. This upheaval in the moral behavior of humanity operated in several ways.

First of all the "clerks" have adopted political passions. No one will deny that throughout Europe to-day the immense majority of men of letters and artists, a considerable number of scholars, philosophers, and "ministers" of the divine, share in the chorus of hatreds among races and political factions. Still less will it be denied that they adopt national passions. Doubtless, the names of Dante, Petrarch, d'Aubigné, certain apologists of Caboche or preachers of the Ligue will suffice to show that certain "clerks" did not wait for our era to indulge in these passions with all the strength of their souls. But, upon the whole, these "clerks" of the forum were exceptions, at least among the great ones. If, in addition to the great masters named above, I evoke the phalanx of Thomas Aquinas, Roger Bacon, Galilei, Rabelais, Montaigue, Descartes, Racine, Pascal, Leibniz, Kepler, Huyghens, Newton, and even Voltaire, Buffon and Montesquieu (to mention only a few) I think I may repeat that until our own days the men of thought or the honest men remained strangers to political passions, and said with Goethe: "Let us leave politics to the diplomats and the soldiers." Of it, like Voltaire, they took these passions into account, they adopted a critical attitude towards them, did not espouse them as passions. Or if, like Rousseau, Maistre, Chateaubriand, Lamartine, even Michelet, they did take these passions to heart, they did so with a generalizing of feeling, a disdain for immediate results, which in fact make the word "passions" incorrect. Today, if we mention Mommsen, Treitschke, Ostwald, Brunetière, Barrès, Lemaître, Péguy, Maurras, d'Annunzio, Kipling, we have to admit that the "clerks" now exercise political passions with all the characteristics of passion — the tendency to action, the thirst for immediate results, the exclusive preoccupation with the desired end, the scorn for argument, the excess, the hatred, the fixed ideas. The modern "clerk" has entirely ceased to let the layman alone descend to the market place. The modern "clerk" is determined to have the soul of a citizen and to make vigorous use of it; he is proud of that soul; his literature is filled with his contempt for the man who shuts himself up with art or science and takes no interest in the passions of the State. He is violently on the side of Michelangelo crying shame upon Leonardo da Vinci for his indifference to the misfortunes of Florence, and against the master of the Last Supper when he replied that indeed the study of beauty occupied his whole heart. The time has long past by since Plato demanded that the philosopher should be bound in chains in order to compel him to take an interest in the State. To have as his function the pursuit of eternal things and yet to believe that he becomes greater by concerning himself with the State — that is the view of the modern "clerk." It is as natural as it is evident that this adhesion of the "clerks" to the passions of the laymen fortifies these passions in the hearts of the latter. In the first place, it abolishes the suggestive spectacle (which I mentioned above) of a race of men whose interests are set outside the practical world. And then especially, the "clerk" by adopting political passions, brings them the tremendous influence of his sensibility if he is an artist, of his persuasive power if he is a thinker, and in either case his moral prestige. . . .

It is concerning national passions that this adhesion seems to me particularly novel and big with results. . . . It was reserved for our own time to see men of thought, or men giving themselves out as such, professing openly that they would not submit their patriotism to any check on the part of their judgment, proclaiming (like Barrès) that "even if the country is wrong, we must think it in the right," denouncing as "traitors to the nation" those of their compatriots who retain their liberty of mind, or at least of speech, in regard to their country. In France we have not forgotten how, during the last war, so many "thinkers" attacked Renan for the liberty of his judgments on the history of his country. Nor have we forgotten how, a little before that, a whole set of young men (who claimed to share in the life of the spirit) bristled up against one of their masters (Jacob) who tried to teach them a patriotism which did not exclude all right of criticism. After the violation of Belgium and other excesses of the Germans, in October, 1914, a German teacher said: "There is nothing for which we need make excuses." Now, if their own countries had been in a similar position, the same thing would have been said by most of the spiritual leaders of that time; by Barrès in France, by d'Annunzio in Italy, by Kipling in England, if we may judge by his conduct during the attack of his nation upon the Boers, and by William James in the United States, if we recall his attitude when his compatriots seized the island of Cuba.[1] I am quite ready to agree that this sort of blind patriotism makes powerful nations, and that the patriotism of Fénelon or of Renan is not the sort which secures empires. It remains to determine whether the function of "clerks" is to secure empires.

This adhesion of the "clerks" to national passion is particularly remarkable among those whom I shall call "preëminently clerks"; I mean the Churchmen. In all European countries during the past fifty years, the immense majority of these men have not only given their adhesion to the national feeling and therefore have ceased to provide the world with the spectacle of hearts solely occupied with God — but they seem to have adopted this feeling with the same passion as that I have pointed out as existing among men of letters, and they too appear to be ready to support their own countries in the most flagrant injustices. During the last war this could be most clearly seen in the German clergy, from whom no one could drag the shadow of a protest against the excesses committed by their nation, and whose silence does not appear to have been caused solely by prudence. In contrast to this attitude I refer the reader to that of the Spanish theologians of the sixteenth century, to men like Bartholomew de las Casas and Vittoria, earnestly denouncing the cruelties committed by their compatriots in the conquest of America. I do not claim that similar behavior was then the rule among Churchmen, but I should like to ask whether there is a single country to-day where they would do likewise, or where they would even wish to be permitted to do so?

I shall point out another characteristic of patriotism in the modern "clerk": xenophobia. The hatred of man for "the man from outside" (the *horsain*), his rejection of and scorn for everything which is not "from his own home," all these impulses, so constant among peoples and apparently necessary to their existence, have been adopted in our days by the so-called men of thought, and adopted with a seriousness of

[1] See his *Letters*, ii, p. 31. [This is a curious statement. The reference is to a letter James wrote in 1896, where he discussed not Cuba but the Venezuelan boundary dispute with Great Britain. He deplored President Grover Cleveland's attempts to rouse a war spirit in the United States and called a war with England "the worst disaster to civilization that our time could bring forth." Two years later, during the Spanish-American War and the invasion of Cuba, James was among the most prominent American anti-imperialists. — Eds.]

application, *an absence of simple-mindedness,* which go far towards making this adoption worthy of notice. We know how systematically the mass of German teachers in the past fifty years have announced the decline of every civilization but that of their own race, and how in France the admirers of Nietzsche or Wagner, even of Kant or Goethe, were treated by Frenchmen who claimed to share in the life of the spirit. You may estimate how curiously new this form of patriotism is among the men of thought in France by thinking of Lamartine, Victor Hugo, Michelet, Proudhon, Renan, to name only patriotic "clerks" in the age immediately preceding that we are considering. Is it necessary to say once again how much the "clerks" have stimulated the passion of the laymen by adopting this xenophobia?

I shall be told that during the past fifty years, and especially during the twenty years before the war, the attitude of foreigners to France was such that the most violent national partiality was forced upon all Frenchmen who wished to safeguard the nation, and that the only true patriots were those who consented to this fanaticism. I say nothing to the contrary; I only say that the "clerks" who indulged in this fanaticism betrayed their duty, which is precisely to set up a corporation whose sole cult is that of justice and of truth, in opposition to the peoples and the injustice to which they are condemned by their religions of this earth. It is true indeed that these new "clerks" declare that they do not know what is meant by justice, truth, and other "metaphysical fogs," that for them the true is determined by the useful, the just by circumstances. All these things were taught by Callicles, but with this difference; he revolted all the important thinkers of his time.

It must be admitted that the German "clerks" led the way in this adhesion of the modern "clerk" to patriotic fanaticism. The French "clerks" were, and long remained, animated with the most perfect spirit of justice towards foreign cultures (think of the cosmopolitanism of the Romantics!), when already Lessing, Schlegel, Fichte, Goerres were organizing in their hearts a violent adoration for "everything German," and a scorn for everything not German. The nationalist "clerk" is essentially a German invention. This, moreover, is a theme which will frequently recur in [*The Treason of the Intellectuals*], i.e. that most of the moral and political attitudes adopted by the "clerks" of Europe in the past fifty years are of German origin, and that in the world of spiritual things the victory of Germany is now complete. . . .

But the modern "clerks" have held up universal truth to the scorn of mankind, as well as universal morality. Here the "clerks" have positively shown genius in their effort to serve the passions of the laymen. It is obvious that truth is a great impediment to those who wish to set themselves up as distinct; from the very moment when they accept truth, it condemns them to be conscious of themselves in a universal. What a joy for them to learn that this universal is a mere phantom, that there exist only particular truths, "Lorrain truths, Provencal truths, Britanny truths, the harmony of which in the course of centuries constitutes what is beneficial, respectable, *true in France*" (the neighbor similarly speaks of what is *true in Germany*), that in other words Pascal had the mind of a clown, and that what is true on one side of the Pyrenees may perfectly well be error on the other side! Humanity hears the same teaching about the classes and learns that there is a bourgeois truth and a working-class truth; better still, that the functioning of our minds should be different according to whether we are working men or bourgeois. The source of your troubles (Sorel teaches the working classes) is that you do not think in the mental way suited to your class. His disciple, Johannet, says the same thing to the capitalist class. Perhaps we shall soon see the results of this truly supreme art of the "clerks" in exasperating the feeling of their differences among the classes.

The cult for the particular and the scorn for the universal is a reversal of values quite generally characteristic of the teaching of the modern "clerks," who proclaim them in a far higher sphere of thought than politics. The metaphysics adopted in the last twenty years by almost all those who think or pretend to think, set up as the supreme state of human consciousness that state — "duration" — where we succeed in taking cognizance of ourselves in what is most individual, most distinct from everything not ourselves, and in freeing ourselves from those forms of thought (concept, reason, habits of speech) through which we can only become conscious of ourselves in what is common to us and others. These metaphysics put forward as a superior form of cognizance of the world that which grasps each thing by what is unique in it, distinct from every other, and is full of scorn for the mind which seeks to discover general states of being. Our age has seen a fact hitherto unknown, at least from my point of view; and this in metaphysics preaching adoration for the contingent, and scorn for the eternal.[2] Nothing could show better how profound is the modern "clerk's" desire to exalt the real, the practical side of existence, and to degrade the ideal, the truly metaphysical side. In the history of philosophy this veneration for the indi-

[2] The adoration of the contingent *for its own sake;* otherwise, and as a step towards the eternal, the knowledge of "strange things" is highly recommended by Leibniz, and even by Spinoza. Renouvier, so hostile to a certain kind of universalism, never bestows philosophical value on a knowledge of what is "unique and inexpressible" in the object. (See G. Seailles, "Le Pluralisme de Renouvier," *Revue de Metaphysique et de Morale,* 1925.) He would never have signed this charter of modern metaphysics: "That the philosophers since Socrates should have contended as to which should most scorn the knowledge of the particular and should most adore knowledge of the general, is something which passes understanding. For, after all, must not the most honourable knowledge be the knowledge of the most valuable realities! And is there a valuable reality which is not concrete and individual?" (William James.)

vidual comes from the German thinkers (Schlegel, Nietzsche, Lotze), while the metaphysical cult of the universal (added to a certain contempt for the experimental) is preëminently a legacy of Greece to the human mind. So here again, and moreover in its profoundest part, the teaching of the modern "clerks" shows the triumph of Germanic values and the bankruptcy of Hellenism.

I should like to point out another form, not the least remarkable, which this preaching of particularism assumes among the "clerks." I mean their exhortations to consider everything only as it exists *in time*, that is as it constitutes a succession of particular states, a "becoming," a "history," and never as it presents a state of permanence beyond time under this succession of distinct cases. I mean especially their assertion that this view of things in their historical aspect is the only serious and philosophical view, and that the need to look at them in their eternal aspect is a form of the child's taste for ghosts, and should be merely smiled at. Need I point out that this conception inspires the whole of modern thought? It exists among a whole group of literary critics, who, on their own showing, inquire far less whether a work is beautiful than whether it expresses "the present" aspirations of "the contemporary soul." It may be seen in a whole school of moralist-historians who admire a doctrine, not because it is just or good, but because it embodies the morality *of its time*, the scientific spirit *of its time*. (This is the principal reason why Sorel admires Bergsonism and why Nietzsche admires the philosophy of Nicolas de Cuse.) It may be seen especially in all our metaphysicians. Whether they put forward *Entwickelung* or *Duration* or *Creative Evolution* or *Pluralism* or *Integral Experience* or the *Concrete Universal*, they all teach that the absolute is developed *in time*, in the circumstantial, and proclaim the decadence of that form of mind which, from Plato to Kant, hallows existence as conceived beyond change. If, with Pythagoras, we assume that the Cosmos is the place of regulated and uniform existence, and the Ouranos the place of the becoming and the moving, we may say that all modern metaphysics place the Ouranos at the top of their scale of values and hold the Cosmos in very slight esteem. Is it not remarkable to see the "clerks," even in the lofty function of metaphysicians, teaching the laymen that the real alone is worthy of consideration, and that the supersensible is only worthy of derisive laughter? . . .

[The] cult of the strong State and the moral methods which ensure it have been preached to mankind by the "clerks" far beyond the domain of politics, and on a wholly general plane. This is the preaching of *Pragmatism* whose teaching during the past fifty years by nearly all the influential moralists of Europe is one of the most remarkable turning points in the moral history of the human species. It is impossible to exaggerate the importance of a movement whereby those who for twenty centuries taught Man that the criterion of the morality of an act is its disinterestedness, that good is a decree of his reason insofar as it is universal, that his will is only moral if it seeks its law outside its objects, should begin to teach him that the moral act is the act whereby he secures his existence against an environment which disputes it, that his will is moral insofar as it is a will "to power," that the part of his soul which determines what is good is its "will to live" wherein it is most "hostile to all reason," that the morality of an act is measured by its adaptation to its end, and that the only morality is the morality of circumstances. The educators of the human mind now take sides with Callicles against Socrates, a revolution which I dare to say seems to me more important than all political upheavals.

Twilight of Idols

(1917)

RANDOLPH BOURNE

I

Where are the seeds of American promise? Man cannot live by politics alone, and it is small cheer that our best intellects are caught in the political current and see only the hope that America will find her soul in the remaking of the world. If William James were alive would he be accepting the war-situation so easily and complacently? Would he be chiding the over-stimulated intelligence of peace-loving idealists, and excommunicating from the ranks of liberal progress the pitiful remnant of those who struggle "above the battle"? I like to think that his gallant spirit would have called for a war to be gallantly played, with insistent care for democratic values at home, and unequivocal alliance with democratic elements abroad for a peace that should promise more than a mere union of benevolent imperialisms. I think of James now because the recent articles of John Dewey's on the war suggest a slackening in his thought for our guidance and stir, and the inadequacy of his pragmatism as a philosophy of life in this emergency. Whether James would have given us just that note of spiritual adventure which would make the national enterprise seem creative for an American future, — this we can never know. But surely that philosophy of Dewey's which we had been

From *The Seven Arts*, II (October, 1917), 688–702.

following so uncritically for so long, breaks down almost noisily when it is used to grind out interpretation for the present crisis. These articles on "Conscience and Compulsion," "The Future of Pacifism," "What America Will Fight For," "Conscription of Thought," which *The New Republic* has been printing, seem to me to be a little off-color. A philosopher who senses so little the sinister forces of war, who is so much more concerned over the excesses of the pacifists than over the excesses of military policy, who can feel only amusement at the idea that any one should try to conscript thought, who assumes that the war-technique can be used without trailing along with it the mob-fanaticisms, the injustices and hatreds, that are organically bound up with it, is speaking to another element of the younger intelligentsia than that to which I belong. Evidently the attitudes which war calls out are fiercer and more incalculable than Professor Dewey is accustomed to take into his hopeful and intelligent imagination, and the pragmatist mind, in trying to adjust itself to them, gives the air of grappling, like the pioneer who challenges the arid plains, with a power too big for it. It is not an arena of creative intelligence our country's mind is now, but of mob-psychology. The soldiers who tried to lynch Max Eastman [1] showed that current patriotism is not a product of the will to remake the world. The luxuriant releases of explosive hatred for which peace apparently gives far too little scope cannot be wooed by sweet reasonableness, nor can they be the raw material for the creation of rare liberal political structures. All that can be done is to try to keep your country out of situations where such expressive releases occur. If you have willed the situation, however, or accepted it as inevitable, it is fatuous to protest against the gay debauch of hatred and fear and swagger that must mount and mount, until the heady and virulent poison of war shall have created its own anti-toxin of ruin and disillusionment. To talk as if war were anything else than such a poison is to show that your philosophy has never been confronted with the pathless and the inexorable, and that, only dimly feeling the change, it goes ahead acting as if it had not got out of its depth. Only a lack of practice with a world of human nature so raw-nerved, irrational, uncreative, as an America at war was bound to show itself to be, can account for the singular unsatisfactoriness of these later utterances of Dewey. He did have one moment of hestitation just before the war began, when the war and its external purposes and unifying power seemed the small thing beside that internal adventure which should find our American promise. But that perspective has now disappeared, and one finds Dewey now untainted by skepticism as to our being about a business to which all our idealism should rally. That failure to get guaranties that this country's efforts would obligate the Allies to

[1] [Eastman, editor of the radical intellectual magazine the *Masses*, consistently opposed patriotic justification of the war. — Eds.]

a democratic world-order Dewey blames on the defection of the pacifists, and then somehow manages to get himself into a "we" who "romantically," as he says, forewent this crucial link of our strategy. Does this easy identification of himself with undemocratically-controlled foreign policy mean that a country is democratic when it accepts what its government does, or that war has a narcotic effect on the pragmatic mind? For Dewey somehow retains his sense of being in the controlling class, and ignores those anxious questions of democrats who have been his disciples but are now resenters of the war.

What I come to is a sense of suddenly being left in the lurch, of suddenly finding that a philosophy upon which I had relied to carry us through no longer works. I find the contrast between the idea that creative intelligence has free functioning in wartime, and the facts of the inexorable situation, too glaring. The contrast between what liberals ought to be doing and saying if democratic values are to be conserved, and what the real forces are imposing upon them, strikes too sternly on my intellectual senses. I should prefer some philosophy of War as the grim and terrible cleanser to this optimism-haunted mood that continues unweariedly to suggest that all can yet be made to work for good in a mad and half-destroyed world. I wonder if James, in the face of such disaster, would not have abandoned his "moral equivalent of war" for an "immoral equivalent" which, in swift and periodic saturnalia, would have acted as vaccination against the sure pestilence of war.

II

Dewey's philosophy is inspiring enough for a society at peace, prosperous and with a fund of progressive good-will. It is a philosophy of hope, of clear-sighted comprehension of materials and means. Where institutions are at all malleable, it is the only clue for improvement. It is scientific method applied to "uplift." But this careful adaptation of means to desired ends, this experimental working out of control over brute forces and dead matter in the interests of communal life, depends on a store of rationality, and is effective only where there is strong desire for progress. It is precisely the school, the institution to which Dewey's philosophy was first applied, that is of all our institutions the most malleable. And it is the will to educate that has seemed, in these days, among all our social attitudes the most rationally motivated. It was education, and almost education alone, that seemed susceptible to the steady pressure of an "instrumental" philosophy. Intelligence really seemed about to come into conscious control of an institution, and that one the most potent in moulding the attitudes needed for a civilized society and the aptitudes needed for the happiness of the individual.

For both our revolutionary conceptions of what education means, and for the intellectual strategy of its approach, this country is immeasurably indebted to the influence of Professor Dewey's philosophy. With these ideas sincerely felt, a rational nation would have chosen education as its national enterprise. Into this it would have thrown its energy though the heavens fell and the earth rocked around it. But the nation did not use its isolation from the conflict to educate itself. It fretted for three years and then let war, not education, be chosen, at the almost unanimous behest of our intellectual class, from motives alien to our cultural needs, and for political ends alien to the happiness of the individual. But nations, of course, are not rational entities, and they act within their most irrational rights when they accept war as the most important thing the nation can do in the face of metaphysical menaces of imperial prestige. What concerns us here is the relative ease with which the pragmatist intellectuals, with Professor Dewey at the head, have moved out their philosophy, bag and baggage, from education to war. So abrupt a change in the direction of the national enterprise, one would have expected to cause more emotion, to demand more apologetics. His optimism may have told Professor Dewey that war would not materially demoralize our growth — would, perhaps, after all, be but an incident in the nation's life — but it is not easy to see how, as we skate toward the bankruptcy of war-billions, there will be resources available for educational enterprise that does not contribute directly to the war-technique. Neither is any passion for growth, for creative mastery, going to flourish among the host of militaristic values and new tastes for power that are springing up like poisonous mushrooms on every hand.

How could the pragmatist mind accept war without more violent protest, without a greater wrench? Either Professor Dewey and his friends felt that the forces were too strong for them, that the war had to be, and it was better to take it up intelligently than to drift blindly in; or else they really expected a gallant war, conducted with jealous regard for democratic values at home and a captivating vision of international democracy as the end of all the toil and pain. If their motive was the first, they would seem to have reduced the scope of possible control of events to the vanishing point. If the war is too strong for you to prevent, how is it going to be weak enough for you to control and mould to your liberal purposes? And if their motive was to shape the war firmly for good, they seem to have seriously miscalculated the fierce urgencies of it. Are they to be content, as the materialization of their hopes, with a doubtful League of Nations and the suppression of the I. W. W.? Yet the numbing power of the war-situation seems to have kept them from realizing what has happened to their philosophy. The betrayal of their first hopes has certainly not discouraged them. But neither has it roused them to a more energetic expression of the forces through which they intend to realize them. I search Professor Dewey's articles in vain for clues as to the specific working-out of our democratic desires, either nationally or internationally, either in the present or in the reconstruction after the war. No programme is suggested, nor is there feeling for present vague popular movements and revolts. Rather are the latter chided, for their own vagueness and impracticalities. Similarly, with the other prophets of instrumentalism who accompany Dewey into the war, democracy remains an unanalyzed term, useful as a call to battle, but not an intellectual tool, turning up fresh sod for the changing future. Is it the political democracy of a plutocratic America that we are fighting for, or is it the social democracy of the new Russia? Which do our rulers really fear more, the menace of Imperial Germany, or the liberating influence of a socialist Russia? In the application of their philosophy to politics, our pragmatists are sliding over this crucial question of ends. Dewey says our ends must be intelligently international rather than chauvinistic. But this gets us little distance along our way.

In this difficult time the light that has been in liberals and radicals has become darkness. If radicals spend their time holding conventions to attest their loyalty and stamp out the "enemies within," they do not spend it in breaking intellectual paths, or giving us shining ideas to which we can attach our faith and conscience. The spiritual apathy from which the more naive of us suffer, and which the others are so busy fighting, arises largely from sheer default of a clear vision that would melt it away. Let the motley crew of ex-socialists, and labor radicals, and liberals, and pragmatist philosophers, who have united for the prosecution of the war, present a coherent and convincing democratic programme, and they will no longer be confronted with the skepticism of the conscientious and the impossibilist. But when the emphasis is on technical organization, rather than organization of ideas, on strategy rather than desires, one begins to suspect that no programme is presented because they have none to present. This burrowing into war-technique hides the void where a democratic philosophy should be. Our intellectuals consort with war-boards in order to keep their minds off the question what the slow masses of the people are really desiring, or toward what the best hope of the country really drives. Similarly the blaze of patriotism on the part of the radicals serves the purpose of concealing the feebleness of their intellectual light.

Is the answer that clear formulation of democratic ends must be postponed until victory in the war is attained? But to make this answer is to surrender the entire case. For the support of the war by radicals, realists, pragmatists, is due — or so they say — to the fact that the war is not only saving the cause of democracy, but is immensely accelerating its progress. Well, what are those gains? How are they to be conserved? What do they lead to? How can we further them? Into what large idea of society do they group? To ignore these questions, and think only of the war-technique and its accompanying devotions, is to undermine the foundations of these people's own faith.

A policy of "win the war first" must be, for the radical, a policy of intellectual suicide. Their support of the war throws upon them the responsibility of showing inch by inch the democratic gains, and of laying out a charter of specific hopes. Otherwise they confess that they are impotent and that the war is submerging their expectations, or that they are not genuinely imaginative and offer little promise for future leadership.

III

It may seem unfair to group Professor Dewey with Mr. [John] Spargo and Mr. [Samuel] Gompers, Mr. A. M. Simons, and the Vigilantes. I do so only because in their acceptance of the war, they are all living out that popular American "instrumental" philosophy which Professor Dewey has formulated in such convincing and fascinating terms. On an infinitely more intelligent plane, he is yet one with them in his confidence that the war is motivated by democratic ends and is being made to serve them. A high mood of confidence and self-righteousness moves them all, a keen sense of control over events that makes them eligible to discipleship under Professor Dewey's philosophy. They are all hostile to impossibilism, to apathy, to any attitude that is not a cheerful and brisk setting to work to use the emergency to consolidate the gains of democracy. Not, Is it being used? but, Let us make a flutter about using it! This unanimity of mood puts the resenter of war out of the arena. But he can still seek to explain why this philosophy which has no place for the inexorable should have adjusted itself so easily to the inexorable of war, and why, although a philosophy of the creative intelligence in using means toward ends, it should show itself so singularly impoverished in its present supply of democratic values.

What is the matter with the philosophy? One has a sense of having come to a sudden, short stop at the end of an intellectual era. In the crisis, this philosophy of intelligent control just does not measure up to our needs. What is the root of this inadequacy that is felt so keenly by our restless minds? Van Wyck Brooks has pointed out searchingly the lack of poetic vision in our pragmatist "awakeners." Is there something in these realistic attitudes that works actually against poetic vision, against concern for the quality of life as above machinery of life? Apparently there is. The war has revealed a younger intelligentsia, trained up in the pragmatic dispensation, immensely ready for the executive ordering of events, pitifully unprepared for the intellectual interpretation or the idealistic focussing of ends. The young men in Belgium, the officers' training corps, the young men being sucked into the councils at Washington and into war-organization everywhere, have among them a definite element, upon whom Dewey, as veteran philosopher, might well bestow a papal blessing. They have absorbed the secret of scientific method as applied to political administration. They are liberal, enlightened, aware. They are touched with creative intelligence toward the solution of political and industrial problems. They are a wholly new force in American life, the product of the swing in the colleges from a training that emphasized classical studies to one that emphasized political and economic values. Practically all this element, one would say, is lined up in service of the war-technique. There seems to have been a peculiar congeniality between the war and these men. It is as if the war and they had been waiting for each other. One wonders what scope they would have had for their intelligence without it. Probably most of them would have gone into industry and devoted themselves to sane reorganization schemes. What is significant is that it is the technical side of the war that appeals to them, not the interpretative or political side. The formulation of values and ideals, the production of articulate and suggestive thinking, had not, in their education, kept pace, to any extent whatever, with their technical aptitude. The result is that the field of intellectual formulation is very poorly manned by this younger intelligentsia. While they organize the war, formulation of opinion is left largely in the hands of professional patriots, sensational editors, archaic radicals. The intellectual work of this younger intelligentsia is done by the sedition-hunting Vigilantes, and by the saving remnant of older liberals. It is true, Dewey calls for a more attentive formulation of war-purposes and ideas, but he calls largely to deaf ears. His disciples have learned all too literally the instrumental attitude toward life, and, being immensely intelligent and energetic, they are making themselves efficient instruments of the war-technique, accepting with little question the ends as announced from above. That those ends are largely negative does not concern them, because they have never learned not to subordinate idea to technique. Their education has not given them a coherent system of large ideas, or a feeling for democratic goals. They have, in short, no clear philosophy of life except that of intelligent service, the admirable adaptation of means to ends. They are vague as to what kind of a society they want, or what kind of society America needs, but they are equipped with all the administrative attitudes and talents necessary to attain it.

To those of us who have taken Dewey's philosophy almost as our American religion, it never occurred that values could be subordinated to technique. We were instrumentalists, but we had our private utopias so clearly before our minds that the means fell always into its place as contributory. And Dewey, of course, always meant his philosophy, when taken as a philosophy of life, to start with values. But there was always that unhappy ambiguity in his doctrine as to just how values were created, and it became easier and easier to assume that just any growth was justified and almost any activity valuable so long as it achieved ends. The American, in living out this philosophy, has habitually confused results with product, and been content with getting somewhere without asking too closely whether it was the desirable place to get. It is now becoming plain that unless you start with the vividest kind of poetic vision, your instrumentalism is likely to land you just where it has landed this younger intelligentsia which is so happily and busily engaged in the national enterprise of war. You must have your vision and you must have your technique. The practical effect of Dewey's philosophy has evidently been to develop the sense of the latter at the expense of the former. Though he himself would develop them together, even in him there seems to be a flagging of values, under the influence of war. *The New Republic* honorably clamors for the Allies to subordinate military strategy to political ends, technique to democratic values. But war always undermines values. It is the outstanding lesson of the whole war that statesmen cannot be trusted to get this perspective right, that their only motto is, first to win and then grab what they can. The struggle against this statesmanlike animus must be a losing one as long as we have not very clear and very determined and very revolutionary democratic ideas and programmes to challenge them with. The trouble with our situation is not only that values have been generally ignored in favor of technique, but that those who have struggled to keep values foremost, have been too bloodless and too near-sighted in their vision. The defect of any philosophy of "adaptation" or "adjustment," even when it means adjustment to changing, living experience, is that there is no provision for thought or experience getting beyond itself. If your ideal is to be adjustment to your situation, in radiant cooperation with reality, then your success is likely to be just that and no more. You never transcend anything. You grow, but your spirit never jumps out of your skin to go on wild adventures. If your policy as a publicist reformer is to take what you can get, you are likely to find that you get something less than you should be willing to take. Italy in the settlement is said to be demanding one hundred in order to get twenty, and this machiavellian principle might well be adopted by the radical. Vision must constantly outshoot technique, opportunist efforts usually achieve less even than what seemed obviously possible. An impossibilist élan that appeals to desire will often carry further. A philosophy of adjustment will not even make for adjustment. If you try merely to "meet" situations as they come, you will not even meet them. Instead you will only pile up behind you deficits and arrears that will some day bankrupt you.

We are in the war because an American Government practised a philosophy of adjustment, and an instrumentalism for minor ends, instead of creating new values and setting at once a large standard to which the nations might repair. An intellectual attitude of mere adjustment, of mere use of the creative intelligence to make your progress, must end in caution, regression, and a virtual failure to effect even that change which you so clear-sightedly and desirously see. This is the root of our dissatisfaction with much of the current political and social realism that is preached to us. It has everything good and wise except the obstreperous vision that would drive and draw all men into it.

IV

The working-out of this American philosophy in our intellectual life then has meant an exaggerated emphasis on the mechanics of life at the expense of the quality of living. We suffer from a real shortage of spiritual values. A philosophy that worked when we were trying to get that material foundation for American life in which more impassioned living could flourish no longer works when we are faced with inexorable disaster and the hysterias of the mob. The note of complacency which we detect in the current expressions of this philosophy has a bad taste. The congruous note for the situation would seem to be, on the contrary, that of robust desperation, — a desperation that shall rage and struggle until new values come out of the travail, and we see some glimmering of our democratic way. In the creation of these new values, we may expect the old philosophy, the old radicalism, to be helpless. It has found a perfectly definite level, and there is no reason to think that it will not remain there. Its flowering appears in the technical organization of the war by an earnest group of young liberals, who direct their course by an opportunist programme of State-socialism at home and a league of benevolently-imperialistic nations abroad. At their best they can give us a government by prudent, enlightened college men instead of by politicians. At their best, they can abolish war by making everybody a partner in the booty of exploitation. That is all, and it is technically admirable. Only there is nothing in the outlook that touches in any way the happiness of the individual, the vivifying of the personality, the comprehension of social forces, the flair of art, — in other words, the quality of life. Our intellectuals have failed us as value-creators, even as value-emphasizers. The allure of the martial in war has passed only to be succeeded by the allure of the technical. The allure of fresh and true ideas, of free speculation, of artistic vigor, of cultural styles, of intelligence suffused by feeling, and feeling given fibre and outline by intelligence, has not come, and can hardly come, we see now, while our reigning philosophy is an instrumental one.

Whence can come this allure? Only from those who are thorough malcontents. Irritation at things as they are, disgust at the continual frustrations and aridities of American life, deep dissatisfaction with self and with the groups that give themselves forth as hopeful — out of such moods there might be hammered new values. The malcontents would be men and women who could not stomach the war, or the reactionary idealism that has followed in its train. They are quite through with the professional critics and classicists who have let cultural values die through their own personal ineptitude. Yet these malcontents have no intention of being cultural vandals, only to slay. They are not barbarians, but seek the vital and the sincere everywhere. All they want is a new orientation of the spirit that shall be modern, an orientation to accompany that technical orientation which is fast coming, and which the war accelerates. They will be harsh and often bad-tempered, and they will feel that the break-up of things is no time for mellowness. They will have a taste for spiritual adventure, and for sinister imaginative excursions. It will not be Puritanism so much as complacency that they will fight. A tang, a bitterness, an intellectual fibre, a verve, they will look for in literature, and their most virulent enemies will be those unaccountable radicals who are still morally servile, and are now trying to suppress all free speculation in the interests of nationalism. Something more mocking, more irreverent, they will constantly want. They will take institutions very lightly, indeed will never fail to be surprised at the seriousness with which good radicals take the stated offices and systems. Their own contempt will be scarcely veiled, and they will be glad if they can tease, provoke, irritate thought on any subject. These malcontents will be more or less of the American tribe of talent who used either to go immediately to Europe, or starved submissively at home. But these people will neither go to Europe, nor starve submissively. They are too much entangled emotionally in the possibilities of American life to leave it, and they have no desire whatever to starve. So they are likely to go ahead beating their heads at the wall until they are either bloody or light appears. They will give offense to their elders who cannot see what all the concern is about, and they will hurt the more middle-aged sense of adventure upon which the better integrated minds of the younger generation will have compromised. Optimism is often compensatory, and the optimistic mood in American thought may mean merely that American life is too terrible to face. A more skeptical, malicious, desperate, ironical mood may actually be the sign of more vivid and more stirring life fermenting in America today. It may be a sign of hope. That thirst for more of the intellectual "war and laughter" that we find Nietzsche calling us to may bring us satisfactions that optimism-haunted philosophies could never bring. Malcontentedness may be the beginning of promise. That is why I evoked the spirit of William James, with its gay passion for ideas, and its freedom of speculation, when I felt the slightly pedestrian gait into which the war had brought pragmatism. It is the creative desire more than the creative intelligence that we shall need if we are ever to fly.

XI

LIBERALISM IN THE INTER-WAR PERIOD

The consequences of the Treaty of Versailles and the world-wide Depression of the 1930's posed special threats to capitalism and to the liberal ideology that was its rationale. But as liberalism in Western Europe and America faced challenges from the Fascist right and the Communist left, two brilliant thinkers offered theories and programs for its defense.

The British economist John Maynard Keynes (1883–1946) capped his criticism of orthodox economic theory in 1936 with the publication of the now famous General Theory of Employment, Interest, and Money. *There he explained, contrary to accepted economic belief, that it was possible for an economy to be in equilibrium short of full employment of its resources. Keynes's theory offered an explanation for the depth and duration of the Great Depression and suggested that only massive government spending could effect recovery; the laissez-faire economists pursued a chimerical hope, Keynes insisted, when they argued that the economy would before long right itself.*

Keynes thus added a new dimension to the statist theories that had been building since the late nineteenth century. But though Keynes helped move liberal social thought further along in its endorsement of the positive state, he saw his own work as a compromise between older notions of laissez-faire and modern collectivism. Keynes believed that the essential features of capitalism should be saved, but that substantial reforms, along the lines he suggested in the General Theory, *were necessary.*

John Dewey (1859–1952), one of the most prominent and intellectually prolific American philosophers, shared several conceptions with Keynes. As one of the leaders of the pragmatic movement in philosophy, Dewey was committed to the idea that there could be no absolutes in theory or in practice. He therefore repudiated the monolithic totalitarian philosophies and political regimes that

Keynes likewise rejected. Further, Dewey followed William James in teaching that man's mind was an agent interacting with the environment, and that man, by employing his "creative intelligence" could shape his society. Thus Dewey, with Keynes, condemned the passive approach of laissez-faire economics. Though it was Keynes, the professional economist, who worked out a specific program of governmental action to regulate the economy, the two thinkers agreed on the general principle that modern industrial economies necessitated positive direction by the state.

Just as Keynes tried to effect a compromise between laissez-faire economics and the detailed direction of economic affairs envisioned in socialist theory, Dewey, though more friendly to socialism than Keynes, attempted to reconcile the individualistic values of nineteenth-century liberalism with the necessarily collective character of industrial life. Both men are important figures in the general modification of liberal theory that took place in Europe and America during the early part of the twentieth century.

The End of Laissez-Faire

(1926, 1936)

JOHN MAYNARD KEYNES

Let us clear from the ground the metaphysical or general principles upon which, from time to time, *laissez-faire* has been founded. It is *not* true that individuals possess a prescriptive "natural liberty" in their economic activities. There is *no* "compact" conferring perpetual rights on those who Have or on those who Acquire. The world is *not* so governed from above that private and social interest always coincide. It is *not* so managed here below that in practice they coincide. It is *not* a correct deduction from the Principles of Economics that enlightened self-interest always operates in the public interest. Nor is it true that self-interest generally *is* enlightened; more often individuals acting separately to promote their own ends are too ignorant or too weak to attain even these. Experience does *not* show that individuals, when they make up a

From *Essays in Persuasion* by John Maynard Keynes and *The General Theory of Employment, Interest and Money* by John Maynard Keynes. Reprinted by permission of Harcourt, Brace & World, Inc.

social unit, are always less clear-sighted than when they act separately.

We cannot, therefore, settle on abstract grounds, but must handle on its merits in detail, what Burke termed "one of the finest problems in legislation, namely, to determine what the State ought to take upon itself to direct by the public wisdom, and what it ought to leave, with as little interference as possible, to individual exertion." We have to discriminate between what Bentham, in his forgotten but useful nomenclature, used to term *Agenda* and *Non-Agenda,* and to do this without Bentham's prior presumption that interference is, at the same time, "generally needless" and "generally pernicious."[1] Perhaps the chief task of Economists at this hour is to distinguish afresh the *Agenda* of Government from the *Non-Agenda;* and the companion task of Politics is to devise forms of Government within a Democracy which shall be capable of accomplishing the *Agenda.* I will illustrate what I have in mind by two examples.

(1) I believe that in many cases the ideal size for the unit of control and organisation lies somewhere between the individual and the modern State. I suggest, therefore, that progress lies in the growth and the recognition of semi-autonomous bodies within the State — bodies whose criterion of action within their own field is solely the public good as they understand it, and from whose deliberations motives of private advantage are excluded, though some place it may still be necessary to leave, until the ambit of men's altruism grows wider, to the separate advantage of particular groups, classes, or faculties — bodies which in the ordinary course of affairs are mainly autonomous within their prescribed limitations, but are subject in the last resort to the sovereignty of the democracy expressed through Parliament.

I propose a return, it may be said, towards mediaeval conceptions of separate autonomies. But, in England at any rate, corporations are a mode of government which has never ceased to be important and is sympathetic to our institutions. It is easy to give examples, from what already exists, of separate autonomies which have attained or are approaching the mode I designate — the Universities, the Bank of England, the Port of London Authority, even perhaps the Railway Companies.

But more interesting than these is the trend of Joint Stock Institutions, when they have reached a certain age and size, to approximate to the status of public corporations rather than that of individualistic private enterprise. One of the most interesting and unnoticed developments of recent decades has been the tendency of big enterprise to socialise itself. A point arrives in the growth of a big institution — particularly a big railway or big public utility enterprise, but also a big

[1] Bentham's *Manual of Political Economy,* published posthumously, in Bowring's edition (1843).

bank or a big insurance company — at which the owners of the capital, *i.e.* the shareholders, are almost entirely dissociated from the management, with the result that the direct personal interest of the latter in the making of great profit becomes quite secondary. When this stage is reached, the general stability and reputation of the institution are more considered by the management than the maximum of profit for the shareholders. The shareholders must be satisfied by conventionally adequate dividends; but once this is secured, the direct interest of the management often consists in avoiding criticism from the public and from the customers of the concern. This is particularly the case if their great size or semi-monopolistic position renders them conspicuous in the public eye and vulnerable to public attack. The extreme instance, perhaps, of this tendency in the case of an institution, theoretically the unrestricted property of private persons, is the Bank of England. It is almost true to say that there is no class of persons in the Kingdom of whom the Governor of the Bank of England thinks less when he decides on his policy than of his shareholders. Their rights, in excess of their conventional dividend, have already sunk to the neighbourhood of zero. But the same thing is partly true of many other big institutions. They are, as time goes on, socialising themselves.

Not that this is unmixed gain. The same causes promote conservatism and a waning of enterprise. In fact, we already have in these cases many of the faults as well as the advantages of State Socialism. Nevertheless we see here, I think, a natural line of evolution. The battle of Socialism against unlimited private profit is being won in detail hour by hour. In these particular fields — it remains acute elsewhere — this is no longer the pressing problem. There is, for instance, no so-called important political question so really unimportant, so irrelevant to the reorganisation of the economic life of Great Britain, as the Nationalisation of the Railways.

It is true that many big undertakings, particularly Public Utility enterprises and other business requiring a large fixed capital, still need to be semi-socialised. But we must keep our minds flexible regarding the forms of this semi-socialism. We must take full advantage of the natural tendencies of the day, and we must probably prefer semi-autonomous corporations to organs of the Central Government for which Ministers of State are directly responsible.

I criticise doctrinaire State Socialism, not because it seeks to engage men's altruistic impulses in the service of Society, or because it departs from *laissez-faire*, or because it takes away from man's natural liberty to make a million, or because it has courage for bold experiments. All these things I applaud. I criticise it because it misses the significance of what is actually happening; because it is, in fact, little better than a dusty survival of a plan to meet the problems of fifty years ago, based on a misunderstanding of what some one said a hundred years ago. Nineteenth-century State Socialism sprang from Bentham, free competition, etc., and is in some respects a clearer, in some respects a more muddled, version of just the same philosophy as underlies nineteenth-century individualism. Both equally laid all their stress on freedom, the one negatively to avoid limitations on existing freedom, the other positively to destroy natural or acquired monopolies. They are different reactions to the same intellectual atmosphere.

(2) I come next to a criterion of *Agenda* which is particularly relevant to what it is urgent and desirable to do in the near future. We must aim at separating those services which are *technically social* from those which are *technically individual*. The most important *Agenda* of the State relate not to those activities which private individuals are already fulfilling, but to those functions which fall outside the sphere of the individual, to those decisions which are made by *no one* if the State does not make them. The important thing for Government is not to do things which individuals are doing already, and to do them a little better or a little worse; but to do those things which at present are not done at all.

It is not within the scope of my purpose on this occasion to develop practical policies. I limit myself, therefore, to naming some instances of what I mean from amongst those problems about which I happen to have thought most.

Many of the greatest economic evils of our time are the fruits of risk, uncertainty, and ignorance. It is because particular individuals, fortunate in situation or in abilities, are able to take advantage of uncertainty and ignorance, and also because for the same reason big business is often a lottery, that great inequalities of wealth come about; and these same factors are also the cause of the Unemployment of Labour, or the disappointment of reasonable business expectations, and of the impairment of efficiency and production. Yet the cure lies outside the operations of individuals; it may even be to the interest of individuals to aggravate the disease. I believe that the cure for these things is partly to be sought in the deliberate control of the currency and of credit by a central institution, and partly in the collection and dissemination on a great scale of data relating to the business situation, including the full publicity, by law if necessary, of all business facts which it is useful to know. These measures would involve Society in exercising directive intelligence through some appropriate organ of action over many of the inner intricacies of private business, yet it would leave private initiative and enterprise unhindered. Even if these measures prove insufficient, nevertheless they will furnish us with better knowledge than we have now for taking the next step.

My second example relates to Savings and Investment. I believe that some co-ordinated act of intelligent judgement is required as to the scale on which it is desirable that the community as a whole should save, the scale on which these savings should go abroad in the form of foreign investments, and whether the present organisation of the investment market distributes savings along the most nationally productive channels. I do not think that these matters should be left entirely to the chances of private judgement and private profits, as they are at present.

My third example concerns Population. The time has already come when each country needs a considered national policy about what size of Population, whether larger or smaller than at present or the same, is most expedient. And having settled this policy, we must take steps to carry it into operation. The time may arrive a little later when the community as a whole must pay attention to the innate quality as well as to the mere numbers of its future members.

These reflections have been directed towards possible improvements in the technique of modern Capitalism by the agency of collective action. There is nothing in them which is seriously incompatible with what seems to me to be the essential characteristic of Capitalism, namely the dependence upon an intense appeal to the money-making and money-loving instincts of individuals as the main motive force of the economic machine. Nor must I, so near to my end, stray towards other fields. Nevertheless, I may do well to remind you, in conclusion, that the fiercest contests and the most deeply felt divisions of opinion are likely to be waged in the coming years not round technical questions, where the arguments on either side are mainly economic, but round those which, for want of better words, may be called psychological or, perhaps, moral.

In Europe, or at least in some parts of Europe — but not, I think, in the United States of America — there is a latent reaction, somewhat widespread, against basing Society to the extent that we do upon fostering, encouraging, and protecting the money-motives of individuals. A preference for arranging our affairs in such a way as to appeal to the money-motive as little as possible, rather than as much as possible, need not be entirely *a priori*, but may be based on the comparison of experiences. Different persons, according to their choice of profession, find the money-motive playing a large or a small part in their daily lives, and historians can tell us about other phases of social organisation in which this motive has played a much smaller part than it does now. Most religions and most philosophies deprecate, to say the least of it, a way of life mainly influenced by considerations of personal money profit. On the other hand, most men to-day reject ascetic notions and do not doubt the real advantages of wealth. Moreover it seems obvious to them that one cannot do without the money-motive, and that, apart from certain admitted abuses, it does its job well. In the result the average man averts his attention from the problem, and has no clear idea what he really thinks and feels about the whole confounded matter.

Confusion of thought and feeling leads to confusion of speech. Many people, who are really objecting to Capitalism as a way of life, argue as though they were objecting to it on the ground of its inefficiency in attaining its own objects. Contrariwise, devotees of Capitalism are often unduly conservative, and reject reforms in its technique, which might really strengthen and preserve it, for fear that they may prove to be first steps away from Capitalism itself. Nevertheless a time may be coming when we shall get clearer than at present as to when we are talking about Capitalism as an efficient or inefficient technique, and when we are talking about it as desirable or objectionable in itself. For my part, I think that Capitalism, wisely managed, can probably be made more efficient for attaining economic ends than any alternative system yet in sight, but that in itself it is in many ways extremely objectionable. Our problem is to work out a social organisation which shall be as efficient as possible without offending our notions of a satisfactory way of life.

The next step forward must come, not from political agitation or premature experiments, but from thought. We need by an effort of the mind to elucidate our own feelings. At present our sympathy and our judgement are liable to be on different sides, which is a painful and paralysing state of mind. In the field of action reformers will not be successful until they can steadily pursue a clear and definite object with their intellects and their feelings in tune. There is no party in the world at present which appears to me to be pursuing right aims by right methods. Material Poverty provides the incentive to change precisely in situations where there is very little margin for experiments. Material Prosperity removes the incentive just when it might be safe to take a chance. Europe lacks the means, America the will, to make a move. We need a new set of convictions which spring naturally from a candid examination of our own inner feelings in relation to the outside facts.

The outstanding faults of the economic society in which we live are its failure to provide for full employment and its arbitrary and inequitable distribution of wealth and incomes. The bearing of the foregoing theory on the first of these is obvious. But there are also two important respects in which it is relevant to the second.

Since the end of the nineteenth century significant progress towards the removal of very great disparities of wealth and income has been achieved through the instrument of direct taxation — income tax and surtax and death duties — especially in Great Britain. Many people would wish to see this process carried much further, but they are deterred by two considerations; partly by the fear of making skilful evasions too much worth while and also of diminishing unduly the motive towards risk-taking, but mainly, I think, by the belief that the growth of capital depends upon the strength of the motive towards individual saving and that for a large proportion of this growth we are dependent on the savings of the rich out of their superfluity. Our argument does not affect the first of these considerations. But it may considerably modify our attitude towards the second. For we have seen that, up to the point where full employment prevails, the growth of capital depends not at all on a low propensity to consume but is, on the contrary, held back by it; and only in conditions of full employment is a low propensity to consume conducive to the growth of capital. Moreover, experience suggests that in existing conditions saving by institutions and through sinking funds is more than adequate, and that measures for the redistribution of incomes in a way likely to raise the propensity to consume may prove positively favourable to the growth of capital.

The existing confusion of the public mind on the matter is well illustrated by the very common belief that the death duties are responsible for a reduction in the capital wealth of the country. Assuming that the State applies the proceeds of these duties to its ordinary outgoings so that taxes on incomes and consumption are correspondingly reduced or avoided, it is, of course, true that a fiscal policy of heavy death duties has the effect of increasing the community's propensity to consume. But inasmuch as an increase in the habitual propensity to consume will in general (*i.e.* except in conditions of full employment) serve to increase at the same time the inducement to invest, the inference commonly drawn is the exact opposite of the truth.

Thus our argument leads towards the conclusion that in contemporary conditions the growth of wealth, so far from being dependent on the abstinence of the rich, as is commonly supposed, is more likely to be impeded by it. One of the chief social justifications of great inequality of wealth is, therefore, removed. I am not saying that there are no other reasons, unaffected by our theory, capable of justifying some measure of inequality in some circumstances. But it does dispose of the most important of the reasons why hitherto we have thought it prudent to move carefully. This particularly affects our attitude towards death duties; for there are certain justifications for inequality of incomes which do not apply equally to inequality of inheritances.

For my own part, I believe that there is social and psychological justification for significant inequalities of incomes and wealth, but not for such large disparities as exist to-day. There are valuable human activities which require the motive of money-making and the environment of private wealth-ownership for their full fruition. Moreover, dangerous human proclivities can be canalised into comparatively harmless channels by the existence of opportunities for money-making and private wealth, which, if they cannot be satisfied in this way, may find their outlet in cruelty, the reckless pursuit of personal power and authority, and other forms of self-aggrandisement. It is better that a man should tyrannise over his bank balance than over his fellow-citizens; and whilst the former is sometimes denounced as being but a means to the latter, sometimes at least it is an alternative. But it is not necessary for the stimulation of these activities and the satisfaction of these proclivities that the game should be played for such high stakes as at present. Much lower stakes will serve the purpose equally well, as soon as the players are accustomed to them. The task of transmuting human nature must not be confused with the task of managing it. Though in the ideal commonwealth men may have been taught or inspired or bred to take no interest in the stakes, it may still be wise and prudent statesmanship to allow the game to be played, subject to rules and limitations, so long as the average man, or even a significant section of the community, is in fact strongly addicted to the money-making passion.

There is, however, a second, much more fundamental inference from our argument which has a bearing on the future of inequalities of wealth; namely, our theory of the rate of interest. The justification for a moderately high rate of interest has been found hitherto in the necessity of providing a sufficient inducement to save. But we have shown that the extent of effective saving is necessarily determined by the scale of investment and that the scale of investment is promoted by a *low* rate of interest, provided that we do not attempt to stimulate it in this way beyond the point which corresponds to full employment. Thus it is to our best advantage to reduce the rate of interest to that point relative to the schedule of the marginal efficiency of capital at which there is full employment.

There can be no doubt that this criterion will lead to a much lower rate of interest than has ruled hitherto; and, so far as one can guess at the schedules of the marginal efficiency of capital corresponding to increasing amounts of capital, the rate of interest is likely to fall steadily, if it should be practicable to maintain conditions of more or less continuous full employment — unless, indeed, there is an excessive change in the aggregate propensity to consume (including the State).

I feel sure that the demand for capital is strictly limited in the sense that it would not be difficult to increase the stock of capital up to a point where its marginal efficiency had fallen to a very low figure. This would not mean that the use of capital instruments would cost almost nothing, but only that the return from them would have to cover little more than their exhaustion by wastage and obsolescence together with some margin to cover risk and the exercise of skill and judgement. In short, the aggregate return from durable goods in the course of their life would, as in the case of short-lived goods, just cover their labour-costs of production *plus* an allowance for risk and the costs of skill and supervision.

Now, though this state of affairs would be quite compatible with some measure of individualism, yet it would mean the euthanasia of the rentier, and, consequently, the euthanasia of the cumulative oppressive power of the capitalist to exploit the scarcity-value of capital. Interest to-day rewards no genuine sacrifice, any more than does the rent of land. The owner of capital can obtain interest because capital is scarce, just as the owner of land can obtain rent because land is scarce. But whilst there may be intrinsic reasons for the scarcity of land, there are no intrinsic reasons for the scarcity of capital. An intrinsic reason for such scarcity, in the sense of a genuine sacrifice which could only be called forth by the offer of a reward in the shape of interest, would not exist, in the long run, except in the event of the individual propensity to consume proving to be of such a character that net saving in conditions of full employment comes to an end before capital has become sufficiently abundant. But even so, it will still be possible for communal saving through the agency of the State to be maintained at a level which will allow the growth of capital up to the point where it ceases to be scarce.

I see, therefore, the rentier aspect of capitalism as a transitional phase which will disappear when it has done its work. And with the disappearance of its rentier aspect much else in it beside will suffer a sea-change. It will be, moreover, a great advantage of the order of events which I am advocating, that the euthanasia of the rentier, of the functionless investor, will be nothing sudden, merely a gradual but prolonged continuance of what we have seen recently in Great Britain, and will need no revolution.

Thus we might aim in practice (there being nothing in this which is unattainable) at an increase in the volume of capital until it ceases to be scarce, so that the functionless investor will no longer receive a bonus; and at a scheme of direct taxation which allows the intelligence and determination and executive skill of the financier, the entrepreneur *et hoc genus omne* (who are certainly so fond of their craft that their labour could be obtained much cheaper than at present), to be harnessed to the service of the community on reasonable terms of reward.

At the same time we must recognise that only experience can show how far the common will, embodied in the policy of the State, ought to be directed to increasing and supplementing the inducement to invest; and how far it is safe to stimulate the average propensity to consume, without forgoing our aim of depriving capital of its scarcity-value within one or two generations. It may turn out that the propensity to consume will be so easily strengthened by the effects of a falling rate of interest, that full employment can be reached with a rate of accumulation little greater than at present. In this event a scheme for the higher taxation of large incomes and inheritances might be open to the objection that it would lead to full employment with a rate of accumulation which was reduced considerably below the current level. I must not be supposed to deny the possibility, or even the probability, of this outcome. For in such matters it is rash to predict how the average man will react to a changed environment. If, however, it should prove easy to secure an approximation to full employment with a rate of accumulation not much greater than at present, an outstanding problem will at least have been solved. And it would remain for separate decision on what scale and by what means it is right and reasonable to call on the living generation to restrict their consumption, so as to establish, in course of time, a state of full investment for their successors.

In some other respects the foregoing theory is moderately conservative in its implications. For whilst it indicates the vital importance of establishing certain central controls in matters which are now left in the main to individual initiative, there are wide fields of activity which are unaffected. The State will have to exercise a guiding influence on the propensity to consume partly through its scheme of taxation, partly by fixing the rate of interest, and partly, perhaps, in other ways. Furthermore, it seems unlikely that the influence of banking policy on the rate of interest will be sufficient by itself to determine an optimum rate of investment. I conceive, therefore, that a somewhat comprehensive socialisation of investment will prove the only means of securing an approximation to full employment; though this need not exclude all manner of compromises and of devices by which public authority will co-operate with private initiative. But beyond this no obvious case is made out for a system of State Socialism which would embrace most of the economic life of the community. It is not the ownership of the instruments of production which it is important for the State to assume. If the State is able to determine the aggregate amount of resources devoted to augmenting the instruments and the basic rate of reward to those who own them, it will have accomplished all that is necessary. Moreover, the necessary measures of socialisation can be introduced gradually and without a break in the general traditions of society.

Our criticism of the accepted classical theory of economics has consisted not so much in finding logical flaws in its analysis as in pointing out that its tacit assumptions are seldom or never satisfied, with the result that it cannot solve the economic problems of the actual world. But if our central controls succeed in establishing an aggregate volume of output corresponding to full employment as nearly as is practicable, the classical theory comes into its own again from this point onwards. If we suppose the volume of output to be given, *i.e.* to be determined by forces outside the classical scheme of thought, then there is no objection to be raised against the classical analysis of the manner in which private self-interest will determine what in particular is produced, in what proportions the factors of production will be combined to produce it, and how the value of the final product will be distributed between them. Again, if we have dealt otherwise with the problem of thrift, there is no objection to be raised against the modern classical theory as to the degree of consilience between private and public advantage in conditions of perfect and imperfect competition respectively. Thus, apart from the necessity of central controls to bring about an adjustment between the propensity to consume and the inducement to invest, there is no more reason to socialise economic life than there was before.

To put the point concretely, I see no reason to suppose that the existing system seriously misemploys the factors of production which are in use. There are, of course, errors of foresight; but these would not be avoided by centralising decisions. When 9,000,000 men are employed out of 10,000,000 willing and able to work, there is no evidence that the labour of these 9,000,000 men is misdirected. The complaint against the present system is not that these 9,000,000 men ought to be employed on different tasks, but that tasks should be available for the remaining 1,000,000 men. It is in determining the volume, not the direction, of actual employment that the existing system has broken down.

Thus I agree with Gesell that the result of filling in the gaps in the classical theory is not to dispose of the "Manchester System," but to indicate the nature of the environment which the free play of economic forces requires if it is to realise the full potentialities of production. The central controls necessary to ensure full employment will, of course, involve a large extension of the traditional functions of government. Furthermore, the modern classical theory has itself called attention to various conditions in which the free play of economic forces may need to be curbed or guided. But there will still remain a wide field for the exercise of private initiative and responsibility. Within this field the traditional advantages of individualism will still hold good.

Let us stop for a moment to remind ourselves what these advantages are. They are partly advantages of efficiency — the advantages of decentralisation and of the play of self-interest. The advantage to efficiency of the decentralisation of decisions and of individual responsibility is even greater, perhaps, than the nineteenth century supposed; and the reaction against the appeal to self-interest may have gone too far. But, above all, individualism, if it can be purged of its defects and its abuses, is the best safeguard of personal liberty in the sense that, compared with any other system, it greatly widens the field for the exercise of personal choice. It is also the best safeguard of the variety of life, which emerges precisely from this extended field of personal choice, and the loss of which is the greatest of all the losses of the homogeneous or totalitarian state. For this variety preserves the traditions which embody the most secure and successful choices of former generations; it colours the present with the diversification of its fancy; and, being the handmaid of experiment as well as of tradition and of fancy, it is the most powerful instrument to better the future.

Whilst, therefore, the enlargement of the functions of government, involved in the task of adjusting to one another the propensity to consume and the inducement to invest, would seem to a nineteenth-century publicist or to a contemporary American financier to be a terrific encroachment on individualism, I defend it, on the contrary, both as the only practicable means of avoiding the destruction of existing economic forms in their entirety and as the condition of the successful functioning of individual initiative.

For if effective demand is deficient, not only is the public scandal of wasted resources intolerable, but the individual enterpriser who seeks to bring these resources into action is operating with the odds loaded against him. The game of hazard which he plays is furnished with many zeros, so that the players *as a whole* will lose if they have the energy and hope to deal all the cards. Hitherto the increment of the world's wealth has fallen short of the aggregate of positive individual savings; and the difference has been made up by the losses of those whose courage and initiative have not been supplemented by exceptional skill or unusual good fortune. But if effective demand is adequate, average skill and average good fortune will be enough.

The authoritarian state systems of to-day seem to solve the problem of unemployment at the expense of efficiency and of freedom. It is certain that the world will not much longer tolerate the unemployment which, apart from brief intervals of excitement, is associated — and, in my opinion, inevitably associated — with present-day capitalistic individualism. But it may be possible by a right analysis of the problem to cure the disease whilst preserving efficiency and freedom.

I have mentioned in passing that the new system might be more favourable to peace than the old has been. It is worth while to repeat and emphasise that aspect.

War has several causes. Dictators and others such, to whom war offers, in expectation at least, a pleasurable excitement, find it easy to work on the natural bellicosity of their peoples. But, over and above this, facilitating their task of fanning the popular flame, are the economic causes of war, namely, the pressure of population and the competitive struggle for markets. It is the second factor, which probably played a predominant part in the nineteenth century, and might again, that is germane to this discussion.

I have pointed out . . . that, under the system of domestic *laissez-faire* and an international gold standard such as was orthodox in the latter half of the nineteenth century, there was no means open to a government whereby to mitigate economic distress at home except through the competitive struggle for markets. For all measures helpful to a state of chronic or intermittent under-employment were ruled out, except measures to improve the balance of trade on income account.

Thus, whilst economists were accustomed to applaud the prevailing international system as furnishing the fruits of the international division of labour and harmonising at the same time the interests of different nations, there lay concealed a less benign influence; and those statesmen were moved by common sense and a correct apprehension of the true course of events, who believed that if a rich, old country were to neglect the struggle for markets its prosperity would droop and fail. But if nations can learn to provide themselves with full employment by their domestic policy (and, we must add, if they can also attain equilibrium in the trend of their population), there need be no important economic forces calculated to set the interest of one country against that of its neighbours. There would still be room for the international division of labour and for international lending in appropriate conditions. But there would no longer be a pressing motive why one country need force its wares on another or repulse the offerings of its neighbour, not because this was necessary to enable it to pay for what it wished to purchase, but with the express object of upsetting the equilibrium of payments so as to develop a balance of trade in its own favour. International trade would cease to be what it is, namely, a desperate expedient to maintain employment at home by forcing sales on foreign markets and restricting purchases, which, if successful, will merely shift the problem of unemployment to the neighbour which is worsted in the struggle, but a willing and unimpeded exchange of goods and services in conditions of mutual advantage.

Is the fulfilment of these ideas a visionary hope? Have they insufficient roots in the motives which govern the evolution of political society? Are the interests which they will thwart stronger and more obvious than those which they will serve?

I do not attempt an answer in this place. It would need a volume of a different character from this one to indicate even in outline the practical measures in which they might be gradually clothed. But if the ideas are correct — an hypothesis on which the author himself must necessarily base what he writes — it would be a mistake, I predict, to dispute their potency over a period of time. At the present moment people are unusually expectant of a more fundamental diagnosis; more particularly ready to receive it; eager to try it out, if it should be even plausible. But apart from this contemporary mood, the ideas of economists and political philosophers, both when they are right and when they are wrong, are more powerful than is commonly understood. Indeed the world is ruled by little else. Practical men, who believe themselves to be quite exempt from any intellectual influences, are usually the slaves of some defunct economist. Madmen in authority, who hear voices in the air, are distilling their frenzy from some academic scribbler of a few years back. I am sure that the power of vested interests is vastly exaggerated compared with the gradual encroachment of ideas. Not, indeed, immediately, but after a certain interval; for in the field of economic and political philosophy there are not many who are influenced by new theories after they are twenty-five or thirty years of age, so that the ideas which civil servants and politicians and even agitators apply to current events are not likely to be the newest. But, soon or late, it is ideas, not vested interests, which are dangerous for good or evil.

The Individual in the New Society

(1918, 1930, 1939)

JOHN DEWEY

I. The Individual in the Cultural Crisis [1]

Anthropologically speaking, we are living in a money culture. Our materialism, our devotion to money making and to having a good time, are not things by themselves. They are the product of the fact that we live in a money culture; of the fact that our technique and technology are controlled by interest in private profit. There lies the serious and fundamental defect of our civilization, the source of the secondary and induced evils to which so much attention is given. Critics are dealing with symptoms and effects. The evasion of fundamental economic causes by critics both foreign and native seems to me to be an indication of the prevalence of the old European tradition, with its disregard for the body, material things, and practical concerns. The development of the American type, in the sense of the critics, is an expression of the fact that we

From Joseph Ratner, ed., *Intelligence in the Modern World: John Dewey's Philosophy* (New York: Random House, 1939), 405–433.

[1] From *Individualism Old and New* [1930]. The passages have been selected and arranged from all parts of the book. Ed.

have retained this tradition and the economic system of private gain on which it is based, while at the same time we have made an independent development of industry and technology that is nothing short of revolutionary. When our critics deal with this issue instead of avoiding it there will be something really doing.

Until the issue is met, the confusion of a civilization divided against itself will persist. The mass development, which our European critics tell us has submerged individuality, *is* the product of a machine age; in some form it will follow in all countries from the extension of a machine technology. Its immediate effect has been, without doubt, a subjection of certain types of individuality. As far as individuality is associated with aristocracy of the historic type, the extension of the machine age will presumably be hostile to individuality in its traditional sense all over the world.

There are two "solutions" that fail to solve. One of these is the method of avoidance. This course is taken as far as it is assumed that the only valid type of individuality is that which holds over from the ages that anteceded machine technology and the democratic society it creates. The course that is complementary to the method of escape springs from assumption that the present situation is final; that it presents something inherently ultimate and fixed. Only as it is treated as transitive and moving, as material to be dealt with in shaping a later outcome, only, that is, as it is treated as a *problem*, is the idea of any solution genuine and relevant. We may well take the formula advanced by European critics as a means of developing our consciousness of some of the conditions of the problem. So regarded, the problem is seen to be essentially that of creation of a new individualism as significant for modern conditions as the old individualism at its best was for its day and place.

The first step in further definition of this problem is realization of the collective age which we have already entered.

There is no word which adequately expresses what is taking place. "Socialism" has too specific political and economic associations to be appropriate. "Collectivism" is more neutral, but it, too, is a party-word rather than a descriptive term. Perhaps the constantly increasing role of corporations in our economic life gives a clew to a fitting name. The word may be used in a wider sense than is conveyed by its technical legal meaning. We may then say that the United States has steadily moved from an earlier pioneer individualism to a condition of dominant corporateness. The influence business corporations exercise in determining present industrial and economic activities is both a cause and a symbol of the tendency to combination in all phases of life. Associations tightly or loosely organized more and more define the opportunities, the choices and the actions of individuals. The need of the present is to apprehend the fact that, for better or worse, we are living in a corporate age.

It is of the nature of society as of life to contain a balance of opposed forces. Actions and reactions are ultimately equal and counterpart. At present the "socialization" is largely mechanical and quantitative. The system is kept in a kind of precarious balance by the movement toward lawless and reckless overstimulation among individuals. If the chaos and the mechanism are to generate a mind and soul, an integrated personality, it will have to be an intelligence, a sentiment and an individuality of a new type.

Assured and integrated individuality is the product of definite social relationship and publicly acknowledged functions. Judged by this standard, even those who seem to be in control, and to carry the expression of their special individual abilities to a high pitch, are submerged. They may be captains of finance and industry, but until there is some consensus of belief as to the meaning of finance and industry in civilization as a whole, they cannot be captains of their own souls — their beliefs and aims. They exercise leadership surreptitiously and, as it were, absent-mindedly. They lead, but it is under cover of impersonal and socially undirected economic forces. Their reward is found not in what they do, in their social office and function, but in a deflection of social consequences to private gain. They receive the acclaim and command the envy and admiration of the crowd, but the crowd is also composed of private individuals who are equally lost to a sense of social bearings and uses.

The explanation is found in the fact that while the actions promote corporate and collective results, these results are outside their intent and irrelevant to that reward of satisfaction which comes from a sense of social fulfillment. To themselves and to others, their business is private and its outcome is private profit. No complete satisfaction is possible where such a split exists. Hence the absence of a sense of social value is made up for by an exacerbated acceleration of the activities that increase private advantage and power. One cannot look into the inner consciousness of his fellows; but if there is any general degree of inner contentment on the part of those who form our pecuniary oligarchy, the evidence is sadly lacking. As for the many, they are impelled hither and yon by forces beyond their control.

The unrest, impatience, irritation and hurry that are so marked in American life are inevitable accompaniments of a situation in which individuals do not find support and contentment in the fact that they are sustaining and sustained members of a social whole. They are evidence, psychologically, of abnormality, and it is as idle to seek for their explanation within the deliberate intent of individuals as it is futile to think that they can be got rid of by hortatory moral appeal. Only an acute maladjustment between individuals and the social conditions under which they live can account for such widespread pathological phenomena. Feverish love of anything as long as it is a change which is distracting, impatience, unsettlement, nervous discontentment and desire for excitement, are not native to human nature. They are so abnormal as to demand explanation in some deep-seated cause.

Instances of the flux in which individuals are loosened from the ties that once gave order and support to their lives are glaring. They are indeed so glaring that they blind our eyes to the causes which produce them. Individuals are groping their way through situations which they do not direct and which do not give them direction. The beliefs and ideals that are uppermost in their consciousness are not relevant to the society in which they outwardly act and which constantly reacts upon them. Their conscious ideas and standards are inherited from an age that has passed away; their minds, as far as consciously entertained principles and methods of interpretation are concerned, are at odds with actual conditions. This profound split is the cause of distraction and bewilderment.

Because of the bankruptcy of the older individualism, those who are aware of the breakdown often speak and argue as if individualism were itself done and over with. I do not suppose that those who regard socialism and individualism as antithetical really mean that individuality is going to die out or that it is not something intrinsically precious. But in speaking as if the only individualism were the local episode of the last two centuries, they play into the hands of those who would keep it alive in order to serve their own ends, and they slur over the chief problem — that of remaking society to serve the growth of a new type of individual. There are many who believe that socialism of some form is needed to realize individual initiative and security on a wide scale. They are concerned about the restriction of power and freedom to a few in the present régime, and they think that collective social control is necessary, at least for a time, in order to achieve its advantages for all. But they too often seem to assume that the result will be merely an extension of the earlier individualism to the many.

Such thinking treats individualism as if it were something static, having a uniform content. It ignores the fact that the mental and moral structure of individuals, the pattern of their desires and purposes, change with every great change in social constitution. Individuals who are not bound together in associations, whether domestic, economic, religious, political, artistic or educational, are monstrosities. It is absurd to suppose that the ties which hold them together are merely external and do not react into mentality and character, producing the framework of personal disposition.

The tragedy of the "lost individual" is due to the fact that while individuals are now caught up into a vast complex of associations, there is no harmonious and coherent reflection of the import of these connections into the imaginative and emotional outlook on life. This fact is of course due in turn to the absence of harmony within the state of society. There is an undoubted circle. But it is a vicious circle only as far as men decline to accept — in the intellectual, observing and inquiring spirit — the realities of the social estate, and because of this refusal either surrender to the division or seek to save their individuality by escape or sheer emotional revolt. The habit of opposing the corporate and collective to the individual tends to the persistent continuation of the confusion and uncertainty. It distracts attention from the crucial issue: How shall the individual refind himself in an unprecedentedly new social situation, and what qualities will the new individualism exhibit?

It is not too much to say that the whole significance of the older individualism has now shrunk to a pecuniary scale and measure. The virtues that are supposed to attend rugged individualism may be vocally proclaimed, but it takes no great insight to see that what is cherished is measured by its connection with those activities that make for success in business conducted for personal gain. Hence, the irony of the gospel of "individualism" in business conjoined with suppression of individuality in thought and speech. One cannot imagine a bitterer comment on any professed individualism than that it subordinates the only creative individuality — that of mind — to the maintenance of a regime which gives the few an opportunity for being shrewd in the management of monetary business.

There is at least this much truth in economic determinism. Industry is not outside of human life, but within it. The genteel tradition shuts its eyes to this fact; emotionally and intellectually it pushes industry and its material phase out into a region remote from human values. To stop with mere emotional rejection and moral condemnation of industry and trade as materialistic is to leave them in this inhuman region where they operate as the instruments of those who employ them for private ends. Exclusion of this sort is an accomplice of the forces that keep things in the saddle. There is a subterranean partnership between those who employ the existing economic order for selfish pecuniary gain and those who turn their backs upon it in the interest of personal complacency, private dignity, and irresponsibility.

Every occupation leaves its impress on individual character and modifies the outlook on life of those who carry it on. No one questions this fact as respects wage-earners tied to the machine, or business men who devote themselves to pecuniary manipulations. Callings may have their roots in innate impulses of human nature but their pursuit does not merely "express" these impulses, leaving them unaltered; their pursuit determines intellectual horizons, precipitates knowledge and ideas, shapes desire and interest. This influence operates in the case of those who set up fine art, science, or religion as ends in themselves, isolated from radiation and expansion into other concerns (such radiation being what "application" signifies) as much as in the case of those who engage in industry. The alternatives are lack of application with consequent narrowing and overspecialization, and application with enlargement and increase of liberality. The narrowing in the case of industry pursued apart from social ends is evident to all thoughtful persons. Intellectual and literary folks who conceive themselves devoted to pursuit of pure truth and uncontaminated beauty too readily overlook the fact that a similar narrowing and hardening take place in them. Their goods are more refined, but they are also engaged in acquisition; unless they are concerned with use, with expansive interactions, they too become monopolists of capital. And the monopolization of spiritual capital may in the end be more harmful than that of material capital.

There are, I suppose, those who fancy that the emphasis which I put upon the corporateness of existing society in the United States is in effect, even if not in the writer's conscious intent, a plea for greater conformity than now exists. Nothing could be further from the truth. Identification of society with a level of uniformity, whatever it be, high as well as low, is just another evidence of that distraction because of which the individual is lost. Society is of course but the relations of individuals to one another in this form and that. And all relations are interactions, not fixed molds. The particular interactions that compose a human society include the give and take of participation, of a sharing that increases, that expands and deepens, the capacity and significance of the interacting factors. Conformity is a name for the absence of vital interplay; the arrest and benumbing of communication. It is the artificial substitute used to hold men together in lack of associations that are incorporated into inner dispositions of thought and desire. I often wonder what meaning is given to the term "society" by those who oppose it to the intimacies of personal intercourse, such as those of friendship. Presumably they have in their minds a picture of rigid institutions or some set and external organization. But an institution that is other than the structure of human contact and intercourse is a fossil of some past society; organization, as in any living organism, is the coöperative consensus of multitudes of cells, each living in exchange with others.

We are given to thinking of society in large and vague ways. We should forget "society" and think of law, industry, religion, medicine, politics, art, education, philosophy — and think of them in the plural. For points of contact are not the same for any two persons and hence the questions which the interests and occupations pose are never twice the same. There is no contact so immutable that it will not yield at some point. All these callings and concerns are the avenues through which the world acts upon us and we upon the world. There is no society at large, no business in general. Harmony with conditions is not a single and monotonous uniformity, but a diversified affair requiring individual attack. It is the part of wisdom to note the double meaning of such ideas as "acceptance." There is an acceptance that is of the intellect; it signifies facing facts for what they are. There is another acceptance that is of the emotions and will; that involves commitment of desire and effort. So far are the two from being identical that acceptance in the first sense is the precondition of all intelligent refusal of acceptance in the second sense. There is a prophetic aspect to all observation; we can perceive the meaning of what exists only as we forecast the consequences it entails. When a situation is as confused and divided within itself as is the present social estate, choice is implicated in observation. As one perceives different tendencies and different possible consequences, preference inevitably goes out to one or the other. Because acknowledgment in thought brings with it intelligent discrimination and choice, it is the first step out of confusion, the first step in forming those objects of significant allegiance out of which stable and efficacious individuality may grow. It might even perform the miracle of rendering conservatism relevant and thoughtful. It certainly is the prerequisite of an anchored liberalism.

Individuality is inexpugnable because it is a manner of distinctive sensitivity, selection, choice, response and utilization of conditions. For this reason, if for no other, it is impossible to develop integrated individuality by any all-embracing system or program. No individual can make the determination for anyone else; nor can he make it for himself all at once and forever. A native manner of selection gives direction and continuity, but definite expression is found in changing occasions and varied forms. The selective choice and use of conditions have to be continually made and remade. Since we live in a moving world and change with our interactions in it, every act produces a new perspective that demands a new exercise of preference. If, in the long run, an individual remains lost, it is because he has chosen irresponsibility; and if he remains wholly depressed, it is because he has chosen the course of easy parasitism.

Individuality is at first spontaneous and unshaped; it is a potentiality, a capacity of development. Even so, it is a unique manner of acting in and with a world of objects and persons. It is not something complete in itself, like a closet in a house or a secret drawer in a desk, filled with treasures that are waiting to be bestowed on the world. Since individuality is a distinctive way of feeling the impacts of the world and of showing a preferential bias in response to these impacts, it develops into shape and form only through interaction with actual conditions; it is no more complete in itself than is a painter's tube of paint without relation to a canvas. The work of art is the truly individual thing; and it is the result of the interaction of paint and canvas through the medium of the artist's distinctive vision and power. In its determination, the potential individuality of the artist takes on visible and enduring form. The imposition of individuality as something made in advance always gives evidence of a mannerism, not of a manner. For the latter is something original and creative; something formed in the very process of creation of other things.

The future is always unpredictable. Ideals, including that of a new and effective individuality, must themselves be framed out of the possibilities of existing conditions, even if these be the conditions that constitute a corporate and industrial age. The ideals take shape and gain a content as they operate in remaking conditions. We may, in order to have continuity of direction, plan a program of action in anticipation of occasions as they emerge. But a program of ends and ideals if kept apart from sensitive and flexible method becomes an encumbrance. For its hard and rigid character assumes a fixed world and a static individual; and neither of these things exists. It implies that we can prophesy the future — an attempt which terminates, as someone has said, in prophesying the past or in its reduplication.

II. The Economic Basis of the New Society [2]

The imminence of the "next world war" has caused the last World War to recede from thought, discussion and imagination except in negative ways. During the progress of the World War positive attitudes and hopes were generated and positive plans and objectives put forward for the creation of a better human society. The fact that these hopes were betrayed and objectives failed to be realized is evidence of our failure to take advantage of the opportunity that was unquestionably there. It is not a condemnation of those hopes and objectives.

The constructive thought of that period centered about two comprehensive objectives: the establishment of a system of international law that would ensure peaceful relations between nations; and the reorganization of the social and economic relations within nations. Passing over the former objective, let us consider the latter.

I quote the statement I made then concerning the objectives for internal social reorganization then afoot, plans and programs, it may be pointed out, which claimed the attention not only of progressive individuals but of political parties. Unfortunately, I need make no apology for quoting from an article written nearly twenty years ago. The evils existing then still exist now, the things needing to be done then still need to be done now.

[2] Written specially for [*Intelligence in the Modern World* (1939)].

"The first of the deficiencies which will have to be cared for in any effective reorganization which may take place after the war is the failure of our social order in the past to secure to its members steady and useful employment. It would be difficult to bring any more severe indictment against anything that calls itself a civilization, than the fact that it is not able to utilize the energy, physical, intellectual and moral, of the members who are desirous and anxious of rendering some kind of service, of producing some kind of needed and useful commodity; that it has not been able systematically to give all of its members a chance to do something. The evil, and the unnecessary character of the evil of unemployment is, then, the thing which I would put first, because it represents, in anything that professes to be civilization, the most obvious and definite point of weakness.

"Now, this is serious, not merely from the standpoint of the enormous poverty and misery which insecure and precarious employment entails upon a large part of the population, but, if possible, even more serious because of the undermining of morale, of character, which comes with such a situation as this. We all know how demoralizing charity is. Every society of organized charity is teaching and constantly preaching the evils of indiscriminate charity, how it destroys the character of those who become its recipients. Cannot we generalize this lesson and apply it to the whole industrial situation? What is the effect upon the self-respect of the large classes of men and women who periodically, once in so often, find themselves in large numbers thrown out of employment, and find that they have to beg, not for charity, but for even a chance to do work in turning out commodities or in rendering services which society actually needs? The undermining of confidence in oneself, of respect for oneself, the undermining of faith or belief in the world and in others that comes because of precarious and insecure tenure of employment is I think impossible to overestimate. When people find that they cannot do things that they are capable of doing, the attitude that comes toward the world is either one of impotence and enfeeblement, or else one of bitterness and hostility. Now, these things are, perhaps, sufficiently obvious. They are not new. There was plenty of discussion of the problem of unemployment and the remedies for it, before the war, but the war in its conduct has made the consciousness of it more acute and more general, and it has shown that the problem is not inevitable, that it is capable of human administration and handling. It has proved that it is possible for men, pooling and organizing their intelligence and experience, and having the authority of the government behind them, to take hold of the industrial and economic processes and see to it, even in a period of such great stress as during the war, that no man or woman who is capable of work shall lack useful, steady, and reasonably remunerative employment.

"The second evil is the degraded and inhuman standard, or scale, of living which is found on the part of so many of the industrial population — of course, partly as a consequence of chronic employment or, at least, insecure employment, but partly because of the low rate of return for employment. We are accustomed, of course, to connect low wages and lack of work with poverty and suffering, but we too often fail to translate poverty and the misery that goes with it into terms of the general vitiation, the general deterioration of the scale of life on the part of a large element of the population. We fail to note what an unhuman lowering it means of the standard of physical health — though here again was a point that was being agitated more and more, even before the war, involving a consideration of the question of the socially unnecessary deaths, illnesses, accidents and incapacitations that come from the bad economic conditions under which so much of modern industry is carried on. We need only to think of the conditions under which masses of our populations live, not merely in the slums, but wherever there is a congested industrial population, to realize how low, as compared with the attained standards of the well-to-do element of the population their plane of living really is.

"In the third place, the war has revealed the serious weaknesses and defects which exist with respect to efficiency of production and distribution. Now, this is the particular phase of the matter upon which our existing old social order most prided itself. It might have admitted that it had not done so well with the human side of the problem, but it has been contended that, so far as efficiency in the invention, organization and utilization of the machinery of production and distribution is concerned, the present age is almost infinitely in advance of any that has preceded. Of course, in a certain sense, as compared with older civilizations — those that came before the great industrial revolution — this is true enough; for these mechanical inventions are, of course, the product of scientific discovery. They are the product of the release of men's minds in the study of nature and the mystery of natural forces. It is a great mistake to suppose that our mechanical inventions of machines and implements — the steam engine, the telegraph, the telephone, the motor car, and the other agencies of production and distribution — are the actual fruit of the present industrial order. On the contrary, they are the fruit of the discoveries of a comparatively small number of scientific men who have not labored for recognition and who have never got it, very much — at least, in the way of pecuniary recognition. It simply happened that conditions were such that the men of means, men possessed of the financial and pecuniary resources, could utilize these fruits of natural science.

"Furthermore, efficiency is not an absolute thing; but, of course, as every engineer tells us, it is a matter of ratio. Efficiency is a matter of the ratio which the actual output bears to the available resources; and looked at from that standpoint, not in comparison with the output of past ages, but as a matter of ratio which exists now between the present output and the resources now available, we cannot pride ourselves on having attained any great amount of even industrial efficiency in production. I need hardly remind you of the fact that when greater efficiency was required in England and in this country, the government had to take charge of the distributing agencies, the railroads. I need not remind you of the breakdown in the production and distribution of coal, from which we suffered; and however much or however little the blame for that is to be laid at the doors of any particular individuals, the real difficulty, of course, goes much further back. It goes back to the fact that we have had production and distribution organized on a non-social basis — a basis of pecuniary profit. And when they suddenly had to be switched over to the basis of public need and public service, they naturally broke down. The great inefficiency here is, however, the failure to utilize human power. The great advance has, of course, been in the utilizing of natural power — steam and electricity, the machines, implements, and so on; but we have not succeeded in engaging, enlisting and releasing available human energy.

"The first great demand of a better social order, I should say, then, is the guarantee of the right, to every individual who is capable of it, to work — not the mere legal right, but a right which is enforceable so that the individual will always have the opportunity to engage in some form of useful activity; and if the ordinary economic machinery breaks down through a crisis of some sort, then it is the duty of the state to come to the rescue and see that individuals have something to do that is worth while — not breaking stone in a stone yard, or something else to get a soup ticket with, but some kind of productive work which a self-respecting person may engage in with interest and with more than mere pecuniary profit. Whatever may be said about the fortunes of what has technically been called socialism, it would seem to be simply the part of ordinary common sense that society should reorganize itself to make sure that individuals can make a living and be kept going, not by charity, but by having productive work to do.

"In the second place, war has revealed the *possibilities* of intelligent administration — administration which *could* be used to raise and maintain on a higher level the general standard and scale of living. The minimum wage is not one of the visions of the nations that have been longer in the war than we have; it is not, with them, a dream, an uplift notion: it is an accomplished fact. Great Britain is already spending an immense amount of money for the housing of its laborers, and, as we have found out in connection with our shipping program, we cannot do what we have got to do, unless we first see to it that there are decent, comfortable and sanitary housing facilities for the population. One of the demands which has already been made in England, which would help, also, to take care of the unemployment problem after the war, is that this great work of housing, conducted under national social auspices, shall go on until the slums, with their bad sanitary, moral, and bad esthetic influence, have disappeared and every individual has a home to live in and surroundings to live in which observe the ordinary amenities of human life. The movements for insurance against accident, insurance against illness, insurance against the contingencies of old age, which were already active before the war, have also, of course, been given a tremendous acceleration.

"The third phase that I mention is the need of securing greater industrial autonomy, that is to say, greater ability on the part of the workers in any particular trade or occupation to control that industry, instead of working under these conditions of external control where they have no interest, no insight into what they are doing, and no social outlook upon the consequences and meaning of what they are doing. This means an increasing share given to the laborer, to the wage earner, in controlling the conditions of his own activity. It is so common to point out the absurdity of conducting a war for political democracy which leaves industrial and economic autocracy partically untouched, that I think we are absolutely bound to see, after the war, either a period of very great unrest, disorder, drifting, strife — I would not say actual civil war, but all kinds of irregular strife and disorder, or a movement to install the principle of self-government within industries.

"These three things, then, seem to me the essential minimum elements of an intelligent program of social reorganization."

The idea of reconstruction was at the time the foregoing was written something to conjure with. In retrospect, we may come to the conclusion, widely prevalent today, that the whole idea of social reorganization was an illusion bred of the excited state of mind of the war. If that idea seems an illusion today, it is because we failed to *learn* the lesson, which could be truly learned only by carrying it out into practice. If we fail to learn the lessons of the present day — in fundamental respects identical with those of twenty years ago — then we may be sure that twenty years hence our present most ardent hopes and inspired programs will also be dismissed as illusions.

To quote again:

"Now, in such a situation as this, we are not, I think, entitled to unthinking optimism about the certainty of great progress or about the particular direction which social reorganization will take after the war. There is going to be, of course, a very great demand and a very great pressure, especially from the side of labor, but there will also be a very great inertia, very great obstacles and difficulties to contend with. We are not entitled to assume that automatically there is going to be a desirable reorganization and reconstruction after the war. We may, possibly — it is conceivable — go through a long period of social drifting and social unrest. The question is whether society, because of the experience of the war, will learn to utilize the intelligence, the insight and foresight which are available, in order to take hold of the problem and to go at it, step by step, on the basis of an intelligent program — a program which is not too rigid, which is not a program in the sense of having every item definitely scheduled in advance, but which represents an outlook upon the future of the things which most immediately require doing, trusting to the experience which is got in doing them to reveal the next things needed and the next steps to be taken. Now, the one great thing that the war has accomplished, it seems to me, of a permanent sort, is the enforcement of a psychological and educational lesson. Before the war, most persons would have said, who recognized these evils: Well, they are very great. We all recognize them. We deplore them, but the whole situation is so big and so complicated that it is not possible to do any thing about it. We have got to wait for the slow process of evolution. We have got to wait for the working out of unconscious, natural law to accomplish anything serious and important in the way of reorganization. Well, I think the war has absolutely put an end to the right to the claim of anybody to say things of that sort. It is proved now that it is possible for human beings to take hold of human affairs and manage them, to see an end which has to be gained, a purpose which must be fulfilled, and deliberately and intelligently to go to work to organize the means, the resources and the methods of accomplishing those results.

"It seems to me that we cannot in any good conscience return, after the war, to the old period of drifting, so-called evolution, as a necessary method of procedure. The real question with us will be one of effectively discerning whether intelligent men of the community really want to bring about a better reorganized social order. If the desire, the will and the purpose are strong enough, it has been demonstrated that, under conditions of very great strain — abnormal strain and pressure — human beings can get together coöperatively and bring their physical resources and their intellectual resources to bear upon the problem of managing society, instead of letting society drift along more or less at the mercy of accident." [3]

Events after the war in this country seemed to give the lie to the hopes then entertained. "Return to Normalcy" was not only the slogan but the practice — "normalcy" meaning the old social-economic regime. Attempts at radical social change were defeated in Europe in every coun-

[3] All quotations from an article entitled "Internal Social Reorganization After the War," first printed in the *Journal of Race Development*, April 1918; reprinted in *Characters and Events*, vol, II pp. 745 ff.

try save Russia. Italy and Germany moved into Fascist dictatorships and other European and South American countries in that direction. Social reorganization did take place but in a direction opposite to that of the hopes entertained by liberals and radicals in the earlier period. Nevertheless, the forecast of "serious internal disorder and unrest" has been fulfilled.

After the world depression of 1929, the earlier idea of reconstruction revived, not under that name but, in this country, under the slogan of the New Deal. It has become increasingly evident that the conditions which caused the World War remain in full force, intensified indeed by the growth of exacerbated Nationalism — which is the direction in which "internal social reorganization" has in fact mainly moved. Failure of the world communities to "meet and forestall" needed change with "sympathy and intelligence" has left us with the old problems unsolved and new ones added.

The change is not, however, a matter of mere addition. Re-grouping of forces has crystallized forces which were more or less in solution and has given a new face, theoretically and practically, to the whole set of social problems that is involved. The urgent and central question at the present time is whether the needed economic-social changes (with which legal and political changes are bound up) can be effected in ways which preserve and develop what was fundamental in earlier liberalism, or whether social control is to be instituted by means of coercive governmental control from above in ways which destroy for a time (a time whose length cannot now be measured) all that was best worth conserving in older democratic ideas and ideals: intellectual and moral freedom; freedom of inquiry and expression; freedom of association in work, recreation and for religious purposes; the freedom of intercourse among nations which, always hampered by tariff-walls and fear of war, is now deliberately suppressed in many countries by a multitude of new technical devices.

This new face of the problem is far from being exhibited solely in Fascist nations, although in them the suppression of liberties of thought, expression and teaching; the dissolution of voluntary groupings, such as trade unions; the threat to voluntary association for worship; and the prevention of free intercourse with other nations have their most marked expression. Nor is the problem confined to the one country in which reconstruction in the line of collectivist control during the early period after the World War made the most headway; for, contrary to the earlier belief in the "withering away of the State," governmental restriction of the essential liberties for which democracy stood has reached, through control of thought, expression, propaganda and direct coercion, a point in which there is little difference discernible between the U.S.S.R. and Fascist countries.

The fundamental problem is also acute in the countries that remain democratic in form and that so far have maintained, though with many violations, the ancient democratic liberties of free inquiry, free assembly, and freedom of voluntary association. For in these countries we have to a very large extent a continuation of the older policy of social drifting plus an amount of social tinkering accompanied by social unrest and uncertainty. Experience has proved that this policy is attended by economic collapse and breakdowns of ever increasing severity. As long as the alternatives set before us are rigid governmental control on the one hand, whether of the Fascist or the Russian type, and "democracy" of the drifting type on the other hand, the question to which I referred in the article quoted, "whether society will learn to utilize the intelligence, the insight and foresight which are available to go at the problem" of economic-social readjustment remains and is even more urgent today in this country than it was when the words were first written.

How much progress has been made in the intervening years? How does the situation now stand? We have a recognition which did not exist before of social responsibility for the care of the unemployed whose resources are exhausted in consequence of unemployment. But at best, the method we employ is palliative: it comes after the event. The positive problem of instituting a social-economic order in which all those capable of productive work will do the work for which they are fitted remains practically untouched. As a result, the conduct of relief and charitable care is almost never at what was termed "at the best." The personal deterioration that results from enforced idleness is a coercion which excludes the idle from the factors that contribute most effectively to decent self-respect and to personal development. While the mass of unemployed have met the situation with patience and even dignity, there can be no question that the corroding influence of living without work, upon the charity of others, private and public, is operating. In the long run, it would be difficult to find anything more destructive of the best elements of human nature than a continued prospect of living, at least of subsisting, in more or less parasitical dependence upon charity, even if it is public.

In saying these things, I am expressing no sympathy for those who complain about the growing amount of money spent upon taking care of those thrown out of productive work and the consequent increase in taxation. Much less am I expressing sympathy with the reckless charges brought against the unemployed of loving idleness and wishing to live at the expense of society. Such complaints and charges are the product of refusal to look at the causes which produce the situation and of desire to find an alibi for their refusal to do anything to remove the causes — causes which are inherent in the existing social-economic regime. The problem of establishing social conditions which will make it possible for all who are capable to do socially productive work is not an easy one. I am not engaging in criticism because it has not been solved. I am pointing out that the problem is not even being thought much about, not to speak of being systematically faced. The reason for the great refusal is clear. To face it would involve the problem of remaking a profit system into a system conducted not just, as is sometimes said, in the interest of consumption, important as that is, but also in the interest of positive and enduring opportunity for productive and creative activity and all that that signifies for the development of the potentialities of human nature.

What gain has been made in the matter of establishing conditions that give the mass of workers not only what is called "security" but also constructive interest in the work they do? What gain has been made in giving individuals, the great mass of individuals, an opportunity to find themselves and then to educate themselves for what they can best do in work which is socially useful and such as to give free play in development of themselves? The managers of industries here and there have learned that it pays to have conditions such that those who are employed know enough about what they are doing so as to take an interest in it. Educators here and there are awake to the need of discovering vocational and occupational abilities and to the need of readjusting the school system to build upon what is discovered. But the basic trouble is not the scantiness of efforts in these directions, serious as is their paucity. It is again that the whole existing industrial system tends to nullify in large measure the effects of these efforts even when they are made. The problem of the adjustment of individual capacities and their development to actual occupations is not a one-sided or unilateral one. It is bilateral and reciprocal. It is a matter of the state of existing occupations, of the whole set-up of productive work, of the structure of the industrial system. Even if there were a much more widespread and searching concern with the capacities of individuals and much more preparation of them along the lines of their inherent fitness and needs than now exists, what assurance is there in the existing system that there will be opportunity to use their gifts and the education they have obtained? As far as the mass is concerned, we are now putting the social cart before the social horse.

If we take the question of production, what do we find? I pass by the basic fact that real production is completed only through distribution and consumption, so that mere improvement in the mechanical means of mass production may, and does, intensify the problem instead of solving it. I pass it over here because recurring crises and depressions, with the paradox of want amid plenty, has forced the fact upon the attention of every thoughtful person. The outcome is sufficient proof that the problem of production cannot be solved in isolation from distribution and consumption. I want here to call attention rather to the fact that the present method of dealing with the problem is *restriction* of productive capacity. For scarcity of materials and surplus of those who want to work is the ideal situation for profit on the part of those situated to take advantage of it. *Restriction of production* at the very time when *expan-*

sion of production is most needed had long been the rule of *industrialists*. Now the Government is adopting the same policy for agriculturalists. Those who practice restriction of production in their own businesses cry out loudly when the Government, following their example, intervenes to kill pigs, plow under cotton, and reduce the crop of cereals, and does it, moreover, when there is the most urgent need for food. Here again, as in the case of public relief, critics prefer to complain about symptoms rather than to face the cause: The inherent exigencies of the existing social-economic system. Anyone can wax eloquent about the high social function of those who farm, mine and quarry, providing the raw materials not only of food, clothing and shelter but also of all later forms of production of both capital and consumer goods. Anyone can wax pathetic over the plight of agriculture. But under present conditions, the former course is to put the burden of carrying society upon the class now least competent to bear it, and the latter course is to engage in idle sentiment.

The ultimate problem of production is the production of human beings. To this end, the production of goods is intermediate and auxiliary. It is by this standard that the present system stands condemned. "Security" is a means, and although an indispensable social means, it is not the end. Machinery and technological improvement are means, but again are not the end. Discovery of individual needs and capacities is a means to the end, but only a means. The means have to be implemented by a social-economic system that establishes and uses the means for the production of free human beings associating with one another on terms of equality. Then and then only will these means be an integral part of the end, not frustrated and self-defeating, bringing new evils and generating new problems.

The problem today remains one of using available intelligence, of employing the immense resources science has put at our disposal: a pooled and coördinated social intelligence, not the mere scattered individualized intelligences of persons here and there, however high their I.Q.'s may be. Mere individual intellectual capacities are as ineffective as are mere personal good intentions. The existence of social objective intelligence brings us back to the point where we started. Social control effected through organized application of social intelligence is the sole form of social control that can and will get rid of existing evils without landing us finally in some form of coercive control from above and outside.

A great tragedy of the present situation may turn out to be that those most conscious of present evils and of the need of thorough-going change in the social-economic system will trust to some short-cut way out, like the method of civil war and violence. Instead of relying upon the constant application of all socially available resources of knowledge and continuous inquiry they may rely upon the frozen intelligence of some past thinker, sect and party cult: frozen because arrested into a dogma.

That "intelligence," when frozen in dogmatic social philosophies, themselves the fruit of arrested philosophies of history, generates a vicious circle of blind oscillation is tragically exemplified in the present state of the world. What *claims* to be social planning is now found in Communist and Fascist countries. The *social* consequence is complete suppression of freedom of inquiry, communication and voluntary association, by means of a combination of personal violence, culminating in extirpation, and systematic partisan propaganda. The results are such that in the minds of many persons the very idea of social planning and of violation of the integrity of the individual are becoming intimately bound together. But an immense difference divides the *planned* society from a *continuously planning* society. The former requires fixed blueprints imposed from above and therefore involving reliance upon physical and psychological force to secure conformity to them. The latter means the release of intelligence through the widest form of coöperative give-and-take. The attempt to *plan* social organization and association without the freest possible play of intelligence contradicts the very idea in *social* plann*ing*. For the latter is an operative method of activity, not a predetermined set of final "truths."

When social "planning" is predicated on a set of "*final*" truths, the social end is fixed once for all, and the "end" is then used to justify whatever means are deemed necessary to attain it. "Planning" then takes place only with respect to means of the latter sort, not with respect to ends, so that planning with respect to even means is constrained and coercive. The social result is that the means used have quite other consequences than the end originally set up in idea and afterwards progressively reduced to mere words. As the events of the past twenty years have shown, the seizure of political power by force signifies the continued maintenance of power by force with its continued suppression of the most precious freedoms of the individual spirit. Maintenance of power in order to use force becomes the actual end. Means used determine the end actually reached. The end justifies the means only when the means used are such as actually bring about the desired and desirable end.

Only when reflection upon means and choice of ends are free can there be actual social planning. Every arrest of intelligence (and every form of social dogma is an arrest) obstructs and finally suppresses free consideration and choice of means. The method of social intelligence is primarily concerned with free determination of means to be employed. Until that method of social action is adopted we shall remain in a period of drift and unrest whose final outcome is likely to be force and counterforce, with temporary victory to the side possessed of the most machine guns.

XII

THE INTELLECTUALS AND THE COLD WAR

The decade and a half following the close of the Second World War marked a period of intellectual retrenchment. The most influential thinkers in both Europe and America had come to distrust those ambitious theoretical systems which were held responsible, at least in part, for the triumph of authoritarianism in Nazi Germany and Soviet Russia. Perhaps the most characteristic intellectual product of this period was the theory of totalitarianism, which attempted to subsume under one rubric extreme political systems of both the right and the left. Extremism of any sort was disparaged, as liberal intellectuals on both sides of the Atlantic reaffirmed their allegiance to what Arthur Schlesinger, Jr., has termed "the vital center."

The readings reproduced here are two important examples of the intellectual style of the 1950's. Both the French political theorist and philosopher Raymond Aron (b. 1905) and the American sociologist and political scientist Daniel Bell (b. 1919) proclaim, Aron somewhat more tentatively than Bell, that the age of systematic ideologies is at an end. Both thinkers exhibit a marked suspicion of political intellectuals, reminiscent of Edmund Burke's attack on the "political metaphysicians" of the Enlightenment. Aron and Bell profess an impartial distaste for all political dogmatisms, but the ideological tradition for which they reserve their severest strictures is Marxism. Marxism, they both argue, is best understood as a secular religion, and their essays bristle with deprecatory religious metaphors.

Both of these essays show evidence of a heightened trans-Atlantic dialogue. Perhaps reflecting the impact of the central European intellectual emigration of the 1930's and 1940's, Bell's essay exhibits a greater sensitivity to European intellectual traditions than usually found in the writings of an American thinker. Similarly, the rise of the United States to the status of super-power is reflected in the considerable space Aron devotes to American society, an interest that, with the exception of Alexis de Tocqueville, we are not accustomed to encountering in European intellectuals.

The End of the Ideological Age? (1955)

RAYMOND ARON

It may seem rather paradoxical to envisage the end of the ideological age at a time when Senator McCarthy continues to play a leading role on the Washington stage, when *Les Mandarins* has just won the Prix Goncourt and the flesh-and-blood 'mandarins' are making the pilgrimage to Moscow and Peking. One is not, of course, so naïve as to expect peace to blossom forth in the immediate future: the idealists disillusioned or liquidated, the bureaucrats continue to reign.

The Westerners themselves may dream of political tolerance just as, three centuries ago, they tired of futile slaughter in the name of the same God for the choice of the true religion. But they have communicated to the rest of the world their faith in a radiant future. Nowhere, in Asia or in Africa, has the Welfare State spread enough benefits to stifle the impulse towards irrational and foolish hope. The nations of Europe preceded the others on the road to industrial civilisation. Now, perhaps, moved by the first glimmerings of scepticism, they are beginning to foreshadow, however prematurely, a new shape of things to come.

Let us look back and survey the centuries which have elapsed since the dawn of the philosophy of immanence and of modern science. Every one of the ideologies which, for a few years or for a few decades, has seized the imagination of the crowd or of thinking men, reveals, retrospectively, a simple structure with one or two guiding ideas.

The optimism of the Left was created and maintained by a strong feeling: admiration for the power of reason, certainty that the application of science to industry would revolutionise the order of human society and the condition of its individual members. The ancestral aspiration towards human brotherhood was united with faith in practical science in order to inspire either nationalism or socialism or both.

Freedom of enquiry asserted against Church orthodoxy, and the equality of fighting men established on the field of battle by the introduction of firearms, undermined the edifice of traditional hierarchies. The future would belong to free and equal citizens. After the storm which precipitated the collapse of the most grandiose edifice of aristocratic Europe, after the fall of the French monarchy, the revolutionary fervour, encouraged by flamboyant successes as well as bloody defeats, split into two separate channels, nationalist and socialist.

Called upon to defend the Fatherland at the risk of their lives, the servants of the throne felt entitled to demand a State which they could call their own and rulers whose language they could understand. Historians, philosophers and novelists, stressing the individuality of ethnic or cultural groups or the right of self-determination, sensitive to the unconscious workings of the centuries or to the coherence of the cities of antiquity, elaborated the various theories of the nation. Perhaps, in justifying national passions, they merely succeeded in exacerbating them, sometimes on the level of primitive tribalism, sometimes ennobled by the dream of liberty. At all events, the sort of reasonable administration accepted by several nationalities because foreign to each of them was in the long run rendered anachronistic by the speed of primary education and conscription.

National sentiments are still strong on both sides of the Iron Curtain. In the people's democracies Russian domination is detested. The French are easily aroused against the American 'occupation'. The European Defence Community was denounced as the supreme surrender because it transferred to a supra-national organism some of the prerogatives of sovereignty. The Communist militant follows the orders which are sent from Moscow; in 1939–40 he sabotaged the war effort, in June 1941 he joined the Resistance, but the Party won recruits by the million during the period when the interests of France coincided with those of the Soviet Union.

National feeling remains and must remain the cement of human collectivities, but the nationalist ideology is none-the-less condemned in Western Europe. An ideology presupposes an apparently systematic formalisation of facts, interpretations, desires and predictions. The intellectual who wants to be *essentially* nationalist must interpret history as the permanent struggle of jungle states or prophesy peace between independent nations on a basis of mutual respect. The combination of revolutionary nationalism and Machiavellian diplomacy advocated by Charles Maurras [1] could not survive the weakening of the European states.

[1] [Maurras was the leading literary light of the quasi-Fascist movement known as Action Française. He was sentenced to life imprisonment for his collaborationist activities during the Second World War. — Eds.]

By all means let the rulers defend tooth and nail the interests and rights of their country against the encroachments of strong and tactless allies. But how can one get excited about the temporal grandeur of a collectivity which is incapable of manufacturing its own arms? The American defence budget represents three-quarters of the total military expenditure of the Atlantic alliance. Isolation, neutrality, and the playing off of one bloc against the other, are sometimes possible and always legitimate, but they do not contribute towards an ideological transfiguration. In our century, a second-class nation-state is not an adequate framework for full human expression.

The United States and the Soviet Union are capable of spreading the pride of domination and the will to conquest. Their nationalism is on a different level from that of the European states tied to one soil, one culture, one language. In Russia, whether Tsarist or Soviet, and in the United States, citizenship is accorded to men of many different races, colours and languages. Colour prejudice in the United States has put a brake on the realisation by the negroes of the equality promised by the American constitution. If they have not responded to the appeal of Communism, it is to a large extent because of this promise. Externally the United States, except for a few years at the end of the last century and the beginning of this, have been innocent of imperialism in the European fashion, or of the desire for expansion and the permanent struggle with other states. American citizenship involves not so much the participation in a culture rooted in history as the acquisition of a way of life.

The Soviet Union has carried on in a new form the Tsarist tradition which allowed the ruling classes of neighbouring peoples entry into the aristocracy of the imperial State. Thanks to the Communist Party, it has maintained the unity of the multi-national élite. Soviet citizenship, offered to innumerable nationalities, requires loyalty to a State and adherence to an ideology, but not the renouncing of the nationality of origin.

The Big Two, as a result of their rivalry and of the power vacuum which grew up between them after the Second World War, have been led to set up supra-national systems one against the other. NATO is dominated by the United States which provides arms for the allied divisions and which alone is powerful enough to form a counter-weight to the Soviet mass. Marshal Rokossovsky is in command in Warsaw because the Soviet leaders are doubtful about the loyalty of the Poles and because several divisions of the Red Army are stationed in the heart of Germany. *Lebensraum*, one of the favourite themes of the pundits of the Third Reich, has been realised on both sides of the Iron Curtain, *but only on the military plane*.

One hesitates to use the word empire. There is not the slightest sign of an Atlantic patriotism and it is scarcely likely that Soviet Russian patriotism is very widespread in the satellite states, outside the Communist minorities. The supranational system, in theory unified by the triumph of a common faith, denies itself by isolating the people's democracies one from the other. It is not much easier to travel from Roumania to Poland than from Poland to France. The people's democracies, deprived of the substance of independence, have been given a sort of travesty of it; they are all shut in between their own frontiers as if each state necessary to the total plan had to be closed, even against its allies.

No less than the domination of men of other races and other languages, extreme inequalities of economic conditions seemed to be in contradiction with the spirit of the new times. The miracles of science made human misery scandalous and inexcusable. Nobody doubted that industry must soon eliminate the relics of immemorial poverty; people differed only on the choice of means. The ideal of the social community oscillated between the notion of a balance achieved by all without having been the object of a conscious will, and the notion of prosperity for all thanks to a global plan and the elimination of the exploiters.

Liberalism and socialism continue to inspire convictions and to provoke controversies, but it is becoming more and more difficult reasonably to transform such preferences into doctrines. Western 'capitalist' society today comprises a multitude of socialist institutions. One can no longer count on collective ownership or planning to bring about a dramatic improvement in man's lot.

Technological progress lived up to men's expectations and has gone on increasing by leaps and bounds. Perhaps, some years or some decades hence, it will have overcome the limitations of material resources. But its price and its limits are now generally realised. Mechanised societies are not pacific; they deliver man from the servitudes of poverty and weakness, but they subject millions of workers to the logic of mass production, and they risk turning human beings into machines.

Neither the optimist who conjures up a vision of fraternity thanks to material plenty, nor the pessimist who visualises a consummate tyranny extended over human minds with the help of the new instruments of mass communication and torture, is quite refuted by the experience of the twentieth century. The dialogue between them, begun at the time of the first factories, is still being pursued. But it does not take the form of an ideological debate, since the opposing themes are no longer connected with a particular class or party.

The last great ideology was born of the combination of three elements: the vision of a future consistent with human aspirations, the link between this future and a particular social class, and trust in human values above and beyond the victory of the working class, thanks to planning and collective ownership. Confidence in the virtues of a socio-economic technique has begun to wane and one looks in vain for this class which is supposed to bring about the radical renewal of institutions and ideas.

The theory of the class struggle, which is still current today, is falsified by a spurious analogy: the rivalry between bourgeoisie and proletariat differs in essence from the rivalry between aristocracy and bourgeoisie.

Certain nineteenth-century thinkers transfigured into a promethean exploit the overthrow of the French monarchy and the blood-stained, terror-haunted, faction-ridden adventure of the Republic. Hegel claimed to have seen the spirit of the world passing on horseback, in the form of an officer risen from the ranks whom the god of battles had crowned. Marx and then Lenin painted dream-pictures of the Jacobins, the active minority which stirs up the stagnant pool of popular feeling, the missionary order in the service of the socialist revolution. There could be no doubt about it — the proletariat would finish the work begun by the bourgeoisie.

The ideologists of the proletariat are bourgeois intellectuals. The bourgeoisie, whether it derived its ideas from Montesquieu, Voltaire or Jean-Jacques Rousseau, set up its own conception of human existence and the political order in opposition to the *Ancien Régime* and the Catholic vision of the world. *The proletariat has never had a conception of the world opposed to that of the bourgeoisie; there has been an ideology of what the proletariat should be or should do, an ideology whose historical ascendancy was most powerful when the number of industrial workers was smallest.* The so-called proletarian party, in the countries where it has seized power, has had peasants rather than factory workers as its troops, and intellectuals, exasperated by the traditional hierarchy or by national humiliation, as its leaders.

The values to which the working class spontaneously subscribes differ from those of the bourgeoisie. It is not impermissible to construct antitheses between the two: the sense of solidarity against the desire for possessions, participation in the community against individualism or egoism, the generosity of the penniless against the avarice of the rich, etc. In any case there is no denying the obvious fact that the system and style of living in working-class districts are very different from those of the wealthy middle classes. So-called proletarian régimes, that is régimes governed by Communist parties, owe practically nothing to authentic working-class culture, to the parties or unions whose leaders themselves belong to the working class.

Popular culture in our century has succumbed to the blows of *Pravda*, *France-Soir* or the *Readers' Digest*. Revolutionary syndicalist or anarchist movements cannot resist the unconscious coalition of employers' organisations which fear them, and socialist, especially communist, parties which detest them. The latter have been affected by the thought and action of the intellectuals.

It was in the hope of accomplishing fully the ambitions of the bourgeoisie — the conquest of Nature, social equality or equality of opportunity — that the ideologists handed on the torch to the proletariat. The contrast between technological progress and the misery of the workers was a crying scandal. How could one help but impute to private ownership and the anarchy of the market the survival of ancestral poverty which was in fact due to the exigencies of accumulation (capitalist or socialist), insufficient productivity and increases in population. Soft-hearted intellectuals, revolted by injustice, seized on the idea that capitalism, being in itself evil, would be destroyed by its contradictions and that its victims would eventually overthrow the privileged. Marx achieved an improbable synthesis between the Hegelian metaphysic of history, the Jacobin interpretation of the Revolution, and the pessimistic theory of the market economy developed by British authors. To maintain the continuity between the French Revolution and the Russian Revolution, it was only necessary to call Marxist ideology proletarian. But one has merely to open one's eyes to be rid of the illusion.

The market economy and total planning are rival models — which no existing economy actually reproduces — not successive stages in evolution. There is no necessary link between the phases of industrial development and the predominance of one model or the other. Backward economies approximate more to the model of the planners than do advanced economies. Mixed systems are not monsters incapable of surviving, or transitional forms on the way to the pure type; they are the normal thing. In a planned system one will find most of the categories of the market economy, more or less modified. As the standard of living rises and the Soviet consumer has more freedom of choice, the benefits and the problems of Western prosperity will appear on the other side of the Iron Curtain.

The revolutions of the twentieth century have not been proletarian revolutions; they have been thought up and carried out by intellectuals. They have overthrown the traditional power, ill-adapted to the exigencies of the technological age. The prophets imagined that capitalism would precipitate a revolution comparable to the one which convulsed France at the end of the eighteenth century. Nothing of the sort happened. On the contrary, wherever the ruling classes have been unable or unwilling to reform themselves quickly enough, the dissatisfaction of the bourgeoisie, the impatience of the intellectuals and the immemorial aspirations of the peasants have provoked an explosion.

Neither Russia nor the United States ever fully experienced the struggle between the aristocracy and the bourgeoisie. Tsarism sought to borrow the technical civilisation of the West while discarding its democratic ideas. It has been replaced by a power which has re-established the identification between society and the State, the administrators constituting the only privileged class.

The United States became conscious of its identity through the progressive ideas of the European eighteenth century. It sought to put them into practice on virgin soil which had to be conquered not so much in the face of the Indians, who were doomed to extinction by the gap between their tribal culture and that of the European immigrants, as in the face of recalcitrant Nature and the elements. There was no aristocracy, clinging to its privileges, to restrain the impetus of reason and industry. American religion taught moral strictness, not a creed or orthodoxy. It urged the citizens both to intransigence and conformism, but it did not unite with the State to put a brake on the movement of modern thought. No event comparable to the French Revolution and the secession of the proletariat came to belie the eighteenth-century optimism of the New World. The Civil War was interpreted by the historians — the spokesmen of the victors — as a triumph, proving that the world cannot live half free and half enslaved. The American workers accepted the promises of the American Idea and did not believe in the necessity of an Apocalypse.

Armed with a doctrine which condemned their enterprise in advance, the Bolsheviks were the builders of an industrial society of a kind hitherto unknown. The State took over the responsibility for distributing the collective resources, for managing the factories, for savings and investments. The Western working class in the nineteenth century rose against the employers, not directly against the State. Where the employers and the State are identical, revolt against the one would involve dissidence toward the other. The Marxist ideology offered an admirable justification for the necessities of a State economy: the proletarians owed unconditional obedience to their own collective will embodied in the Party.

Certainly, if criticism had been tolerated, the intellectuals would have denounced the misery of the slums of Leningrad and Moscow in the Russia of 1930, just as their colleagues had denounced those of Manchester or Paris a century earlier. The contrast between the growth of the means of production and the aggravation, apparent or real, of the sufferings of the people would have inspired familiar Utopian visions of progress without tears or of fecund catastrophes.

In any case, what possible programme could the oppositionists offer as an alternative to the Soviet reality? They might demand political liberties, the participation of the workers in the management of industry, but not the individual appropriation of the instruments of production, except perhaps in agriculture. Under a capitalist régime the masses can at least imagine that public ownership would cure or attenuate the evils of industry, but under a collectivist régime they cannot expect the same miracle from a restoration of private ownership. The malcontents dream of a return to Leninism, of a truly proletarian State; in other words they aspire to institutions and a way of life which would be a more faithful expression of the reigning ideology.

In the United States, the proletariat does not think of itself as such. The workers' organisations demand and obtain many of the reforms which in Europe are associated with the Welfare State or socialism; the leaders of the masses are satisfied with the position accorded to them under the present régime, and the masses themselves do not aspire to a different society or different values. Unanimity on 'free enterprise,' on competition and the 'circulation of the élites' does not mean that the American reality accords with these ideas, any more than the obligatory teaching of Marxist-Leninism ensures that Russian society conforms to the official ideology.

Thus, by different routes, either spontaneously or with the help of the police, the two great societies of our time have come to suppress the conditions of ideological debate, have integrated the workers, and imposed a unanimous adherence to the principles of the régime. The debate remains a burning one in those countries of the second rank who are not entirely at home in the ideological camp to which they belong; too proud to accept their *de facto* dependence, too arrogant to admit that the dissidence of the internal proletariat reflects a national failure rather than a decree of history, fascinated by the power which spreads terror, prisoners of the geography which tolerates criticism and abuse but which forbids escape. . . .

The attitude of the French intellectuals is determined by national pride and nostalgia for a universal idea. This attitude has repercussions abroad which are not solely due to the talent of French writers. If the men of culture cease to believe heart and soul in a truth for all men, are they not lapsing into indifference?

An intellectual's religion, Communism recruits disciples among the intellectuals of Asia and Africa, whereas the reasonable democracy of the West, though it often wins free elections, finds scarcely any supporters ready to sacrifice all for the triumph of the cause.

"In offering to China and Japan a secularised version of our Western civilisation, we have been offering them a stone instead of bread, while the Russians, in offering them Communism as well as technology, have been offering them bread of a sort — a gritty, black bread, if you like to call it so; but that is still an edible substance that contains in it some grain of nutriment for the spiritual life without which man cannot live." [2]

Communism is a degraded version of the Western message. It retains its ambition to conquer nature, to improve the lot of the humble, but it sacrifices what was and must remain the heart and soul of the unending human adventure: freedom of enquiry, freedom of controversy, freedom of criticism, and the vote.

Must it be said that the Communist version succeeds because of its intellectual weakness? No true theory will suppress the uncertainties of the present; it will maintain and encourage controversy, it will offer no hope of speedy progress, it will not liberate the Asian intellectuals from their complexes. The secular religion retains the prestige and the force of the prophetism; it creates a small number of fanatics, and these in their turn mobilise and control the masses, who themselves are not so much seduced by the vision of the future as revolted by the miseries of the present.

The content of the Communist faith differs scarcely at all from the content of the other ideologies to which left-wing intellectuals everywhere adhere. For the most part the latter remain on the threshold, unamenable to the discipline of the sect. The minority who take the final step, overcoming all their doubts and scruples, are possessed by the faith which 'moves mountains.' The liberals are consumed with doubts and uncertainties and sometimes feel vaguely guilty for being on the 'wrong side' — the side of the Right, of Reaction, of Feudalism. The climate of the Western universities has rendered students from all over the world susceptible to the Marxist-Leninist doctrine which is not the logical fulfilment but the dogmatic hardening of the progressivist philosophy.

Communism, it is said, is the first essentially European belief to have succeeded in converting millions of Asians. The first of the new catechumens were intellectuals. They had not been converted by Christianity, which ran counter to the traditional system of values and customs, whose teachings were belied by the behaviour of the invaders, and which did not accord with scientific thought, the essence of the military superiority of the imperialists. Communism attracts not because it is a Christian heresy but because it seems to be the extreme form, the definitive interpretation, of the rationalist and optimist philosophy. It gives a coherent expression to the political hopes of the West.

Simple people are susceptible to these hopes, but indifferent to the interpretative scholasticism. In allowing themselves to be mobilised by the Party they do not become true believers in the Church. The peasants do not aspire to collective ownership but to individual ownership. The workers do not visualise in advance the building up of socialism by

[2] Arnold Toynbee, *The World and the West.*

the *Gleichschaltung* of the trade unions. It is the prophetism which confers on Communism a sort of spiritual substance.

What remains of this when the conquerors of the future have become the planners of the economy? "The deified militarist has been a flagrant scandal. Alexander, as the Tyrrhenian pirate told him to his face in the story as we have it from St. Augustine, would have been called not a god but a gangster if he had done what he did with a couple of accomplices instead of doing it with a whole army. And what about the deified policeman? Augustus, now, has made himself into a policeman by liquidating his fellow-gangsters, and we are grateful to him for that; but, when we are required to register our gratitude by worshipping this reformed gangster as a god, we cannot comply with much conviction or enthusiasm." [3] What could possibly be our feeling towards Stalin when he liquidates Zinoviev and Bukharin, or towards Malenkov when he liquidates Beria? Does Communism, when it is installed in power, still contain a spiritual substance?

How long will the exaltation of the builders continue to sustain the militants? How long will national grandeur continue to testify to the mandate of the historical powers-that-be? Perhaps China will find in this mandarins' religion a durable peace. Christian Europe will not. The official orthodoxy will decline into a ritual language, or else the only authentic faith, that which no temporal good can satisfy, will revolt against the secular clericalism. Perhaps men can live without adoring a God in spirit and in truth. They will not live long, after the 'proletarian' victory, in the expectation of a paradise on this earth.

Is there, then, no alternative to faith in the proletariat but faith in Christ? Can the West offer a spiritual truth in opposition to Soviet materialism? We must be careful not to compromise religion in the struggles of temporal powers, to attribute to the system we defend virtues which it does not possess.

The liberal democracies do not represent a 'Christian' civilisation. They have developed in societies whose religion was Christian, and they have been inspired to a certain extent by the absolute value which Christianity gives to the individual soul. Neither electoral and parliamentary practices nor the mechanism of the market, as such, are either Christian or contrary to the Christian spirit. Doubtless the free play of initiative, competition between buyers and sellers, would be unthinkable if human nature had not been sullied by the Fall. The individual would give of his best in the interests of others without hope of recompense, without concern for his own interests. Man being what he is, the Church, which cannot approve unbridled competition or the unlimited desire for wealth, is not obliged to condemn the economic institutions which are characteristic of industrial civilisation. The planners, too, are

[3] Arnold Toynbee, *op. cit.*, p. 182.

compelled to appeal to the appetite for money or personal glory. No régime can afford to ignore human egotism.

Communism comes into conflict with Christianity because it is atheist and totalitarian, not because it controls the economy. It arrogates to itself the sole right to educate the young. The Communist State allows religious rites to be celebrated and the sacraments to be administered; but it does not consider itself neutral, it calls religious beliefs superstitions, doomed to disappear with the progress of socialist construction. It enrols the hierarchy in political crusades; 'popes,' priests, bishops and Metropolitans are invited to lead the campaign in favour of peace, to denounce the conspiracies of the Vatican.

It is not for those of us who belong to no Church to recommend a choice to the believers, but it behoves us all, incorrigible liberals who tomorrow would return again to the struggle against clericalism, to fight today against this totalitarianism from which professing Christians happen to suffer as much as free-thinking scientists and artists. The tyranny we denounce is not solely directed against a faith we do not share; it is one which affects us all. The State which imposes an orthodox interpretation of day-to-day events also imposes on us an interpretation of global development and ultimately of the meaning of human existence. It seeks to subordinate all the achievements of the mind, all the activities of autonomous individuals and groups, to its pseudo-truth. In defending the freedom of religious teaching, the unbeliever defends his own freedom.

What essentially distinguishes the West from the Soviet universe is the fact that the one admits itself to be divided and the other 'politicises' the whole of existence. The least important aspect of plurality, although it is more readily cited than any other, is the party system. This is not without its disadvantages; it maintains an atmosphere of division and discord in the body politic, it blurs the sense of communal responsibilities and jeopardises internal peace and friendship. It is tolerated, in spite of everything, as a means of limiting arbitrary power and ensuring a legal expression to discontent, and as a symbol of the lay impartiality of the State and the autonomy of the human mind.

The Westerners, especially the intellectuals, suffer from the fragmentation of their universe. Diffusion and obscurity in poetry, and abstraction in painting, isolate poets and artists from the big public which they affect to despise but which, in their heart of hearts, they long to serve. Physicists or mathematicians can extract energy from the atom but cannot extract freedom of movement, opinion and friendship from suspicious politicians, from a sensation-hungry Press, from anti-intellectualist demagogues or the secret police. Masters of nuclear fission but slaves of 'security,' the scientists, enclosed in their narrow community, feel that they lose all control over their discoveries as soon as they transmit their secrets to the generals and the politicians. The specialist has control over but a limited field of knowledge; present-day science seems to leave him as ignorant of the answers to the ultimate questions as a child awakening to consciousness. The astronomer can foretell an eclipse of the sun with faultless precision; neither the economist nor the sociologist knows whether humanity is progressing towards an atomic holocaust or Utopian peace.

That is where ideology comes in — the longing for a purpose, for communion with the people, for something controlled by an idea and a will. The feeling of belonging to the elect, the security provided by a closed system in which the whole of history as well as one's own person find their place and their meaning, the pride in joining the past to the future in present action — all this inspires and sustains the true believer, the man who is not repelled by the scholasticism, who is not disillusioned by the twists in the party line, the man who lives entirely for the cause and no longer recognises the humanity of his fellow-creatures outside the party.

Such fanaticism is not for us. We can admire the sombre grandeur of these armies of believers. We can admire their devotion, their discipline and self-sacrifice: such warrior virtues are of the kind that lead to victory. But what will remain tomorrow of the motives that led them to fight? Without a scintilla of doubt or guilt or regret, we can leave the fanatics their inevitable superiority.

Does the rejection of fanaticism encourage a reasonable faith, or merely scepticism?

One does not cease to love God when one gives up converting the pagans or the Jews and no longer reiterates: "No salvation outside the Church." Will one cease to desire a less unjust society and a less cruel lot for humanity as a whole if one refuses to subscribe to a single class, a single technique of action and a single ideological system?

True, the comparison is not unreservedly valid. Religious experience gains in authenticity as one comes to distinguish better between moral virtue and obedience to the Church. The secular religions dissolve into politico-economic opinions as soon as one abandons the dogma. Yet the man who no longer expects miraculous changes either from a revolution or an economic plan is not obliged to resign himself to the unjustifiable. It is because he likes individual human beings, participates in living communities, and respects the truth, that he refuses to surrender his soul to an abstract ideal of humanity, a tyrannical party, and an absurd scholasticism.

Perhaps it will be otherwise. Perhaps the intellectual will lose interest in politics as soon as he discovers its limitations. Let us accept joyfully this uncertain promise. Indifference will not harm us. Men, unfortunately, have not yet reached the point where they have no further occasion or motive for killing one another. If tolerance is born of doubt, let us teach everyone to doubt all the models and utopias, to challenge all the prophets of redemption and the heralds of catastrophe.

If they alone can abolish fanaticism, let us pray for the advent of the sceptics.

The End of Ideology in the West (1960)

DANIEL BELL

Men commit the error of not knowing when to limit their hopes.
— Machiavelli

There have been few periods in history when man felt his world to be durable, suspended surely, as in Christian allegory, between chaos and heaven. In an Egyptian papyrus of more than four thousand years ago, one finds: ". . . impudence is rife . . . the country is spinning round and round like a potter's wheel . . . the masses are like timid sheep without a shepherd . . . one who yesterday was indigent is now wealthy and the sometime rich overwhelm him with adultation." The Hellenistic period as described by Gilbert Murray was one of a "failure of nerve"; there was "the rise of pessimism, a loss of self-confidence, of hope in this life and of faith in normal human effort." And the old scoundrel Talleyrand claimed that only those who lived before 1789 could have tasted life in all its sweetness.

This age, too, can add appropriate citations — made all the more wry and bitter by the long period of bright hope that preceded it — for the two decades between 1930 and 1950 have an intensity peculiar in written history: world-wide economic depression and sharp class struggles; the rise of fascism and racial imperialism in a country that had stood at an advanced stage of human culture; the tragic self-immolation of a revolutionary generation that had proclaimed the finer ideals of man; destructive war of a breadth and scale hitherto unknown; the bureaucratized murder of millions in concentration camps and death chambers.

From *The End of Ideology* (New York: The Free Press, 1960), 393–407.

For the radical intellectual who had articulated the revolutionary impulses of the past century and a half, all this has meant an end to chiliastic hopes, to millenarianism, to apocalyptic thinking — and to ideology. For ideology, which once was a road to action, has come to be a dead end.

Whatever its origins among the French *philosophes*, ideology as a way of translating ideas into action was given its sharpest phrasing by the left Hegelians, by Feuerbach and by Marx. For them, the function of philosophy was to be critical, to rid the present of the past. ("The tradition of all the dead generations weighs like a nightmare on the brain of the living," wrote Marx.) Feuerbach, the most radical of all the left Hegelians, called himself Luther II. Man would be free, he said, if we could demythologize religion. The history of all thought was a history of progressive disenchantment, and if finally, in Christianity, God had been transformed from a parochial deity to a universal abstraction, the function of criticism — using the radical tool of alienation, or self-estrangement — was to replace theology by anthropology, to substitute Man for God. Philosophy was to be directed at life, man was to be liberated from the "specter of abstractions" and extricated from the bind of the supernatural. Religion was capable only of creating "false consciousness." Philosophy would reveal "true consciousness." And by placing Man, rather than God, at the center of consciousness, Feuerbach sought to bring the "infinite into the finite."

If Feuerbach "descended into the world," Marx sought to transform it. And where Feuerbach proclaimed anthropology, Marx, reclaiming a root insight of Hegel, emphasized History and historical contexts. The world was not generic Man, but men; and of men, classes of men. Men differed because of their class position. And truths were class truths. All truths, thus, were masks, or partial truths, but the real truth was the revolutionary truth. And this real truth was rational.

Thus a dynamic was introduced into the analysis of ideology, and into the creation of a new ideology. By demythologizing religion, one recovered (from God and sin) the potential in man. By the unfolding of history, rationality was revealed. In the struggle of classes, true consciousness, rather than false consciousness, could be achieved. But if truth lay in action, one must act. The left Hegelians, said Marx, were only *littérateurs*. (For them a magazine was "practice.") For Marx, the only real action was in politics. But action, revolutionary action as Marx conceived it, was not mere social change. It was, in its way, the resumption of all the old millenarian, chiliastic ideas of the Anabaptists. It was, in its new vision, a new ideology.

The analysis of ideology belongs properly in the discussion of the intelligentsia. One can say that what the priest is to religion, the intellectual is to ideology. This in itself gives us a clue to the dimensions of the word and the reason for its multivariate functions. The word *ideology* was coined by the French philosopher Destutt de Tracy, at the end of the 18th century. Together with other Enlightenment philosophers, notably such materialists as Helvetius and Holbach, de Tracy was trying to define a way of discovering "truth" other than through faith and authority, the traditional methods encouraged by Church and State. And, equally, under the influence of Francis Bacon, these men were seeking some way to eliminate the accidents of bias, the distortions of prejudice, the idiosyncracies of upbringing, the interventions of self-interest or the simple will to believe, all of which, like shadows in Plato's cave, created illusions of truth. Their aim was to "purify" ideas in order to achieve "objective" truth and "correct" thought. Some of them, Helvetius, for example, believed that one had to go back to the origin and development of ideas in order to see how distortions entered. De Tracy believed that one "purified" ideas by reducing them to sense perceptions — a belated French variant of British empiricism with a barely concealed anti-religious bias — and this new science of ideas he called "ideology."

The negative connotations of the term arose with Napoleon. Having consolidated his power, he forbade the teaching of moral and political science at the Institut National and denounced the "ideologues" as irresponsible speculators who were subverting morality and patriotism. As a republican, Napoleon had been sympathetic to the ideas of the philosophers; as Emperor, he recognized the importance of religious orthodoxy for the maintenance of the State.

But it was with Marx that the word "ideology" went through some curiously different transmutations. For Marx, as in his work *The German Ideology*, ideology was linked to philosophical idealism, or the conception that ideas are autonomous, and that ideas, independently, have the power to reveal truth and consciousness. For Marx, as a materialist, this was false since "existence determined consciousness" rather than vice versa; any attempt to draw a picture of reality from ideas alone could produce only "false consciousness." Thus, for example, in following Feuerbach — from whom Marx drew most of his analysis of ideology and alienation — he considered religion to be a false consciousness: Gods are the creation of men's minds and they only appear to exist independently and determine man's fate; religion therefore is an ideology.

But Marx went one step further. Ideologies, he said, are not only false ideas, but they mask particular interests. Ideologies claim to be truth, but reflect the needs of specific groups. In his early essays on *The Jewish Question*, one of the few places where he dealt specifically with the philosophical problems of State and Society, Marx sharply attacked the concept of "natural rights" as it appeared in the French

Revolution's Declaration of the Rights of Man, and as these rights were specified in the State constitutions of Pennsylvania and New Hampshire. The presumption of "natural rights" — the freedom to worship or the freedom to own property — was that they were "absolute" or "transcendant" rights; for Marx, they were only 'bourgeois rights," historically achieved, which made false claim to universal validity. The function of the State, Marx pointed out, was to create some basis for the "general will." In the "civil society" which the bourgeoisie had created, the State presumably was to be negative or neutral. Each man would pursue his own self-interest, and a social harmony would prevail. But in fact, he argued, the State was used to enforce the rights of particular groups. Thus the claim of "natural rights" simply masked the demand of the bourgeoisie to be able to use property to their own advantage. Marx believed that the individualism of "natural rights" was a false individualism, since man could only "realize" himself in community, and that true freedom was not freedom *of* property or freedom *of* religion, but freedom *from* property and freedom *from* religion — in short, from ideology. The attempt, therefore, to claim universal validity for what was in fact a class interest, was ideology.

Marx differed from Bentham, and other utilitarians, in recognizing that individuals were not always motivated by direct self-interest. (This was "vulgar hedonism.") Ideology, he said, was a meaningful force. "One must not form the narrow-minded idea," he wrote in *The Eighteenth Brumaire*, "that the petty-bourgeoisie wants on principle to enforce an egoistic class interest. It believes, rather, that the *special* conditions of its emancipation are the *general* conditions through which alone modern society can be saved and the class struggle avoided." The "unmasking" of ideology, thus, is to reveal the "objective" interest behind the idea, and to see what function the ideology serves.

The implications of all this are quite direct. For one, a rationalistic analysis of politics alone is inadequate. What people say they believe cannot always be taken at face value, and one must search for the structure of interests beneath the ideas; one looks not at the *content* of ideas, but their *function*. A second, more radical conclusion is that if ideas mask material interests, then the "test of truth" of a doctrine is to see what class interests it serves. In short, truth is "class truth." Thus, there is no objective philosophy, but only "bourgeois philosophy" and "proletarian philosophy"; no objective sociology but only "bourgeois sociology" and "proletarian sociology." But Marxism is not, simply, a relativistic doctrine: there is an "objective" ordering of the social universe, which is revealed through "history." History, for Marx as for Hegel, is a progressive unfolding reason, in which society, through man's conquest of nature and the destruction of all mythologies and superstitions, moves on to "higher stages." The "truth" of doctrine, therefore, is to be determined by its "closeness of fit" to the development of history; and in practice, it has meant that "truth" was determined by whether or not it contributed to the advancement of revolution.

There are many difficulties to the theory of the "social determination of ideas." One is the role of science. Marx did not speak of the natural sciences as ideologies. Yet a number of Marxists, particularly in the Soviet Union in the 1930's, did claim that there was a "bourgeois science" and a "bourgeois physics" and a "proletarian science" and a "proletarian physics." Thus, the relativity theories of Albert Einstein were attacked as "idealistic." And while today in the Soviet Union, there is hardly any talk of "bourgeois physics," the theories of Sigmund Freud are officially condemned as "idealistic." Yet if science is not class-bound, is this equally true of the social sciences? The question of the autonomy of science is one that has never been satisfactorily resolved in Marxian thought.

A second difficulty is the deterministic presumption that there is a *one-to-one* correspondence between a set of ideas and some "class" purpose. Yet this is rarely the case. Empiricism is usually associated with liberal inquiry. Yet David Hume, the most "radical" empiricist, was a Tory, and Edmund Burke, who had argued the most vigorously against rationalist efforts to blueprint a new society, was conservative. Hobbes, one of the most profound of materialists, was a royalist, and T. H. Green, one of the leaders of the idealist revival in Great Britain, a liberal.

And the third difficulty is the definition of class. For Marx (though class was never rigorously defined in his work) the key social divisions in society arose out of the distribution of property. Yet in a politico-technological world, property has increasingly lost its force as a determinant of power, and sometimes, even, of wealth. In almost all modern societies, technical skill becomes more important than inheritance as a determinant of occupation, and political power takes precedence over economic. What then is the meaning of class?

And yet, one cannot wholly discount the force of the proposition that "styles of thought" are related to historic class groups and their interests, or that ideas emerge as a consequence of the different world-views, or perspectives, of different groups in the society. The problem is how to specify the relationships between the existential base and the "mental production." Max Weber, the sociologist, argued, for example, that there is an "elective affinity" between ideas and interests. The social origin of an idea, or of a theorist, or a revolutionist, is less relevant than the fact that certain ideas become "selected out," so to speak, by social groups that find them congenial and thus espouse them. This was the basis for the theory of the "Protestant Ethic," in which he argued that certain features of Calvinistic thought, and the kind of personality that such a doctrine sanctioned, became necessary, and causal, in the development of capitalism, despite the other-worldly foundation of these ideas. Karl Mannheim, another sociologist, sought to divide social thought into two fundamental styles, which he called "ideological" and "utopian." He accepted the proposition, derived from Marx, that ideas are "time-bound," but insisted that Marx's ideas, as those of all socialists, came within the same stricture. Since all ideas serve interests, those which defended the existing order he called "ideological" and those which sought to change the social order he called "utopian." But was all effort, then, at objective truth hopeless? Was Bacon's quest therefore a mirage? Mannheim felt that one social group could be relatively objective — the intellectuals. Since the intelligentsia were a "floating stratum" in society, and therefore were less bound than other class groups, they could achieve multi-perspectives that transcended the parochial limits of the other social groups.

In the development of the social sciences, the problem raised by Bacon, de Tracy, Marx and others — the clarification of the role of ideas in social change — has become part of a technical field known as the "sociology of knowledge." (For a clear discussion of these issues, see the chapter by Robert K. Merton in his *Social Theory and Social Structure*.) But in popular usage the word *ideology* remains as a vague term where it seems to denote a world-view or belief-system or creeds held by a social group about the social arrangements in society, which is morally justified as being right. People then talk of the "ideology of the small businessman," or of liberalism, or fascism, as an "ideology." Or some writer will talk of "the dream-world of ideology (in which) Americans see their country as a place where every child is born to 'equality of opportunity,' where every man is essentially as good as every other man if not better." In this sense, ideology connotes a "myth" rather than just a set of values.

Clearly, such usages, by mixing together many things, create only confusion. Some distinctions, therefore, are in order.

We can, perhaps, borrow a distinction from Mannheim, and distinguish between what he called "the *particular* conception of ideology," and "the *total* conception of ideology." In the first sense, we can say that individuals who profess certain values do have interests as well, and we can better understand the meaning of these values or beliefs, or the reasons why they come forth where they have, by linking them up with the interests they have — though the interests may not always be economic; they may be status interests (such as an ethnic group that wants higher standing or social approval in a society), political interests, such as representation, and the like. It is in this sense that we can talk of the *ideology* of business, or of labor, or the like. (When Charles E. Wilson, the Secretary of Defense in the Eisenhower Administration and one-time president of General Motors, said, "What is good for the United States is good for General Motors, and vice-versa," he was expressing ideology — i.e., the view that economic policy should be geared to the needs of the business community, since the welfare of the country depended on the health of business.) A *total* ideology is an all-inclusive system of comprehensive reality, it is a set of beliefs, infused with passion, and seeks to transform the whole of a way of life. This commitment to ideology — the yearning for a "cause," or the satisfaction of deep moral feelings — is *not* necessarily the reflection of interests in the shape of ideas. Ideology, in this sense, and in the sense that we use it here, is a secular religion.

Ideology is the conversion of ideas into social levers. Without irony, Max Lerner once entitled a book "Ideas Are Weapons." This is the language of ideology. It is more. It is the commitment to the consequences of ideas. When Vissarion Belinsky, the father of Russian criticism, first read Hegel and became convinced of the philosophical correctness of the formula "what is, is what ought to be," he became a supporter of the Russian autocracy. But when it was shown to him that Hegel's thought contained the contrary tendency, that dialectically the "is" evolves into a different form, he became a revolutionary overnight. "Belinsky's conversion," comments Rufus W. Mathewson, Jr., "illustrates an attitude toward ideas which is both passionate and myopic, which responds to them on the basis of their immediate relevances alone, and inevitably reduces them to tools."

What gives ideology its force is its passion. Abstract philosophical inquiry has always sought to eliminate passion, and the person, to rationalize all ideas. For the ideologue, truth arises in action, and meaning is given to experience by the "transforming moment." He comes alive not in contemplation, but in "the deed." One might say, in fact, that the most important, latent, function of ideology is to tap emotion. Other than religion (and war and nationalism), there have been few forms of channelizing emotional energy. Religion symbolized, drained away, dispersed emotional energy from the world onto the litany, the liturgy, the sacraments, the edifices, the arts. Ideology fuses these energies and channels them into politics.

But religion, at its most effective, was more. It was a way for people to cope with the problem of death. The fear of death — forceful and inevitable — and more, the fear of violent death, shatters the glittering, imposing, momentary dream of man's power. The fear of death, as Hobbes pointed out, is the source of conscience; the effort to avoid violent death is the source of law. When it was possible to believe, really believe, in heaven and hell, then some of the fear of death could be tempered or controlled; without such belief, there is only the total annihilation of the self.

It may well be that with the decline in religious *faith* in the last century and more, this fear of death as total annihilation, unconsciously expressed, has probably increased. One may hypothesize, in fact, that here is a cause of the breakthrough of the irrational, which is such a marked feature of the changed moral temper of our time. Fanaticism, violence, and cruelty are not, of course, unique in human history. But there was a time when such frenzies and mass emotions could be displaced, symbolized, drained away, and dispersed through religious devotion and practice. Now there is only this life, and the assertion of self becomes possible — for some even necessary — in the domination over others. One can challenge death by emphasizing the omnipotence of a movement (as in the "inevitable" victory of communism), or overcome death (as did the "immortality" of Captain Ahab) by bending others to one's will. Both paths are taken, but politics, because it can institutionalize power, in the way that religion once did, becomes the ready avenue for domination. The modern effort to transform the world chiefly or solely through politics (as meant that all other religious transformation of the self) has meant that all other institutional ways of mobilizing emotional energy would necessarily atrophy. In effect, sect and church became party and social movement.

A social movement can rouse people when it can do three things: simplify ideas, establish a claim to truth, and, in the union of the two, demand a commitment to action. Thus, not only does ideology transform ideas, it transforms people as well. The nineteenth-century ideologies, by emphasizing inevitability and by infusing passion into their followers, could compete with religion. By identifying inevitability with progress, they linked up with the positive values of science. But more important, these ideologies were linked, too, with the rising class of intellectuals, which was seeking to assert a place in society.

The differences between the intellectual and the scholar, without being invidious, are important to understand. The scholar has a bounded field of knowledge, a tradition, and seeks to find his place in it, adding to the accumulated, tested knowledge of the past as to a mosaic. The scholar, qua scholar, is less involved with his "self." The intellectual begins with *his* experience, *his* individual perceptions of the world, *his* privileges and deprivations, and judges the world by these sensibilities. Since his own status is of high value, his judgments of the society reflect the treatment accorded him. In a business civilization, the intellectual felt that the wrong values were being honored, and rejected the society. Thus there was a "built-in" compulsion for the free-floating intellectual to become political. The ideologies, therefore, which emerged from the nineteenth century had the force of the intellectuals behind them. They embarked upon what William James called "the faith ladder," which in its vision of the future cannot distinguish possibilities from probabilities, and converts the latter into certainties.

Today, these ideologies are exhausted. The events behind this important sociological change are complex and varied. Such calamities as the Moscow Trials, the Nazi-Soviet pact, the concentration camps, the suppression of the Hungarian workers, form one chain; such social changes as the modification of capitalism, the rise of the Welfare State, another. In philosophy, one can trace the decline of simplistic, rationalistic beliefs and the emergence of new stoic-theological images of man, e.g. Freud, Tillich, Jaspers, etc. This is not to say that such ideologies as communism in France and Italy do not have a political weight, or a driving momentum from other sources. But out of all this history, one simple fact emerges: for the radical intelligentsia, the old ideologies have lost their "truth" and their power to persuade.

Few serious minds believe any longer that one can set down "blueprints" and through "social engineering" bring about a new utopia of social harmony. At the same time, the older "counter-beliefs" have lost their intellectual force as well. Few "classic" liberals insist that the State should play no role in the economy, and few serious conservatives, at least in England and on the Continent, believe that the Welfare State is "the road to serfdom." In the Western world, therefore, there is today a rough consensus among intellectuals on political issues: the acceptance of a Welfare State; the desirability of decentralized power; a system of mixed economy and of political pluralism. In that sense, too, the ideological age has ended.

And yet, the extraordinary fact is that while the old nineteenth-century ideologies and intellectual debates have become exhausted, the rising states of Asia and Africa are fashioning new ideologies with a different appeal for their own people. These are the ideologies of industrialization, modernization, Pan-Arabism, color, and nationalism. In the distinctive difference between the two kinds of ideologies lies the great political and social problems of the second half of the twentieth century. The ideologies of the nineteenth century were universalistic, humanistic, and fashioned by intellectuals. The mass ideologies of Asia and Africa are parochial, instrumental, and created by political leaders. The driving forces of the old ideologies were social equality and, in the largest sense, freedom. The impulsions of the new ideologies are economic development and national power.

And in this appeal, Russia and China have become models. The fascination these countries exert is no longer the old idea of the free society, but the new one of economic growth. And if this involves the wholesale coercion of the population and the rise of new elites to drive the people, the new repressions are justified on the ground that without such coercions economic advance cannot take place rapidly enough. And even for some of the liberals of the West, "economic development" has become a new ideology that washes away the memory of old disillusionments.

It is hard to quarrel with an appeal for rapid economic growth and modernization, and few can dispute the goal, as few could ever dispute an appeal for equality and freedom. But in this powerful surge — and its swiftness is amazing — any movement that instates such goals risks the sacrifice of the present generation for a future that may see only a new exploitation by a new elite. For the newly-risen countries, the debate is not over the merits of Communism — the content of that doctrine has long been forgotten by friends and foes alike. The question is an older one: whether new societies can grow by building democratic institutions and allowing people to make choices — and sacrifices — voluntarily, or whether the new elites, heady with power, will impose totalitarian means to transform their countries. Certainly in these traditional and old colonial societies where the masses are apathetic and easily manipulated, the answer lies with the intellectual classes and their conceptions of the future.

Thus one finds, at the end of the fifties, a disconcerting caesura. In the West, among the intellectuals, the old passions are spent. The new generation, with no meaningful memory of these old debates, and no secure tradition to build upon, finds itself seeking new purposes within a framework of political society that has rejected, intellectually speaking, the old apocalyptic and chiliastic visions. In the search for a "cause," there is a deep, desperate, almost pathetic anger. The theme runs through a remarkable book, *Convictions*, by a dozen of the sharpest young Left Wing intellectuals in Britain. They cannot define the content of the "cause" they seek, but the yearning is clear. In the U.S. too there is a restless search for a new intellectual radicalism. Richard Chase, in his thoughtful assessment of American society, *The Democratic Vista*, insists that the greatness of nineteenth-century America for the rest of the world consisted in its radical vision of man (such a vision as Whitman's), and calls for a new radical criticism today. But the problem is that the old politico-economic radicalism (pre-occupied with such matters as the socialization of industry) has lost its meaning, while the stultifying aspects of contemporary culture (e.g., television) cannot be redressed in political terms. At the same time, American culture has almost completely accepted the avant-garde, particularly in art, and the older academic styles have been driven out completely. The irony, further, for those who seek "causes" is that the workers, whose grievances were once the driving energy for social change, are more satisfied with the society than the intellectuals. The workers have not achieved utopia, but their expectations were less than those of the intellectuals, and the gains correspondingly larger.

The young intellectual is unhappy because the "middle way" is for the middle-aged, not for him; it is without passion and is deadening. Ideology, which by its nature is an all-or-none affair, and temperamentally the thing he wants, is intellectually devitalized, and few issues can be formulated any more, intellectually, in ideological terms. The emotional energies — and needs — exist, and the question of how one mobilizes these energies is a difficult one. Politics offers little excitement. Some of the younger intellectuals have found an outlet in science or university pursuits, but often at the expense of narrowing their talent into mere technique; others have sought self-expression in the arts, but in the wasteland the lack of content has meant, too, the lack of the necessary tension that creates new forms and styles.

Whether the intellectuals in the West can find passions outside of politics is moot. Unfortunately, social reform does not have any unifying appeal, nor does it give a younger generation the outlet for "self-expression" and "self-definition" that it wants. The trajectory of enthusiasm has curved East, where, in the new ecstasies for economic utopia, the "future" is all that counts.

The end of ideology is not — should not be — the end of utopia as well. If anything, one can begin anew the discussion of utopia only by being aware of the trap of ideology. The point is that ideologists are "terrible simplifiers." Ideology makes it unnecessary for people to confront individual issues on their individual merits. One simply turns to the ideological vending machine, and out comes the prepared formulae. And when these beliefs are suffused by apocalyptic fervor, ideas become weapons, and with dreadful results.

There is now, more than ever, some need for utopia, in the sense that men need — as they have always needed — some vision of their potential, some manner of fusing passion with intelligence. Yet the ladder to the City of Heaven can no longer be a "faith ladder," but an empirical one: a utopia has to specify *where* one wants to go, *how* to get there, the costs of the enterprise, and some realization of, and justification for the determination of *who* is to pay.

The end of ideology closes the book, intellectually speaking, on an era, the one of easy "left" formulae for social change. But to close the book is not to turn one's back upon it. This is all the more important now when a "new Left," with few memories of the past, is emerging. This "new Left" has passion and energy, but little definition of the future. Its outriders exult that it is "on the move." But where it is going, what it means by Socialism, how to guard against bureaucratization, what one means by democratic planning or workers' control — any of the questions that require hard thought, are only answered by bravura phrases.

It is in attitudes towards Cuba and the new States in Africa that the meaning of intellectual maturity, and of the end of ideology, will be tested. For among the "new Left," there is an alarming readiness to create a *tabula rasa*, to accept the word "Revolution" as an absolution for outrages, to justify the suppression of civil rights and opposition — in short, to erase the lessons of the last forty years with an emotional alacrity that is astounding. The fact that many of these emerging social movements are justified in their demands for freedom, for the right to control their own political and economic destinies, does not mean they have a right to a blank check for everything they choose to do in the name of their emancipation. Nor does the fact that such movements take power in the name of freedom guarantee that they will not turn out to be as imperialist, as grandeur-concerned (in the name of Pan-Africanism or some other ideology), as demanding their turn on the stage of History, as the States they have displaced.

If the end of ideology has any meaning, it is to ask for the end of rhetoric, and rhetoricians, or "revolution" of the day when the young French anarchist Vaillant tossed a bomb into the Chamber of Deputies, and the literary critic Laurent Tailhade declared in his defense: "What do a few human lives matter; it was a *beau geste*." (A *beau geste* that ended, one might say, in a mirthless jest: two years later, Tailhade lost an eye when a bomb was thrown into a restaurant.) Today, in Cuba, as George Sherman, reporting for the *London Observer* summed it up: "The Revolution is law today although nobody has said clearly what that law is. You are expected to be simply for or against it and judge and be judged accordingly. Hatred and intolerance are wiping out whatever middle ground may have existed."

The problems which confront us at home and in the world are resistant to the old terms of ideological debate between "left" and "right," and if "ideology" by now, and with good reason, is an irretrievably fallen word, it is not necessary that "utopia" suffer the same fate. But it will if those who now call loudest for new utopias begin to justify degrading *means* in the name of some Utopian or revolutionary *end,* and forget the simple lessons that if the old debates are meaningless, some old verities are not — the verities of free speech, free press, the right of opposition and of free inquiry.

And if the intellectual history of the past hundred years has any meaning — and lesson — it is to reassert Jefferson's wisdom (aimed at removing the dead hand of the past, but which can serve as a warning against the heavy hand of the future as well), that "the present belongs to the living." This is the wisdom that revolutionists, old and new, who are sensitive to the fate of their fellow men, rediscover in every generation. "I will never believe," says a protagonist in a poignant dialogue written by the gallant Polish philosopher Leszek Kolakowski, "that the moral and intellectual life of mankind follows the law of economics, that is by saying today we can have more tomorrow; that we should use lives now so that truth will triumph or that we should profit by crime to pave the way for nobility."

And these words, written during the Polish "thaw," when the intellectuals had asserted, from their experience with the "future," the claims of humanism, echo the protest of the Russian writer Alexander Herzen, who, in a dialogue a hundred years ago, reproached an earlier revolutionist who would sacrifice the present mankind for a promised tomorrow: "Do you truly wish to condemn all human beings alive today to the sad role of caryatids . . . supporting a floor for others some day to dance on? . . . This alone should serve as a warning to people: an end that is infinitely remote is not an end, but, if you like, a trap; an end must be nearer — it ought to be, at the very least, the labourer's wage or pleasure in the work done. Each age, each generation, each life has its own fullness. . . ."

XIII

THE NEW RADICALISM

Perhaps the most dramatic development in European and American intellectual life during the 1960's has been the resurgence of that intellectual habit that Daniel Bell pronounced dead in the 1950's: ideological thinking. To be sure, the radical intellectuals of the 1960's have not attempted to revive the classic ideologies of the nineteenth century — "those great ossified monsters," as Sartre calls them. Despite their indebtedness to Marx, explicitly acknowledged by all three of the thinkers here represented, they are openly hostile to Soviet communism and argue that the traditional Marxian proletariat can no longer be the agency of liberation. In general their radicalism is inspired less by a systematic political world view than by moral indignation. Nevertheless, Daniel Bell would not hesitate to call them ideologists. They are united in their opposition to the matter-of-fact thinking celebrated by Bell and Aron and in their insistence on the critical function of social theory. Above all, they maintain that contemporary industrial society and the contemporary international order are irrevocably repressive and violent. Nothing short of a complete structural transformation of our civilization, they suggest, can insure a peaceful and just existence for the citizens of the world.

Jean-Paul Sartre (b. 1905) is unquestionably the most influential European intellectual of the postwar era. His novels, plays, and systematic philosophical writings have established him as the leading French exponent of existentialism. He appears here in his guise of social and political critic — a role that, since his active participation in the French resistance during the Second World War, he has regarded as following necessarily from his philosophical vision. It would be incorrect to suggest that Sartre's radicalism is a product of the 1960's. Throughout the years of the Cold War, in a series of confrontations with the popular novelist and essayist Albert Camus and with the philosopher Maurice Merleau-Ponty, Sartre consistently defended the radical position. In the last decade, how-

ever, he has become even more militant in his political opposition. In "Ideology and Revolution," which first appeared in Spanish, he treats a topic close to the hearts of radicals on both sides of the Atlantic: the exploitation of the Third World by the capitalist nations of the West, particularly the United States, and the struggle of colonized peoples to achieve independence. The article also makes clear the sources of Sartre's ambivalence about ideological systems of the traditional monolithic variety.

C. Wright Mills (1916–1962), perhaps the most important American social thinker of the post-war years, takes on the Western intellectual establishment — the "NATO intellectuals," Mills calls them — in his article "On the New Left," a direct response to Daniel Bell's essay "The End of Ideology in the West" reprinted in Section XII. Mills established his radical credentials in the late 1950's, most notably in The Power Elite *(1956) and* The Sociological Imagination *(1959). The first of these books argued that American society was in effect run by an elite of businessmen, politicians, and generals, who conspired to perpetuate the Cold War in order to sustain the military economy on which their power, prestige, and profits were based. In* The Sociological Imagination *Mills first took up the theme that concerns him in the present essay, and which Herbert Marcuse echoes in* One-Dimensional Man: *the uncritical and implicitly conservative empiricism of the American academic establishment.*

The selection by Herbert Marcuse (b. 1898) provides a fitting climax for this anthology. His work is the most rigorous manifestation of the new radicalism and marks a significant confluence of the American and European intellectual traditions. A German émigré schooled in the writings of Marx and Hegel, and the author of a major theoretical treatise on Freud, Marcuse has become in the 1960's a trenchant — and surprisingly popular — critic of American society. Moreover, despite his basically European intellectual orientation, Marcuse explicitly acknowledges the contribution of American radicals, above all C. Wright Mills, to the development of his most recent thinking.

In "The New Forms of Control," the first chapter of his book One-Dimensional Man, *Marcuse treats an issue that has preoccupied the new radicals almost as much as the role of Western imperialism in the Third World: the development of a repressively affluent society at home. Marcuse's prose is demanding — he enjoys paradoxical and ironic formulations — but the main themes of his critique are clear enough. In the affluent society, he tells us, repression and exploitation have assumed much more subtle, and therefore more insidious, forms than in previous cultures. The very success of our society in providing an apparently endless supply of goods and services makes oppositional action — even oppositional thinking — all but impossible. Yet, like Mills, Marcuse continues to hope that critical social theory will find a receptive audience. And again like Mills, Marcuse has, in his most recent writings, turned to the young — "the young intelligentsia," in Mills's language — to provide that audience.*

Ideology and Revolution
(1960)

JEAN-PAUL SARTRE

A few days ago at the University I was asked a question that I reproach myself with having answered too briefly: "Can there be a Revolution without an ideology?" Since *Lunes de Revolucion* has seen fit to offer me its pages, I propose to analyze the problem more fully. One can guess that it is not just a matter of constructing some theory or other about Revolutions in general and about the abstract notions which guide them. It is Cuba which is the case in point: the nature of the tie which unites actions and ideas is a very special characteristic of the social movement which is developing here. In what follows below I will set forth the observations which impress themselves upon a foreign observer.

Ideology Defined

But before anything else we must define our terms. Let us say, therefore, that an ideology is a system of theoretical and practical ideas whose entirety ought, at one and the same time, to be founded upon, interpret, and surpass experience in the unity of rational and technical projections. We shall not say that it is a science, although science may sustain it; indeed, it is less a question of disinterested knowledge than of the thoughts formed by the people of a particular society, inasmuch as they are both the witnesses and the members of the said society. These are practical thoughts, as can be seen, and ones which not only try to seize social structures in their essence, but above all try to maintain them or to change them. Ideology brings a practical vision to objective circum-

From *Studies on the Left*, I (1960), 7–16. This article appeared as a translation of an article Sartre wrote for *Lunes de Revolucion* (No. 51, March 21, 1960), while visiting Cuba.

stances. It means that it [ideology] itself establishes a *program*. Even on occasions when it seems to describe, it prepares the action; it acts. The reactionary formula, "No sugar, no Cuba" ["Without sugar there is no country"], was put forth as an empirical contention. The cultivation of sugar cane has in fact produced a particular kind of community, and the phrase I have just quoted is nothing more than an ideology in a primitive state: under its false objectivity, it reveals itself to be a rejection of everything that tries to change the "status quo." It tries to discourage rebellion against the social order by presenting the latter as the expression of a natural order; that phrase gives the Cubans their misery in the form of a destiny. It is the same as saying that it embodies a pessimistic view of man: since man cannot change his life, let him resign himself to one which has been imposed upon him. Behind the rigors of nature, primitive ideology already permits us to divine the supernatural consolations. One could oppose this conservative thought with the optimism which knows how to transform the conditions of life and which trusts in man to make history on the basis of past events. Whatever the progressive ideology that is adopted, in all cases, as we understand it, it bears with it a practical judgment on men. Thus what we are doing is nothing less than deciding on the human condition when we present it as if it were smothered in this world by inflexible laws; and, similarly, we are deciding on the human condition when we take our destiny into our own hands. And all ideology which deals with man in the social community defines man starting from the basis of the practical task of conserving or of changing his common structures; there is nothing surprising here since that ideology has been produced in everyone by the situation itself, and by the depth of passions and interests. It is the reflection of a social medium upon itself that defines men, starting from the practical task of defending their privileges or of conquering their fundamental rights.

Ideological Constructs

I said that there were primitive ideologies; there are others that are very elaborate. It happens also that some of them contain, at the same time, a judgment on men, a definite political and social program, and even the study of the necessary means to realize them. In this last instance, knowledge allows for the clarification of every practical measure: empiricism and its costly errors are avoided, dangers can be foreseen, and plans can be established. The advantage of so minutely developed a system escapes no one: it knows where it is going; it can also be added that an agreement on precise ideas, on immediate or long range objectives, should be a unifying factor. The more vague the ideas are, the greater the risk of misunderstanding and, finally, of internal dissension; but if a group accepts an ideology that is without ambiguity, this will inevitably lead it to integration. On the other hand, what it gains in force it will lose in flexibility: everything is foreseen but the unforeseen — which emerges to shake the edifice and which it is more comfortable to deny by asserting that nothing has occurred, nothing has happened. The danger of those great ossified monsters constitutes what is called voluntarism. The program is made in advance; upon it, particular plans are calculated: there will be produced so much wheat, so much cotton, so many machines and tools within five or ten years. I have seen men of my own age, in a great Empire, making plans for the final years of this century. I knew that we would all be dead by then and they also knew it — but the ideology would live on.

What is first surprising in Cuba — especially if one has visited the countries of the East — is the apparent absence of ideology. Ideologies, however, are not what this century lacks; right here they have representatives who are offering their services from all sides. Your leaders do not ignore them. They simply do not make use of them. Their adversaries formulate the most contradictory reproaches. For some of them, that absence of ideas is only a deception; it hides a rigorous Marxism which does not yet dare to reveal its name: some day the Cubans will take off their mask and Communism will be implanted in the Caribbean, just a few miles from Miami. Other enemies — or, at times, the same ones — accuse them of not thinking at all: "They are improvising," I have been told, "and then after having done something they make up a theory." Some politely add, "Try to speak to the members of the government; perhaps they know what they are doing. Because as far as we are concerned, I must confess that we know absolutely nothing at all." And a few days ago at the University, a student declared, "To the extent that the Revolution has not defined its objectives, Autonomy becomes all the more indispensible to us."

"The Revolution Is a Praxis"

I have heard all this answered a thousand times: "The Revolution is a *praxis* which forges its ideas in action." That reply is logically unassailable, but one has to admit that it turns out to be a little abstract. To be sure, one must understand the uneasiness — sincere or pretended — of those who say they know nothing about it at all, or who reproach the revolutionary movement for not having defined its goals. As a matter of fact, in Paris, several months ago, some Cuban friends came to see me. They spoke to me heatedly for a long time about the Revolution, but I tried in vain to get them to tell me whether or not the new regime would be socialist. Today I have to admit that I was wrong in stating the problem in those terms. But when a person is far away he is rather abstract and he tends to fall into those great words that today constitute symbols more than programs. Socialism? A Liberal Economy? Many minds ponder: they are convinced in good faith that a Revolution should know where it is going.

In fact, they are mistaken. Our Revolution, the French Revolution of 1789, was completely blind. The bourgeoisie — who carried it out — believed they were the universal goddess; they understood too late the conflict which opposed them to the people. These same people who voted for the Republic had been monarchists two years earlier. It all ended with a military dictatorship which saved the rich and restored the Monarchy. And behind the mirages of an inflexible rigor, how many vacillations, how many errors, how many setbacks, were produced during the first years of the Russian Revolution! The N.E.P. was imposed because of the circumstances; the U.S.S.R. did not foresee the failure of the revolutionary movements in Europe, nor its own isolation. New ideas were expressed within the framework of an inflexible ideology; they became ruptures: Socialism in one country, the permanent Revolution — inventions which they believed could be justified by means of quotations. And Marxist thought was disarmed in the face of peasant resistance: they made a turn to the right, then to the left, then a new turn to the right. No matter how rigorous, or how wide its experiments, an ideology outlives the present by a very narrow margin.

Nevertheless, the question continues to be raised and it will be enough to answer those who ask, "Are you going to establish Socialism?" by saying that the *praxis* will itself define its ideology. Perhaps it would be better to show the theoretical consequences of the action that is developing in Cuba. Perhaps the dialectical ties which unite action with thought will be better seen. Even though I myself, who am a stranger to Cuba, have had to follow the path of an outsider, I saw beyond the things which were explained to me: that deeds produce ideas. Therefore, I do not think it useless to retrace my itinerary here.

Rebound and Radicalization

Ideas come in pairs and they contradict one another; their opposition is the principal engine of reflexion [*motor principal de la reflexión*]. Here is the first conflict I became aware of: someone who was speaking to me of your Revolution, a leader, stated that your action could not set itself a long range objective, "because it is a *re-action*, or if you wish, a rebound."

By that he meant that your people, placed next to a much too powerful neighbor, never had absolute initiative, and were obliged to use all their resources of intelligence and energy in order to *invent* a counterblow. And he added, "How can we make long range plans when we might be invaded tomorrow, or when we might have to bear the most intense economic pressure? The guerilla warfare, the resistance to an economic block, will necessarily change the structure of our society. The one thing we do know is this: we will not be defeated. But the conditions of our struggle will change us; a *different* Cuba will know the victory." I understood that he meant that your "improvisations" were, in fact, nothing but a defensive technique; the Cuban Revolution had to *adjust* itself constantly to the enemies' tactics. Can it be the case that these *counter-measures* will give birth to a counter-ideology?

And yet, more or less in those days, other leaders spoke to me of themselves. I questioned them about their lives, about the evolution of their thought. All told me that the Revolution had pulled them much further than their original positions. Violent shocks had occurred and they had had to confront severe realities; some of their old friends had not continued to follow the movement; others, at first reluctantly, had become *radicalized.*

The shock of rebound, or radicalization? The two concepts seemed to me, at first, incompatible. In the first instance, I thought, one adapts oneself, one contemporizes, everything has to remain fluid, and principles should not constitute a hindrance. In the second place, the revolutionary movement becomes more profound in a sure and regular manner; there exists, therefore, an advancing order, reference points, a direction. Perhaps it would be too ambitious to call the discovery of an orientation "ideology," but we must at least admit that the exigencies of the praxis have changed the ideas of those revolutionary leaders.

"La Coubre"

At that stage of my reflections, the sabotage of the steamship "La Coubre" occurred. I saw Fidel Castro in the tribunal and the people standing before him. Castro spoke. The afternoon sun set on those sombre faces; then the night came. The aggression, whoever had been responsible for it, produced that shock, Castro's speech, the assembly of citizens. In order to adjust to the enemy's attack the head of the government had to demand even more of your people, and, in turn, they had to trust him even more; he called for an indissoluble unity, and justly enough, the criminal act of the evening before united you in rage and in the mobilization of all your energies. If, two days before, there still remained in the depths of some souls a little laxity, a desire to rest, a lazy negligence, or a comfortable optimism, the affront swept away all those cowardly ideas: one had to fight an implacable enemy; one had to win. Castro identified himself with the people, his sole support; the people at the same time manifested their approbation and intransigence. The aggressor had taken the initiative, but the counter-blow provoked by his insensibility was the radicalization of the people through their leaders, and of the leaders through the people — that is to say, the least favored classes. At that moment I understood that the enemy, because of his tactics, had only accelerated an internal process which was developing according to its own laws. The Revolution had adapted itself to the acts of the foreign power; it was inventing its counter-thrusts. But the very situation of this country which was strangled for so long, caused its counter-blows to be always more radical, conceding more strongly each time to the just reclamations [*a las revindicaciones*] of the masses. By trying to crush your Revolution, the enemy allowed it to convert itself into what it was. I believe I discovered in the history of your struggles the inflexible rigor of an idea.

To sum up, I will say that a movement — which began in the form of a "putsch" — saw its objectives disappear one after another, each time discovering new objectives, more popular and more profound; in a word, more revolutionary. And you understood, it seems to me — some of you right away, others little by little — that the order of your goals had been presenting itself inversely: in order to arrive at the most immediate and apparently most simple objectives, you had, from the beginning, to aim at the most complicated and distant ones. But the opposite is also true; in order to carry along the entire nation, you had to propose in the first place universal objectives which would not be achieved until the end.

Old Corruption and New Optimism

What were, then, those abstract objectives which seemed to be within reach and which produced the unification of all the classes? They are well known; others — in 1933, and in 1944 — had already defined them: a sovereign Nation, honorable leaders, free citizens. During the first half of the century more than one attempt was made to realize this ideal, but they all ended in failure. One could observe, nevertheless, that the demands might seem modest. They constitute the most clear and simple affirmation of Democracy under its parliamentary and middle class form: citizens ought to defend their rights by means of their vote; they delegate their powers to representatives whose honesty must be controlled by universal suffrage (if they steal, they should not be re-elected), and whose task should be to defend from within and from without the interests of that totality which is the country.

That abstract idea could, in a given moment, unite the entire world. Who would not demand freedom against tyranny, honesty against corruption? Without any doubt — and especially in the cities — the 26th of July Movement reached all social classes, because in the beginning it wanted no more than this. Batista had to be overthrown. No one asked himself then, why, in 1933 and in 1944, men who had in the beginning been honest and rebellious in the face of the corruption of the rest, had let themselves in turn be corrupted little by little, and ended by betraying the country. No one asked himself that, and yet, in a certain form, the question was in everyone's mind, and it even received an *ideological* and pessimistic answer. The uneasiness of the Cubans, their scepticism

— at the moment the 26th of July Movement was about to be born — was founded upon a deep contempt for politicians; and that contempt, justified by long experience, rendered, in a certain form, service to the conservatives. The same quietism which made the country people [*campesinos*] resign themselves when they were told "No sugar, no Cuba" ["Without sugar there is no country"], the same discouragement, real or pretended, the same misanthropy, led some to despair: men do not change, power ruins them, they will always have their price. Once again, from the shadows, a *theory* of human nature crept in, which converted your miseries into an immutable destiny. And with respect to those who refused to accept that total submission, who tried to unite themselves against the tyrant, their contempt for parliamentarianism and their very uneasiness demonstrated that they had nothing with which to oppose those crafty ideologies of despair, except their youth, courage, and will to change. However, while they were so involved on the abstract plane of parliamentarianism, experience spoke against it. And, from that moment on, they felt the necessity of *another* ideology to support their efforts and to return confidence to them. It was, if you wish, the diagram of a theory of man and of his powers; it came, *called forth by the counter-blow;* no one had planned it, but it already contained the germ of radicalism since it provided the Cubans with a way of *thinking* about their condition and of changing it.

The first elements of that new theory were given by practice: Fidel Castro landed on the Island one day and climbed up to the Sierra Maestra. The romantic heroism of that landing covered with a brilliant veil the other aspect of his attempt: the rigorous development of a thought which was, at the same time, inventing its conclusions and its method, so that the first ideas, the beginnings of the doctrine, were developed in the shadows and went winning spirits without their being aware of it. The politician would always be for sale; Cuba could not live without sugar cane — Castro brought together those two pessimistic decrees and saw clearly that both constituted a whole. The example of your reform politicians, of their failures and corruption, could be compared to other efforts and to other defeats: in Latin America and even in China, anyplace where the apparent existence of a parliamentary and sovereign democracy conceals the semi-colonial nature of the economic regime. In Cuba itself the corruption could not have been the simple consequence of human nature: it had its origin in the degrading mixture of power and impotence which had characterized all your governments. Institutions that pretend to be founded on liberty are necessarily degraded when their real foundation is servitude. The development of a one-crop economy presents itself as the *apparent* outcome of a free choice; Cuba seems to have freely accepted American investments. The transformation of the social structure which resulted from this could no longer be regarded as freely accepted. The regime of the one-crop system had to give your country one of the most typical characteristics of "semi-colonialism": it forced all your national activities to submit to a dependence upon one sector of production controlled by the foreign power, directly linked to exportation. Your economy was completely conditioned by variations in the price of sugar in foreign markets; it could not direct itself and it remained at the mercy of a fall in price and values. Those cataclysms which menaced your economy from outside, its instability, the inevitable succession of "lean" and "fat" years were not the consequence of general and absolute laws, but must be seen as the results — rigorous, in effect — of a semi-colonial economy. No decree of Nature or of Providence had ever impeded the development of a multi-crop system or of national industries. But one of the necessities of "semi-colonialism" is that the semi-colonial power — in this case the United States — oppose itself to the industrialization of the semi-colonized country in order to avoid the risks of competition, and so that the industries necessary to the "semi-colony" remain under the permanent control of the semi-colonizers, and are converted into a source of profit. One of the most obvious consequences of that system is exemplified by the fact that your country, strangled by the one-crop system, imported nearly half of the food products it consumed. In the midst of that almost total dependence, what could the politicians who governed you have done? For the country, nothing. Their impotence came not from their vices but from their servitude; and their vices, on the other hand, were born from their impotence. Those men who perhaps had been in the opposition, dreaming sincerely of serving the public interest, found themselves, due to a species of mystification of which they were first the victims and then the accomplices, with nothing else to defend when they attained power but their own private interests. So that the corruption seemed, in the eyes of your revolutionary leaders, since 1952, to be an effect and not a cause. If one wished the government to be honest, then one had to act precisely upon the causes that had corrupted the ruling officials. In other words, the bourgeois democracy was nothing more than a flat joke if it were not founded upon national sovereignty. And that sovereignty, in turn, even if all the countries in the world recognized it verbally, would continue to be an empty abstraction so long as it was not the concrete consequence of economic independence. The first objectives of the revolutionary struggle were already manifesting themselves, revealing a more radical and more imperative finality.

But though the immense majority of Cubans should have understood and demanded that independence, an infamous but powerful minority found it was not in their interest. What then appeared in a manifest way was the fact that the economic imperialism of the Foreign Power necessarily created its own accomplices in the very countries it was crushing. The faulty structure of your society had its origin in the one-crop system.

The one-crop system in its turn created the privileged and the victims; that is to say, the colonial structures of super-exploitation. The internal markets of the country, also controlled by the United States, continued to be limited; the one-crop system went along jointly with the *latifundias*. That backward form of cultivation, the only extensive one, not only left immense tracts of land uncultivated, but it likewise created a handful of privileged people who were the owners of everything and who kept the mass of the country people in poverty: national production could find no outlet in the internal market because the vast majority of the country people [*campesinos*] completely lacked purchasing power. In that way, the great landowners — whether they were conscious of it or not — were the representatives of foreign imperialism on their own soil: to fight for the independence of the Cuban economy, for the sovereignty of your State and for the honesty of your ruling officials, was *first* to fight against them. The political objective had vanished before the economic objective and the latter, in turn, has vanished before the social objective. Students and the petit bourgeoisie wanted at first to reform the institutions. But the revolutionaries, upon *thinking* of their just claims for reform [*sus revindicaciones reformistas*], quickly discovered the only instrument capable of carrying them out: the people — and especially the most numerous and disinherited class: the agricultural workers.

The Liberation of Cuba

The liberation of Cuba, in this moment of revolutionary thought, is found in the hands of its people. Doubly so: only the people can sustain themselves until the end in the fight for independence, because the people suffer in their bodies from the hunger, poverty, sickness, and inexorable fatigue of Cuba's dependency. And only by means of raising the people's standard of living, only in that way, will the sterilizing structure of the economy be broken, and a new impetus be given to the movement for industrialization, and to the development of a multi-crop system. The radicalization of the ideology is also found here through practice. Fidel Castro and his soldiers landed near Santiago; the reason was very simple, but it had to be discovered. That *practical* discovery which will condition all the revolutionary ideology will constitute Castro's historic merit. Nehru said of Gandhi: he looked for the weak point in the system and, once he had discovered it, he struck at it without resting and the entire system toppled. In other terms, in order to overcome the caste system, Gandhi conceived the practical and radical idea of attacking the weakest and most fundamental element: the problem of the pariah. For Castro, whose thought seems, on this point, to be close to Gandhi's, it was not sufficient to overthrow the semi-colonial regime: he had to find the weakest point of the entire edifice and strike hard. He realized what the weakness of the preceding revolutionary movements in Cuba and in Latin

American countries had been: the revolutions had always been carried out with the consent of the national Army. But this Army, whose leaders belonged to the privileged class, identified their interests with those of the great land-owners; they accepted as a matter of course the overthrow of a tyrant who was too unpopular, but only in order to carry out an imperceptible undermining of the new regime, to neutralize its attempts to reform and finally, by means of a *coup d'etat,* to make it abandon power. The Cuban army protected the large landholdings [*latifundias*] and was, without being clearly aware of it, the instrument of foreign imperialism. That army would be opposed to any structural reform. Since, however, it constituted the only strength of the large landowners, if it disappeared, all possibilities of sabotaging a reform would disappear with it. The Army, therefore, had to be attacked first and it had to be attacked where it was weakest: in the country, and not in the cities, counting on the help of the country people who were being oppressed. With it the semi-colonial system would topple. That clear and practical vision, which was concretized in the struggles in the Sierra Maestra, put the revolutionaries in direct contact with the class of country people [*la clase campesina*] and inflexibly produced its radicalization. They first discovered the rural poverty, exploitation, unhappiness: that discovery constituted for most of them a total shock; little by little they began to understand its full importance. But, in addition, if the rural population was to take the struggle for independence into their own hands, they had to begin by being shown that independence was *their* affair and in *their* fundamental interest. The very nature of the struggle had to reveal to the rebels the profound exigencies of the people: to attack Batista's army in the country and to promote Agrarian Reform were at bottom one and the same thing. And, at the conclusion of this long development, one could see the first elements of an ideology appear: the sovereignty of Cuba, its independence, the honesty of its leaders, and the Agrarian Reform were indissolubly linked; the raising of the people's standard of living and the radical change of the old structures, reciprocally conditioned each other. There is no middle ground between the defeatist ideology of bourgeois parliamentarianism, individualism, and the humanistic ideology of the people. Man is capable of changing the conditions of his life. But he cannot change whatever he wishes and however he wishes; indeed, only by changing *himself* can he change objective needs. He can obtain national sovereignty and freedom, but he can only do it by overthrowing the false bourgeois democracy which preserved the misery of the regime of property. He can do it only if he stops thinking of himself and stops loving himself as a *separate individual* who is proud of his differences and perfectly important, so that he may transform himself into the people, and through the people into a free person in the midst of all the rest.

I shall stop my reflections here. We have seen how a lucid practice has changed in Cuba even the very notion of man. We have also seen how human abstract problems (honesty, sovereignty) lead to the concrete problems of production and of social structures, and how those problems constitute the practical and material aspect of the entire human and humanistic question. The method of thought appears very clear here: never to separate the exigencies of production and the exigencies of man. The dual aspect of the Agrarian Reform is a clear example of this: It grants a new purchasing power to the rural classes and breaks foreign domination by creating an internal market. But, at the same time, the Agrarian Reform is *just:* it overcomes privileges and poverty; it lets the worker be the master of the land and build a house on it. Those two indissoluble characteristics constitute perhaps the originality of the Cuban ideology: the human problem must be resolved in terms of production; the only viable development of production will be that which satisfies, in everyone, all of the needs of man.

After this we can understand why the government does not worry about formulating socialist and liberal declarations: what it does day after day under foreign pressure takes on, in its eyes, an original and profound meaning. Radical socialization would be today an abstract objective, and it would only be desirable in the name of a prefabricated ideology, since objective necessities do not require it at the moment. If some day it were necessary to restore to it, it would first be done, for example, to resist a blockade and as a war economy measure. But, at any rate, the phenomenon will emerge with a dual characteristic which we find in all measures adopted by the revolutionary government: it will be a reaction, a counterblow, and if they had to maintain it, it would be the expression of the authentic sentiment of the Cuban Revolution and the termination of its self-radicalization. On the other hand, at the moment we would feel sure that the aforementioned socialization would satisfy the new exigencies of production and of the just and human claims [*revindicaciones*] of the Cuban people. It is very certain that practice creates the idea which clarifies it. But we now know that it deals with a concrete and particular practice, which discovers and makes the Cuban man in action.

On the New Left

(1960)

C. WRIGHT MILLS

It is no exaggeration to say that since the end of World War II, smug conservatives, tired liberals and disillusioned radicals in Britain and the United States have carried on a weary discourse in which issues are blurred and potential debate muted; the sickness of complacency has prevailed, the bi-partisan banality flourished. There is no need to explain again why all this has come about among "people in general" in the NATO countries; but it may be worthwhile to examine one style of cultural work that is in effect an intellectual celebration of apathy.

Many intellectual fashions, of course, do just that; they stand in the way of a release of the imagination — about the cold war, the Soviet bloc, the politics of peace, about any new beginnings at home and abroad. But the fashion I have in mind is the weariness of many NATO intellectuals with what they call "ideology," and their proclamation of "the end of ideology." So far as I know, this fashion began in the mid-fifties, mainly in intellectual circles more or less associated with the Congress for Cultural Freedom and the magazine *Encounter*. Reports on the Milan Conference of 1955 heralded it; since then, many cultural gossips have taken it up as a posture and an unexamined slogan. Does it amount to anything?

I

Its common denominator is not liberalism as a political philosophy, but the liberal rhetoric, become formal and sophisticated and used as an uncriticized weapon with which to attack Marxism. In the approved style, various elements of this rhetoric appear simply as snobbish assumptions. Its sophistication is one of tone rather than of ideas: in it, the *New Yorker* style of reportage has become politically triumphant. The disclosure of fact — set forth in a bright-faced or in a dead-pan manner — is the rule. The facts are duly weighed, carefully balanced, always hedged. Their power to outrage, their power truly to enlighten in a political way, their power to aid decision, even their power to clarify some situation — all that is blunted or destroyed.

So reasoning collapses into reasonableness. By the more naive and snobbish celebrants of complacency, arguments and facts of a displeasing

From *Studies on the Left*, II (1961), 63–72.

kind are simply ignored; by the more knowing, they are duly recognized, but they are neither connected with one another nor related to any general view. Acknowledged in a scattered way, they are never put together: to do so is to risk being called, curiously enough, "one-sided."

This refusal to relate isolated facts and fragmentary comment to the changing institutions of society makes it impossible to understand the structural realities which these facts reveal or the longer-run trends of which they might be tokens. In brief, fact and idea are isolated, so the real questions are not even raised, analysis of the meanings of facts not even begun.

Practitioners of the no-more-ideology school do, of course, smuggle in general ideas under the guise of reportage, by intellectual gossip, and by their selection of the notions they handle. Ultimately, the-end-of-ideology is based upon a disillusionment with any real commitment to socialism in any recognizable form. *That* is the only "ideology" that has really ended for these writers. But with its ending, *all* ideology, they think, has ended. *That* ideology they talk about; their own ideological assumptions, they do not. Yet these assumptions, which they snobbishly take for granted, provide the terms of their rejection of "all ideology"; and upon these assumptions they themselves stand.

Underneath this style of observation and comment there is the assumption that in the West there are no more real issues or even problems of great seriousness. The mixed economy plus the welfare state plus prosperity — that is the formula. U.S. capitalism will continue to be workable; the welfare state will continue along the road to ever greater justice. In the meantime, things everywhere are very complex; let us not be careless; there are great risks.

This posture — one of "false consciousness" if there ever was one — stands in the way, I think, of considering with any chances of success what may be happening in the world.

First and above all, this posture rests upon a simple provincialism. If the phrase "the end of ideology" has any meaning at all, it pertains to self-selected circles of intellectuals in the richer countries. It is in fact merely their own self-image. The total population of these countries is a fraction of mankind; the period during which such a posture has been assumed is very short indeed. To speak in such terms of much of Latin-America, Africa, Asia, the Soviet bloc is merely ludicrous. Anyone who stands in front of audiences — intellectual or mass — in any of these places and talks in such terms will merely be shrugged off (if the audience is polite) or laughed at out loud (if the audience is more candid and knowledgeable). The end-of-ideology is a slogan of complacency, circulating among the prematurely middle-aged, centered in the present, and in the rich Western societies. In the final analysis, it also rests upon a disbelief in the shaping by men of their own futures — as history and as biography. It is a consensus of a few provincials about their own immediate and provincial position.

Second, the end-of-ideology is of course itself an ideology — a fragmentary one, to be sure, and perhaps more a mood. The end-of-ideology is in reality the ideology of an ending: the ending of political reflection itself as a public fact. It is a weary know-it-all justification, by tone of voice rather than by explicit argument, of the cultural and political default of the NATO intellectuals.

II

All this is just the sort of thing that I at least have always objected to, and do object to, in the "socialist realism" of the Soviet Union.

There too, criticism of milieux are of course permitted, but they are not to be connected with criticism of the structure itself: one may not question "the system." There are no "antagonistic contradictions."

There too, in novels and plays, criticisms of characters, even of party members, are permitted, but they must be displayed as "shocking exceptions"; they must be seen as survivals from the old order, not as systematic products of the new.

There too, pessimism is permitted, but only episodically and only within the context of the big optimism; the tendency is to confuse any systematic or structural criticism with pessimism itself. So they admit criticisms, first of this and then of that, but engulf them all by the long-run historical optimism about the system as a whole and the goals proclaimed by its leaders.

I neither want nor need to overstress the parallel, yet in a recent series of interviews in the Soviet Union concerning socialist realism I was very much struck by it. In Uzbekistan and Georgia, as well as in Russia, I kept writing notes to myself at the end of recorded interviews: "This man talks in a style just like Arthur Schlesinger Jr." "Surely this fellow is the counterpart of Daniel Bell, except not so — what shall I say? — so gossipy; and certainly neither so petty nor so vulgar as the more envious status-climbers. Perhaps this is because here they are not thrown into such a competitive status-panic about the ancient and obfuscating British models of prestige." "The would-be enders of ideology," I kept thinking, "are they not the self-coordinated or, better, the fashion-coordinated, socialist realists of the NATO world?" And: "Check this carefully with the files of *Encounter* and *The Reporter*." I have now done so; it is the same kind of thing.

Certainly there are many differences: above all, the fact that socialist realism is part of an official line, while the end of ideology is self-managed. But the differences one knows. It is more useful to stress the parallels, and the generic fact that both of these postures stand opposed to radical criticisms of their respective societies.

In the Soviet Union, only political authorities at the top, or securely on their way up there, can seriously tamper with structural questions and ideological lines. These authorities, of course, are much more likely to be intellectuals (in one or another sense of the word — say a man who actually writes his own speeches) than are American politicians. Moreover, since the death of Stalin, such Soviet authorities *have* begun to tamper quite seriously with structural questions and basic ideology, although for reasons peculiar to the tight and official joining of culture and politics in their set-up, they must try to disguise this fact.

The end-of-ideology is very largely a mechanical reaction, not a creative response, to the ideology of Stalinism. As such it takes from its opponent something of its inner quality. What it all means is that these people have become aware of the uselessness of vulger Marxism, but are not yet aware of the uselessness of the liberal rhetoric.

III

But the most immediately important thing about the "end of ideology" is that it *is* merely a fashion, and fashions change. Already this one is on its way out. Even a few diehard anti-Stalinists are showing signs of a reappraisal of their own past views; some are even beginning to recognize publicly that Stalin himself no longer runs the Soviet party and state. They begin to see the poverty of their comfortable ideas as they come to confront Khrushchev's Russia.

We who have been, in moral terms, consistently radical in our work throughout the postwar period are often amused nowadays that various writers, sensing another shift in fashion, are beginning to call upon intellectuals to work once more in ways that are politically explicit. But we should not be merely amused; we ought to try to make their shift more than a fashion change.

The end-of-ideology is on the decline because it stands for the refusal to work out an explicit political philosophy. And alert men everywhere today do feel the need for such a philosophy. What we should do is to continue directly to confront this need. In doing so, it may be useful to keep in mind that to have a working political philosophy means to have a philosophy that enables you to work, and that at least four kinds of work are needed, each of them at once intellectual and political.

In these terms, think for a moment longer of the end-of-ideology:

(1) It is a kindergarten fact that any political reflection that is of possible public significance is *ideological;* in its terms policies, institutions, and men of power are criticized or approved. In this respect, the end-of-ideology stands, negatively, for the attempt to withdraw oneself and one's work from political relevance; positively, it is an ideology of political complacency which seems the only way now open for many writers to acquiesce in or to justify the status quo.

(2) So far as orienting *theories* of society and of history are concerned, the end-of-ideology stands for, and presumably stands upon, a fetishism of empiricism: more academically, upon a pretentious methodology used to state trivialities about unimportant social areas; more essayistically, upon a naive journalistic empiricism — which I have already characterized above — and upon a cultural gossip in which "answers" to the vital and pivotal issues are merely assumed. Thus political bias masquerades as epistomological excellence, and there are no orienting theories.

(3) So far as the *historic agency of change* is concerned, the end-of-ideology rests upon the identification of such agencies with going institutions, perhaps upon their piecemeal reform, but never upon the search for agencies that might be used for, or that might themselves operate toward, a structural change of society. The problem of agency is never posed as a problem to solve, as "our problem." Instead there is endless talk of the need to be pragmatic, flexible, open. Surely all this has already been adequately dealt with: such a view makes sense politically only if the blind drift of human affairs is in general beneficent.

(4) So far as political and human *ideals* are concerned, the end-of-ideology stands for a denial of their relevance, except as abstract ikons. Merely to hold such ideals seriously is in this view "utopian."

IV

But enough. Where do *we* stand on each of these four aspects of political philosophy? Various of us are of course at work on each of them, and all of us are generally aware of our needs in regard to each. As for the articulation of ideals, there I think your magazines have done their best work so far.[1] That is *your* meaning — is it not? — of the emphasis upon cultural affairs. As for ideological analysis and the rhetoric with which to carry it out, I do not think any of us is nearly good enough. But that will come with further advance on the two fronts where we are weakest: theories of society, history, and human nature, and — the major problem — ideas about the historical agencies of structural change.

We have frequently been told by an assorted variety of dead-end people that the meanings of left and of right are now liquidated, by history and by reason. I think we should answer them in some such way as this:

The *Right*, among other things, means what you are doing: celebrating society as it is, a going concern. *Left* means, or ought to mean, just the opposite. It means structural criticism and reportage and theories of society, which at some point or another are focussed politically as demands and programs. These criticisms, demands, theories, programs are guided morally by the humanist and secular ideals of Western civilization —

[1] This refers to *The New Left Review, The New Reasoner*, and *Universities & Left Review*, all of Great Britain. Eds.

above all, the ideals of reason, freedom and justice. To be "left" means to connect up cultural with political criticism, and both with demands and programs. And it means all this inside *every* country of the world.

Only one more point of definition: absence of public issues there may well be, but this is not due to any absence of problems or of contradictions, antagonistic and otherwise. Impersonal and structural changes have not eliminated problems or issues. Their absence from many discussions is an ideological condition, regulated in the first place by whether or not intellectuals detect and state problems as potential *issues* for probable publics, and as *troubles* for a variety of individuals. One indispensible means of such work on these central tasks is what can only be described as ideological analysis. To be actively left, among other things, is to carry on just such analysis.

To take seriously the problem of the need for a political orientation is not, of course, to seek for A Fanatical and Apocalyptic Vision, for An Infallible and Monolithic Lever of Change, for Dogmatic Ideology, for A Startling New Rhetoric, for Treacherous Abstractions, and all the other bogeymen of the dead-enders. These are, of course, "the extremes," the straw men, the red herrings used by our political enemies to characterize the polar opposite of where they think they stand.

They tell us, for example, that ordinary men cannot always be political "heroes." Who said they could? But keep looking around you; and why not search out the conditions of such heroism as men do and might display? They tell us that we are too "impatient," that our "pretentious" theories are not well enough grounded. That is true, but neither are our theories trivial. Why don't they get to work to refute or ground them? They tell us we "do not really understand" Russia and China today. That is true; we don't; neither do they. We at least are studying the question. They tell us we are "ominous" in our formulations. That is true: we do have enough imagination to be frightened, and we don't have to hide it. We are not afraid we'll panic. They tell us we are "grinding axes." Of course we are: we do have, among other points of view, morally grounded ones, and we are aware of them. They tell us, in their wisdom, that we do not understand that The Struggle is Without End. True: we want to change its form, its focus, its object.

We are frequently accused of being "utopian" in our criticisms and in our proposals and, along with this, of basing our hopes for a new left *politics* "merely on reason," or more concretely, upon the intelligentsia in its broadest sense.

There is truth in these charges. But must we not ask: What now is really meant by *utopian?* And is not our utopianism a major source of our strength? *Utopian* nowadays, I think, refers to any criticism or proposal that transcends the up-close milieux of a scatter of individuals, the milieux which men and women can understand directly and which they can reasonably hope directly to change. In this exact sense, our theoretical work is indeed utopian — in my own case, at least, deliberately so. What needs to be understood, and what needs to be changed, is not merely first this and then that detail of some institution or policy. If there is to be a politics of a new left, what needs to be analyzed is the *structure* of institutions, the *foundation* of policies. In this sense, both in its criticisms and in its proposals, our work is necessarily structural, and so — for *us*, just now — utopian.

This brings us face to face with the most important issue of political reflection and of political action in our time: the problem of the historical agency of change, of the social and institutional means of structural change. There are several points about this problem I would like to put to you.

V

First, the historic agencies of change for liberals of the capitalist societies have been an array of voluntary associations, coming to a political climax in a parliamentary or congressional system. For socialists of almost all varieties, the historic agency has been the working class — and later the peasantry, or parties and unions composed of members of the working class, or (to blur, for now, a great problem) of political parties acting in its name, "representing its interests."

I cannot avoid the view that both these forms of historic agency have either collapsed or become most ambiguous. So far as structural change is concerned, neither seems to be at once available and effective as *our* agency any more. I know this is a debatable point among us, and among many others as well; I am by no means certain about it. But surely, if it is true, it ought not to be taken as an excuse for moaning and withdrawal (as it is by some of those who have become involved with the end-of-ideology); and it ought not to be bypassed (as it is by many Soviet scholars and publicists, who in their reflections upon the course of advanced capitalist societies simply refuse to admit the political condition and attitudes of the working class).

Is anything more certain than that in 1970 — indeed, at this time next year — our situation will be quite different, and — the chances are high — decisively so? But of course, that isn't saying much. The seeming collapse of our historic agencies of change ought to be taken as a problem, an issue, a trouble — in fact, as *the* political problem which *we* must turn into issue and trouble.

Second, it is obvious that when we talk about the collapse of agencies of change, we cannot seriously mean that such agencies do not exist. On the contrary, the means of history-making — of decision and of the enforcement of decision — have never in world history been so enlarged and so available to such small circles of men on both sides of The Curtains as they now are. My own conception of the shape of power, the theory of the power elite, I feel no need to argue here. This theory has been fortunate in its critics, from the most diverse political viewpoints, and I have learned from several of these critics. But I have not seen, as of this date, an analysis of the idea that causes me to modify any of its essential features.

The point that is immediately relevant does seem obvious: what is utopian for us, is not at all utopian for the presidium of the Central Committee in Moscow, or the higher circles of the Presidency in Washington, or, recent events make evident, for the men of SAC and CIA. The historic agencies of change that have collapsed are those which were at least thought to be open to *the left* inside the advanced Western nations, to those who have wished for structural changes of these societies. Many things follow from this obvious fact; of many of them, I am sure, we are not yet adequately aware.

Third, what I do not quite understand about some new-left writers is why they cling so mightily to "the working class" of the advanced capitalist societies as *the* historic agency, or even as the most important agency, in the face of the really impressive historical evidence that now stands against this expectation.

Such a labor metaphysic, I think, is a legacy from Victorian Marxism that is now quite unrealistic.

It is an historically specific idea that has been turned into an a-historical and unspecific hope.

The social and historical conditions under which industrial workers tend to become a-class-for-themselves, and a decisive political force, must be fully and precisely elaborated. There have been, there are, there will be such conditions. These conditions vary according to national social structure and the exact phase of their economic and political development. Of course we cannot "write off the working class." But we must *study* all that, and freshly. Where labor exists as an agency, of course we must work with it, but we must not treat it as The Necessary Lever, as nice old Labour Gentlemen in Britain and elsewhere tend to do.

Although I have not yet completed my own comparative studies of working classes, generally it would seem that only at certain (earlier) stages of industrialization, and in a political context of autocracy, *etc.*, do wage-workers tend to become a class-for-themselves, *etc.* The *etceteras* mean that I can here merely raise the question.

VI

It is with this problem of agency in mind that I have been studying, for several years now, the cultural apparatus, the intellectuals, as a possible, immediate, radical agency of change. For a long time, I was not much happier with this idea than were many of you; but it turns out now, at the beginning of the 1960's, that it may be a very relevant idea indeed.

In the first place, is it not clear that if we try to be realistic in our utopianism — and that is no fruitless contradiction — a writer in our countries on the left today *must* begin with the intellectuals? For that is what we are, that is where we stand.

In the second place, the problem of the intelligentsia is an extremely complicated set of problems on which rather little factual work has been done. In doing this work, we must, above all, not confuse the problems of the intellectuals of West Europe and North America with those of the Soviet Bloc or with those of the underdeveloped worlds. In each of the three major components of the world's social structure today, the character and the role of the intelligentsia is distinct and historically specific. Only by detailed comparative studies of them in all their human variety can we hope to understand any one of them.

In the third place, who is it that is getting fed up? Who is it that is getting disgusted with what Marx called "all the old crap"? Who is it that is thinking and acting in radical ways? All over the world — in the bloc, outside the bloc and in between — the answer is the same: it is the young intelligentsia.

I cannot resist copying out for you, with a few changes, some materials I recently prepared for a 1960 paperback edition of a book of mine on war:

"In the spring and early summer of 1960, more of the returns from the American decision and default are coming in. In Turkey, after student riots, a military junta takes over the state, of late run by Communist Container Menderes. In South Korea, too, students and others knock over the corrupt American-puppet regime of Syngman Rhee. In Cuba, a genuinely left-wing revolution begins full-scale economic reorganization, without the domination of U.S. corporations. Average age of its leaders: about 30 — and certainly a revolution without Labor As Agency. On Taiwan, the eight million Taiwanese under the American-imposed dictatorship of Chiang Kai-shek, with his two million Chinese, grow increasingly restive. On Okinawa, a U.S. military base, the people get their first chance since World War II ended to demonstrate against U.S. seizure of their island; and some students take that chance, snake-dancing and chanting angrily to the visiting President: 'Go home, go home — take away your missiles.' (Don't worry, 12,000 U.S. troops easily handle the generally grateful crowds; also the President is 'spirited out the rear end of the United States compound' — and so by helicopter to the airport). In Japan, weeks of student rioting succeed in rejecting the President's visit, jeopardizing a new treaty with the U.S.A., and displacing the big-business, pro-American Prime Minister, Kishi. And even in our own pleasant Southland, Negro and white students are — but let us keep that quiet: it really *is* disgraceful.

"That is by no means the complete list; that was yesterday; see today's newspaper. Tomorrow, in varying degree, the returns will be more evident. Will they be evident enough? They will have to be very obvious to attract real American attention: sweet complaints and the voice of reason — these are not enough. In the slum countries of the world today, what are they saying? The rich Americans, they pay attention only to violence — and to money. You don't care what they say, American? Good for you. Still, they may insist; things are no longer under the old control; you're not getting it straight, American: your country — it would seem — may well become the target of a world hatred the like of which the easy-going Americans have never dreamed. Neutralists and Pacifists and Unilateralists and that confusing variety of Leftists around the world — all those tens of millions of people, of course they are misguided, absolutely controlled by small conspiratorial groups of trouble-makers, under direct orders from Moscow and Peking. Diabolically omnipotent, it is *they* who create all this messy unrest. It is *they* who have given the tens of millions the absurd idea that they shouldn't want to remain, or to become, the seat of American nuclear bases — those gay little outposts of American civilization. So now they don't want U-2's on their territory; so now they want to contract out of the American military machine; they want to be neutral among the crazy big antagonists. And they don't want their own societies to be militarized.

"But take heart, American: you won't have time to get really bored with your friends abroad: they won't be your friends much longer. You don't need *them;* it will all go away; don't let them confuse you."

Add to that: In the Soviet bloc, who is it that has been breaking out of apathy? It has been students and young professors and writers; it has been the young intelligentsia of Poland and Hungary, and of Russia, too. Never mind that they have not won; never mind that there are other social and moral types among them. First of all, it has been these types. But the point is clear, isn't it?

That is why we have got to study these new generations of intellectuals around the world as real live agencies of historic change. Forget Victorian Marxism, except when you need it; and read Lenin again (be careful) — Rosa Luxemburg, too.

"But it is just some kind of moral upsurge, isn't it?" Correct. But under it: no apathy. Much of it is direct non-violent action, and it seems to be working, here and there. Now we must learn from the practice of these young intellectuals and with them work out new forms of action.

"But it's all so ambiguous — Cuba, for instance." Of course it is; history-making is always ambiguous. Wait a bit; in the meantime, help them to focus their moral upsurge in less ambiguous political ways. Work out with them the ideologies, the strategies, the theories that will help them consolidate their efforts: new theories of structural changes of and by human societies in our epoch.

"But it is utopian, after all, isn't it?" No, not in the sense you mean.

Whatever else it may be, it's not that. Tell it to the students of Japan. Tell it to the Negro sit-ins. Tell it to the Cuban Revolutionaries. Tell it to the people of the Hungry-nation bloc.

The New Forms of Control

(1964)

HERBERT MARCUSE

A comfortable, smooth, reasonable, democratic unfreedom prevails in advanced industrial civilization, a token of technical progress. Indeed, what could be more rational than the suppression of individuality in the mechanization of socially necessary but painful performances; the concentration of individual enterprises in more effective, more productive corporations; the regulation of free competition among unequally equipped economic subjects; the curtailment of prerogatives and national sovereignties which impede the international organization of resources. That this technological order also involves a political and intellectual coordination may be a regrettable and yet promising development.

The rights and liberties which were such vital factors in the origins and earlier stages of industrial society yield to a higher stage of this society: they are losing their traditional rationale and content. Freedom of thought, speech, and conscience were — just as free enterprise, which they served to promote and protest — essentially *critical* ideas, designed to replace an obsolescent material and intellectual culture by a more productive and rational one. Once institutionalized, these rights and liberties shared the fate of the society of which they had become an integral part. The achievement cancels the premises.

To the degree to which freedom from want, the concrete substance of all freedom, is becoming a real possibility, the liberties which pertain to a state of lower productivity are losing their former content. Independence of thought, autonomy, and the right to political opposition are being deprived of their basic critical function in a society which seems increasingly capable of satisfying the needs of the individuals through the way in which it is organized. Such a society may justly demand acceptance of its principles and institutions, and reduce the opposition to the discussion and promotion of alternative policies *within* the status

From *One-Dimensional Man* by Herbert Marcuse. Reprinted by permission of the Beacon Press, quo. In this respect, it seems to make little difference whether the increasing satisfaction of needs is accomplished by an authoritarian or a non-authoritarian system. Under the conditions of a rising standard of living, non-conformity with the system itself appears to be socially useless, and the more so when it entails tangible economic and political disadvantages and threatens the smooth operation of the whole. Indeed, at least in so far as the necessities of life are involved, there seems to be no reason why the production and distribution of goods and services should proceed through the competitive concurrence of individual liberties.

Freedom of enterprise was from the beginning not altogether a blessing. As the liberty to work or to starve, it spelled toil, insecurity, and fear for the vast majority of the population. If the individual were no longer compelled to prove himself on the market, as a free economic subject, the disappearance of this kind of freedom would be one of the greatest achievements of civilization. The technological processes of mechanization and standardization might release individual energy into a yet uncharted realm of freedom beyond necessity. The very structure of human existence would be altered; the individual would be liberated from the work world's imposing upon him alien needs and alien possibilities. The individual would be free to exert autonomy over a life that would be his own. If the productive apparatus could be organized and directed toward the satisfaction of the vital needs, its control might well be centralized; such control would not prevent individual autonomy, but render it possible.

This is a goal within the capabilities of advanced industrial civilization, the "end" of technological rationality. In actual fact, however, the contrary trend operates: the apparatus imposes its economic and political requirements for defense and expansion on labor time and free time, on the material and intellectual culture. By virtue of the way it has organized its technological base, contemporary industrial society tends to be totalitarian. For "totalitarian" is not only a terroristic political coordination of society, but also a nonterroristic economic-technical coordination which operates through the manipulation of needs by vested interests. It thus precludes the emergence of an effected opposition against the whole. Not only a specific form of government or party rule makes for totalitarianism, but also a specific system of production and distribution which may well be compatible with a "pluralism" of parties, newspapers, "countervailing powers," etc.

Today political power asserts itself through its power over the machine process and over the technical organization of the apparatus. The government of advanced and advancing industrial societies can maintain and secure itself only when it succeeds in mobilizing, organizing, and exploiting the technical, scientific, and mechanical productivity available to industrial civilization. And this productivity mobilizes society as a whole, above and beyond any particular individual or group interests. The brute fact that the machine's physical (only physical?) power surpasses that of the individual, and of any particular group of individuals, makes the machine the most effective political instrument in any society whose basic organization is that of the machine process. But the political trend may be reversed; essentially the power of the machine is only the stored-up and projected power of man. To the extent to which the work world is conceived of as a machine and mechanized accordingly, it becomes the *potential* basis of a new freedom for man.

Contemporary industrial civilization demonstrates that it has reached the stage at which "the free society" can no longer be adequately defined in the traditional terms of economic, political, and intellectual liberties, not because these liberties have become insignificant, but because they are too significant to be confined within the traditional forms. New modes of realization are needed, corresponding to the new capabilities of society.

Such new modes can be indicated only in negative terms because they would amount to the negation of the prevailing modes. Thus economic freedom would mean freedom *from* the economy — from being controlled by economic forces and relationships; freedom from the daily struggle for existence, from earning a living. Political freedom would mean liberation of the individuals *from* politics over which they have no effective control. Similarly, intellectual freedom would mean the restoration of individual thought now absorbed by mass communication and indoctrination, abolition of "public opinion" together with its makers. The unrealistic sound of these propositions is indicative, not of their utopian character, but of the strength of the forces which prevent their realization. The most effective and enduring form of warfare against liberation is the implanting of material and intellectual needs that perpetuate obsolete forms of the struggle for existence.

The intensity, the satisfaction and even the character of human needs, beyond the biological level, have always been preconditioned. Whether or not the possibility of doing or leaving, enjoying or destroying, possessing or rejecting something is seized as a *need* depends on whether or not it can be seen as desirable and necessary for the prevailing societal institutions and interests. In this sense, human needs are historical needs and, to the extent to which the society demands the repressive development of the individual, his needs themselves and their claim for satisfaction are subject to overriding critical standards.

We may distinguish both true and false needs. "False" are those which are superimposed upon the individual by particular social interests in his repression: the needs which perpetuate toil, aggressiveness, misery, and injustice. Their satisfaction might be most gratifying to the individual, but this happiness is not a condition which has to be maintained and protected if it serves to arrest the development of the ability (his own and others) to recognize the disease of the whole and grasp the chances of curing the disease. The result then is euphoria in unhappiness. Most of the prevailing needs to relax, to have fun, to behave and consume in accordance with the advertisements, to love and hate what others love and hate, belong to this category of false needs.

Such needs have a societal content and function which are determined by external powers over which the individual has no control; the development and satisfaction of these needs is heteronomous. No matter how much such needs may have become the individual's own, reproduced and fortified by the conditions of his existence; no matter how much he identifies himself with them and finds himself in their satisfaction, they continue to be what they were from the beginning — products of a society whose dominant interest demands repression.

The prevalence of repressive needs is an accomplished fact, accepted in ignorance and defeat, but a fact that must be undone in the interest of the happy individual as well as all those whose misery is the price of his satisfaction. The only needs that have an unqualified claim for satisfaction are the vital ones — nourishment, clothing, lodging at the attainable level of culture. The satisfaction of these needs is the prerequisite for the realization of *all* needs, of the unsublimated as well as the sublimated ones.

For any consciousness and conscience, for any experience which does not accept the prevailing societal interest as the supreme law of thought and behavior, the established universe of needs and satisfactions is a fact to be questioned — questioned in terms of truth and falsehood. These terms are historical throughout, and their objectivity is historical. The judgment of needs and their satisfaction, under the given conditions, involves standards of *priority* — standards which refer to the optimal development of the individual, of all individuals, under the optimal utilization of the material and intellectual resources available to man. The resources are calculable. "Truth" and "falsehood" of needs designate objective conditions to the extent to which the universal satisfaction of vital needs and, beyond it, the progressive alleviation of toil and poverty, are universally valid standards. But as historical standards, they do not only vary according to area and stage of development, they also can be defined only in (greater or lesser) *contradiction* to the prevailing ones. What tribunal can possibly claim the authority of decision?

In the last analysis, the question of what are true and false needs must be answered by the individuals themselves, but only in the last analysis; that is, if and when they are free to give their own answer. As long as they are kept incapable of being autonomous, as long as they are indoctrinated and manipulated (down to their very instincts), their answer to this question cannot be taken as their own. By the same token, however, no tribunal can justly arrogate to itself the right to decide which needs should be developed and satisfied. Any such tribunal is reprehensible, although our revulsion does not do away with the question: how can the people who have been the object of effective and productive domination by themselves create the conditions of freedom?

The more rational, productive, technical, and total the repressive administration of society becomes, the more unimaginable the means and ways by which the administered individuals might break their servitude and seize their own liberation. To be sure, to impose Reason upon an entire society is a paradoxical and scandalous idea — although one might dispute the righteousness of a society which ridicules this idea while making its own population into objects of total administration. All liberation depends on the consciousness of servitude, and the emergence of this consciousness is always hampered by the predominance of needs and satisfactions which, to a great extent, have become the individual's own. The process always replaces one system of preconditioning by another; the optimal goal is the replacement of false needs by true ones, the abandonment of repressive satisfaction.

The distinguishing feature of advanced industrial society is its effective suffocation of those needs which demand liberation — liberation also from that which is tolerable and rewarding and comfortable — while it sustains and absolves the destructive power and repressive function of the affluent society. Here, the social controls exact the overwhelming need for the production and consumption of waste; the need for stupefying work where it is no longer a real necessity; the need for modes of relaxation which soothe and prolong this stupefication; the need for maintaining such deceptive liberties as free competition at administered prices, a free press which censors itself, free choice between brands and gadgets.

Under the rule of a repressive whole, liberty can be made into a powerful instrument of domination. The range of choice open to the individual is not the decisive factor in determining the degree of human freedom, but *what* can be chosen and what *is* chosen by the individual. The criterion for free choice can never be an absolute one, but neither is it entirely relative. Free election of masters does not abolish the masters or the slaves. Free choice among a wide variety of goods and services does not signify freedom if these goods and services sustain social controls over a life of toil and fear — that is, if they sustain alienation. And the spontaneous reproduction of superimposed needs by the individual does not establish autonomy; it only testifies to the efficacy of the controls.

Our insistence on the depth and efficacy of these controls is open to the objection that we overrate greatly the indoctrinating power of the "media," and that by themselves the people would feel and satisfy the needs which are now imposed upon them. The objection misses the point. The preconditioning does not start with the mass production of radio and television and with the centralization of their control. The people enter this stage as preconditioned receptacles of long standing; the decisive difference is in the flattening out of the contrast (or conflict) between the given and the possible, between the satisfied and the unsatisfied needs. Here, the so-called equalization of class distinctions reveals its ideological function. If the worker and his boss enjoy the same television program and visit the same resort places, if the typist is as attractively made up as the daughter of her employer, if the Negro owns a Cadillac, if they all read the same newspaper, then this assimilation indicates not the disappearance of classes, but the extent to which the needs and satisfactions that serve the preservation of the Establishment are shared by the underlying population.

Indeed, in the most highly developed areas of contemporary society, the transplantation of social into individual needs is so effective that the difference between them seems to be purely theoretical. Can one really distinguish between the mass media as instruments of information and entertainment, and as agents of manipulation and indoctrination? Between the automobile as nuisance and as convenience? Between the horrors and the comforts of functional architecture? Between the work for national defense and the work for corporate gain? Between the private pleasure and the commercial and political utility involved in increasing the birth rate?

We are again confronted with one of the most vexing aspects of advanced industrial civilization: the rational character of its irrationality. Its productivity and efficiency, its capacity to increase and spread comforts, to turn waste into need, and destruction into construction, the extent to which this civilization transforms the object world into an extension of man's mind and body makes the very notion of alienation questionable. The people recognize themselves in their commodities; they find their soul in their automobile, hi-fi set, split-level home, kitchen equipment. The very mechanism which ties the individual to his society has changed, and social control is anchored in the new needs which it has produced.

The prevailing forms of social control are technological in a new sense. To be sure, the technical structure and efficacy of the productive and destructive apparatus has been a major instrumentality for subjecting the population to the established social division of labor throughout the modern period. Moreover, such integration has always been accompanied by more obvious forms of compulsion: loss of livelihood, the administration of justice, the police, the armed forces. It still is. But in the contemporary period, the technological controls appear to be the very embodiment of Reason for the benefit of all social groups and interests — to such an extent that all contradiction seems irrational and all counteraction impossible.

No wonder then that, in the most advanced areas of this civilization, the social controls have been introjected to the point where even individual protest is affected at its roots. The intellectual and emotional refusal "to go along" appears neurotic and impotent. This is the socio-psychological aspect of the political event that marks the contemporary period: the passing of the historical forces which, at the preceding stage of industrial society, seemed to represent the possibility of new forms of existence.

But the term "introjection" perhaps no longer describes the way in which the individual by himself reproduces and perpetuates the external controls exercised by his society. Introjection suggests a variety of relatively spontaneous processes by which a Self (Ego) transposes the "outer" into the "inner." Thus introjection implies the existence of an inner dimension distinguished from and even antagonistic to the external exigencies — an individual consciousness and an individual unconscious *apart from* public opinion and behavior.[1] The idea of "inner freedom" here has its reality: it designates the private space in which man may become and remain "himself."

Today this private space has been invaded and whittled down by technological reality. Mass production and mass distribution claim the *entire* individual, and industrial psychology has long since ceased to be confined to the factory. The manifold processes of introjection seem to be ossified in almost mechanical reactions. The result is, not adjustment but *mimesis:* an immediate identification of the individual with *his* society and, through it, with the society as a whole.

This immediate, automatic identification (which may have been characteristic of primitive forms of association) reappears in high industrial civilization; its new "immediacy," however, is the product of a sophisticated, scientific management and organization. In this process, the "inner" dimension of the mind in which opposition to the status quo can take root is whittled down. The loss of this dimension, in which the power of negative thinking — the critical power of Reason — is at home, is the ideological counterpart to the very material process in which advanced industrial society silences and reconciles the opposition. The impact of progress turns Reason into submission to the facts of life, and to the dynamic capability of producing more and bigger facts of the same sort of life. The efficiency of the system blunts the individ-

[1] The change in the function of the family here plays a decisive role: its "socializing" functions are increasingly taken over by outside groups and media. See my *Eros and Civilization* (Boston: Beacon Press, 1955), p. 96 ff.

uals' recognition that it contains no facts which do not communicate the repressive power of the whole. If the individuals find themselves in the things which shape their life, they do so, not by giving, but by accepting the law of things — not the law of physics but the law of their society.

I have just suggested that the concept of alienation seems to become questionable when the individuals identify themselves with the existence which is imposed upon them and have in it their own development and satisfaction. This identification is not illusion but reality. However, the reality constitutes a more progressive stage of alienation. The latter has become entirely objective; the subject which is alienated is swallowed up by its alienated existence. There is only one dimension, and it is everywhere and in all forms. The achievements of progress defy ideological indictment as well as justification; before their tribunal, the "false consciousness" of their rationality becomes the true consciousness.

This absorption of ideology into reality does not, however, signify the "end of ideology." On the contrary, in a specific sense advanced industrial culture is *more* ideological than its predecessor, inasmuch as today the ideology is in the process of production itself. In a provocative form, this proposition reveals the political aspects of the prevailing technological rationality. The productive apparatus and the goods and services which it produces "sell" or impose the social system as a whole. The means of mass transportation and communication, the commodities of lodging, food, and clothing, the irresistible output of the entertainment and information industry carry with them prescribed attitudes and habits, certain intellectual and emotional reactions which bind the consumers more or less pleasantly to the producers and, through the latter, to the whole. The products indoctrinate and manipulate; they promote a false consciousness which is immune against its falsehood. And as these beneficial products become available to more individuals in more social classes, the indoctrination they carry ceases to be publicity; it becomes a way of life. It is a good way of life — much better than before — and as a good way of life, it militates against qualitative change. Thus emerges a pattern of *one-dimensional thought and behavior* in which ideas, aspirations, and objectives that, by their content, transcend the established universe of discourse and action are either repelled or reduced to terms of this universe. They are redefined by the rationality of the given system and of its quantitative extension.

The trend may be related to a development in scientific method: operationalism in the physical, behaviorism in the social sciences. The common feature is a total empiricism in the treatment of concepts; their meaning is restricted to the representation of particular operations and behavior. The operational point of view is well illustrated by P. W. Bridgman's analysis of the concept of length: [2]

> We evidently know what we mean by length if we can tell what the length of any and every object is, and for the physicist nothing more is required. To find the length of an object, we have to perform certain physical operations. The concept of length is therefore fixed when the operations by which length is measured are fixed: that is, the concept of length involves as much and nothing more than the set of operations by which length is determined. In general, we mean by any concept nothing more than a set of operations; *the concept is synonymous with the corresponding set of operations.*

Bridgman has seen the wide implications of this mode of thought for the society at large: [3]

> To adopt the operational point of view involves much more than a mere restriction of the sense in which we understand 'concept,' but means a far-reaching change in all our habits of thought, in that we shall no longer permit ourselves to use as tools in our thinking concepts of which we cannot give an adequate account in terms of operations.

Bridgman's prediction has come true. The new mode of thought is today the predominant tendency in philosophy, psychology, sociology, and other fields. Many of the most seriously troublesome concepts are being "eliminated" by showing that no adequate account of them in terms of operations or behavior can be given. The radical empiricist onslaught (I shall subsequently . . . examine its claim to be empiricist) thus provides the methodological justification for the debunking of the mind by the intellectuals — a positivism which, in its denial of the transcending elements of Reason, forms the academic counterpart of the socially required behavior.

Outside the academic establishment, the "far-reaching change in all our habits of thought" is more serious. It serves to coordinate ideas and goals with those exacted by the prevailing system, to enclose them in the system, and to repel those which are irreconcilable with the system. The reign of such a one-dimensional reality does not mean that materialism rules, and that the spiritual, metaphysical, and bohemian occupations are petering out. On the contrary, there is a great deal of "Worship together this week," "Why not try God," Zen, existentialism, and beat ways of life, etc. But such modes of protest and transcendence are no longer contradictory to the status quo and no longer negative. They are rather the ceremonial part of practical behaviorism, its harmless negation, and are quickly digested by the status quo as part of its healthy diet.

[2] P. W. Bridgman, *The Logic of Modern Physics* (New York: Macmillan, 1928), p. 5. . . .

[3] P. W. Bridgman, *The Logic of Modern Physics,* loc. cit., p. 31.

One-dimensional thought is systematically promoted by the makers of politics and their purveyors of mass information. Their universe of discourse is populated by self-validating hypotheses which, incessantly and monopolistically repeated, become hypnotic definitions or dictations. For example, "free" are the institutions which operate (and are operated on) in the countries of the Free World; other transcending modes of freedom are by definition either anarchism, communism, or propaganda. "Socialistic" are all encroachments on private enterprises not undertaken by private enterprise itself (or by government contracts), such as universal and comprehensive health insurance, or the protection of nature from all too sweeping commercialization, or the establishment of public services which may hurt private profit. This totalitarian logic of accomplished facts has its Eastern counterpart. There, freedom is the way of life instituted by a communist regime, and all other transcending modes of freedom are either capitalistic, or revisionist, or leftist sectarianism. In both camps, non-operational ideas are non-behavioral and subversive. The movement of thought is stopped at barriers which appear as the limits of Reason itself.

Such limitation of thought is certainly not new. Ascending modern rationalism, in its speculative as well as empirical form, shows a striking contrast between extreme critical radicalism in scientific and philosophic method on the one hand, and an uncritical quietism in the attitude toward established and functioning social institutions. Thus Descartes' *ego cogitans* was to leave the "great public bodies" untouched, and Hobbes held that "the present ought always to be preferred, maintained, and accounted best." Kant agreed with Locke in justifying revolution *if and when* it has succeeded in organizing the whole and in preventing subversion.

However, these accommodating concepts of Reason were always contradicted by the evident misery and injustice of the "great public bodies" and the effective, more or less conscious rebellion against them. Societal conditions existed which provoked and permitted real dissociation from the established state of affairs; a private as well as political dimension was present in which dissociation could develop into effective opposition, testing its strength and the validity of its objectives.

With the gradual closing of this dimension by the society, the self-limitation of thought assumes a large significance. The interrelation between scientific-philosophical and societal processes, between theoretical and practical Reason, asserts itself "behind the back" of the scientists and philosophers. The society bars a whole type of oppositional operations and behavior; consequently, the concepts pertaining to them are rendered illusory or meaningless. Historical transcendence appears as metaphysical transcendence, not acceptable to science and scientific thought. The operational and behavioral point of view, practiced as a "habit of thought" at large, becomes the view of the established universe of discourse and action, needs and aspirations. The "cunning of Reason" works, as it so often did, in the interest of the powers that be. The insistence on operational and behavioral concepts turns against the efforts to free thought and behavior *from* the given reality and *for* the suppressed alternatives. Theoretical and practical Reason, academic and social behaviorism meet on common ground: that of an advanced society which makes scientific and technical progress into an instrument of domination.

"Progress" is not a neutral term; it moves toward specific ends, and these ends are defined by the possibilities of ameliorating the human condition. Advanced industrial society is approaching the stage where continued progress would demand the radical subversion of the prevailing direction and organization of progress. This stage would be reached when material production (including the necessary services) becomes automated to the extent that all vital needs can be satisfied while necessary labor time is reduced to marginal time. From this point on, technical progress would transcend the realm of necessity, where it served as the instrument of domination and exploitation which thereby limited its rationality; technology would become subject to the free play of faculties in the struggle for the pacification of nature and of society.

Such a state is envisioned in Marx's notion of the "abolition of labor." The term "pacification of existence" seems better suited to designate the historical alternative of a world which — through an international conflict which transforms and suspends the contradictions within the established societies — advances on the brink of a global war. "Pacification of existence" means the development of man's struggle with man and with nature, under conditions where the competing needs, desires, and aspirations are no longer organized by vested interests in domination and scarcity — an organization which perpetuates the destructive forms of this struggle.

Today's fight against this historical alternative finds a firm mass basis in the underlying population, and finds its ideology in the rigid orientation of thought and behavior to the given universe of facts. Validated by the accomplishments of science and technology, justified by its growing productivity, the status quo defies all transcendence. Faced with the possibility of pacification on the grounds of its technical and intellectual achievements, the mature industrial society closes itself against this alternative. Operationalism, in theory and practice, becomes the theory and practice of *containment*. Underneath its obvious dynamics, this society is a thoroughly static system of life: self-propelling in its oppressive productivity and in its beneficial coordination. Containment of technical progress goes hand in hand with its growth in the established direction. In spite of the political fetters imposed by the status quo, the more technology appears capable of creating the conditions for pacification, the more are the minds and bodies of man organized against this alternative.

The most advanced areas of industrial society exhibit throughout these two features: a trend toward consummation of technological rationality, and intensive efforts to contain this trend within the established institutions. Here is the internal contradiction of this civilization: the irrational element in its rationality. It is the token of its achievements. The industrial society which makes technology and science its own is organized for the ever-more-effective domination of man and nature, for the ever-more-effective utilization of its resources. It becomes irrational when the success of these efforts opens new dimensions of human realization. Organization for peace is different from organization for war; the institutions which served the struggle for existence cannot serve the pacification of existence. Life as an end is qualitatively different from life as a means.

Such a qualitatively new mode of existence can never be envisaged as the mere by-product of economic and political changes, as the more or less spontaneous effect of the new institutions which constitute the necessary prerequisite. Qualitative change also involves a change in the *technical* basis on which this society rests — one which sustains the economic and political institutions through which the "second nature" of man as an aggressive object of administration is stabilized. The techniques of industrialization are political techniques; as such, they prejudge the possibilities of Reason and Freedom.

To be sure, labor must precede the reduction of labor, and industrialization must precede the development of human needs and satisfactions. But as all freedom depends on the conquest of alien necessity, the realization of freedom depends on the *techniques* of this conquest. The highest productivity of labor can be used for the perpetuation of labor, and the most efficient industrialization can serve the restriction and manipulation of needs.

When this point is reached, domination — in the guise of affluence and liberty — extends to all spheres of private and public existence, integrates all authentic opposition, absorbs all alternatives. Technological rationality reveals its political character as it becomes the great vehicle of better domination, creating a truly totalitarian universe in which society and nature, mind and body are kept in a state of permanent mobilization for the defense of this universe.

SUGGESTIONS FOR FURTHER READING

The most rewarding further reading, of course, will be in the works of the thinkers so briefly represented here. The titles listed below are intended to serve as guides to those works, rather than as a general bibliography of writings on European or American intellectual history.

General

The most recent survey of European intellectual history is Roland Stromberg, *An Intellectual History of Modern Europe* (New York: Appleton-Century-Crofts, 1966), the second part of which has been published in paperback under the title *European Intellectual History Since 1789* (New York: Appleton-Century-Crofts, 1968). The nineteenth and twentieth centuries are also covered in George Mosse, *The Culture of Western Europe* (Chicago: Rand McNally, 1961), a book that places special emphasis on the intellectual origins of Fascism. Two older, and more inclusive, accounts might also be consulted: John Herman Randall, Jr., *The Making of the Modern Mind* (Boston: Houghton Mifflin, 1926) is particularly good on scientific developments, while Crane Brinton, *Ideas and Men* (Englewood Cliffs, N.J.: Prentice-Hall, 1950) remains, for all its popularizing and loose chronology, the most readable and entertaining of the existing surveys. The Introduction and last eight chapters of *Ideas and Men*, treating the period from the Renaissance to the present, have been published in paperback under the title *The Shaping of Modern Thought* (Englewood Cliffs, N.J.: Prentice-Hall, 1963). A book of a slightly different sort is Robert Kelley's imaginative study, *The Transatlantic Persuasion: The Liberal-Democratic Mind in the Age of Gladstone* (New York: Alfred A. Knopf, 1969), which explicitly compares the American and English manifestations of the liberal tradition.

Standard textbooks in American intellectual history are Vernon Louis Parrington, *Main Currents in American Thought*, 3 vols. (New York: Harcourt, Brace and World, 1927–30), one of the outstanding achievements of progressive historical scholarship; Ralph Henry Gabriel,

The Course of American Democratic Thought (New York: The Ronald Press, 1940), which treats the history of ideas in America as the history of the "democratic faith"; and Stow Persons, *American Minds: A History of Ideas* (New York: Holt, Rinehart and Winston, 1958), a discriminating study of the unifying elements in successive phases of American thought. Henry Steele Commager, *The American Mind: An Interpretation of American Thought and Character Since the 1880's* (New Haven: Yale University Press, 1950) is a valuable general account concentrating on the period from Reconstruction to the Second World War. Joseph Dorfman, *The Economic Mind in American Civilization*, 6 vols. (New York: Viking Press, 1946–59) is encyclopedic on its subject. Clinton Rossiter, *Conservatism in America: The Thankless Persuasion* (New York: Vintage, 1955; 2d ed., 1962) cogently traces the history of an important theme. Paul Conkin, *Puritans and Pragmatists: Eight Eminent American Thinkers* (New York: Dodd, Mead, 1968) offers good summaries of several leading American intellectual careers. David W. Minar, *Ideas and Politics: The American Experience* (Homewood, Ill.: Dorsey Press, 1964) is a useful history of American political thinking by a political scientist.

I. The Enlightenment

The best synoptic treatment of the European Enlightenment remains Ernst Cassirer, *The Philosophy of the Enlightenment* (Boston: Beacon Press, 1955), originally published in 1932. Peter Gay, *The Enlightenment: An Interpretation*, 2 vols. (New York: Alfred A. Knopf, 1966, 1969) is less demanding than Cassirer, and contains lengthy bibliographical essays. Gay has also published a solid book on Voltaire, *Voltaire's Politics* (Princeton: Princeton University Press, 1959). A famous critique of the European Enlightenment, written by an American scholar in the 1930's, is Carl Becker, *The Heavenly City of the Eighteenth-Century Philosophers* (New Haven: Yale University Press, 1932), to which a number of the Enlightenment's friends have responded in Raymond Rockwood, ed., *Carl Becker's Heavenly City Revisited* (Ithaca: Cornell University Press, 1958). On Rousseau, see Ernst Cassirer's essay *The Question of Jean-Jacques Rousseau* (Bloomington: Indiana University Press, 1963), which defends Rousseau against the accusation of totalitarianism. Peter Gay's "The Enlightenment," in C. Vann Woodward, ed., *The Comparative Approach to American History* (New York: Basic Books, 1968) suggestively compares the Enlightenment in Europe and America.

Bernard Bailyn, *The Ideological Origins of the American Revolution* (Cambridge, Mass.: The Belknap Press of Harvard University Press, 1967) traces the sources of Revolutionary political thought to early eighteenth-century England. Paul W. Conner, *Poor Richard's Politicks: Benjamin Franklin and His New American Order* (New York: Oxford

University Press, 1965) is an analytical study of Franklin's social thought. Ralph L. Ketcham, *Benjamin Franklin* (New York: Washington Square Press, 1965) is a good brief survey of Franklin's principal ideas and has a short but helpful bibliography. Daniel J. Boorstin, *The Lost World of Thomas Jefferson* (New York: Holt, 1948), and Adrienne Koch, *The Philosophy of Thomas Jefferson* (New York: Columbia University Press, 1943) are both good analyses of another leading American *philosophe*. Adrienne Koch has made easily accessible a valuable collection of documents from the period in *The American Enlightenment* (New York: George Braziller, 1965).

II. The Revolt against the Enlightenment: Conservatism

There is no good general treatment of the conservative revolt of the early nineteenth century. Russell Kirk, *The Conservative Mind* (Chicago: Henry Regnery Company, 1953) provides a useful starting point, but Kirk is concerned less with the nineteenth century than with the history of conservative thinking in its entirety—"from Burke to Eliot," as his subtitle has it. Moreover, with but few exceptions, Kirk's treatment is limited to the English-speaking world. There are, however, useful books on individual conservative thinkers and conservative national traditions. Klaus Epstein, *The Genesis of German Conservatism* (Princeton: Princeton University Press, 1966) and Alfred Cobban, *Edmund Burke and the Revolt against the Eighteenth Century* (London: G. Allen and Unwin, 1929) are both fair-minded. Among the most stimulating pieces on Burke is Conor Cruise O'Brien's Introduction to the Pelican Classics edition of the *Reflections* (Baltimore: Penguin Books, 1968). As an introduction to the greatest French conservative of the early nineteenth century, see Jack Lively, ed., *The Works of Joseph de Maistre* (New York: Macmillan, 1965).

In *John Adams and the Prophets of Progress* (Cambridge, Mass.: Harvard University Press, 1952), Zoltan Haraszti has reprinted the marginal notes Adams made in his copies of the works of Bolingbroke, Rousseau, Voltaire, and others, and has offered valuable comments of his own on Adams's political ideas. Edward Handler, *America and Europe in the Political Thought of John Adams* (Cambridge, Mass.: Harvard University Press, 1964) explores Adams's own comparisons with Europe in the development of his thinking about America. John R. Howe, *The Changing Political Thought of John Adams* (Princeton: Princeton University Press, 1966) discusses the development of Adams's ideas in the context of his public career.

John C. Miller, *Alexander Hamilton: Portrait in Paradox* (New York: Harper and Brothers, 1959) is an able biography with some discussion of Hamilton's intellectual accomplishments. Stuart Gerry Brown, *Alexander Hamilton* (New York: Washington Square Press, 1967) presents a helpful synopsis of Hamilton's thought.

III. The Revolt against the Enlightenment: Romanticism

The literature on Romanticism is vast. A useful starting point is the pamphlet edited by John B. Halstead, *Romanticism: Definition, Explanation, and Evaluation* (Boston: D. C. Heath, 1965). Treatments of Romanticism are often polemical. The classic attack was written half a century ago by Irving Babbitt, *Rousseau and Romanticism* (Boston: Houghton Mifflin, 1919). A more recent version of the Babbitt thesis, which attempts to link Romanticism with political irresponsibility and irrationalism, is J. H. Talmon, *Political Messianism* (New York: F. A. Praeger, 1960). Romanticism, however, has not been without its defenders. Probably the most ardent is Jacques Barzun, *Classic, Romantic, and Modern* (Garden City, N.J.: Doubleday, 1961), a revision of *Romanticism and the Modern Ego* (Boston: Little, Brown, 1943). A very interesting general treatment of Romanticism is Mario Praz, *The Romantic Agony* (Cleveland: World Publishing Company, 1933), which seeks the essence of Romanticism in its "erotic sensibility." A good selection of Romantic writings can be found in Howard E. Hugo, ed., *The Portable Romantic Reader* (New York: Viking Press, 1957).

There are several fine books on Alexis de Tocqueville. The most recent general treatment is Jack Lively, *The Social and Political Thought of Alexis de Tocqueville* (Oxford: Clarendon Press, 1965). Also of use are George Wilson Pierson, *Tocqueville and Beaumont in America* (New York: Oxford University Press, 1938), an account of the journey on which *Democracy in America* was based, and Richard Herr, *Tocqueville and the Old Regime* (Princeton: Princeton University Press, 1962), an insightful analysis of Tocqueville's final masterpiece, *The Old Regime and the French Revolution.*

F. O. Mathiessen, *American Renaissance: Art and Expression in the Age of Emerson and Whitman* (New York: Oxford University Press, 1941) is a standard work on American Romanticism. Perry Miller, in his collection of readings *The Transcendentalists* (Cambridge, Mass.: Harvard University Press, 1950), contributed a short but characteristically cogent and valuable introductory essay. See also Miller's *The Life of the Mind in America: From the Revolution to the Civil War* (New York: Harcourt, Brace and World, 1965), the first installment of a planned multi-volume history of American intellectual life that death in 1963 prevented Miller from completing. Marvin Meyers, *The Jacksonian Persuasion: Politics and Belief* (Stanford: Stanford University Press, 1957) is a provocative discussion of political ideas and attitudes.

On Emerson, see Sherman Paul, *Emerson's Angle of Vision: Man and Nature in the American Experience* (Cambridge, Mass.: Harvard University Press, 1952), and the essays collected by Carl Bode, ed., *Ralph Waldo Emerson: A Profile* (New York: Hill and Wang, 1969).

IV., V. Responses to Industrialism

On pre-Marxian responses to industrialism, consult Frank Manuel, *The Prophets of Paris* (Cambridge, Mass.: Harvard University Press, 1962), which treats the French utopian socialists Henri de Saint-Simon and Charles Fourier. See also George Lichtheim, *The Origins of Socialism* (New York: F. A. Praeger, 1969). John D. Rosenberg is the author of a fine book on Ruskin, *The Darkening Glass: A Portrait of Ruskin's Genius* (New York: Columbia University Press, 1961), as well as an anthology of Ruskin's writings, *The Genius of John Ruskin* (Boston: Houghton Mifflin, 1963). Jackson Holbrook, *Dreamers of Dreams: The Rise and Fall of Nineteenth-Century Idealism* (London: Faber and Faber, 1948) discusses the thought and reciprocal influences of Thomas Carlyle, John Ruskin, William Morris, Ralph Waldo Emerson, Henry David Thoreau, and Walt Whitman. Joseph Wood Krutch, *Henry David Thoreau* (New York: W. Sloane Associates, 1948), and James G. Murray, *Henry David Thoreau* (New York: Washington Square Press, 1968) are both general accounts of Thoreau's life and thought. Leo Stoller, *After Walden: Thoreau's Changing Views on Economic Man* (Stanford: Stanford University Press, 1957) focusses on Thoreau's social thought in later life. Yehoshua Arieli, *Individualism and Nationalism in American Ideology* (Cambridge, Mass.: Harvard University Press, 1966) traces the relationship of those two important themes in the years from the Revolution to the Civil War.

Marx's *Economic and Philosophical Manuscripts*, the essential source for all discussions of his early thought, are reproduced and sympathetically analyzed in Erich Fromm, *Marx's Concept of Man* (New York: Frederick Ungar, 1961). For a more critical study of the young Marx, see Robert Tucker, *Philosophy and Myth in Karl Marx* (Cambridge, Eng.: Cambridge University Press, 1967). Two very good general treatments of Marxism are Edmund Wilson, *To the Finland Station* (Garden City, N.J.: Doubleday, 1940) and George Lichtheim, *Marxism: An Historical and Critical Study* (New York: F. A. Praeger, 1961). Isaiah Berlin's short biography, *Karl Marx* (London: Oxford University Press, 1939), is a useful introduction; it contains clear, though not over-simplified, analyses of Marx's most important ideas.

Arnold W. Green, *Henry Charles Carey, Nineteenth-Century Sociologist* (Philadelphia: University of Pennsylvania Press, 1951) treats all of Carey's many intellectual interests. Joseph Dorfman, *The Economic Mind in American Civilization*, Vol. 2 (New York: Viking Press, 1946) discusses the context of economic ideas in which Carey worked.

VI. Darwinism

Two books that recreate the cultural milieu in which European Darwinism flourished are Carlton J. H. Hayes, *A Generation of Materialism*

(New York: Harper and Brothers, 1941), and G. M. Young, *Victorian England: Portrait of an Age* (London: Oxford University Press, 1936). Walter Simon, *European Positivism in the Nineteenth Century* (Ithaca: Cornell University Press, 1963) deals only with the positivism of Auguste Comte and his disciples, but it succeeds, despite its narrow focus, in suggesting something of the general intellectual atmosphere of the late nineteenth century.

Loren Eiseley, *Darwin's Century* (Garden City, N.J.: Doubleday, 1958) is concerned primarily with the scientific aspects of Darwin's theory and its reception. Eiseley's treatment of this difficult, and potentially boring, topic is so lucid and gracefully written that even the most uncompromising humanist will be delighted by it. Gertrude Himmelfarb, *Darwin and the Darwinian Revolution* (Garden City, N.J.: Doubleday, 1959) is both an intellectual biography, rather hostile to its subject, and an account of Darwin's impact on European intellectual life.

The best general account of American Darwinism is Richard Hofstadter, *Social Darwinism in American Thought* (Philadelphia: University of Pennsylvania Press, 1944). See also Robert Green McCloskey, *American Conservatism in the Age of Enterprise* (Cambridge, Mass.: Harvard University Press, 1951), a study of William Graham Sumner, Stephen J. Field, and Andrew Carnegie. Sidney Fine, *Laissez-Faire and the General Welfare State* (Ann Arbor: University of Michigan Press, 1956) describes the late nineteenth-century modification of conservative Darwinian thought.

VII. The Revolt against Positivism and Formalism: Fictionalism

The two books that have principally defined this period in European and American thought are H. Stuart Hughes, *Consciousness and Society: The Reorientation of European Social Thought 1890–1930* (New York: Alfred A. Knopf, 1958), and Morton White, *Social Thought in America: The Revolt against Formalism* (Boston: Beacon Press, 1957). Both are indispensable starting points for the serious student of turn-of-the-century intellectual history.

Charles Peirce, neglected in his own time and long neglected by intellectual historians as well, has recently been the subject of revived scholarly interest, principally among philosophers. Three of the best studies are: W. B. Gallie, *Peirce and Pragmatism* (Harmondsworth, Middlesex: Penguin Books, 1952), a philosophically technical discussion; Hjalmar Wennerberg, *The Pragmatism of C. S. Peirce: An Analytical Study* (Lund, Sweden: CWK Gleerup, 1962), which provides an exegesis of Peirce's chief ideas; and A. J. Ayer, *The Origins of Pragmatism: Studies in the Philosophy of Charles Sanders Peirce and William James* (San Francisco: Freeman, Cooper, 1968). Horace Standish Thayer, *Meaning and Action: A Critical History of Pragmatism* (Indianapolis: Bobbs-Merrill, 1968) discusses the pragmatic movement in both Europe and America and contains an extensive bibliography. See also Edward C. Moore, *American Pragmatism: Peirce, James, and Dewey* (New York: Columbia University Press, 1961) and Philip P. Wiener, *Evolution and the Founders of Pragmatism* (Cambridge, Mass.: Harvard University Press, 1949).

On William James, see Ralph Barton Perry, *The Thought and Character of William James,* 2 vols. (Boston: Little, Brown, 1935), both a biography and a rich source of James's letters, which Perry printed generously along with his account of James's life. A good brief account of James's varied intellectual career is Edward C. Moore, *William James* (New York: Washington Square Press, 1965). John Wild, *The Radical Empiricism of William James* (Garden City, N.J.: Doubleday, 1969) is a detailed analysis by a philosopher who argues that James was one of the first existentialists. In *The Thirteen Pragmatisms and Other Essays* (Baltimore: Johns Hopkins Press, 1963) Arthur O. Lovejoy attacks pragmatism from several different angles.

Georges Sorel's intellectual affinities with the pragmatists, as well as his debt to Henri Bergson are treated by Hughes in *Consciousness and Society.* See also Richard Humphrey, *Georges Sorel: Prophet without Honor: A Study in Anti-intellectualism* (Cambridge, Mass.: Harvard University Press, 1951).

VIII. The Revolt against Positivism and Formalism: the Psychology of the Unconscious

The standard biography of Freud is Ernest Jones, *The Life and Work of Sigmund Freud,* 3 vols. (New York: Basic Books, 1953–57), which Lionel Trilling and Steven Marcus have condensed into one volume (New York: Basic Books, 1961). It is authoritative and moving. A very good survey of psychoanalytic thought is J. A. C. Brown, *Freud and the Post-Freudians* (Baltimore: Penguin Books, 1961). We can recommend two analytical treatments of Freud's work: Paul Roazen, *Freud: Political and Social Thought* (New York: Alfred A. Knopf, 1968), and Philip Rieff, *Freud: The Mind of the Moralist* (New York: Viking Press, 1959), difficult, but rigorous in placing Freud in the larger context of modern intellectual history.

The history of psychological thought in America has not received the attention it deserves from scholars. A general survey is Abraham Roback, *History of American Psychology* (New York: Collier Books, 1964). John Wild's book, *The Radical Empiricism of William James* (Garden City, N.J.: Doubleday, 1969), devotes considerable space to William James's psychological theories. On Freud in America, see David Shakow and David Rapaport, *The Influence of Freud on American Psychology* (Cleveland: World Publishing Company, 1968), and Clarence P. Oberndorf, *A History of Psychoanalysis in America* (New York: Grune and Stratton, 1953).

IX. The Revolt against Positivism and Formalism: New Approaches in the Social Sciences

Two important books treat the major European sociologists of the early twentieth century. Talcott Parsons, *The Structure of Social Action*, 2 vols. (New York: McGraw-Hill, 1937) is intensely analytical and, regrettably, somewhat prolix; volume I discusses Alfred Marshall, Vilfredo Pareto, and Emile Durkheim, while volume II is devoted entirely to Max Weber. Raymond Aron, *Main Currents in Sociological Thought*, Vol. II (New York: Basic Books, 1967) offers shorter and more graceful studies of Pareto, Durkheim, and Weber. Also on Weber, see Reinhard Bendix, *Max Weber: An Intellectual Portrait* (Garden City, N.J.: Doubleday, 1960), and the Introduction to H. H. Gerth and C. Wright Mills, eds., *From Max Weber* (New York: Oxford University Press, 1946).

Joseph Dorfman's biography of Veblen, *Thorstein Veblen and His America* (New York: Viking Press, 1934) is exhaustive. More concise are David Riesman, *Thorstein Veblen* (New York: Charles Scribner's Sons, 1953), and the excellent Introduction in Max Lerner, ed., *The Portable Veblen* (New York: Viking Press, 1948). David W. Noble, in *The Paradox of Progressive Thought* (Minneapolis: University of Minnesota Press, 1958), discusses a number of important social thinkers in Veblen's time. See also Noble's *The Progressive Mind, 1890–1917* (Chicago: Rand McNally, 1970).

X. World War I and the Crisis of Liberalism

Benda is the subject of a book by Robert J. Niess: *Julian Benda* (Ann Arbor: University of Michigan Press, 1956). On Randolph Bourne, see Louis Filler, *Randolph Bourne* (Washington, D.C.: American Council on Public Affairs, 1943). For a general description of the trends to which Bourne objected, see Sidney Kaplan, "Social Engineers as Saviors," *Journal of the History of Ideas*, XVII (1956), 347–69.

XI. Liberalism in the Inter-war Period

Roderick Nash, *The Nervous Generation: American Thought, 1917–1930* (Chicago: Rand McNally, 1970), and Charles C. Alexander, *Nationalism in American Thought, 1930–1945* (Chicago: Rand McNally, 1969), are general treatments of this period. Roy F. Harrod, *The Life of John Maynard Keynes* (New York: Harcourt, Brace, 1951), is the definitive biography. Anabel Helen Phillips, *J. M. Keynes, Vision and Technique* (Stanford, Calif.: Stanford University Press, 1951), is a short but insightful essay.

Alvin Hansen, *A Guide to Keynes* (New York: McGraw-Hill, 1953) provides valuable assistance in understanding Keynesian economics. Both Harlan L. McCracken, *Keynesian Economics in the Stream of Economic Thought* (Baton Rouge: Louisiana State University Press, 1961) and Lawrence R. Klein, *The Keynesian Revolution* (New York: Macmillan, 1954) explain Keynes's thought and attempt to place it historically.

The scholarship on John Dewey is immense. Perhaps the best general introduction to the extraordinarily broad scope of his thought is Sidney Hook, *John Dewey, an Intellectual Portrait* (New York: John Day, 1939), a sympathetic exegesis by one of Dewey's most prominent students. Morton Levitt, *Freud and Dewey on the Nature of Man* (New York: Philosophical Library, 1960) compares the psychological theories of two central figures in modern thought.

XII. The Intellectuals and the Cold War

Daniel Bell, ed., *The Radical Right* (Garden City: Doubleday, 1963) exemplifies the sort of social analysis in which intellectual cold warriors engaged. Michael Rogin has severely criticized that kind of analysis in *The Intellectuals and McCarthy: The Radical Specter* (Cambridge, Mass.: M.I.T. Press, 1967).

On the European side, H. Stuart Hughes, *The Obstructed Path: French Social Thought in the Years of Desperation 1930–1960* (New York: Harper and Row, 1968), while not explicitly concerned with responses to the Cold War, offers the best introduction to the major French intellectuals of the period, including Raymond Aron. For a general evaluation of Aron as a political thinker, see Roy Pierce, *Contemporary French Political Thought* (London: Oxford University Press, 1966), Chapter 8. Also helpful for this period is the collection of essays edited by Donald Fleming and Bernard Bailyn, *The Intellectual Migration: Europe and America, 1930–1960* (Cambridge, Mass.: The Belknap Press of Harvard University Press, 1969). It contains articles on a number of important émigrés in the sciences and the humanities, as well as a biographical index with 300 entries.

XIII. The New Radicalism

There are already a number of studies on Sartre. Perhaps the most relevant to an understanding of his political thought is Wilfrid Desan, *The Marxism of Jean-Paul Sartre* (Garden City, N.J.: Doubleday, 1965), an exegesis of Sartre's most important writing of the 1960's, *Critique of Dialectical Reason*. See also Walter Odajnyk, *Marxism and Existentialism* (Garden City, N.J.: Doubleday, 1965).

Paul Jacobs and Saul Landau, *The New Radicals* (New York: Vintage Books, 1966) and Marvin E. Gettleman and David Mermelstein, *The Great Society Reader: The Failure of American Liberalism* (New York: Vintage Books, 1967) contain valuable documents and analyses of the recent radical movement in America. See also Jack Newfield, *A Prophetic Minority* (New York: New American Library, 1966). For a provocative though premature general discussion of the contemporary intellectual climate, see Ronald Berman, *America in the Sixties: An Intellectual History* (New York: The Free Press, 1968). On Herbert Marcuse, see Paul A. Robinson, *The Freudian Left* (New York: Harper and Row, 1969), and Robert W. Marks, *The Meaning of Marcuse* (New York: Ballantine Books, 1970).